Big African States

Edited by Christopher Clapham
Jeffrey Herbst and Greg Mills

Big African States

Edited by Christopher Clapham
Jeffrey Herbst and Greg Mills

WITS UNIVERSITY PRESS

Wits University Press
1 Jan Smuts Avenue
Johannesburg
2001
South Africa

http://witspress.wits.ac.za

ISBN 1 86814 425 9
ISBN 978 1 86814 425 9

First published 2006

Cover design by LimeBlue, Johannesburg
Design and layout by Acumen Publishing Solutions, Johannesburg
Printed and bound by Creda Communications, Cape Town

Contents

Acknowledgements

This compendium is based on the findings of a research project led by Jeffrey Herbst, then of Princeton University and Greg Mills, then of the South African Institute of International Affairs and funded by the Ford Foundation and the Anglo American Chairman's Fund, bringing together analysts from Europe, Africa and North America at three international conferences at which the country case studies and cross cutting thematic papers were discussed: that hosted by the Stiftung Wissenschaft und Politik (SWP) at Cadenabbia in Italy in November 2002; at the Tswalu Dialogue in South Africa in May 2003; and at Princeton University in October 2003.

Grateful appreciation is expressed to the funders and paper writers, and also to Jonathan and Jennifer Oppenheimer who kindly hosted the second meeting at Tswalu in the Kalahari in May 2003.

Christopher Clapham, Jeffrey Herbst & Greg Mills,
Cambridge UK, Oxford Ohio & Johannesburg South Africa,
April 2006

Contributors

Garth Abraham is an Associate Professor in the School of Law, University of the Witwatersrand, Johannesburg, South Africa.

Joseph Ayee is a Professor/Dean in the Faculty of Social Studies, University of Ghana, Legon, Ghana.

Daniel C Bach is Research Director at the French National Centre for Scientific Research, Centre d'Etude d'Afrique Noire, and professor at Institut d'Etudes Politiques, University Montesquieu Bordeaux IV (France).

Christopher Clapham is an Associate of the Centre of African Studies, Cambridge University. He has written extensively on the politics of Ethiopia and north east Africa, including *Haile Selassie's Government*, in 1969; and *Transformation and Continuity in Revolutionary Ethiopia* in 1988.

Jeffrey Herbst is Provost and Executive Vice President for Academic Affairs at Miami University, Ohio. He initially explored some of the the themes of state consolidation and political geography in 'States and Power in Africa' (Princeton University Press, 2000).

Tim Hughes is the Parliamentary Research Fellow at the South African Institute of International Affairs. He is based in Cape Town.

Claude Kabemba is Chief Research Manager, in Society, Culture and Identity at the Human Sciences Research Council in Pretoria.

Dr Jack Kalpakian is an Assistant Professor in the School of Humanities and Social Sciences at Al Akhawayn University, Ifrane, Morocco. He would like to acknowledge his intellectual debt to Dr Francis Deng in preparing this paper.

Greg Mills heads the Brenthurst Foundation dedicated to strengthening economic performance in Africa and was, from 1996-2005, the National Director of the SA Institute of International Affairs (SAIIA) based at the University of the Witwatersrand in Johannesburg when this chapter was originally written.

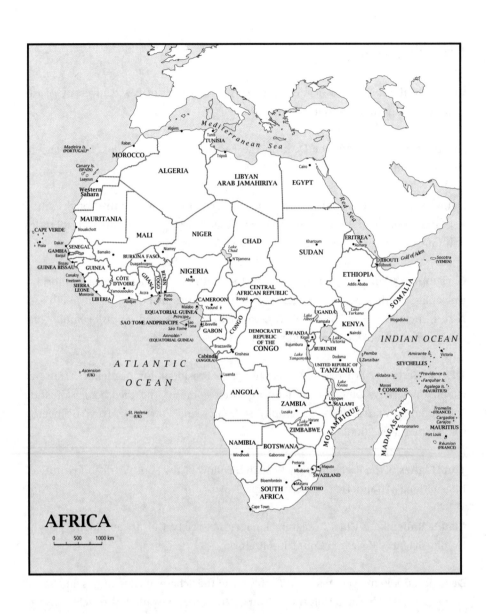

AFRICA

0   500   1000 km

Africa's big dysfunctional states:

an introductory overview

Jeffrey Herbst and Greg Mills

One of the least challenged assumptions in the political analysis of the viability of states is that 'bigger is better'. Throughout the academic literature, across the policy debates, and in almost all public debate, large states are assumed to have a better chance for development and small states are assumed to be problematic. However, in sub Saharan Africa, large states (Nigeria, Ethiopia, and the Democratic Republic of Congo (DRC) by population; Sudan, the DRC, and Niger by landmass) have performed poorly. There are, of course, a great number of small states in Africa that have poor development records, but it is the large states that are especially disappointing. Indeed, the development tragedies of Nigeria, Ethiopia, and the DRC have not only profoundly affected the 242.6 million people in those countries (36.8% of the 659.7 million in Africa) but have also depressed the prospects of the countries around them because the big states have acted more like cabooses than locomotives in the drive to develop.

This book seeks to understand why Africa's largest, and therefore presumably most important, countries have performed so poorly. It includes case studies of Angola (fourteenth in population, fifth in landmass), the DRC (third in population, second in landmass), Ethiopia (second in population, ninth in landmass), Nigeria (first in population, tenth in landmass), South Africa (fourth in population, sixth in landmass), and Sudan (seventh in population, first in landmass), all of which are in the top five in either population or landmass or both.

In all six countries selected in this study, the state exhibits varying conditions of dysfunctionality (defined in this study as the lack of provision of welfare and opportunity to the population) and, excluding to a degree South Africa, a sustained period of civil unrest, economic decline, state atrophy and social corrosion. These large states are diverse, incorporating large numbers of ethnic groupings within their territory, which, coupled with religious tensions, may act as fault lines for

Table 1.1   Africa's big states: population, landmass and economy

	Population (million) % annual growth (1980–2000)	GNI per cap ($) 2000 (1990)	% GDP average annual real growth (1990–2000)	ODA flows, ($ per capita) (2000)	Landmass ('000 km²)
Angola	13 (3.1)	290	-1.8	23	1.246
DRC	50.9 (3.2)	80	-8.2	4	2.267
Ethiopia	64.3 (2.7)	100	2.4	24	1.000
Nigeria	126.9 (2.9)	260	-0.4	1	.910
South Africa	42.8 (2.2)	3 020	.0	11	1.221
Sudan	21.1 (2.4)	310	5.6	7	2.376
Sub-Saharan Africa	658.9 (2.7)	470		20 (13,453mn)	23.603

Source: World Bank, *World Bank Africa Database on CD-Rom.* Washington, DC: The World Bank, 2002.

social and geographic fission. The economies of most, with the exception of Ethiopia, are dependent on mineral exports. In extreme examples, they are countries with big hinterlands, which are hard to police and govern. More generally, it is impossible to see how Africa as a whole can develop without impressive progress by its largest countries.

Apart from sheer size, these countries were selected to be representative of the various regions in Africa and because of the special political role that they play or may play, now or in the future. (This was a particularly important consideration for Angola, given its potential to be a rising power in southern and central Africa). We have not only selected those countries which have weak, failed or crisis ridden state systems, but also the one that may be regarded as a success – South Africa. The book also reviews a series of cross cutting issues that affect all of the big states in Africa. Finally, it explores the policy implications of the poor record of Africa's large states and what can be done about it.

In this volume, we hope to provide a new perspective on the development challenges facing Africa. Indeed, it is surprising that there has not, in general, been a focus on country size when discussing Africa's problems. Size, and the particular dysfunctionality of the large states, should be the context in every discussion concerning Africa.

Figure 1.1   GDP per capita by population group

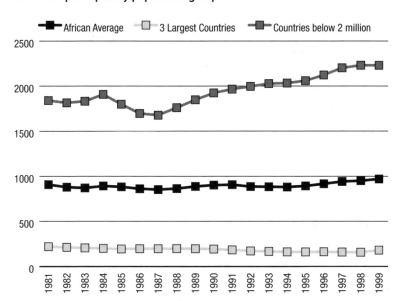

As the graph above shows, since 1981 (the first year that there is data for Ethiopia), the three African giants have had considerably lower per capita incomes than the African average. Their performance worsened over the eighteen year period - per capita incomes declined by a total of eighteen per cent, compared to an overall average increase of seven per cent in African per capita income during the same period. In contrast, the thirteen countries with populations under two million[1] have higher overall per capita incomes and managed to grow by a total of twenty one per cent during the same period. The problem, of course, is that these thirteen countries with relatively high per capita incomes and (again relatively) high growth rates account for only 1.7 per cent of the total African population. Indeed, the fundamental problem affecting Africa is that, overall, the countries that have done especially well have few people and the countries that have performed worse than average are extremely large and populous.

Published figures for 'average' continental per capita income and growth rates often misleadingly take the mean level for *national* income and growth, without weighting these for population size. Thus, the income of Mauritius ($4,120 per person in 1999, with a population of 1.2 million) is 'averaged' with that of Ethiopia ($112, with a population of 63 million), to produce a mean of $2,116 per person. When the figure is weighted for Ethiopia's much larger population, the actual mean sinks to $187. Figure 1.1 contrasts the 'average' continental per capita income (without weighting for population size) with the weighted incomes for Africa's largest and smallest states. These 'weighted by population' figures represent essentially what the 'average' African experienced between 1981 and the present. As the chart suggests, the experience of the 'average' person has been even worse than the simple continental statistics imply because the countries where most African people live have been doing much worse than the African average.

Poor performance is not only measurable in economic terms. Africa's large states have a low, and in some cases declining, Human Development Index ranking, combining standards of literacy and schooling, and life expectancy along with economic indicators.[2]

Table 1.2   Africa's big states: Human Development Index

	HDI ranking 2003 (out of 175)	HDI ratings for 1975–2001					
		1975	1980	1985	1990	1995	2001
South Africa	111	0.66	0.68	0.70	0.73	0.74	0.68
Sudan	138	0.35	0.38	0.40	0.43	0.47	0.50
Nigeria	152	0.32	0.38	0.40	0.43	0.45	0.46
Angola	–	–	–	–	–	–	0.38
the DRC	167	0.42	0.43	0.43	0.42	0.38	0.36
Ethiopia	169	–	–	0.28	0.31	0.32	0.36

This situation is exacerbated by a high degree of inequality in living standards and by the prevalence of disease, including HIV/Aids. The number of adults (aged 15-49) living with HIV/Aids in 2001 in the states in question was: South Africa 20.1 per cent, Sudan 2.6 per cent, Nigeria 5.8 per cent, Angola 5.5 per cent, the DRC 4.9 per cent, and Ethiopia 6.41 per cent.[3] Where scores are available, South Africa scores 59.3 on the *Gini* co efficient index (where a value of 0 represents perfect equality in society and 100 perfect inequality), Nigeria 50.6, and Ethiopia 57.2. In each of these countries, addressing poverty is, or should be, a priority challenge. Yet there remain varying concerns about governance and political stability in each of them.

The assumed advantages of bigness

Since a realistic discussion of national design has not been on the agenda recently, many of the assumptions from the critical period of European state building have been imported with little hesitation into the analysis of developing countries. In particular, what analysis there has been has inevitably reflected a European bias in favour of larger states. The nation state rose to dominance in Europe largely because of its unique ability to unite market and population under sovereign rule. This provided leaders in successive centuries with important 'economies of scale' in military, economic, and political affairs that could not be achieved any other way. Such economies were especially important, given the constant threats faced by many European states and the need for states to garner resources to survive external competition. The comparative advantages of the post feudal state became progressively more important as warfare became more expensive and increasingly involved the long term funding of standing armies. These were conscripted from the national population, funded through domestic taxes, and led by a professional staff that had to be able to adapt to continual changes in military technology. After some failed experiments with mercenary armies, it became clear by 1800 that only the new type of state could support the new type of warfare.[4] Such were the advantages offered by the nation state that Joseph Strayer was forced to conclude that:

> The development of the modern state ... made possible such a concentrated use of human resources that no other type of social organization could avoid being relegated to a subordinate role.[5]

Similarly, from Adam Smith to current times, economists have argued, in the words of Charles Kindleberger, that 'the state should be large to achieve economies of scale'.[6] Economists continue to believe that larger internal markets are intrinsically better because the boundaries of the nation state, in accordance with the theory of comparative advantage, are seen as barriers to economic exchange. As Robinson suggested in 1960:

> [t]he boundary of the nation represents a point of discontinuity; it represents a change in the degree of mobility of almost all the factors of production, of labour more especially, but in hardly less degree also of capital and credit, since currency and banking systems are co terminous with nations; it represents above all a discontinuity in the mobility of goods.[7]

In the third world, industrialisation through import substitution (ISI), the dominant development ideology from the 1950s until the 1980s, exemplified the fixation on the size of the domestic market. The larger the domestic market, the more viable the strategy became, because the approach assumed that growth would be governed by domestic demand. Thus the Fabian Society, when it examined the prospects for Eritrean independence, argued:

> Looking further ahead, Eritrea is almost certainly not a viable unit on its own. If we are to think in terms of eventual independence, its people can stand no chance unless they link themselves to bigger and more viable neighbours.[8]

More generally, the small size of many African countries has been cited as a structural problem. For instance, Stock complains that 'there are forty six independent states, some of which are too small to be considered economically viable.'[9]

The perceived material advantages of size were also translated into virtues by political theorists. Classical political theory stressed the importance of small political units, ideally city states.[10] Plato calculated the optimal number of citizens at 5,040 while Aristotle believed that all citizens should be able to assemble in one place and hear a speaker. Later, Montesquieu and Rousseau also stressed the importance of the relationship between size and democracy.[11] The framers of the American constitution were particularly concerned that Montesquieu, who had a profound influence on Jefferson, seemed to be a size determinist, arguing not only that city states would be democratic but also that larger units would inevitably be ruled by despots.

As a result, from the foundation of the US and, especially, during the period of great state consolidation in Europe in the nineteenth century, there was a furious effort on the part of theorists and practitioners to prove that the relative largeness of their nation states was an unambiguous advantage. James Madison brilliantly turned the argument on size and democracy on its head by suggesting not only that large political units were not inherently undemocratic but also that they had substantial advantages over smaller units by being able to limit the damage of 'factions.'[12] After Madison, there developed a long term bias in favour of viewing size as positively associated with prospects for viability. Thus, Alexis de Tocqueville predicted at the end of the first book of *Democracy in America* that the United States and Russia would be the two great superpowers because they were the only ones that could still expand.[13]

The distribution of country size in Africa

The unexamined assumptions regarding size and the viability of nations in Africa constitute a particularly important issue because of the way that population is distributed. The average population of sub Saharan Africa's forty eight countries is 13.7 million but the median is only 7.6 million, immediately suggesting an uneven distribution.

Table 1.3   African states by population size

Population size	Number of countries in Africa
Under two million	13
>2 million and <10 million	15
>10 million and <25 million	13
>25 million	7

The seven largest countries (Nigeria, Ethiopia, the DRC, South Africa, Tanzania, Kenya and Sudan - a total of 379 million or fifty seven per cent of the population of the continent) tend to dominate the continent. After all, Nigeria alone has a population equivalent to the sum of the thirty one smallest countries. Each of Africa's regions can be said to have at least one big country that is the centre of gravity for much of the political and economic activity. Thus, South Africa dominates southern Africa, the DRC dwarfs the rest of central Africa, Nigeria is recognised as the centre of west Africa, and Sudan and Ethiopia are the major countries in the Horn of Africa.

Without getting into a debate as to whether the big countries of Africa are pivotal states,[14] it is easy to claim that each of these countries has a profound effect on its region. For instance, economic disturbances in Nigeria clearly send reverberations throughout the west African region. Correspondingly, if there was ever a Nigeria that began to develop quickly, the positive effects throughout the neighbourhood would quickly be felt. Similarly, in South Africa, negative developments in the 1980s and positive developments in the 1990s clearly affected neighbouring countries although, as the differing paths that Mozambique and Zimbabwe have taken demonstrate, these were not the only determinants of the progress of other countries. Similarly, the chronic instability experienced by Ethiopia and Sudan has had profoundly negative effects on their neighbours. Finally, the political vacuum in Congo has attracted the armies of almost all of the neighbouring countries; indeed, the political situation in Burundi, Rwanda, and Uganda cannot be understood except with reference to Congo.

The international response

Despite the many problems caused by the poor performance of large states, the international community has largely ignored the problem. For instance, Nigeria is repeatedly cited as a leading state by Western governments when it is, in fact, in the process of a long term collapse. Indeed, it is far more likely that Nigeria will be a threat to its neighbours than that it will provide any meaningful assistance. Even the extreme measures of peace keeping have largely been reserved for small countries (e.g. Liberia, Sierra Leone) and small parts of larger countries (e.g. Bunia). The development of a force that would actually provide security throughout large parts of Congo is simply beyond the capabilities of the international community, as most would admit, and therefore the problem of developing a regime that encourages peace in Congo is ignored.

Indeed, the latest African proposal to develop better governance on the continent – the New Partnership for Africa's Development (Nepad) – is also crippled by the failures of large states. The most important way that Nepad differs from all previous African plans for economic development that have failed is the proposal for 'peer review'. This is essentially a kind of Africa sponsored reporting on governments that would replace IMF/World Bank conditionality. However, if the large countries in Africa are failing, who is actually going to put pressure on the continent to improve governance? Nigeria, for instance, is one of the founders of Nepad but it is not in a position to argue that other countries should improve their governance.

There are many reasons why the poor performance of large states has been ignored. Poor performance or outright failure in large states generates too many problems for the international community to handle. Thus peacekeeping strategies have been developed for small countries but not for large ones. The international community has sent 13,000 peacekeepers to tiny Sierra Leone but could never send that number per square mile to Congo. The international community would rather pretend that large states are part of the solution rather than part of the problem. The systematic ignoring of the endless decline of Nigeria is certainly strong evidence of this avoidance behaviour. The African aversion to boundary change of any type has also retarded any real discussion of the problems of big states. Finally, large states are also leaders in Africa and therefore have impeded any systematic discussion of their problems.

Indeed, the large states find many allies in avoiding discussions of the structural problems associated with state design in Africa. There are enough dysfunctional small states in Africa to ensure that any systematic questioning of what could be done to reduce or eliminate the pathologies of large states could also threaten other leaders.

What is meant by dysfunctional?

The importance of Africa's big states and their relatively poor performance are clear and will be further set out in the essays that follow. However, we go beyond saying that their record is disappointing and argue that they are, with the notable exception of South Africa, dysfunctional. Here we are making two claims: first, the actual size of these states is itself a problem for governance. In other words there are, to use the economists' language, decreasing political returns to scale in Africa. Secondly, the big states, instead of playing their natural leadership role in Africa, are actually problems for their associated regions. Both claims are counter intuitive and go against the (admittedly unexamined) assumptions in much of the literature. If these suggestions are true, they have important implications for the way in which we understand the evolution of these countries and for the future of African politics more generally.

Decreasing returns to scale

Large African states have generally performed poorly, but sub optimal economic performance is common across the continent. To tie the actual size of Africa's large countries to poor performance is admittedly difficult, in part because we cannot run controlled experiments with countries and also because there is probably only one large country (South Africa) that has even a moderately good record. There are some reasons to believe that size and dysfunctionality are related. First, scattered populations in a large state automatically present a physical challenge to the extension of state authority over a large percentage of the population. An extensive population distribution also yields a more complex ethnic situation because African minority groups are more highly concentrated in single geographic areas than minorities in other regions. Gurr and his colleagues code seventy per cent of black African minorities as located in one region as compared to sixty one per cent for Latin America and forty eight per cent in the rest of the world.[15]

Thus African states with difficult geographies face the continual problem of a relatively large number of outlying groups that are not only spatially distinct but also can be mobilised around ethnic and cultural symbols that can compete with the state. Leaders in these states often respond by trying to placate potentially restive groups through patronage, with the result that they may have a proportionally larger patronage bill to pay. However, as the Nigerian case clearly demonstrates, there is seldom enough patronage to go round.

More generally, big states tend to have multiple centres of power.[16] In small states, the capital city is almost inevitably the biggest city and the centre of economic activity. All citizens in those countries automatically take their problems to the capital. Quite often, resolution of these political conflicts is messy and incomplete but at least there is agreement about the locus of authority. In contrast, due to the opportunities presented by more land and people, as well as the corresponding weakness of the central state, many Africans in big states are not automatically oriented toward the capital. Important provincial cities, ancient capitals, and even the capitals of neighbouring states are often much closer than their own national authorities and present attractive alternative sources of authority and conflict resolution. As a result, conflicts are more difficult to resolve because there is not even agreement about who should resolve them, more actors are involved, and the state has even fewer cards to play. Thus, Nigerians in the north promulgate their own state level laws based on *shar'ia*, Ethiopians outside of the main regions look to their ethnically inspired regions to champion their causes, Congolese look to whatever authority, domestic or foreign, can provide them with some sense of order, and southern Sudanese and Angolans were motivated to fight in part to seal their own autonomy. Only South Africa, of the big states, has definitively established that the national capital is the source of all authority and conflict resolution.

Secondly, large countries, due to their geographies, are the sites of kinds of battles which differ from those of small countries. Insurgencies in Africa tend to begin very small and are therefore, by definition, harder to detect in large countries. Perhaps more importantly, in small African countries, fighting will often (but by no means always) revolve around who can take the capital, because that is the ultimate political prize, given that the international community awards recognition to those who control the seat of government. On the other hand, in geographically large countries, it is often impossible for the rebels to take the capital because the government is at least strong enough to provide point defence and the rebel home base may be far away. At the same time, the vast distances and logistical problems that African militaries face mean that it is often difficult for them to defeat an insurgency far from the capital. As a result, in large countries, a rough equilibrium can be reached where neither side can defeat the other but both can continue to fight. The civil wars in Angola and Ethiopia went on for many years until one side collapsed, while in Congo and Sudan violence continues. Again, small countries also have wars but at least there is a prospect of their ending more rapidly. Museveni's relatively quick conquest of Kampala is perhaps a model of the possibilities of victory in a small country.

Thirdly, the general but all too real logistical problems that affect all African countries are especially evident in big countries. In these states, the capital can be hundreds of kilometres from many of the people and it is therefore harder for leaders to know what is going on. Government ministries, agricultural extension officers, and other elements of the administrative backbone may not be present in significant numbers in parts of large states, giving the impression to the populace that the state is uninterested in them. As the current international system does not demand that African states control the countryside in order for them to be recognized as sovereign, there may often be no good reason for leaders to expand their administrative nets in a way that would make the state better governed. Indeed, it is one of the paradoxes of modern politics that the international system, via the norm of sovereignty, protects the state as a geographic expression but little attention is paid to how a particular state is governing the area it supposedly rules.

At the same time, some of the advantages of bigness are not as obvious as they used to be. In an age of a dynamic international economy, countries get rich by trading with the rest of the world. Even if one of Africa's big countries were to become stable and prosperous, it would still represent an economically insignificant market. For instance, South Africa - the economic giant of the continent - has a gross domestic product of $427 billion, roughly only half that of Spain.[17] South Africa cannot become rich trading with itself and has recognised that it must engage with the international economy. The size of Congo, Ethiopia and the other African giants offer them few or no economic advantages and considerable political problems. Thus the economic returns to size are becoming less impressive, while big countries find the consolidation of their territories a daunting task.

Threats to the neighbourhood

Recent reasoning has tended to deny that big states pose disproportionate threats to their neighbourhoods but this is easy to prove. In theory, big states should dominate their regions, providing markets for goods and, hopefully, stability. In fact, instability in big states has often been the cause of considerable problems for the region. West African countries must continually worry that events in Nigeria will destabilise them, while the political vacuum in the Congo has incited many of the neighbouring countries to join Africa's continental war. At the very least, the political troubles of Ethiopia and Sudan have had a negative effect on their regions and fighting has often spilled across their borders. The positive developments in southern Africa since the transition in South Africa, especially the ending of the war in Mozambique, demonstrate the positive regional effects that big states can generate when they are well ordered and prosperous.

Indeed, one of the most interesting phenomena in Africa is that big states that should be regional leaders have been so dysfunctional that it makes sense for smaller neighbouring states to try to protect themselves from big states. Thus, a continual topic of conversation in west Africa is how countries can prevent the shock waves emanating from a deteriorating Nigeria from affecting them. Congo is the extreme case, because tiny Rwanda decided that it had to invade its neighbour in order to protect its interests, notably disrupting the sanctuary given to Hutu rebels. This is precisely the opposite of the benign vision of regional trade that is usually posited, in which the big state leads an increasingly dynamic region. It also explains why regional integration has so often failed in Africa: it is, in fact, a bad idea for countries to tie their fates too closely to the state that is the region's putative leader.

As a result, the diagnosis of dysfunctionality in large states is not merely the judgement that they have done badly by their people. Unfortunately, that is a common situation in Africa. Rather, we are making a more direct observation that large size in Africa may be a formidable barrier for leaders to address when they are building their states. Further, it may not be helpful to have a large state as a neighbour: many countries have only experienced the negative effects of a nearby giant and have yet to benefit from larger markets. South Africa demonstrates that relatively large size need not be an absolute barrier to governance, but, during much of the history of the country, white governments did not attempt to rule over significant territories designated for a short period as 'homelands'. As a result, Pretoria's present day attempt to rule over its entire territory is a new experiment in South African history and one from which few lessons can yet be drawn. The argument that 'big' may not be desirable when it comes to designing political units would not be unfamiliar to the ancient Greeks but is a direct challenge to what might be called the post Madison consensus.

Organisation of this volume

The analysis of big dysfunctional states has thus to start from a recognition of the inherent problems of governance in Africa and of the peculiar impact on African states of the international system, which created most of these states in the first place, and has since attempted to maintain them. However, it is also necessary to build into the analysis recognition of the specific histories of different African states. Despite the tendency to group them all together, African states (and perhaps especially the largest African states) have developed in distinctive ways, which in turn have had a profound bearing on their ability to perform the functions associated with statehood. Thus the volume begins with case studies of each of the large African states. Each of the country specific papers considers the critical factors shaping the functions and cohesion of states, notably:

·   the geographic, demographic, religious and ethnic context in each country;
·   the set of political, economic, and security policies that have been adopted by successive rulers since independence;
·   the role of outsiders, including other African states, criminal networks, the diaspora, and westerners, and how they have affected the countries' trajectories; and
·   the threat posed by internal and external groups to the integrity of the state.

Case studies, even when they are as persuasive and co ordinated as those in this volume, cannot address all of the analytic questions posed. We have therefore included a series of papers that examine cross cutting issues that affect all of the big states: leadership, rebellion, lootable commodities, and engagement with the international political and economic system. When combined with the case studies, what emerges is a rich description of the nuances of each country with attention to their common problems and unique challenges. Finally, the conclusion by Christopher Clapham describes some of the policy implications that emerge from the project.

Conclusion

It is hardly surprising that large African states are failing. State creation is an inherently difficult process. If small African states are failing, it is almost inevitable that big African states will also have their viability even more strongly challenged.

One of the most difficult aspects of state creation – reorienting allegiances from local and regional leaders to a distant capital – goes directly to the heart of the vulnerability of large states. What is new in the current period is the expectation that big states will continue to exist, no matter how dysfunctional they are and how much damage they do to their own citizens and to their neighbourhoods. The first step in trying to develop realistic solutions to the problem of big state viability is to recognise, at last, the important problems associated with scale in Africa rather than ignoring them because the problems they raise are too daunting.

Endnotes

1   By increasing size, Seychelles, Mayotte, Sao Tomé, Cape Verde, Equatorial Guinea, Comoros, Swaziland, Mauritius, Guinea Bissau, Gabon, Gambia, Botswana, and Namibia.

2   The HDI is a summary measure of development, where 1.0 is the maximum and zero the minimum score, combining measures of life expectancy, school enrolment, literacy, income, poverty and gender empowerment and development. As a result, countries are classified into three human development groups: an HDI of 0.800 or more indicates high human development; 0.500-0.799 represents medium human development; and low human development is represented by a score of less than 0.500. The top ranking state in 2003 was Norway (0.944) and the lowest was Sierra Leone (0.275). United Nations Development Programme, *Human Development Report* 2003. New York: Oxford University Press, 2003.

3   *Ibid.*

4   Tilly C, *European Revolutions*, 1492-1992. Oxford: Blackwell, 1993, p. 32.

5   Strayer JR, *On the Medieval Origins of the Modern State.* Princeton: Princeton University Press, 1970, p. 4.

6   Kindleberger CP, *Multinational Excursions.* Cambridge: MIT Press, 1984, p. 28.

7   Robinson EAG, 'Introduction', in Robinson EAG (ed.), *Economic Consequences of the Size of Nations.* New York: St. Martin's Press, 1960, p. xiv.

8   Fabian Society, *The Fate of Italy's Colonies.* London: Fabian Publications, 1948, p. 89.

9   Stock R, *Africa South of the Sahara: A Geographical Interpretation.* New York: The Guilford Press, 1995, p. 15.

10   This discussion relies heavily on Dahl RA & ER Tufte, *Size and Democracy.* Stanford: Stanford University Press, 1973, pp. 4-7.

11   See especially, *The Spirit of the Laws*, 1, II; and Rousseau J J, *The Social Contract and Discourses*. London: J.M Dent, 1952, pp. 46-55.

12   See especially, *Federalist*, 10 reprinted in *The Federalist Papers*. PA: Westvaco, 1995, p. 61.

13   De Tocqueville A, *Democracy in America*, 1. New York: Alfred A Knopf, 1945, p. 434.

14   See Chase R, Hill E & P Kennedy (eds), *The Pivotal States: A New Framework for US Policy in the Developing World*. New York: WW Norton, 1999.

15   Scarritt JR, 'Communal conflict and contention for power in Africa south of the Sahara', in Gurr TR (ed.), *Minorities at Risk: A Global View of Ethnopolitical Conflicts*. Washington, DC: US Institute of Peace, 1993, p. 256.

16   We are grateful to Christopher Clapham for making this point to us.

17   Central Intelligence Agency, *The World Factbook*, 2003. Found at: http://www.cia. gov/cia/publications/factbook/geos/sp.html.

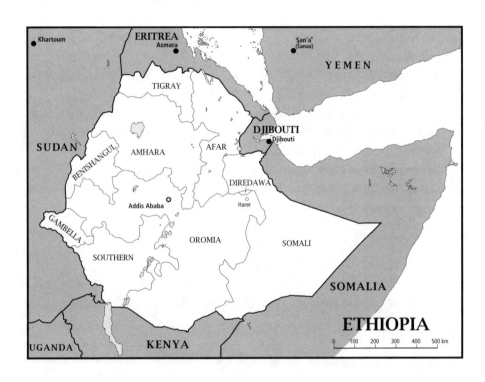

1

Ethiopia

Christopher Clapham

Introduction

A mong African states, Ethiopia ranks second only to Nigeria in the size of its
population. It is also, by a long way, sub Saharan Africa's oldest state, with a
written history stretching back over 700 years and plausible historical antecedents
for one and a half millennia before that. In contrast to the other states examined
in this volume which have had to cope with the territoriality imposed on them by
colonialism, Ethiopia illustrates the struggles of Africa's sole, large indigenous state
to come to terms with the problems imposed by size: all other African states that
derive from pre colonial monarchies - Burundi, Lesotho, Rwanda, Swaziland - are
extremely small. Ethiopia retains a strong sense of its own identity, a pervasive
awareness of its history and an enormous pride in being the only indigenous African
state to retain its independence through the period of the colonial scramble. Despite
considerable upheavals, it has never come close to collapse and indeed, in many
respects, may be regarded as a strong state rather than a weak one.

Set against the criterion of 'functionality', however, Ethiopia's shortcomings are
apparent. Its proverbial and continuing famines and its lowly position on any league
table of global per capita income testify to its inability to provide even the most
basic necessities for most of its people. It was riven by warfare for much of the
twentieth century and, despite a massive and well equipped army, it was the first
African state in the modern era to be forced to acknowledge the secession of part
of its territory with the independence of Eritrea in 1993. It has never maintained
a system of government with any plausible claim to democracy, in the sense of
permitting free and fair competition between rival contenders for power. However,
the structure of the state itself has come under increasing challenge, leading to
the introduction of a constitution which acknowledges, uniquely in Africa, the
right of each of its constituent 'nations, nationalities and peoples' to secede and
form separate states of their own. If 'functionality' is measured, not by the state's

survival but by its capacity to secure the peace, welfare and loyalty of its people, then the Ethiopian state is in trouble.

Geography

All of Africa's large states encompass high levels of geographical variation, and Ethiopia is no exception; yet the peculiar configuration of the country's climate and population zones is, at least in some respects, conducive rather than otherwise to state maintenance. The critical variable is altitude. Central Ethiopia largely comprises a plateau zone, much of it over 2 000m above sea level, with a temperate climate that (with relatively high rainfall) supports high population densities. The northern part of this plateau forms the traditional heartland of the Ethiopian state. Around this central area, the altitude declines, with the result that the densely inhabited highlands are surrounded by lowland areas, with a much lower rainfall, a harsher climate and a sparser population. At its crudest, state maintenance in Ethiopia is therefore a matter of sustaining a critical level of coherence among the peoples of the highlands, who, provided that they are not too badly divided themselves, can then continue to control the lowland peripheries.

However, this has never been an easy task. The highlands are divided by deep gorges which separate different centres of population from one another, and support peoples with disparate languages and cultures. The people of the northern highlands, Orthodox Christian since the fourth century AD, are divided between Tigrinya speaking peoples to the north (broadly, modern Tigray and highland Eritrea), and Amharic speakers further south. The settlements of the Oromo people extend into a significant portion of the northern plateau, as well as much of the south. Other peoples – Sidamas, Gurages, Welaytas, Kambattas, Hadiyas and many more – occupy densely populated areas in the south and west. The peripheral lowlands, large in area but sparse in population, are inhabited principally by Afars to the north east, Somalis to the south east and south, and a variety of Sudanic peoples along the western frontier. To some extent, as a result, the highland/lowland difference broadly corresponds to a frontier between Christianity and Islam, though Islam has also spread into parts of the highlands, especially in the south. Projecting power in Ethiopia is difficult, and regional insurgency has been a feature of the state since the earliest times.

Two further features of Ethiopia's geography are critical. First, the historical vulnerability of north eastern Ethiopia to famine (a result of periodic failures in rainfall), environmental degradation, warfare and misconceived policies has prompted the movement of population towards the south and west, providing strong incentives for a corresponding extension of political control to the relatively fertile and productive areas that provide most of the country's marketable surplus. Secondly, the country's proximity to Arabia, the Red Sea and the Nile valley has linked it to civilisations to the north and east (in contrast it has been relatively isolated, until the modern era, from most of sub Saharan Africa). Christianity and a written language were among the earliest legacies of these linkages; engagement with the politics of the Middle East is one of the more recent ones.

Historicities

The origins of the Ethiopian state, which are a source of great pride to many of its citizens, are also the seed of many of its problems. Formally designated the Empire of Ethiopia until the deposition of its last emperor, Haile Selassie in 1974, it was imperial not only in the title of its ruler but in the way that the state itself was put together. A hegemonic role was historically accorded to the peoples of the northern highlands, and especially the Amhara, who dominated the state from at least the thirteenth century onwards. To its own members, the culture of the northern highlands – including Christianity, the Amharic language, and distinctive dress and food – was not so much 'Amhara' as simply Ethiopian. Amharas and others readily intermarried over many generations, and anyone who adopted the lifestyle of the ruling group, of which Orthodox Christianity was the critical defining element, could rise to the highest positions. But all the same, the premise of inequality built into the original Ethiopian state could not easily be overcome. Muslims were defined as outsiders, and Somalis, Afars and other peoples of the Muslim lowlands were treated as enemies of the state or at best as subordinate clients. Still more damaging, the rapid expansion of Ethiopian territory in the later nineteenth century – when the state used its powerful military force and imported firearms to conquer huge areas south and west of the historic core – incorporated numerous subordinate and potentially dissident peoples. Tracts of conquered land were handed over, either as personal fiefdoms to the leading officials of the imperial regime or in small plots to soldiers, who thus became established as the local guarantors of central power. Anywhere in the world this is a practice fraught with long term dangers and Ethiopia was no exception.

The expansion of Ethiopia's imperial power in the late nineteenth century and the first half of the twentieth was associated with the rise in eminence of Shoa, the region surrounding Addis Ababa. In some respects this was conducive to national unity: Shoa is both centrally placed and multi ethnic, although most of its population are Oromo. But its dominance also helped to alienate the peoples of northern Ethiopia, historically the heartland of the state, who provided the most effective resistance to central government rule. The northernmost area, inhabited by Tigrinya speakers, was divided in 1890 when the Italian colony of Eritrea was formed. This in turn provided the launching pad for Italian invasions of Ethiopia in 1895-96 and 1935-36. Although Eritrea was federated with Ethiopia in 1952, by decision of the UN, it retained a separate sense of identity and political trajectory carried over from its period of Italian (and briefly British) rule. This in turn provided the momentum for a formidable and eventually successful challenge to the Ethiopian state.

Argument has long raged over whether Ethiopia suffered or benefited as a result of not being colonised. Many Ethiopians believe that Ethiopia's exceptionally low level of economic development and its retention of a political structure that eventually came to seem both anachronistic and discriminatory represent a high price to pay for the honour of being the one long established state in Africa to defeat colonialism. Given that any large African country is of necessity multi ethnic, there is something to be said for having diversity imposed by external conquest, which subjects all indigenous peoples to a common colonialism, rather than by the imposition of the power of one of those peoples over the others. The extreme levels of violence suffered by a high proportion of those African states – including Burundi, Rwanda, Liberia and in some degree Sudan – that owed their origin to internal rather than external processes of state formation, testify that this is not solely an Ethiopian problem.

Ethiopia also has a *culture* of statehood, derived both from the hierarchical social structures of the northern highlands, and from the sense of 'manifest destiny' through which it has imposed its rule over neighbouring peoples, that is exceptionally resistant to political accommodation. In striking contrast to that often misleading stereotype that pictures Africans as sitting together and talking until they agree, highland Ethiopian culture is instinctively authoritarian. Whereas inculcating habits of obedience has been a major problem of governance in those parts of Africa not historically subject to state control, the Ethiopian problem has lain in the difficulty of developing the habits of discussion and compromise that are essential to successful government of a large and diverse population. Any questioning, let alone criticism, of leaders is readily equated with treason.

Ethiopia also missed the decolonisation period in the 1950s and early 1960s, when the foundations of multiparty democracy, however shallow, were being laid in many other African states. By that time, many of the younger educated Ethiopians were already intensely alienated from the regime. It was this alienation, the land question and the 'national question' (as the problem of internal ethnic differences is generally referred to) that led in 1974 to what is, as yet, Africa's one unquestioned social revolution. The emperor was deposed and murdered, and power was seized by a committee of radical soldiers, the Derg, who soon announced their commitment to Marxism Leninism, and abandoned Ethiopia's long standing alliance with the US for one with the Soviet Union.

For many observers, this is where things really went wrong. Some have identified, in the idealism of the early years of the revolution, the birth of a liberal democracy that was then cruelly aborted by military dictatorship. I am more sceptical: military dictatorship is the usual outcome of violent revolution, and the Ethiopian revolutionaries, almost all of whom were fervently Marxist, made unconvincing democrats. The Derg's programme of revolutionary centralisation was too thoroughly in line with the historical trajectory of the Ethiopian state to be dismissed as an aberration imposed by a crazed dictator. The consequences for that country were, however, disastrous.

Though the great famine of 1984–85 was not entirely due to mistaken agricultural policies – it was most immediately caused by drought – these policies certainly contributed to its impact. So did the civil wars, especially in the north of the country, which were fostered (or at least greatly exacerbated) by the rigid centralism of the regime, which became enmeshed in unwinnable conflicts fought out in terrain perfectly adapted to guerrilla warfare, against dedicated and exceptionally well organised opponents. The alliance with the Soviet superpower provided not only an inappropriate economic and political model for its Ethiopian acolytes, but also a seemingly inexhaustible source of weaponry that encouraged the regime to believe that its problems could be solved by force. Though it is easy to ascribe the collapse of the Derg in 1991 to that of the Soviet Union itself, its demise was internal every bit as much as external. The attrition of its once highly effective military, and the alienation resulting from conscription and economic failure resulted in its massive armies crumbling away before a smaller but more determined foe.

Resources

Though resources everywhere form an important part of the story of state effectiveness or dysfunctionality, Ethiopia differs from all of the other large

African states that we are considering, in that it does *not* have any significant mineral deposits, in the form either of oil (as in Angola, Nigeria and Sudan), or of other minerals (as in the Democratic Republic of Congo (DRC) and South Africa). One result is that it is far less embroiled with organised crime or the activities of dubious multinational companies than other large African states. Historically, the Ethiopian state derived its resources in part from direct exactions from the peasantry, and in part from control over the trade routes between the African interior and the Red Sea coast. In the modern era, the principal export has been coffee, and while this has made it necessary for the state to control the south western regions in which the crop is grown, it has not created the kind of *rentier* state that characterises the other countries with which we are concerned. Nor has the recent rapid expansion in the production and export of the narcotic *chat*, which is widely consumed, especially in Yemen, become criminalised: it is treated as a legitimate crop. The northern heartland of the state is so degraded that it is highly vulnerable to famine, and extracting any resources from most of it is out of the question. Indeed, a significant element in the current political economy of Ethiopia, which is governed by a regime drawn heavily from the most famine prone part of the country, is the government's need to take revenues away from the principal producing areas, and redistribute them in favour of its own home base.

The critical resources available, both to those who seek to maintain the central Ethiopian state and to those who seek to disrupt or dismember it, have therefore been external. (In this Ethiopia is again unlike other large African states.) Ever since the late nineteenth century, when the emperor Menilek used externally supplied firearms to impose control over rebellious vassals and greatly expand the national territory, the state has skilfully adapted external resources to domestic goals. A key element of this process has been military. Emperor Haile Selassie formed a strategic alliance with the United States, while the Derg, by shifting its allegiance to the Soviet Union, was able to gain access to massive quantities of weaponry. From the period of the great famine in 1984-85, food from foreign sources was added to military hardware as a vital resource for state maintenance, the key difference being that this could only be supplied from the West. In the post Cold War era, with weapon supply a sharply reduced priority for Ethiopia, foreign development aid has to some extent replaced it as a means through which the central government can both maintain itself and secure its control over the national territory.

The critical change, which in this part of Africa preceded the end of the Cold War, has been the capacity of organisations opposed to the central government - splitters, in short - to gain access to external resources which, until the mid 1970s, had largely been monopolised by the state. The Horn of Africa has never been subject to continental norms prohibiting intervention in neighbouring states, and governments throughout the region have been prepared to give covert support to insurgencies directed against rival regimes. From the mid 1970s - with the Ethiopian revolution, the escalation of the Eritrean war, and the 1977-78 Somali invasion of Ethiopia - this covert intervention increased. From the time of the 1984 famine, food was directed by Western relief agencies not only through the official channels controlled by the Ethiopian state but through routes controlled by anti government insurgencies in Ethiopia, especially through Sudan. Though the formidable dedication and organisation of the insurgents were the major sources of their eventual victory, this could scarcely have been achieved without access to supplies from outside. These, rather than the control of indigenous resources such as oil, diamonds, or coltan, have fuelled conflict in the Horn. Though patterns have changed in some degree after the Cold War, with the decline of superpower engagement and the rise of other networks connected especially to radical Islam, the fundamentals remain.

Splitters and controllers

The challenge to the state in Ethiopia comes from actors who have been excluded from it. The closest resemblance is clearly with Sudan, where the 'ownership' of the state is likewise not merely a matter of who happens to hold power at a particular moment, as might be the case in the DRC or Nigeria, but is built into the very origins of the state itself.

The first 'splitters' were the Somalis, who occupied (albeit sparsely) vast areas of south east Ethiopia that had been incorporated into the state during the late nineteenth century, but had nothing whatever in common with it. Their repudiation of the state was fomented by the development in the 1950s of an irredentist Somali nationalism that sought to unite Somalis in five different territories - Italian Somalia, British Somaliland, Djibouti, Ethiopia, and Kenya - into a single state. From 1960, the movement was backed by an independent Somali Republic that had united the first two of these. In practice, however, the Somalis lacked the resources (especially in population and social organisation) to mount a sustained campaign of defiance, and the disastrous reversal of the attempt to launch a pre emptive strike in 1977, while Ethiopia was incapacitated by revolution, made a major contribution to the eventual collapse of the Somali state.

The Eritrean secessionist movement, which was launched in the early 1960s and attained formidable proportions by the mid 1970s, was by contrast successful. Yet Eritrea is itself an artificial and multi ethnic colonial creation, many of whose people had historically formed part of Ethiopia. There was nothing inevitable about this success, which derived from the failure of successive Ethiopian regimes (both imperial and revolutionary) to devise any political formula that could secure the allegiance of highland Christian Eritreans (many of whom had actively supported union with Ethiopia in the 1940s and early 1950s). It was also a result of the corresponding ability of the main insurgent movement, the Eritrean People's Liberation Front (EPLF), to devise a counter formula based on a multi ethnic Eritrean nationalism.

The EPLF provides a very clear example of Herbst's comment that 'rebels structure their forces according to the amount of force that states can project'. The defeat of a massive and heavily armed Ethiopian military required an extraordinary organisational effort, not only at the military level, but also in restructuring local society in the 'liberated areas', and creating very effective external linkages. Though Eritrea's independence (effectively from 1991, formally from 1993) removed it from the equation, it remains a critical splitting factor, first through its example, and second through the support that it has given to other separatist groups since its defeat in the 1998-2000 war against Ethiopia. Conversely, the redefinition of Ethiopian nationalism *against* Eritrea during the 1998-2000 war has helped to promote a greater sense of identity. Eritrea nonetheless remains anomalous, as a multi ethnic state whose claim to independence derived from Italian colonial rule, whereas other challenges to the Ethiopian state have derived from ethnicity.

A third 'splitter', particularly intriguing since it forms the core of the present Ethiopian government, was the Tigray People's Liberation Front (TPLF), based in the northern Tigray region adjoining Eritrea. Like the EPLF, this benefited from the organisational technologies required to fight against the Derg, though it did not acquire the same formidable structure. Despite some early aspirations to independence or even union with Eritrea, the TPLF soon settled on a policy of ethnic federalism - based closely on Stalin's theory of nationalities, applied in the Soviet Union - under which each 'nationality' would have the right to internal self government, with secession as an ultimate resort. This policy made sense in Tigray, which had a truculent sense of self identity but no plausible case for independence from Ethiopia, and also needed the economic security that it could gain only from incorporation into a larger unit. The same formula was much trickier when applied to other peoples (especially in southern and western Ethiopia) who lacked the historic Tigrayan commitment to the state, and formed much less manageable and coherent potential federal units.

The Oromo, who have emerged over recent years as the most important of the potential splitters, are particularly problematic. They are not only the largest group in Ethiopia (if only marginally), comprising some thirty two per cent of the population according to the 1994 census, but they are also the most centrally placed. They are not, like Somalis or Eritreans, peripheral peoples whose secession would leave the core of the state intact. Were they to secede, Ethiopia would no longer exist. This gives the Oromo issue a peculiar sensitivity, but also helps to explain divisions among the Oromo themselves. At one level, why would Oromos want to secede from a state in which they are the largest and most strategically placed group? At another, the Oromo themselves are divided in numerous ways, notably by religion - with significant populations of Orthodox, Lutherans, and Muslims - and also by greatly varying levels of historical association with the Ethiopian state. The major Oromo political organisation, the Oromo Liberation Front (OLF), probably commands the loyalty of most Oromos, even though few of them share its secessionist agenda. It is engaged in a low level insurgency in western Ethiopia, backed by the Eritreans, but has been unable to create the level of political and military effectiveness that marked the EPLF and TPLF insurgencies against the Derg. This in turn reflects divisions, not only within the organisation but also within the constituent elements of the Oromo population. Given the failure of the Ethiopian government's attempt to incorporate the Oromo in any effective way into the ruling coalition, however, the threat remains a live one.

But unlike most of the other large African states with which we are concerned, Ethiopia also has a tradition of statehood, and a profound sense of its own identity that is not merely the property of a single ethnic group. Not only Amharas and Tigrayans, but many Oromos and most of the peoples of south western Ethiopia think of themselves as Ethiopian, and have no secessionist agenda. Indeed, one of the reasons why the country has been so prone to conflict is that substantial sections of the population have had a real commitment to the Ethiopian state and a corresponding determination to defend it. This has been most recently reflected in the sense of outrage with which Ethiopians from many ethnic groups greeted the Eritrean occupation of a small disputed frontier zone in May 1998. The resultant outburst of Ethiopian nationalism even surprised the government itself. Even the former dictator, Mengistu Haile Mariam, retains a measure of support among those who respect his unquestionable commitment to the national identity and territorial integrity of Ethiopia. It is symptomatic that Mengistu belonged to a small group in south western Ethiopia, the Kulo Konta, and made his career in the most nationalist of state institutions, the army.

Leadership and the response to diversity

There are only a limited number of ways in which a state such as Ethiopia can respond to the challenge of diversity. Historically, diversity was accommodated through the impossibility of maintaining close central control over a large geographical area with extremely poor communications – a situation that enabled the state to combine an ideology of deference to an all powerful emperor with a high level of effective regional devolution. This relationship was itself unstable, and varied (with the capacities of individual emperors and the resources available to them and their rivals) between strong central leadership on the one hand, and the virtual disappearance of any central state authority on the other. As increasingly effective central control from the mid nineteenth century onwards made this balance more difficult to maintain, so it became necessary to articulate alternative responses to the central dilemmas of a multi ethnic Ethiopia.

In this process, leadership has played a critical role. Highland Ethiopian political culture, as already indicated, places enormous emphasis on relations of domination and deference, and accords a corresponding respect to leaders. Conversely, no leader who fails to live up to the expectations placed on him is likely to survive. The two generals, Aman Andom and Teferi Benti, who were successive leaders of the revolutionary governments between 1974 and 1977, paid with their lives for their incapacity to establish their personal dominance. They were replaced by a junior officer, Mengistu Haile Mariam, whose ruthlessness and determination enabled him to claw his way to the top.

Once established, an Ethiopian leader can benefit from the respect for authority that is built into the Ethiopian tradition of statehood, and articulate his own approach to the challenges of national governance. Unsurprisingly, then, three very different approaches correspond to the three rulers who have governed the country over most of the last sixty years.

The first of these approaches to governance, pursued by emperor Haile Selassie up to 1974, can be described as assimilationist. Haile Selassie was a manipulative individual, with a strong aversion to violence, who operated within the social and intellectual confines of a court administration. He assumed that the traditions and identities of Christian highland Ethiopia provided a model for the entire country, whose peoples could – by adopting Christianity, using the Amharic language, and generally associating themselves with the customs and institutions of the core – simply become Ethiopian and play a full role in the state. This aspiration did not seem far fetched. Indeed, both the central region of Shoa from which the emperor and most of his leading officials originated, and Haile Selassie himself (genealogically a mixture of Oromo, Amhara and Gurage), exemplified it. During his reign, the expression of ethnic identities was effectively suppressed. The image of the emperor as a benevolent father figure, combined with the extension of the Amharic language through radio and a still modest educational system, helped to present the impression of a country without major internal divisions. At the elite level, Haile Selassie pursued the same vision in a characteristically dynastic fashion, through marriages between members of his own family and the nobility, especially that of Tigray and the western Oromo.

This approach, however, failed to address real problems that could not be ignored indefinitely. Such issues, of which land tenure was the most pressing, were bound eventually to find political expression. Once this happened, a system that worked fairly well for incorporating a small number of favoured individuals into a central elite - and this was essentially all that Ethiopian politics under the imperial regime consisted of - was unable to cope with the mobilisation of political identities on a larger scale. Its failure was most clearly illustrated in Eritrea, where the imperial government sought to associate leading politicians with the central government through the time honoured mechanisms of imperial patronage. However, it could not manage organised political parties (which existed only in Eritrea, and were completely absent from the rest of Ethiopia), or allow the Eritrean government, established under the terms of the UN sponsored federation, to exercise any autonomy. Exactly the same problem undermined the imperial regime at the centre, where it could find no place for the new political ideologies espoused by urban groups - and especially students - and was incapable of managing the inevitable mobilisation of ethnic identities. The imperial government fell because it possessed no plausible formula through which it could govern.

The revolution, on the other hand, rapidly led to the emergence of a Marxist military regime with limitless confidence in its capacity to create both development and national unity, and to a proliferation of other political organisations, almost all of them Marxist. After a murderous bout of in fighting that culminated in the 'red terror' of 1976-77, a 'red emperor', Mengistu Haile Mariam, re established the old pattern of autocracy. He assumed a much more ruthless and violent leadership style than his predecessor, and sought to harness the forces unleashed by the revolution through a nationalist formula under which the 'feudalism' of the old regime was swept away, and all Ethiopians were to unite to defend the nation and its revolution against feudalists, reactionaries, secessionists and narrow nationalists.

The Ethiopian revolutionaries were Jacobins, like their French counterparts of

1792. They believed that by sweeping away the corrupt old order, and introducing social reforms, they could lay the basis for a centralised and effective national state. The key to this was the nationalisation of land, the use of which was then to be allocated to local farmers through peasants' associations. In this way the discriminatory land tenure system imposed by conquest on much of the country would be destroyed. Divisions within the revolutionary elite were ruthlessly suppressed and a Somali invasion was defeated, with Soviet and Cuban assistance, in 1977–78. For a time, it seemed that the revolutionary state, its armies massively expanded, was gaining the upper hand over the secessionists in Eritrea. State farms and co operatives were established, a Leninist vanguard ruling party was set up, and Ethiopia set out on a new course as a people's democratic republic in close alliance with the Soviet bloc. There was very limited recognition of ethnic diversity, notably in a literacy campaign that was conducted in a variety of languages. There was also a minimal recognition of different nationalities within the structures established in 1987 by the People's Democratic Republic of Ethiopia, only a few years before the regime fell; but the entire ethos of the regime was centralist.

Again, the new formula had something to be said for it. In the early years of the revolution, peasants in much of the country gained real benefits from land reform, and their dedication to the new regime helped to secure its victory over opponents both at home and abroad. These gains were, however, eroded by the inefficiency of socialist economic management and the increasing exactions from the peasantry – especially in terms of taxes and military conscription – required to impose the regime's control over its obdurate and extremely well organised opponents in Eritrea and Tigray. The failure of that effort led to the collapse of the revolutionary government in 1991.

The third response to the inherent problems of Ethiopian diversity was that of the Ethiopian Peoples' Revolutionary Democratic Front (EPRDF) government, led by Meles Zenawi, which seized power in May 1991. Meles is a very different leader from any of his predecessors. He is an intellectual, and self effacing to the point of seeking anonymity (unlike almost all other African leaders, he had no desire to be head of state and contented himself with the post of prime minister). He remains imbued with the Marxist Leninist principles common to almost all Ethiopian students of his generation, including an approach to issues of ethnic diversity derived from Stalin's writings on 'the national question' in the USSR. The EPRDF accordingly sought to rebuild Ethiopia from the base up, through voluntary union between its different constituent 'nations, nationalities, and peoples'. Each of these was to have the right to internal self government, and to engage with the others in forming a federal central government, from which, as already noted, they retained the right to secede. Only thus, the EPRDF argued, could the legacies of inequality and highland Christian hegemony be removed and the bases for participatory democracy be laid. This was a remarkable programme, diametrically opposed to the way in which the Ethiopian state had been constituted in the past, and sharply at variance also with the common commitment of African states to maintaining the territorial structures inherited from the colonial partition. Now in place for a dozen years, it has inevitably had a bumpy ride and faces an uncertain future. However, it provides a unique approach to the problems of Africa's ethnic diversity.

The most striking feature of the new political order is that people can participate in it *only* through the medium of a specifically ethnic organisation: there is no such thing as a national political party, and all elections (outside Addis Ababa, which retains a federal status) are conducted within the framework of a particular ethnic state. The contrast with the rest of Africa, where 'tribalism' is generally disapproved, and ethnically based parties sometimes prohibited, is dramatic. The new system likewise dismisses the experience of Ethiopian nationalism as mere 'Amhara chauvinism', and denies a place in the political order for those who wish to identify themselves simply as 'Ethiopians'. Though ethnicity has now been embedded in Ethiopian politics to an extent that will be very difficult (and perhaps impossible) to remove, my feeling is that there remain reservoirs of Ethiopian nationhood that are likely to reassert themselves in the event of any serious challenge to the state. Indeed, the EPRDF government, despite its own commitment to ethnic federalism, had to draw on precisely these reservoirs during the 1998–2000 war against Eritrea.

A second problem is that the redefinition of Ethiopia on ethnic lines has created conflicts of its own, especially over the demarcation of the territories of the different federal units. In Ethiopia as throughout Africa, the boundaries between groups are often blurred – by migration, by the ambivalent identities of individuals, and by the shared use of resources by different groups: pastoralists and agriculturalists, for example, overlap and interact along a long and fuzzy frontier. Under the new system, not only must everyone identify themselves as belonging to a single specific group, but the boundaries of the territory belonging to that group must be demarcated on the ground. Within that territory, in turn, the group to which it is allocated has proprietary rights, and those who do not belong to that group are liable to be regarded as strangers and aliens, and accordingly discriminated against, expelled, or even (in extreme cases) killed. The dangers of 'ethnic cleansing' are limitless, and comparison with Yugoslavia, where a previously multi ethnic state was likewise reconstructed along ethnic lines, is by no means inappropriate. A large number of conflicts over boundary demarcation, several of them bloody, have broken out.

Thirdly, there are real questions over whether the EPRDF government is prepared to allow - or can indeed *afford* to allow - the regional autonomy that it has promised. In part, of course, the interests and perspectives of an incumbent central government are very different from those of the regionally based guerrillas they once were. They now have a commitment to maintain the state against which they once fought, and have taken over the central government institutions, including the bureaucracy, that once served the Mengistu regime. In part, too, the promised autonomy has always incorporated a considerable sleight of hand: in particular, the ethnic parties to which power within the federal system has been devolved are all constituent parties of the EPRDF and formed from the top down, under the aegis of a leadership heavily dominated by the TPLF, rather than developing from indigenous peoples themselves. Opposition parties formed with local support, even when they posed no threat to the federal government, have been harassed and suppressed by the EPRDF, in collaboration with an administrative structure that retains its old centralist instincts.

Even in south western Ethiopia, inhabited by small and historically disadvantaged groups who have everything to gain from local autonomy and have no secessionist agenda, there is a palpable sense of alienation from an EPRDF regime that is widely regarded as merely the vehicle for Tigrayan hegemony. In the case of the largest of the southern peoples, the Sidama, this was massively intensified in March 2002, when government forces opened fire on a peaceful demonstration protesting at a proposed change in the status of the regional capital, Awassa, killing a significant number of demonstrators. The inability of the regime to manage even this low level of dissent revealed the continuing mentality of autocratic control behind the façade of regional self government. Characteristically, the regime's reaction was not to discipline those responsible for the massacre, but to blame the demonstrators and purge anyone in the regional administration who was suspected of sympathising with them. As this case sharply illustrates, Ethiopia - unlike, notably, Nigeria - has not developed a federal *politics*, in which relations between different groups, and between groups and the central government, are subject to constant renegotiation and debate. At base, Ethiopia remains the top down polity that it always was.

Another difference from Nigeria lies in the fact that the territories of the main ethnic groups are not divided between a number of states within the federal system, but are consolidated into single units. The dangers that this poses are most intense in Oromiya, where the government has been quite unable to reach any accommodation with the OLF (a failure for which the divisions between, and inadequacies of, the OLF leadership bear a significant part of the responsibility), and has alienated most of the population. The party that formally represents the Oromo within the EPRDF, the Oromo People's Democratic Organisation (OPDO), is no more than an administrative shell. The EPRDF, in short, has been unable to break away from that inability to compromise or establish genuine bargaining relationships with autonomous political forces that has proved the bane of Ethiopian state culture. Having greatly enhanced the level of ethnic consciousness in Ethiopia - to an extent that is now difficult to control, and quite impossible to remove - it has failed to develop the political institutions that are essential to manage the social forces that it has unleashed.

The regional setting

Ethiopia is the dominant state within the Horn of Africa. The only regional state that remotely matches it, Sudan, has multiple alternative agendas from the DRC to the Middle East, and its other neighbouring states - Eritrea, Djibouti, Somaliland, Somalia and Kenya - are much smaller and in most cases much weaker than itself. Ethiopia should therefore be expected to control its regional environment. In practice, however, this has been an extremely difficult task, not least because the tensions inherent in the composition of Ethiopia itself spill over into relations with its neighbours, which have their own intractable problems that reach into Ethiopia. The Horn of Africa has long been a region with a high level of conflict in which, as already noted, the conventions that (for a time at least) limited conflicts between states in other parts of Africa have not applied. The territorial integrity of existing states has been openly contested - notably in Somalia/Somaliland, in Eritrea, and in southern Sudan - and all governments in the region have been quite prepared to intervene in the domestic politics of their neighbours. These practices persist. Since Eritrean independence in 1991-93 and especially since the outbreak of war between Ethiopia and Eritrea in 1998, the regional stakes have been greatly raised by Ethiopia's loss of direct access to the sea. Now the largest landlocked state in the world (measured by population), Ethiopia has a vital interest in access to a port, which could in principle be attained through any of its six neighbours, but which in practice most affects its relations with Djibouti and Eritrea.

Though Ethiopia is too strong to suck in the armies of neighbouring states in the way that has happened in the DRC, it has sensitive relations with all of its neighbours, and faces acute problems in dealing with two of them, Somalia/ Somaliland and Eritrea. The Somali frontier is closely associated with the problems of governing the Somali regional state within Ethiopia itself, which has been the most lawless and unstable of all the ethnic units established since 1991. In much of this large and sparsely inhabited zone, government control is at best nominal and the central government has resorted to the time honoured tactics of playing off different Somali clans and factions against one another. These tactics extend into Somalia itself: Ethiopia has an interest in maintaining the effectively independent, though still unrecognised, government of Somaliland, and has become deeply involved in the factional politics of 'Puntland', the largely self governing region of eastern Somalia. Since 9/11, the identification by the US of Somalia as an area of state collapse conducive to support for al Qaeda, the presence of US forces in Djibouti and the Islamist agendas of some of the local factions, have enabled Ethiopia to link its own security interests in the region to the 'global war on terror'.

To the north, any hope of stable relations with Eritrea was shattered by the Eritrean seizure of disputed areas in May 1998, and – after Ethiopian victory in the war that followed – by a badly bungled international attempt at demarcation. At the very least, rapprochement remains impossible so long as the Isayas Afewerki regime remains in power in Asmara; while the border issue is likely to remain a bone of contention between the two states for long into the future. One result of this conflict has been support by the Eritrean government for incursions by OLF guerrillas into western Ethiopia, taking advantage of the large areas along the eastern frontier of the Sudan that are beyond the control of the government in Khartoum. These incursions have as yet proved ineffectual, but demonstrate the close connections between regional and domestic instability in a deeply volatile area of the continent. Sudan itself has historically uneasy relations with Ethiopia, deriving from the fault line between Orthodox Christianity and Arabic Islam. Even tiny Djibouti, though heavily dependent on the transit trade with Ethiopia, has sought to counterbalance this dependence by fostering relations with Arabia, while its two domestic communities, Afars and Issa Somalis, clash within Ethiopia over their respective territorial boundaries, and over control of the trade between the highlands and the Red Sea coast. In practice, therefore, any attempt to resolve the problems of state dysfunctionality in Ethiopia must necessarily have a regional component.

International engagement

As already noted, international actors have long had a critical role in the politics of Ethiopia and the Horn, from the period of the scramble (when the Ethiopian government of the time adeptly manipulated the rivalries between Britain, France and Italy), through the Second World War and the Cold War (when Ethiopia sided first with the US, then with the Soviet Union), and into the post Cold War era. Ethiopia's leader since 1991, Meles Zenawi, a man of great charm, intelligence and apparent modesty, has been extraordinarily adept at presenting his regime in such a way as to attract the sympathy and support of the major Western powers - far more so than in his management of domestic politics. In addition to becoming a favourite of the international donor community, he has been able to establish Ethiopia - notably in the eyes of the US - as a pole of regional stability, and as a favoured partner in the 'global war on terror'.

Ethiopia does indeed have significant interests in common with the US and other Western powers in maintaining stability in the region. For reasons entrenched in the country's history, political structure and geographical location, Ethiopian rulers have long had an intense suspicion of radical Islam. This is currently enhanced both by a government with strong Islamist credentials in Sudan, and the appeal of Islam as a potentially unifying ideology to some of the warring factions in Somalia. The latter carries a powerful threat to Ethiopia. The one regional conflict not exacerbated by the Islamic factor is that between Ethiopia and Eritrea, which has a suspicion of Islam every bit as great as Ethiopia's, a fact that has enabled both of these bitter rivals to sign up with the 'coalition of the willing' in the conflict against Iraq.

Ethiopia, however, has been able to manipulate international support while remaining highly resistant to any external pressure against itself. The stereotype that sees African states as mere tools of external powers has been reversed in the case of Ethiopia, which - not only under the present regime, but also under both Haile Selassie and Mengistu - has been far more skilful at using the outside world than the other way round. The 'global war on terror', for example, has provided the perfect umbrella under which Ethiopia has been able to promote its interests in Somalia with the tacit backing of the US. Similarly, Ethiopia has been able to pursue domestic economic policies which serve largely to maintain state control, while benefiting from development assistance and food aid which can be used to compensate for the deficiencies of its own policies. It has proved very difficult - indeed, virtually impossible - for donors to turn Ethiopia's aid dependence into any effective leverage designed to reverse the dysfunctionalities of the Ethiopian state.

Alternative futures

The central problems of Ethiopian state dysfunctionality lie not so much with its size as with its culture. Ethiopia is not an ungovernable state, and has indeed been governed over much of the recent past with a high degree of efficiency. The revolutionary government was for example able to implement nationwide land reform and to establish institutions down to the lowest level – the peasants' associations and urban residents' associations or *kebelles* – which imposed central government policies even over such unpopular tasks as taxation and military conscription. These have largely survived the change of regime in 1991. When the Eritrean war broke out in 1998, for example, a regime that had drastically cut down the armed forces after 1991 (under the mistaken assumption that the country faced no serious external military threat) was able to recruit and train a large army that, despite heavy casualties, was able to win a decisive military victory against a formidable opponent within two years. These are not the actions of a 'failed state'.

They are however the actions of a state that has historically conceived its role in terms of control, and has proved inept at extending that role into activities that call for a different kind of state: a state, notably, that is able to allow any significant autonomy to actors operating independently from it, or to institutionalise mechanisms allowing discussion and compromise within the structure of the government itself. Partly as a result of the EPRDF government's own policies, but also as a result of a diversity enhanced by social change and increasing demands for participation, Ethiopia is now too complex a society to be governed in the way that it once was. A remarkably free press expresses a wide range of often dissident opinions. Opposition parties have, under donor pressure, been allowed to form and organise. Regional and ethnic interests can be openly expressed in a way that was until recently completely impermissible. Yet dissent is still instinctively regarded in terms appropriate to rebellion or even treason, and even local administrations have in practice been denied the autonomy formally guaranteed to them by the nominally federal constitution. There is, in short, a dangerous mismatch between the development of social and political forces on the one hand, and the opportunities for these to be incorporated into the political structure on the other.

Similar problems affect entrepreneurs who seek economic opportunities that are likewise nominally made available by the conversion of a leadership steeped in student Marxist radicalism to the virtues of the market. Despite its formally capitalist economy, the Ethiopian government places endless obstacles in the way of any investor who seeks to establish a business in the country (the 'start up time' for obtaining the necessary licences and legal status is one of the longest in Africa), and continues to maintain a large number of 'partystatal' enterprises, spread across every significant area of the economy, which are owned by the ruling party and enjoy significant advantages in competition with independent companies. Urban development, outside a few centres favoured by administrative expansion (of which the Tigrayan capital, Mekelle, is the most striking and the most resented), has been neglected by economic policies which are designed to favour agriculture, and have enjoyed only limited success even there. A large and potentially volatile urban population clamours for employment, and may easily turn to violence.

These contradictions were dramatically exposed by the national elections of May 2005, in which – effectively for the first time in Ethiopia's long history – opposition parties were able to compete for popular support on even roughly equal terms with those already in power. Two principal opposition coalitions were able to mount campaigns which challenged the regime at each of its two principal points of weakness. The Coalition for Unity and Democracy sought to mobilise the nationalist constituency against a government that was readily portrayed as regionalist and divisive; it gained support especially from urban populations, and from Amharas and some other peoples who tended to favour a strong central state; its economic policy sought to dismantle the continuing elements of state control that the EPRDF had inherited from its Marxist past. On the other side, the Union of Ethiopian Democratic Forces sought to mobilise ethnic constituencies, notably in Oromia and parts of the Southern Region, which resented the government's evident failure to concede in practice the levels of regional autonomy that it had promised in principle.

Both of these coalitions were led by Addis Ababa based elites, with a high proportion of intellectuals, a fact that may have misled the government as to the danger that they posed. But the most striking fact about the election was the high turnout that it attracted from Ethiopian voters, in the countryside as well as the towns – a level of participation that placed it on a par with 'founding elections', such as those in South Africa in 1994 or in other African states in the run up to independence. A high proportion of these votes were cast for the opposition, and (so far as one can tell) especially for the CUD, which swept every single seat in Addis

Ababa, as a high proportion of those in other towns and parts of the countryside. The UEDF likewise scored well, notably in its regional heartlands.

What would have happened had the votes been honestly counted, and had the results been allowed to stand, can only be a matter for speculation. The preceding discussion has already indicated how deeply entrenched are the obstacles to liberal multi party democracy in Ethiopia. The opposition coalitions were themselves fragile; it cannot be assumed that they would have respected in office the democratic norms that they upheld in opposition; and there were very significant policy differences between the two major opposition groupings that would have called for compromises to which Ethiopian political culture has been deeply antithetical. At all events, the option never arose. Stunned, as was the opposition itself, by the completeness of the CUD victory in Addis Ababa, where the results were among the first to come through, the government announced that it had achieved a majority, issued a tally of seats won long before the necessary results had been declared by the election board, and proceeded to rig the outstanding results in conformity with the totals that it had declared. Under these figures, together with the Somali region where the elections were held later, the EPRDF was accorded 327 seats, with 109 for the CUD, 52 for the UEDF, and the remainder of the 545 seats going to a variety of local parties. The European Union election observer mission declared these results to be manifestly flawed. Opposition demonstrations called in protest were suppressed by force with significant loss of life, and the principal opposition leaders (along with many others) were imprisoned on charges of fomenting rebellion.

The resulting impasse remains unresolved at the time of writing. The possibility of any negotiated settlement between the government and opposition parties has effectively been excluded, and although the government remains in power, its standing both domestically and internationally has been badly damaged. The loss of international support is particularly dangerous, because of the government's dependence both on foreign aid flows, which are likely to be curtailed, and on diplomatic pressure to prevent a recurrence of the war with Eritrea. Still more important, however, has been the inability of the government to manage a successful balance between the demands of statehood and Ethiopian nationalism on the one hand, and of regional and ethnic autonomy and representation on the other. Indeed, by encouraging demands for autonomy that it has failed to meet, while remaining closely associated with its own home region of Tigray, the EPRDF may prove to have exacerbated the divisions and inequalities that it had made it its mission to ameliorate.

One scenario is, therefore, that if Ethiopians cannot manage their problems together, then they must do so apart. It has been said of Stalin's theory of nationalities – on which Ethiopia's current political order is closely based – that it had life only *after* death. That is to say, the formal division of the Soviet Union into its fifteen different union republics counted for nothing so long as the communist government remained in power; but as soon as it collapsed, this division provided the formula for splitting the USSR into fifteen different independent states. Similarly, the EPRDF regime has divided Ethiopia into 'national states', which have little autonomy while they are all subject to EPRDF control, but which have established territorial boundaries and internal governmental structures. They are entrenching the idea of ethnicity as the basis for political organisation and may in turn make possible the fragmentation of a post EPRDF Ethiopia into independent Tigray, Afar, Amhara, Somali, Oromo and Southern Peoples' states.

This is certainly a possibility, and I cannot be certain whether it is my own long association with the country that leads me to discount it. Ethiopia has a sense of its own identity, implicit even in the actions of those who contest central rule, that continues to override the centrifugal pull of ethnicity. Even among the Oromo, who are in this respect the critical group, it is difficult to discern any real commitment to independent statehood or any sense that it is an option on the practical political agenda. Demands for Oromo independence come almost entirely from exiles, whose grasp of political developments within the country is at best extremely limited. Most of Ethiopia's peoples, including not only the core highlands of Amhara and Tigray but the southern nationalities as well, have much to lose from fragmentation and may be expected to resist it. Oromos themselves have far more to gain from ruling the country in which they are the largest single group, than from separating themselves from it.

It is certainly possible to conceive that *some* of the newly independent states of a fragmented Ethiopia might better be able to respond to the challenges of development, political pluralism and human welfare than the current Ethiopian state in the way that some of the states of the former Soviet Union have done. However, it is difficult to imagine a post Ethiopian state system *as a whole* being able to create an improved social, political and economic environment. Part of the problem lies in the levels of territorial uncertainty and conflict, already intense within the current federal structure. These could only be exacerbated by separate sovereignty. Issues of land lockedness and communications would become even more acute. But the biggest problem of all would be the presence at the centre of the post Ethiopian cluster of a deeply problematic Oromiya, amoebic in shape, riven by internal rivalries, and lacking any evident capacity to generate an effective statehood. Though there are certainly some limited and practical steps that political actors both within Ethiopia and outside might be able to take to help reduce some of the country's problems and enhance the welfare of its people, this case study as a whole lends weight to the warning in the Introduction that external actors in particular must retain a modest assessment of what can be achieved.

2

War over identity: the case of Sudan

Jack Kalpakian

Introduction

This chapter analyses the slow, gradual collapse of the Sudanese state since its independence in 1956. Identity is central to this analysis, because it is a constant factor that interacts with many variables, such as conflict over resources and the colonial map.

Independent Sudan has suffered civil war throughout its history, except for the decade 1973-1983. Although the country's natural resources, if properly used, could meet the needs of the population, the continual conflict has hindered development. When oil was discovered in the South, the hope was that it would lift the country from poverty. Instead, oil became a primary bone of contention between the government and the Sudanese People's Liberation Army (SPLA), representing the Southern Sudanese communities. These communities were included in Sudan thanks to the British and the Egyptians.[1] Indeed, the map of Sudan is largely the handiwork of the British Colonial Office, which decreed that Nilotic, Sudanic, Hamitic and Arabic speaking peoples should share a state. None of these peoples were consulted about their incorporation into Sudan, and the identity policies of the independent Sudanese state have not been inclusive. Cultural and linguistic differences, when combined with religious division and conflict over resources, have helped break down the country.

The problem for Southern Sudan is not a case of national self determination, although the government in Khartoum has recently agreed to grant the South that right. Over time, a complex system of relationships has emerged among the various Sudanese peoples. An independent Southern Sudan will have to address issues such as the seasonal movement of nomads from the North to the South, and the status of Southern people living in the North and of Arabs living in the South. Apart from legal and international issues, there is the matter of oil wealth and the Southern share of the revenues. It is fair to state that the Northern and Southern elites are both

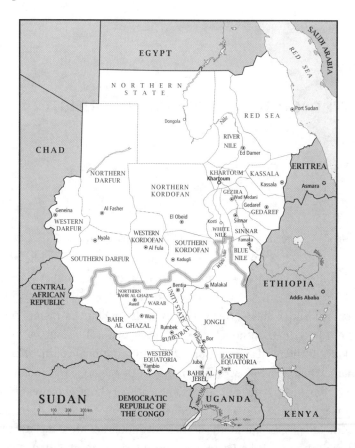

The most recent (Jan 2006) map of the provincial boundaries showing the border of the proposed 'Southern Sudan'. The areas of the Blue Nile and Southern Kordofan are disputed by the South.

motivated by the wish to obtain (or retain) access to oil revenues, and that greed is a malady that infects both sides. The SPLA is asking that the South receive eighty five per cent of the country's oil revenues during the transitional period (see details of the Machakos Protocol below), while the Khartoum government is offering twenty five per cent. Yet the debate over the distribution of wealth presumes the existence of two sides in Sudan. These two sides are not Muslims and non Muslims per se, *but offer two differing alternative definitions of the national identity of Sudan.*

This chapter examines the geography, infrastructure, ethnology and the dysfunctionality of the Sudanese state. In addition, it examines responses to the question of Sudanese national identity, the failure of leadership, the first Sudanese civil war, the Addis Ababa Peace Agreement, the second Sudanese civil war, the Machakos peace proposal, the Niavasha peace settlement, the death of John Garang de Mabior and the catastrophe in Darfur. It concludes with some reflections on the past, and the prospects for peace in Sudan.

Geography

One of the tags memorised by every Sudanese schoolchild is the size of the Sudanese state. Its territory is traditionally referred to as one million square miles, but Sudan is actually somewhat smaller at 966,757 square miles or 2,505,810 square kilometres. In comparative terms, the country is one quarter the size of the US (including Alaska), more than twice the size of South Africa, and four and a half times the size of France. In short, the area of its land mass approaches that of India. Sudan can be described as a huge basin, or a *tasht* (a large flat washing tub used in Sudan, with stones along the side and at certain other points).

The Ethiopian border marks the beginning of the Ethiopian highlands; the Red Sea portion of Sudan is hilly and in places mountainous; mountain chains can also be found near the centre of the country, in the Ngessana portions of the Blue Nile province and the Nuba Mountains area of Kurdufan. In the Darfur region, in the western portion of the country, the Jebel Marra mountains break the dry plains, rising to cooler, wetter and greener altitudes. A huge swamp dominates the central southern portion of the country. This is Sudd, which is surrounded by savannah grasslands that eventually give way southwards to highland forests on the Ugandan, Congolese and Central African borders. To the north, these grasslands are replaced by stony deserts and the northern riparian agricultural settlements.[2]

The country is bound together by the Nile river system, which reaches every province in the country except for northern Darfur, and gives the country a large measure of its geographic coherence. But the Nile is still an unknown, despite having been explored by Europeans and Ottomans in the 19th century. There is some dispute as to the extent of the Nile river basin, the countries within its limits, and the length of the actual river.[3] Sudan dominates the Nile basin in all ways but one: most of the water actually originates in Ethiopia, outside Sudanese controlled areas.

Infrastructure

To a great extent, infrastructure in Sudan means the transport system. The railway network is a legacy of the Anglo–Egyptian period. There are two railway concerns:

Sudan Railways and the Gezira Light Railway. Nominally, Sudan Railways covers about 4,578 kilometres of track, but it does not serve the whole of the country and has not constructed any new extensions since the 1950s. SPLA activities in Bahar al Ghazal have also put the Railways' southern terminus, Wau, out of regular service. The Gezira Light Railway, which comprises about 1,400 kilometres of narrow tracks, is used to move agricultural products out of the Gezira scheme areas and to move in agricultural inputs. However, its operations are sometimes suspended owing to flooding and other weather related problems. Unlike Sudan Railways, the Gezira Light Railway has been adding to its tracks, despite the unreliability of its service.[4]

Alternative forms of transport infrastructure include roads and waterways. The overwhelming majority of Sudan's roads remain unpaved and suitable only for use in dry weather. The country has about 4,320 kilometres of paved roads, and about 12,000 kilometres of unpaved ones. In comparison, South Africa, with a similar sized population and about forty per cent of Sudan's landmass, has about 60,000 kilometres of paved and 360,000 kilometres of unpaved roads. (A similar comparison can be made between the railway systems in the two countries.) In Sudan, many roads in the South have been rendered impassable by heavy rains and/or the laying of landmines by the army and the SPLA.

Use of Sudan's waterways is also affected by conflict. Nominally, the river boats can cover about 5,000 kilometres of the Nile system, but service to most of the South has been disrupted by the civil war. A similar state of deterioration exists in other categories of infrastructure, from hospitals to schools.

The peoples of Sudan

There are 134 extant languages in the Sudan.[5] Although about half the population have Arabic as their mother tongue, most Sudanese people are bilingual. This high degree of linguistic multiplicity is correlated with ethnic and religious diversity. Sudan's ethnic structure can be summarised as fifty two per cent African, forty per cent Arab, and six per cent Beja. Although there are significant exceptions to any classification of the ethnic and cultural communities of Sudan, it is useful to distinguish the various peoples of the country by religion.[6] However, it is important to remember that there are Arabic speaking Christians and Dinka Muslims in the country. What often seem to be clear dividing lines are often a spectrum of shades instead. It should also be noted that distinguishing between the communities of Sudan for the purpose of exposition should not be regarded as advocacy for separatism.

Arabs

Sudanese Arabs constitute the largest Muslim community in the Sudan. While it is possible to talk about Sudanese Arabs as a group, it is important to note that they are a diverse and heterogeneous group of tribes and peoples. They are generally divided into three sub communities: Ja'alayin, Juhayna and the Kawahla. Each of these tribal confederations is further divided into smaller units, until one reaches the level of individual tribes or bands. The Ja'alayin confederation, which includes the Ja'alyin proper, the Shayqiyah and the Rubtab, dominates the northern reaches of the Nile River. The two diarchies in pre Egyptian Northern Sudan were Ja'alyin and the Shayqiyah.

The Juhayna tribal confederation includes the Shukriyah, the Baqqarah and the Kababish sub confederations, which in turn are divided into tribes like the Humr and Rizigat. These peoples live in the Northern Blue Nile, Kurdufan and the Sudanese North east. The Kawahla tribal confederation dominates the regions around Khartoum, and is composed of thirteen tribes.

Even though they represent only forty per cent of the population, Sudanese Arabs have traditionally dominated the Sudanese state. They have provided it with an identity, a language, a religion and a culture. Some Arabic speakers are of Egyptian and Syrian Christian origin, so an Arab identity does not necessarily connote Islam, even in the Sudan. Arab identity also does not mean that Sudanese Arabs look different from other Sudanese: in appearance, almost all Sudanese are African, the only exceptions being Mediterranean transplants and the Rashaydah.

Muslim African Peoples

The Nubians constitute the second most important Muslim majority community in Sudan. Displaced by the Aswan High Dam, they have been resettled in New Halfa, Kassala and Port Sudan. They have put their high level of literacy to good use in government service and education. The Nubians tend to be a close knit community, zealous about maintaining its separate identity and language. They share Port Sudan and the Red Sea province with Beja peoples. Once derided as 'fuzzy wuzzies' by some of the British, the Beja come from four distinct tribal confederations: the Bashariya, the Amarar, the Bani Amir and the dominant Hadendowa, whose name is sometimes used to refer to all Beja. Some of these Beja groups are settled, while others are nomadic. The Beja speak a language akin to Somali and constitute six to ten per cent of the people of Sudan.

In Darfur, the Fur people and their royal family are oriented to the linguistic and cultural traditions of Chad and northern Nigeria. Along with the Fur, the Masalit, Daju, Berti and Zaghawa practise Africanised Islam and speak Nilo-Saharan and other African languages. They do not generally think of themselves as Arabs. In the case of the Fur and the Masalit, there is also a long history of local autonomy and a national identity centred on the royal households of each community.

West African people are also present in large numbers in Sudan. About ten per cent of the population of the northern provinces may be of west African origin. About sixty per cent are said to be from Nigeria. Borno, Takari, Fulani and Hausa peoples are also members of the west African community, which has generally integrated well with the Sudanese social tapestry.

Nilotes

'Nilotes' refers to people who speak languages within the Eastern Sudanic branch of Nilo-Saharan languages and share a myth of common origin. Nilotic peoples make up about sixty per cent of the population of the Southern Sudan. The largest Nilotic group, the Dinka (Ngok in their own language), represents over forty per cent of the population of the Southern provinces, and about ten per cent of the population of Sudan. In addition to the Dinka, two other Nilotic tribes retain a great deal of influence. The Nuer are about one quarter as numerous as the Dinka. Like the Arabs, the Dinka and the Nuer are divided into smaller groups. The Dinka represent a confederation of twenty five distinct tribal identities, and the Nuer about ten. The Shilluk, the third largest Nilotic group, are about one quarter the number of the Nuer. The Shilluk's importance resides in their development of a state centralised around the idea of a sacred king. There are other Nilotic groups besides the Dinka, Nuer and the Shilluk, but they are very small in number and widely scattered. While some Nilotes have adopted Christianity and/or Islam, they remain committed to their tribal loyalties. Cattle raising is the primary economic activity of Sudanese Nilotes and cattle are also central to Nilotic religious traditions.

Nuba and other groups

The Nuba live outside Southern Sudan, in the province of Kurdufan. They speak Kurdufanian languages, which are unrelated to Arabic. Islam and the Arabic language have not found many adherents among them. The group is diverse internally, and consists of about thirty to forty communities, some speaking mutually unintelligible Kurdufanian dialects. The Nuba practise traditional African religions and Christianity, and have generally sided with the South during the civil war. While their name suggests a relationship with the Nubians of the North, the exact link is unclear.

In the South, about forty per cent of the people are not Nilotes. Of these, the Azande constitute around seven to eight per cent. They speak a Niger-Congo language which is also used in central Africa. Most of the two dozen or so remaining groups in the South speak Nilo-Saharan languages that are not Nilotic. Of these, the Muslim Ingessana of the Ngessana Hills in the Blue Nile province have sided with the SPLA during the civil war.

The Sudanese diaspora

There are two categories of Sudanese and former Sudanese overseas residents. The first group left Sudan largely for economic reasons, and migrated to the Gulf Co operation Council States (GCC), Europe and North America in search of employment opportunities. The second group left in order to flee the civil war and the political unrest associated with it. There are about two million Sudanese people in the former category; the number of the latter is not known. It is nevertheless clear that there are now overseas communities of Sudanese in places as diverse as Egypt, Bulgaria, Iowa, Canada, Australia and the United Kingdom. Several NGOs have been created by overseas and diaspora Sudanese to provide assistance, information, legal services and other forms of help for each other. The Sudanese workers in the GCC states are able to make contributions to investment funds and charities in Sudan through GCC banks.

Sudanese law includes an elaborate exit visa regime, which prevents the departure of expatriated Sudanese who have failed to pay special fees and taxes. These taxes make keeping Sudanese citizenship an expensive proposition, which many refugees cannot afford. As a result, Sudanese refugees often feel obliged to naturalise in their new homes. They sometimes become politically active on behalf of the Sudanese government or its opponents. The NGOs of the diaspora are divided along North–South lines, and have different viewpoints on a wide range of issues. Tapping the potential of Sudanese expatriates would entail a change in Sudanese law to allow dual citizenship and the limitation of taxes on income earned on Sudanese soil.

State dysfunction

By any measure, Sudan qualifies as a failed state. Despite claims to the contrary by the current government, literacy remains beneath thirty per cent after forty seven years of independence. Estimates made in 1990 showed that only twenty seven per cent of the men and twelve per cent of the women could read.[7] Official estimates by the Central Intelligence Agency (CIA) put the number of HIV positive people at about one per cent of the population, and the number of people living with Aids at about 200,000. The real numbers are probably much higher. Many areas of the country, particularly in the South, totally lack government services such as education, health and police protection. Life expectancy for both men and women is less than sixty years. One in fifteen Sudanese infants dies before reaching his or her first birthday. More than twenty five per cent of the government's budget is spent on defence, and some have estimated the indirect costs of the Sudanese civil war to be as much as a million dollars a day. Per capita income, adjusted for purchasing parity, stands at less than $1,400 a year. There is a very small middle class and immense income inequality, coupled with an unemployment rate of twenty per cent. Aside from oil, Sudan exports only agricultural products. Agriculture employs about eighty per cent of the labour force but accounts for only forty three per cent of the GDP. The Sudanese dinar, which was introduced to replace the Sudanese pound at the rate of one dinar per ten Sudanese pounds,[8] has seen its value fall from about 160 dinars per US dollar in 1997 to about 247 dinars per US dollar, its current value in January 2006. Much of the blame for this state of affairs lies with the continual state of civil war that plagues the country.

Given the country's diversity, it makes sense to examine how the Sudanese define their common nationality.

Sudanese identity

For many Sudanese living in the North, the Sudan is a profoundly Muslim country whose government must reflect Islamic values and laws. The roots of this view of the country are very old.[9] To many Northerners, Sudan cannot be understood without Islam as the heart of the state. Professor Abd al Latif al Buni, a Sudanese political scientist, argues that Islam is the central component of Sudanese national identity. He attacks missionaries and the Christian churches for preventing the 'spread of Islam' in the South through their 'establishment of an educated Christian class in the South with views incompatible to its sister class in the North.' Al Buni argues that the Islamisation of the South is essential to ensure the region's 'national unification with the North.' He goes further to claim that 'Southern political parties ... resorted to Christianity only to give the South an identity distinct from that of the North'.[10] For al Buni, who speaks for many other Northern Sudanese, religion is the defining element of Sudanese national identity: to be Sudanese is to be a Muslim. It follows that to be a Christian, a traditional religionist, a Jew or a Hindu is not to be Sudanese.[11]

In contrast to these Northern views, the SPLA prefers to regard the country as a territorial entity whose inhabitants have rights and responsibilities on the basis of political citizenship rather than religion. They favour 'Sudanism' instead of 'Islamism/Arabism' or 'Africanism.' Their vision presupposes the equal legitimacy of Islam, Christianity and traditional religions within the country's national identity. John Garang de Mabior argued that the 'New' Sudan would have the same degree of tolerance and comfort with religious issues for all of the country's belief systems. In order to accomplish this goal, the SPLA calls for the separation of church, mosque and state and the establishment of a federal, decentralised government in the Sudan to account for the size and diversity of the country.[12] Arabic is accepted as the official language of the Sudan, but the SPLM/A insists that its acceptance of the language does not entail an exclusively Arab identity for the state.[13] The rejection of an Arabic identity for the country stems from the 'othering' of Northerners in the South. From the Southern perspective, the 'other' is the Northerner who tries to impose his faith on an unwilling South.

According to Francis Deng, the two visions described above have become alternative national identities for Sudan. He argues that the SPLA's positions represent a last ditch effort to maintain the unity of the Sudan, because if the North continues to insist that the Sudan is Arab, despite its African heritage, and continues to attempt to impose an Islamic Arab identity on the South, the only solution left for the Sudan would be partition.

Leadership issues

Coups and military intervention have defined leadership in Sudan. Officers such as Abboud, Nimeiry, and Bashir have ruled the country within the framework of dictatorship for more than thirty six years. While the Sudanese military has generally kept internal discipline and has not collapsed into internal warring factions, it has failed to end civil war. Abboud, who became the country's leader in 1958, realised the importance of using Arab and Islamic identity as a way to win the support of elites in the North. He probably also understood that Nasser would play the Islamic card against any Sudanese government trying to defend its interests in the Nile waters. Rejecting the Aswan dam would have been portrayed by the dominant Egyptian media as tantamount to apostasy and implicit support for Israel. Abboud's primary failure was his inability to understand that attempting to Arabise and Islamise the South would lead to an intensification of the civil war and strike a tremendous blow against hopes for Sudan's economic development. He miscalculated the cost of giving in to Nasser's ideas, because he believed in the centrality of both Islam and Egypt to the national identity of the Sudan.

With regard to the civil war, Nimeiry tried to achieve what Abboud could not, but he was only temporarily successful. Nimeiry's rule can be divided into two periods that correspond with changes in his behaviour. In the first period, Nimeiry was a secular man, with tolerant religious and ethnic attitudes. True enough, he was the dictator who ordered the execution of coup plotters and banned political parties, but he did not attempt to impose his religious beliefs or culture on anyone: in short, he was capable of accepting cultural, albeit not political, pluralism. At some time in the early 1980s, he entered into an alliance with the Sudanese Muslim Brotherhood in an attempt to curb the influence of the banned Umma Party. He also began to ponder his personal religious status. As Nimeiry found himself increasingly attached to his faith, his secularism waned. In September 1983, he imposed Islamic Law over the whole country.

In 1985, Nimeiry's rule was ended by a bloodless coup that brought in General Abdul Rahman Siwar al Dahab as caretaker president for a period of two years. Siwar al Dahab was replaced by an elected civilian administration, which was overthrown within three years by General Omar al Bashir. Both coups had potential for ending the civil war, but this did not happen. Al Bashir initially ruled in conjunction with the political arm of the Sudanese Muslim Brotherhood, the National Islamic Front (NIF), as represented by its leader, Hassan al Turabi. But instead of building a common Sudanese home for all of the country's peoples, all three major Sudanese dictators (Abboud, Nimeiry and Bashir) found the temptation to use religious justifications for their rule too strong to ignore. Nimeiry's secular period was the sole exception, and it too ended with a return to the Islamisation and Arabisation policies of Abboud.

At the risk of a certain amount of overlap, I will not discuss the political context within which Sudan's civil war took place, adopting a wider perspective than that of the country's leaders.

The first Sudanese civil war

The most recent Sudanese civil war is the country's second internal conflict. The background to the first civil war was as follows. Coming to power in a coup in 1958, General Abboud aimed to impose Islam and the Arabic language on the Southern Sudan. He forbade Christian missionaries to operate in the South, and took over Christian schools. Naturally, the people of the Southern Sudan were unwilling to accept the forceful imposition of an alien language and an alien religion. By the 1960s, the Southern Sudan had developed a political party opposed to Northern rule, the Sudan African National Union (SANU), and a loosely organised independent rebel army whose nucleus was some of the Torit rebels who had rejected Governor General Helm's pardon. The rebels, known as the *Anya Nya* or 'Snake Poison', received support from the Democratic Republic of the Congo, Uganda, Israel, and other countries.[14]

As early as the mid sixties, the strain imposed by the war resulted in intense opposition to Abboud in Northern Sudan. By 1964, professional, student and labour unions began to indicate their opposition to the government. Junior officers in the army were plotting to overthrow Abboud, and no solution to the Southern problem seemed to be in sight. In response to these pressures, Abboud dismissed his cabinet, appointed a transitional, apolitical prime minister and introduced an all party government which included two independent Southern Sudanese ministers. However, after his troops had fired on protesters and killed twenty people, Abboud realised that he could not continue to rule the Sudan. He resigned as chief of state on 14 November 1964, and the *de jure* democracy was restored.[15]

The succession of weak coalition governments that followed failed to develop the economy or solve the problem of the civil war in Southern Sudan. The army and the *Anya Nya* began a cycle of atrocities that continued until the end of the war in 1972. As had happened in 1958, the instability of the polity tempted the army to depose the elected government, and Colonel Ja'afar Mohammed al Nimeiry and a junta of colonels and junior officers took power in a bloodless coup on 25 May 1969.[16]

The Addis Ababa peace accords

Nimeiry immediately promoted himself to Major General, and began negotiations with the *Anya Nya's* nascent political arm, the Southern Sudan Liberation Movement (SSLM), in Addis Ababa, Ethiopia. Through the mediation of the Ethiopian emperor, Haile Selassie, the government and the SSLM/*Anya Nya* agreed on a formula for the autonomy of the Southern Sudan on 27 February 1972. Nimeiry's government implemented its agreement with the SSLM in the *Regional Self Government Act for the Southern Provinces.* In terms of this agreement, an autonomous government would be provided for the Southern Sudan, with an elected assembly and a cabinet. The Southern Sudanese would control their own local government, educational policies, public health, mineral and natural resources, and police forces, while the central government in Khartoum would retain jurisdiction over foreign relations, defence, currency and intra regional affairs. The *Anya Nya's* troops were to be incorporated into the Sudanese People's Armed Forces.[17]

The agreement worked for more than a decade, and the guns remained silent until 1983, when the second Sudanese civil war erupted. Nimeiry's desire to abandon the Addis Ababa accords was the primary reason for the renewal of the war. First, on 1st June 1983, Nimeiry abolished the Southern region and created three regions in the South that corresponded to the three Southern Provinces of old. Second, he imposed Islamic law over the whole country. Four months later, the Southern units in the Sudanese army revolted.[18]

The second Sudanese civil war

To complicate matters, the Southern Sudanese soon split into three factions: the mainline SPLA, SPLA Bahr al Ghazal, and the Nasir SPLA. Unlike the mainline SPLA, the smaller dissident factions preferred either to settle with the government or to argue for the independence of Southern Sudan - a goal renounced by the mainline (Torit) SPLA.[19] The Bahr al Ghazal SPLA has since returned to the fold. Initially, the SPLA itself was a junior competitor of the *Anya Nya* II, but the SPLA soon eclipsed and absorbed its rival, despite considerable initial difficulty. John Garang de Mabior, the then leader of the SPLA, estimated that some sixty per cent of his troops came from the *Anya Nya* II.[20]

With the growth of the SPLA, Nimeiry turned to his primary overseas ally – the US – for assistance. As the only Arab leader who stood with Egypt after the Sinai accords, Nimeiry could count on some measure of US assistance. Also, Nimeiry had buttressed his relationship with America through what seemed to be his firm commitment to secularism and multiculturalism. Libya had been aiding the SPLA, and this provided yet another reason for the US to support Nimeiry. The Sudanese president visited the US on 27 March 1985, and was welcomed by President Reagan. However, during his plane's refuelling stop in Egypt on his return, the Sudanese Army, led by General Siwar al Dahab, deposed Nimeiry. The new caretaker president promised a return to democracy and an end to the civil war. Much to the consternation of the US and Egypt, he normalised relations with Libya, which promptly withdrew its support from the SPLA. General Siwar al Dahab failed to accomplish his goal of bringing peace to the South, partly because the NIF rejected a peaceful solution. He did, however, restore democracy to the Sudan. The Umma Party won the April 1986 elections, and Sadiq al Mahdi formed a broad based government, which included the Democratic Unionist Party (DUP), the National Islamic Front (NIF) and several Southern parties.

But with no end to the civil war in sight, Sadiq lost his credibility. The NIF, with support from certain sectors in the army, overthrew Sadiq on 30 June 1989. The new government, dominated by the NIF and its sympathisers in the military, declared its opposition to an agreement reached under the previous government, between the DUP and the SPLA. The government of Lieutenant General Omar al Bashir and Hassan al Turabi continued the war against the SPLA, and consistently refused to compromise on the issue of the 'September laws', as Islamic law came to be known in the Sudan.[21] The arrest and imprisonment of al Turabi, long seen as the main ideologue behind Bashir's Islamist government, initially seemed to suggest a softer line by the government towards the issue of religion and politics, but these hopes were dashed by the government's constant refusal to accept a secular state.

After a short pause and even a show of support for the Sudanese government, the new governments in Ethiopia and Eritrea continued the policy adopted by their previous governments in supporting the SPLA, because the Sudan government began to throw its weight behind new Islamic insurgencies within their borders. Ethiopia, Eritrea, Uganda, the US, and perhaps Israel have been aiding the SPLA.

Egypt shifts sides so often that it is fair to interpret its actions as indicating that Egypt's interests lie in endless war in Sudan. The sympathies of the US were clearly on the Southern side even before the events of 11 September 2001. In a speech in Kampala, Uganda, in 1997, the then US Secretary of State, Madeleine K Albright, indicated that the US supported the SPLA and its allies in the Sudanese civil war and was offering $20 million in military aid and weapons to Eritrea, Ethiopia, and Uganda. Albright also met the leaders of the six factions in the rebel National Democratic Alliance (NDA), which includes the SPLA.[22]

The Machakos peace proposal and the Sudan Comprehensive Peace Agreement (Naivasha Accord)

The Machakos Protocol of 20 July 2003 was a direct product of US pressure exerted on the Sudanese government and the SPLA through the Intergovernmental Authority on Development (IGAD) framework. It was negotiated without Egypt, and therefore represents a decline in Egyptian influence over Sudan. Egypt's obstructive response to the agreement confirms such a conclusion. The agreement foresees two possibilities for the Sudan: Southern independence through self determination, or a federate, secular Sudan. Both of these outcomes are contrary to Egypt's perceptions of its national interest in Sudan.

Articles 1.2 and 1.3 of Part A (Agreed Principles) of the Machakos agreement include language that makes independence (or at least autonomy) a real possibility:[23]

1.2 That the people of South Sudan have the right to control and govern affairs in their region and participate equitably in the National Government.
1.3 That the people of South Sudan have the right to self determination, inter alia, through a referendum to determine their future status.

Articles dealing with the possibility of a united, if federated, Sudan use words that emphasise the country's religious, cultural, ethnic, racial and linguistic diversity. 'Islam' does not appear anywhere in the agreement; neither do the words 'Arab' or 'African' as terms of reference to Sudan, or in defining the identity of its population. Articles 6.1–6.6 of the agreement divorce religion from national politics, although they clearly allow the *shari'ah* to be used in personal affairs among those embracing it. Properly understood, the text of the Machakos agreement reflects the total capitulation of the Sudanese government to all SPLA demands. To that extent, it also represents a massive blow to Egyptian interests in Sudan, because of Egypt's traditional function as the country's bridge to Arab and Islamic culture.

Northern people wishing to be ruled by Islamic principles and the *shari'ah* can find some consolation in that the *shari'ah* can be used under Article 3.2.2 as a basis for legislation in states outside the South. Yet even this provision is undermined by a nullification provision that allows non Muslim areas to nullify the Islamic laws which apply to their territories under Machakos Agreement Article 3.2.4. In essence, the Machakos protocol envisions a Sudan where religion and politics are separate matters at the national level.

The chances of the agreement being implemented depend on several factors. These include the survival of the SPLA and the strength of its military performance; continued US support for the Machakos process; and non intervention by the Egyptians. At a deeper level, the success of the agreement will also depend on the North's ability to accept the South's right to do things differently, whether in an independent or an autonomous context. Given the events of 9/11 and the current US focus on terrorism, it seems likely that the agreement, in some form or another, will be implemented.

There is no consensus yet over whether Islamic law will apply in the capital of a united Sudan. In addition, the issue of the inclusion of the Southern Blue Nile (Ngessana Hills Tract), Abiye and the Nuba Hills in the South has not been resolved. To complicate matters, there are now non NDA, SPLA aligned armed movements in Darfur, such as the Party of Justice and Equality and the Sudan Liberation Front, which are not party to the negotiations. Nevertheless, it is abundantly clear that the agreement will be implemented in one form or another owing to US pressure and the changed nature of international relations since September 2001.

US interests and intentions are an inescapable part of the current discourse on the future of Sudan. There are two views concerning America's motives. The first holds that the US is in favour of a united Sudan, because the presence of a significant number of non Muslim communities in the country and their inclusion in the political process reduces the possibility of a return to a fundamentalist regime in Khartoum. Another reason is that Egypt is vital to US security structures in the Middle East and a divided Sudan is not in Egypt's interest. The second view is that US interests lie in the division of the country into two, so as to secure the South's oil under an agreement with a non Muslim government. Supporters of this view can point to the remarkable bi partisan alliance over Sudan between African-American activists and the Christian Right that has emerged in Washington. They can also argue that the US has come to view the divisions within Sudan as a clash of civilisations.

The agreement envisions that a referendum on partition will be held after six years of autonomy for the South. While it is very hard to predict how people will behave in six years' time, it is likely, *ceteris paribus,* that the South will vote for independence. There are simply too many grievances, too many prejudices and too many massacres to forget within the framework of a united Sudan. Egypt's recent actions lend credence to this point of view. It is busy offering development aid to the Southern Sudanese so that they will choose to stay in a united Sudan. This suggests that the Egyptians are finally beginning to face the consequences of their Sudanese policy: that there is a high price to pay for their repeated intervention in their neighbour's internal affairs, especially with regard to cultural policy.

Defeating the pro independence camp would require several changes. First, the Sudanese state would have to become totally secular, and not half secular/half Islamic, as the current agreement proposes. Second, the Southern elites would have to be integrated into the national power structure and persuaded of the need to remain within one Sudanese state. Given the location of the oil reserves in the South, it is unlikely that the South's elites will reach a unionist conclusion in six years' time. Instead, they may view their relationship with the North as a costly way of doing business with the oil market – a cost to be cut so that they can enjoy the savings. An independent Republic of the Nile in the South could pipe its oil to Kenya instead of the Red Sea, to be sold on the world oil market.

Should the current negotiations collapse or fail, the alternative is a continuation of conflict and the total isolation of Sudan from the rest of the international system. In the post 9/11 world, the present government's interpretation of Sudanese national identity is neither tolerable nor acceptable, at least not in the US. It is therefore likely that the SPLA will start receiving military assistance from the US and its close allies. The Sudanese government will rely heavily on Saudi Arabia and other Arab states for support, and the situation may quickly evolve into a proxy war, pitting two ostensibly friendly states (the US and Saudi Arabia) against each other. The results of such an escalation would be increased famine and starvation, more massacres, and aggravated abuse of human rights by both sides. The SPLA would resort to bringing unconventional warfare to Northern cities, and the final stage of the conflict might see a unilateral declaration of independence by the South and the subsequent recognition of a Southern state by its Western allies. Capping the conflict and bringing it to a peaceful conclusion before this final scenario is played out is therefore essential. Within the Sudanese context, this means limiting the role of ethnic and religious identity in the lives of Sudanese people.

Signed on 31 December 2004, the Sudan Comprehensive Peace Agreement represents the practical implementation of the Machakos peace proposal. The text includes some modifications of the Machakos agreement that are basically fig leaves for the Sudanese government, such as renaming South Sudan to Southern Sudan among other minor changes. The heart of the agreement lies in the military provisions that regulate and define the relationship between the Sudanese Armed Forces and the SPLA. The permanent ceasefire does not envision the unification of the two armed forces in the immediate execution of the peace agreement. Instead, it sets up joint integrated units during the six year transition period, followed by the merger of the two military forces in the case of unionist vote in the South; if the South votes for independence, the SPLA will form the main military force of the newly independent Republic of the (Upper?) Nile.[24]

The death of John Garang de Mabior

John Garang de Mabior's life followed a remarkable trajectory. A Sudanese officer with a Ph.D. from Iowa State University in International Development, Garang had already served as a professional soldier by the time of his graduate studies. He joined the 1983 mutiny after being sent to quell it.[25]

Garang's death in July 2005 in a helicopter crash resulted in massive rioting in cities in both Northern and Southern Sudan. The crash itself was regarded as suspicious by many Southerners, especially those who felt that the hands of Khartoum, Cairo or Kampala were behind the incident. The rioting revealed an option that the SPLA had held in reserve throughout the war – the prospect of bringing the war to the homes of people in the North. Shops and enterprises owned by Northerners were a primary target of the rioters. Garang's positions as Sudanese First Vice President and the Leader of the SPLA/M were transferred to Salva Kiir Mayardit, his second in command.[26]

Garang's death makes the secession of the South all the more likely. Khartoum and other Northern cities experienced severe tensions recently when rumours circulated suggesting the death of Salva Kiir Mayardit. A massive uprising of Sudanese Southerners living in the North is now a possibility that cannot be ignored by the Sudanese government. Consequently, the Sudanese government has tried to demonstrate continuity in its policies with the rapid appointment of Kiir Mayardit as First Vice President.

In many ways, Garang's death represents a severe setback for Southern Sudanese unionism. Despite the well known preferences of his soldiers for separation, he patiently argued for a 'New Sudan', which includes all the components of the state into a territorial nation. There were negative aspects of his leadership such as authoritarianism and human rights abuses, but it is hard to see how any Southern leader would have been able to avoid such behaviour in a movement that had to be forged from dozens of tribal, ethnic and religious communities. In addition, Garang's rivals in the South hardly boasted better human rights records. From the author's perspective, Garang's approach to Sudan included a hopeful optimism, reflected in his cornucopian references in his dissertation to the potential for Sudan to become a regional or global breadbasket.

Darfur

Sudan's future prospects and prosperity are also blighted by the continuing crisis in Darfur. The region's population includes both African Muslims and Baqqarah Arabs. Like all other regions of Sudan, the populations are often impossible to distinguish by colour. Like the conflict in the South, the crisis in Darfur pits the indigenous population against the government in Khartoum. That having been said, there are two main differences between Darfur and the conflict in the South. First, religion is a non factor in Darfur, with Islam being the religion of all the combatants. Darfur's only Christian community is drawn from Egyptian Copts who hold Sudanese citizenship, and its size does not exceed a few hundred. Second, Darfur has a significant Arab population, albeit one that has not been in the majority. In times of drought, conflict between the mainly but not entirely Arab pastoral and the mostly African agricultural communities tends to escalate in the region. The African Muslim communities of Darfur are concentrated in Northern (the Zaghawa) and Western Darfur (the Fur and the Masalit). The Zaghawa are cattle and camel breeders, while the Fur and the Masalit are highland peasants, by and large. Southern Darfur is dominated by Baqqarah Arabs who tend cattle. Traditionally drought has provided the catalyst for conflict in the region between the Baqqarah and other groups in the region. In the late eighties and early nineties, these conflicts metamorphosed into a conflict between Arab paramilitaries supported by the government in Khartoum and the SPLA's Darfur branch.[27] The SPLA sent Daud Yahya Bolad, an engineer and a convert to secularism, to organise its Darfur branch in August 1991. Bolad was initially successful, but was captured and executed by forces loyal to Khartoum.[28]

The current round of conflict pits the SPLA Darfur's eventual successor, the Sudan Liberation Movement/Army (SLA), along with an offshoot of the Muslim Brotherhood, the Justice and Equality Movement (JEM), against the government and its local paramilitary allies, the *janjaweed*.

JEM and the SLA began their uprising against the government in Khartoum in the early months of the 2003. The government responded by letting its paramilitaries conduct campaigns of ethnic cleansing in Darfur, forcing tens of thousands of Fur, Masalit and Zaghawa residents to flee. The *Economist* estimates that at least 180,000 people have been killed by the government paramilitaries and by the SLA and the JEM.[29] A ceasefire was signed by the government and the two movements in April 2004. The government of Chad acted as a mediator, but it is increasingly being seen as biased in favour of the government by the two rebel movements. Despite the ceasefire, the ongoing peace process in Abuja and United Nations resolutions enjoining the Sudanese government to disarm the *janjaweed*, peace has remained out of reach. SLA and JEM forces clash regularly with the government's troops, the *janjaweed*, and with each other. In addition, there is now tension within the SLA itself. The insurgents are divided by tribal and clan loyalties, and in the absence of a unified rebel position, a peaceful end to the conflict is extremely unlikely.[30] The involvement of several foreign players in Darfur, including Libya, and the eruption of a significant insurgency in Eastern Sudan among the Beja does not bode well for Darfur or the rest of Sudan. In many ways, Darfur and the East illustrate the futility of attempting to impose Khartoum's rule on unwilling populations that have known their own political arrangements. The only viable Sudanese state, within its current borders, would be a state that reaches out to its periphery and includes its elites and populations in its development policies through wealth and power sharing.

Conclusion: challenges for both a united and a divided Sudan

Neither side in the Sudanese civil war can claim the moral high ground. The SPLA suffers from as much corruption and has committed as many human rights abuses as has the Sudanese government. Morality may be a legitimate issue for social inquiry, but accounts that highlight the abuses of one side alone ultimately serve the other side's agenda. Consequently, this account of the role of identity in the Sudanese civil war has relied on the war aims and definitions of nationality as stated by the two sides themselves, which means that this chapter is a trans subjective exercise.

There are about ten realities that inform Sudan's situation. First, Sudan is a multi ethnic, multi religious and multi racial country. Second, military dictators have ruled Sudan for thirty six out of the forty six years since independence. Third, no non Muslim or non Arab has served in the capacity of head of state. Fourth, Sudan has known civil war for all but nine years of its history since independence. Fifth, all of Sudan's neighbours have intervened in its internal affairs. Sixth, Egypt has tried to impede the latest attempts at peace, and has attempted to prevent the creation of a Southern Sudanese state, either within or outside Sudan. Seventh, the Addis Ababa peace accord fell apart after the introduction of the September Laws and the suspension of the South's autonomy. Eighth, Sudan is an African as well as an Arab country. Ninth, Islam in Sudan is influenced by African religious practices, and *Zar* (invoking the spirits) ceremonies are held in communities on the Egyptian border. Tenth, many Northern peoples do not speak Arabic, despite having embraced Islam.

To the extent that several Sudanese governments have attempted by coercive means to alter some of the givens mentioned above, the ultimate responsibility for the war rests with them. Peace will not be possible in the North or the South if governments try to force a language and certain interpretations of Islam on unwilling peoples. And to the extent the conflict took a military form early on, the issue of whether the Southern Sudanese, or any other Sudanese communities, have a 'right' to secede or to engage in war to improve their political position is moot. Furthermore, the government has implicitly acknowledged the SPLA by negotiating with it.

The secession of the South will not necessarily end conflict and insurgency in Northern areas such as the Nuba Mountains and the Blue Nile Province. The only solution overall is a government or governments that embrace Sudan for what it is instead of trying, in a desperate attempt to overcome feelings of inferiority, to transform it into another Egypt or Saudi Arabia. Sudan is black and brown, Muslim and non Muslim, and Arab and African. Unfortunately, the government of Sudan has consistently rejected its own people in favour of an abstraction that is probably impossible to realise.

To the extent that the SPLA has accepted the Arabic language and included Muslim members, it has shown a greater ability to understand the nature of the country than the government. Because the SPLA is not a government, its alternative definition of Sudanese identity has never been imposed over all the country. This definition is policy only in areas it controls.

It is not possible to have peace in the country without including the SPLA in negotiations. To the credit of the current Sudanese government, such negotiations are under way. Prodded on by threats from the US, the Sudanese government may come to accept a level of religious and cultural pluralism in the country. This is essential even if the South secedes, because both new states will include substantial religious and cultural minorities.

Equality among the various peoples of the Sudan is meaningless unless some of the economic issues that also underlie the conflict are addressed. These and better access to development aid will figure prominently in the post civil war Sudan(s). The government's previous focus on imposing its interpretation of Sudanese identity came at the expense of economic development and the national interest of the country. The war has created a vast Sudanese diaspora which has access to hard currency and savings. Encouraging ex Sudanese to invest in the old country in order to create jobs and to reduce poverty should become a priority for future governments. If and when peace comes to Sudan, the various political actors also need to ensure that differences over identity do not escalate into war again. In short, both sides need to make sure that the hut of peace is well maintained: its roof properly thatched, its mud walls repaired and renewed, and its interior clean and swept. The mistakes of the early eighties must be avoided. A continuous peace maintenance programme will be required, whether Sudan is one state or two. The focus must quickly shift to the prevention of future war after the conclusion of Machakos, regardless of the shape of Sudan on the map.

Endnotes

1   An Administrative Conference in Khartoum in 1946 advocated the amalgamation of South Sudan with the North, a position adopted by the British and the North Sudanese, and supported by Egypt. The South Sudanese were not consulted.

2   The Central Intelligence Agency, *The World Factbook: Sudan.* Online at *http://www. cia.gov.* Accessed 18 April 2003.

3   Kliot N, *Water Resources and Conflict in the Middle East.* New York: Routledge, 1994, p. 15.

4   See note 3. Metz HC (ed.), *Sudan: A Country Study.* Washington DC: Federal Research Division, 1991. *http://lcweb2.loc.gov/frd/cs/cshome.html.*

5   SIL International, *http://www.ethnologue.com.* Accessed 15 April 2003.

6   Metz HC, op. cit.

7   'Sudan', *Global Arab Encyclopaedia.* Riyadh, Saudi Arabia: Encyclopaedia Works

Publishing, 1996, p. 179.

8   The Central Intelligence Agency, *The World Factbook: Sudan, http://www.cia.gov.* Accessed 18 April 2003. As recently as 1985, 6-8 Sudanese pounds purchased a US dollar.

9   Holt PM & MW Daly, *A History of the Sudan: From the Coming of Islam to the Present Day.* New York: Longman, 1988, p. 72.

10   Al Buni A a L, *Nimeiry's Islamic Experiment in the Sudan.* Khartoun, Sudan: The Institute for Social Studies and Research, 1995, pp. 6-9. In Arabic.

11   For more on this, see Al Sayir HA, *The Sudan From Nimeiry to Bashir.* Khartoum, Sudan: Khartoum University Press, 1995, p. 15. In Arabic.

12   Khalid M (ed), *The call for democracy in the Sudan,* New York: Kegan Paul International, 1995, pp. 118-141; 204, 209-210; 213, 215, 216-220; 251-254; and 257-261.

13   Deng FM, *War of Visions: Conflict of Identities in the Sudan.* Washington DC: The Brookings Institution, 1995, pp. 450-451.

14   *Ibid.,* p.12. See also Holt PM & MW Daly, op. cit., pp. 181-183; 200.

15   *Ibid*

16   Holt PM & MW Daly, *op. cit.,* pp. 181-194.

17   *Ibid.,* pp. 194-202.

18   Harir S & T Tvedt, 'Forward', in Harir S & T Tvedt (eds), *Shortcut to Decay: The Case of the Sudan.* Uppsala, Sweden: Nordiska Afrikainstitutet, 1995, p. 5.

19   Badal R, 'Political cleavages within the Southern Sudan: An empirical analysis of the re division debate', in Harrir S & T Tvedt (eds.), ibid., pp. 105-126.

20   Garang de Mabior J, *op. cit.,* pp. 54-55.

21   *Ibid.* pp.54 55, 268 270; and Holt PM & MW Daly, *op. cit.,* pp. 217-225.

22   McKinley J Jr., 'Albright in Uganda, steps up attack on Sudan's reign of terror,' *The New York Times,* 11 December 1997, p.A7. For Sudan's problems with Uganda and Eritrea, see Miheisi Y, 'Sudan-Uganda tug of war'; 'Intensified exchange of accusations'; and 'Opposition victories,' *Sudan News and Views,* 27, 1 July 1997, http://webzone1.co.uk/www/sudan. Accessed 20 December 1997.

23   IGAD Secretariat on Peace in the Sudan, Machakos Protocol, 23 July 2003.

24   The Government of The Sudan and the Sudan People's Liberation Army, Agreement on Permanent Ceasefire and Security Arrangements: Implementation Modalities during the Pre Interim and Interim Periods, Naivasha, Kenya, 31 December 2004. http://www.igad.org. Accessed 8 December 2005.

25   Gary Phombeah, 'Obituary: John Garang,' BBC News, 3 August 2005. Available at

http://news.bbc.co.uk/1/hi/world/africa/2134220.stm

26   BBC News, 'Profile Salva Kiir,' 2 August 2005. Available at http://news.bbc.co.uk/1/
     hi/world/africa/4738295.stm

27   Human Rights Watch, Sudan: Darfur in Flames, Vol. 16, No (A), April 2004,
     pp. 6 8.

28   Kwaje S, SPLM Position on Developmnets in Darfur, SPLA/M News Agency,
     20 March 2003. Available at the SLA official website: http://www.slma.tk

29   The Economist, 'It'll do what it can get away with,' 3 December 2005, p. 24.

30   The International Crisis Group, 'Unifying Darfur's Rebels: A Prerequisite for Peace,'
     Policy Briefing, Africa Briefing No. 32, 6 October 2005.

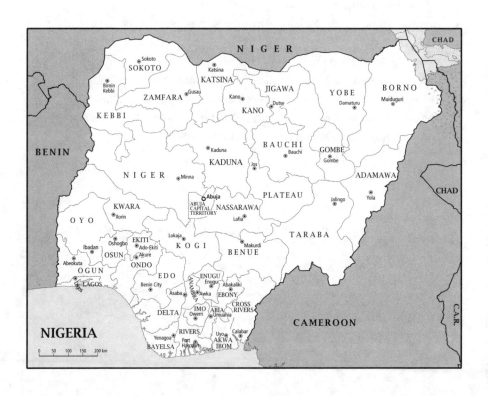

NIGER

CHAD

CHAD

BENIN

SOKOTO
Sokoto⊙

KATSINA
Katsina⊙

JIGAWA

YOBE

BORNO
Maiduguri⊙

Birnin
Kebbi⊙

ZAMFARA
Gusau⊙

Kano⊙

KANO

Damaturu⊙

KEBBI

Dutse⊙

BAUCHI
Bauchi⊙

GOMBE
Gombe⊙

ADAMAWA

Kaduna⊙

KADUNA

Jos⊙

NIGER
Minna⊙

PLATEAU

Jalingo⊙

Yola⊙

Abuja⊙
ABUJA
CAPITAL
TERRITORY

KWARA
Ilorin⊙

NASSARAWA

Lafia⊙

OYO

Lokaja⊙

TARABA

Oshogbo⊙
EKITI
Ado-Ekiti⊙

Ibadan⊙

OSUN
Akure⊙

KOGI

Makurdi⊙

BENUE

Abeokuta⊙

ONDO

OGUN

LAGOS⊙

EDO
Benin City⊙

ENUGU
Enugu⊙

Abakaliki⊙

ANAMBRA

Asaba⊙

Awka⊙

EBONY

DELTA

IMO
Owerri⊙

ABIA
Umuahia⊙

CROSS
RIVERS

RIVERS

Calabar⊙

CAMEROON

C.A.R.

Yenagoa⊙

Port
Harcourt⊙

Uyo⊙

AKWA
IBOM

BAYELSA

NIGERIA

0   50   100   150   200 km

3

Inching towards a country without a state:

prebendalism, violence and state betrayal in Nigeria

Daniel C Bach[1]

Nigeria is Africa's foremost, and the world's sixth most important, oil producer. It is also the tenth largest state of the continent, with a landmass of 924,000 square kilometres and an 853 kilometre long coastline. Nigeria's population, tentatively estimated at 126 million in 2001, also makes it the most populous country in Africa and one of those in which the rate of urbanisation is at its highest. In the course of the last thirty years, several million Nigerians have also settled elsewhere: in neighbouring African countries, in South Africa, in Europe and in the Americas. The communities they form are often very successful in business or academia and many maintain close contacts with Nigeria, sending remittances to family left behind.[2]

Nigeria shares territorial boundaries with four francophone countries (Cameroon, Chad, Niger and Benin), and straddles a great variety of ecosystems. Indeed, Nigeria is frequently described as the only west African state which spans, on a large and balanced scale, the milieus, cultures and populations associated with both Sahelian and coastal regions. The variety of ecosystems supported by the country is considerable. These include the Niger delta, Africa's largest wetlands; tropical forests in the lowlands of the south; savanna on the middle belt plateau and semi aridity in the far north, where the droughts of the seventies and Lake Chad's dramatic contraction over the last four decades[3] have contributed to the region's desertification. Nigeria's diverse ecosystems mean that the country possesses abundant fertile land as well as substantial mineral resources. The Niger and its subsidiary, the Benue, define the frontier between northern and southern Nigeria.

Three major ethno regional clusters have historically been dominant both within their areas of origin and Nigeria as a whole: the Hausa Fulani in the north; the Yoruba in the south west; and the Igbo in the south east. During the pre colonial period, the 'big three', as they are known today, sought to establish control, sometimes through forced incorporation but also through co optation over smaller polities in their respective areas. Colonial rule and post colonial politics did not assuage what remains an ongoing history of uneasy interaction between the dominant tribes and the 350 or so other groups in Nigeria, improperly known as 'the minorities'.[4]

The ad hoc combination of federalism with consociationalism[5]

The establishment of the contemporary Nigerian state is usually traced to the so called 'amalgamation' of the northern and southern protectorates decreed by the British in 1914. Colonial administration in the north was practised through indirect rule that relied upon, and at times supported, the hierarchical systems of pre colonial authority associated with the Sokoto caliphate and the Borno kingdom. Preservation of the social status quo in northern Islamic societies was encouraged by restrictions on the spread of missionary influence. In contrast, in the southern parts of Nigeria the spread of Christianity encouraged better access to western education. From the inter war period onwards it also stimulated nationalist agitation.

By the end of the Second World War, the British colonial administration had undertaken to respond to demands for change. Following a succession of draft constitutions and a final constitutional conference, the administration allowed general elections to be held in 1959. Britain's largest colonial territory in Africa achieved independence in a largely peaceful atmosphere (apart from the Tiv riots in central Nigeria) on 1 October 1960.

Nigeria became independent as a federal state, an institutional framework that had been agreed upon in 1953. Federalism was expected to meet the demands for regional autonomy, while addressing the need to share the country's limited and unevenly spread resources. In adopting federalism the country charted an original path, given that the trend of the time was towards the dissolution of the customs and monetary unions or broader federal arrangements set up by colonial powers.[6]

The Nigerian political system was at that time structured around three hegemonic cores. Competition among these eventually brought Nigeria's First Republic to a violent end with the coup d'état of January 1966, followed that same year by another and, a year later, a bitter civil war, which lasted for over two years. By the time the conflict ended, a profound transformation of the Nigerian federal system had begun. The country was evolving a model of consociationalism that shapes the workings of the Nigerian polity to this day.

Federalism through hegemonic leadership

In 1960, the unity of Nigeria was fragile. Besides the exclusively federal areas of jurisdiction, such as defence and external affairs, considerable legislative and residual powers had been entrusted to the regions. Nigeria's weak centre was accompanied by an institutionally embedded dominance by the northern region of federal assemblies, and the superior power exerted by all three geo ethnic clusters within their own regions. Hegemonic control could have contributed to state or nation building; but this was not to be the case.

The dominance of the north within the federation soon became a source of tension and instability. Considerable inequalities existed in the size, population, revenues and spread of education of the three regions. The northern region alone accounted for seventy nine per cent of the territory of the federation and fifty five per cent of its population (1953-54 census figures). This pre eminence translated into the allocation in its constitution of half of Nigeria's parliamentary seats to representatives from the northern region. Far from providing an inbuilt guarantee of stability, this became a cause of increasing dissatisfaction. Another source of conflict was the contrast between Nigeria's formally open and competitive federal system and the politics of single party rule that prevailed within the regions. Regionally based political parties sought to establish exclusive control over the regional assemblies and parastatals through co optation. They also used intimidation and violence against opposition forces. A third aspect of Nigerian federalism that proved highly problematic during this period was the revenue allocation formula, based on the derivation principle. This principle favoured the regions deriving substantial income from exportable commodities or crude oil deposits, which meant sharp discrepancies in the funds available to the regional governments and created uneven levels of dependency on the federal centre.

The discrepancy between the constitutional allocation of power and its real distribution in society eventually caused the collapse of the First Republic in January 1966 after a successful military coup. By then, the western region, a political battle ground since the elections of 1964, was in a state of utter chaos. Constitutional reforms were subsequently adopted as a remedy for the excesses for 'regionalism' and 'tribalism', but they served only to exacerbate them. Indeed, plans for the transformation of Nigeria into a unitary state were interpreted as an attempt by southerners, more specifically the educationally advanced Igbos, to assert and entrench their domination. Outbursts of violence in the north accompanied a second coup d'état in July 1966. Yacubu Gowon emerged as the new head of state and the secession of the northern region was narrowly avoided.[7] Following renewed violence in the north, aborted constitutional talks between delegates from the four regions in Lagos and the cancellation of an agreement reached at Aburi (Ghana), the eastern region decided in May 1967 to proclaim itself independent under the name of the Republic of Biafra. The war that ensued was to cause the deaths of over one million people.

The restoration of Nigerian unity was the result of the superior capacity of the federal government in terms of military force and diplomatic influence. The ability to mobilise broad domestic support proved equally essential and largely stemmed from the radical reconfiguration of Nigerian federalism. In 1967 Gowon had announced the division of the (then) four regions into twelve new states. The promise of autonomy now offered to the populations of the middle belt and the south east rekindled their commitment to the federal cause. In the former eastern region, this was to undermine rapidly any support the 'Biafrans' could secure from non Igbo populations. On the federal side, the announcement was equally decisive since many soldiers in the infantry originated from the middle belt region, an area where Christianity and traditional religions went along with resistance to the emirate system and its permeation of politics in the northern region.[8]

Regulation through consociational engineering

During the period of the civil war, ad hoc attempts were made to regulate both geo ethnic tensions and access to political representation and resources by means of consociational arrangements. Nigeria's *de facto* evolution towards a decentralised unitary state also reduced opportunities for secession or state control by a single ethno regional grouping. These risks were also contained through a set of constitutional prescriptions generically described as the 'federal character principle' (see below).

The original division of the northern region into six states[9] contributed to a consolidation of the powers of the federal government and opened up the prospect of a more balanced political game. Military rule also meant that numerous areas of jurisdiction which, during the sixties, fell under the responsibility of the regions, were taken over by the federal government in the seventies. Relations between the states and the federal government became increasingly unequal as the government's oil revenues soared. The federal government also consolidated its powers at the expense of the states when, in 1988, federal resources allocated to the local governments were paid directly to them instead of being managed by the states. The autonomy of the states in the management of their domestic affairs, commonly considered as a factor of differentiation between federalism and unitary forms of government,[10] was severely curtailed.

The transformations of Nigerian federalism involved the widespread use of fissiparity, that is, the fragmentation of existing politico administrative units (whether states or local governments) into new ones with identical functional characteristics. This trend gathered momentum in the seventies, and has remained since then a powerful instrument for the management of centre–periphery relations. Nigeria's most recent state creation exercise occurred in 1996. Since then, the federation has comprised 36 states and 774 local governments, a dramatic increase compared with the original 3 regions and 301 local governments.[11] Unlike the regions of the 1960s, the current states are much smaller and, except for a few cases, extremely dependent on resource transfers from the centre. Secession has thus become less than ever a feasible option.

The desire to avoid state control by a single geo ethnic cluster or by a small group of states is encapsulated in what has become known as the 'federal character' doctrine. This term was first used by General Murtala Mohammed, then Nigeria's head of state, in his inaugural address to the Constitution Drafting Committee (CDC) in October 1975.[12] The principle was subsequently endorsed by the CDC and inserted into the 1979 constitution where it was loosely defined as the need to ensure that 'there shall be no predominance of persons from a few states or from a few ethnic or other sectional groups in that government [of the federation] or in any of its agencies'.[13] The notion of federal character was the most innovative feature of Nigeria's new constitution.[14] Within the following two decades, the principle has also acquired increasing pre eminence. Now, the federal character 'doctrine', a term first inserted in the 1989 constitution, is meant to apply to the formation of political parties,[15] the election of the president and governors,[16] presidential appointments and the composition of the federal cabinet (at least one minister must come from each of the thirty six states). The doctrine is also relevant to the composition of the officer corps and other ranks in the armed forces, recruitment to the public service and federal institutions. Within the thirty six states of the federation, the doctrine is matched by a symmetrical requirement that 'the diversity of the people' be reflected in the composition of the state, local government or any other agency and also be observed in the conduct of their affairs.[17] Nigeria's 1999 constitution has contributed to a further broadening and deepening of the doctrine. A Federal Character Commission (FCC) is to be established for the purpose of monitoring implementation, setting the basis for strict compliance and:

work[ing] out an equitable formula subject to the approval of the National Assembly for the distribution of all cadres of posts in the public service of the Federation and of the states, the armed forces of the Federation, the Nigeria Police Force and other government security agencies, government owned companies and parastatals of the states.[18]

Nigerian federalism portrays a rarely discussed experimentation with consociational mechanisms. These also offer a unique illustration of the boomerang effects of prescriptions suggested by Lijphart and his imitators for conflict management in plural societies. Nigerian constitutional engineering clearly displays features that classically differentiate federalism from consociationalism. Nigeria's successive constitutions have endorsed a cumulative array of dispositions to promote the involvement of 'all significant segments of the society'[19] in accordance with the 'grand coalition principle'. The protection of 'vital minority interests', another feature stressed by consociationalism, has, in Nigeria, been interpreted as requiring the creation of new states and local governments. The guarantees offered to 'minorities' have also been of a financial nature. The pre eminence conferred on the criterion of equity in the sharing of federal account revenues among states guarantees resource transfers separately from the value of internally generated revenues.

Most significantly, Nigeria is perfectly attuned to the consociational model's stringent emphasis on proportionality as, 'the principal standard of political representation, civil service appointments and allocation of public funds'.[20] Proportionality has acquired, at least formally, an increasingly pervasive influence over the conduct of politics and the making of policies in Nigeria. The FCC is in charge of monitoring and enforcing implementation of the federal character doctrine across the country. In addition, access to resources or positions is increasingly being appraised through the notion of rotation, a trend underscored by the division of the country into six geo political zones. Already during the Second Republic (1979-1983), what is known as 'zoning' permeated nominations and office allocation within political parties. Since 1999, zoning has become even more deeply engrained in politics and policy implementation, both at national and state level.[21]

Resources and revenue sharing

Nigeria's oil production ranges between 1.7 and 2.0 million barrels per day. In addition to its oil wealth, Nigeria has proven natural gas reserves estimated at 120 trillion cubic feet, with recoverable gas reserves of 45 tcf, which makes these the ninth largest source in the world. Nigeria's reserve-production ratio is also estimated at 125 years for gas, compared with less than 30 years for oil. This spectacular imbalance explains why petroleum experts sometimes present Nigeria as a country that possesses natural gas as well as some oil.

Within the last thirty years, the share of oil in the Nigerian economy has risen sharply. Oil accounts for seventy per cent of the government's fiscal resources, provides ninety eight per cent of export earnings and contributes forty per cent to the country's GDP. Nigeria's other exports include cocoa, rubber, cassava and shrimps. The dominance of oil, together with the volatility of oil prices, has made a decisive contribution to the Nigerian federal system. Oil revenues increased dramatically during the seventies as the expansion of production following the end of the civil war translated into billions of dollars. Nigeria's oil revenues sprang from $250 million to $1.2 billion between 1970 and 1972 and then accelerated as they went from $6.6 billion in 1974 to $23.4 billion in 1980. The Nigerian oil boom was then at its peak. During 1981, international oil prices fell sharply and Nigerian oil revenues dropped to $16.7 billon.[22] The period during which oil revenues could easily underwrite the growing cost of Nigeria's new federalism was over.

Nigeria's oil predicament

Nigeria's oil predicament reflects what has been described as the 'paradox of plenty'.[23] It is estimated that Nigeria earned nearly $200 billion between 1970 and 1990,[24] mostly drawn from oil. This wealth has had an adverse impact on the standard of living of the vast majority of Nigerians. Real incomes have declined by an average 1.5 per cent over the past twenty five years; and about seventy per cent of the population lives on less than $1 per day. Nigeria was ranked 148th out of 178 in the United Nations Human Development Report for 2002. The effects of the dominance of oil revenues combined with volatile 'boom-bust' cycles have locked the country into a development trap. Nigeria's rural, mostly traditional agriculture based sector employs about two thirds of the population, and contributes twenty eight per cent to the GDP. Yet Nigeria, which was an exporter of food at independence, has become a massive importer of foodstuffs, whose share of total imports has grown from eight per cent in 1990 to 14.4 per cent in 2000. During 2002, Nigeria had to import thirty per cent of the rice it consumed and ranked as the second largest world market for this staple.

The United Nations Conference on Trade and Development (UNCTAD) characterised Nigeria as an 'under performer' in its assessment of the country's FDI inflows for the period 1999-2001.[25] Since then, FDI inflows have shown a modest increase, from $1.1 to $1.3 billion between 2001 and 2002. However, they have remained almost exclusively concentrated in the oil and gas sectors, leaving other areas in a state of under development.[26] The legislation that severely constrained foreign investment in the 1970s (Nigeria's famous indigenisation decrees) has had a lasting imprint. The business sector in Nigeria also suffers heavily from an erratic energy supply and poor infrastructure. According to the Nigerian Electricity Power Authority (NEPA), only thirty per cent of the Nigerian population has access to electricity.[27] And even where electricity is available, the supply is so erratic that generators are a necessity if any business activity is to be pursued. The acronym of NEPA is popularly interpreted as 'Never Expect Power Always'. Since the 1970s, gas distribution has been equally unsteady, for reasons which point both to the state of rampant violence in the delta and to the ability of well placed groups of individuals to engage in illegal bunkering, policy capture[28] and speculation on the parallel market.[29] Nigerian industries, despite the size of the country's market, chronically operate below capacity. Because of fluctuations in the supply of fuel at petrol stations, transport and communications are unreliable. The extensive use of generators also causes severe pollution in urban centres.

The degradation of ecosystems and conditions of living has been most extreme in the Niger delta. In the early 1980s, a geologist attached to the Petroleum Inspectorate of the Nigerian National Petroleum corporation (NNPC) noted the adverse effects of gas flaring,[30] surface water pollution[31] and land pollution. The land pollution was primarily attributed to the contamination of soils by crude oil spills or chemical waste. Between 1976 and 1996, 4,835 oil spills, estimated at 1.8 million barrels, were formally reported to the NNPC. Other sources consider that, due to under reporting, the real figures were possibly as much as ten times higher.[32] Not surprisingly, in the early 1980s, the communities of the Niger delta, the area most seriously affected, were described as feeling[33]

badly cheated and neglected by both the oil companies and Federal Government whose officials allegedly show no sympathy to their cause. In sharp reaction to the feelings of human exploitation, some of the villagers resort to stealing, sabotage and deliberate acts of vandalism to avenge their injustice.

The Niger delta garnered all the ingredients that, during the following decade, would transform it into what it still is today: a region plagued by chronic unrest and violence.

The politics of revenue allocation

The oil windfall of the seventies allowed the Nigerian government to pay scant attention to the notions of cost and productivity when it reshuffled federal-state relations. In 1970 the revenue allocation formula was revised. Ever since, the formula has consistently minimised the previously existing principle of derivation (redistribution to the states in accordance with their resources) in favour of such criteria as equality among states and demographic weighting. This shift enabled the government to consider the creation of new states and local governments independently of their internal revenue generating capacity. In 1976, the Irikefe panel on the creation of new states advised that the Federal Government should not 'attach undue emphasis on the requirements for economic viability ... [since] all the existing states except possibly Lagos are heavily dependent on the Federal Government for a substantial percentage of their revenue'. Nor did the panel feel particular concern at the prospect that creating new states meant for them a 'lower percentage of internally raised revenue'.[34] There is little need to emphasise that such a perspective would have been impossible without the sense of optimism conferred by Nigeria's seemingly inexhaustible oil revenues.

Today, Nigeria's revenue allocation formula has evolved only marginally. The country's 36 states and 774 local governments statutorily receive about half of Nigeria's oil revenue in terms of the current revenue sharing arrangement.[35] Most Nigerian states are heavily dependent on these revenues, a pattern that stimulates a debilitating 'cake sharing psychosis towards resource mobilisation and wealth creation'.[36] Fiscal discipline and market driven reforms are key features of the National Economic Empowerment and Development Strategy (NEEDS), the ambitious poverty reduction strategy for 2004-2007 officially launched on 29 May 2004.[37] With respect to Nigeria's revenue allocation formula, NEEDS specifically advocates that it be underpinned by macro economic co ordination between the federal and the state governments. If carried through, such a reform would radically alter relationships between the federal, state and local tiers of government. In the process, Nigeria's 'share of the national cake' ideology and its *rentier* approach to development would be drastically curtailed.

Revenue sharing is, like population counts, one of the most sensitive issues in Nigerian politics because of its direct financial implications. How the allocation formula should evolve is at the core of debates on what is called the 'national question', namely how power and resources should be distributed within the federation. Control of resources has been used to shape and re configure centre periphery relations in Nigeria throughout its history.[38] Most recently, during the first term of Olusegun Obasanjo's presidency (1999-2003), revenue sharing remained at the forefront of federal politics. In the case of the oil producing states, this issue was a source of bitter political and legal wrangling with the federal government. The 1990s had seen military rule transform the Niger delta into a powder keg as brutal repression followed the politicisation of demands for improved socio economic facilities and better control over the environmental impact of oil exploitation. As power was being handed over to the elected civilian administration of Nigeria in May 1999, violence exploded again in the delta region. Its demands for an increased allocation of resources and autonomy were not assuaged by the 1999 constitution's prescription of an increase from two and a half per cent to thirteen per cent in the mineral producing states' share of the distributable pool account. Fresh controversy also broke out with the decision of Olusegun Obasanjo to limit the federal government's loss of revenue by establishing a dichotomy between onshore and offshore oil production. The federal government claimed that the thirteen per cent owed to mineral producing states should be calculated on the basis of onshore extraction only, excluding revenues accruing from the forty per cent of Nigeria's oil production drilled offshore. Nigeria's five oil producing states became irate when the Supreme Court, in April 2002, ruled that the seaward boundary of Nigeria's eight littoral states terminated at the low water mark. This endorsed the position held by Obasanjo, who then altered the Revenue Sharing Act. The federal government's revenue share was thereby increased from 48.5 per cent to 56 per cent, with retroaction to 29 May 1999. By October, dissatisfaction with the Act acquired a new dimension as the national assembly passed a bill erasing the onshore/offshore dichotomy. Relations between the House of Assembly and the president had become difficult and a procedure requesting his impeachment was also instituted. This and the elections due in April 2003 were sufficient warning to the government of impending danger. The president suggested as a compromise that the seaward boundary of Nigeria's littoral states should be extended to twelve miles. The bill subsequently presented to the federal assemblies failed to resolve the issue. The assemblies responded with the adoption of an amendment extending the seaward boundary to 200 miles, thus erasing the onshore/offshore dichotomy. Obasanjo refused to sign the bill into law, but later backed down. Within a few weeks of the general elections, he ordered that the outstanding (offshore) component of the thirteen per cent derivation funds be released to the coastal oil producing states.[39] Much agitation and tension had been generated by what amounted to a reinstatement of the *status quo ante.*

Prebendalism versus predation: governance as a quagmire

Nigeria's consociational dispensation was once more fully operational as the country returned to civilian rule in 1979. Politics under the Second Republic (1979–1983) had gone along with an exacerbated expansion of patronage. Public office was exploited to advance private pursuits, a pattern which, due to its strong *rentier* and state centric slant was described as a striking combination of clientelism with prebendalism.[40] During the Second Republic, appointments to government positions became a much favoured way of distributing patronage, quite often under the pretence of taking into account the 'federal character' principle or the diversity of geo ethnic interests within the states. The principle was regularly called upon as a cover for the partisan or arbitrary allocation of state resources. Scholarships, study trips abroad, appointments, recruitments and promotions in the public sector were distributed in the same way as import licences or industrial and commercial contracts. Employment in the public sector alone increased from 2.1 to 3.7 million. Whereas until 1 October 1979 each state was limited to nine commissioners, their number subsequently rose in some states to as many as twenty. By December 1983, the total number of ministerial portfolios, at federal and state levels, reached 350, not including the numerous special advisers recruited by the governors or the president, without any legislative control. As a means of comparison, on the eve of the creation of the midwest region in 1964, Nigeria had about eighty ministers and commissioners. By January 1981, the total number of permanent secretaries was estimated at 515, a figure ten times greater than in the United Kingdom.[41]

The overthrow of the Second Republic by the military coup of December 1983 did not bring an end to patronage or to the misuse of public office for private enrichment. In the course of the fifteen subsequent years of military rule, recruitment in the public sector continued to expand without much control.[42] Additional states and local governments were carved out, and this meant establishing new civil services, new secretariats, roads and infrastructures, new hospitals, staff schools and houses; not to mention the creation of hundreds of new parastatals. Nor were the other characteristics of Nigeria's consociational dispensation ever questioned. The aborted transitions successively organised by Ibrahim Babangida (1985-1993) and Sani Abacha (1993-1998) involved drafting new constitutions which would have reinforced the formal dispositions on both 'federal character' and 'power sharing'.[43] In fact, what marked Nigeria's governance during these years was the sharp erosion of the fairly codified traditional patterns of neo patrimonial governance associated with prebendalism. Personal rule and dictatorship prevailed instead. Economic decline and military rule combined to trigger a shift from prebendalism to 'predation'.[44]

When Nigeria returned to civilian rule in 1999, a survey of the politics of oil in the country stated that[45]

> Nigerian politics revolve around the distribution of the oil money, whether officially (in the form of debates over revenue allocation) or unofficially (as military and civilian politicians seek favour with those in a position to reward them with opportunities to 'chop').

This was still the case during the first term of Obasanjo's presidency. As the term drew to a close, democratisation and the reinstatement of Nigeria's complex consociational and federal architecture[46] had done little more than reinvigorate the politics of prebendalism.

In his inauguration speech of 29 May 1999, Obasanjo had earmarked eradicating corruption as his major priority. Federal ministers were subsequently asked to sign letters of resignation with a blank for the date; all contracts, licences, awards and appointments made by the departing Abubakar regime were frozen and reviewed; the past activities of key public institutions were probed; and serious investigations were undertaken with the aim of recovering the funds looted by Sani Abacha, his family and their cronies. An anti corruption bill was passed by the federal assemblies in 2000. This new legislation established an Independent Corrupt Practices Commission (ICPC). But by mid 2003 little had been achieved to curb the endemic corruption in the country.[47] Attempts to recover the money stolen by the Abachas were partly successful.[48] This achievement had the aura of a much publicised but isolated case, prone to sustain the persistence of a culture of impunity among past and current ruling elites. At federal level, the sense of immunity of the new politicians showed most explicitly when, on the eve of the

April 2003 elections, the outgoing federal assemblies passed an anti corruption bill that sought both to curb the powers of ICPC and the presidency.[49]

Since its establishment in 2000, the ICPC had spent considerable resources and time in investigating personalities on corruption charges. It managed to secure the conviction of only one minor official, the chairman of a local government in Kogi state. Material and budgetary constraints, corruption within the police and the courts and disregard for ICPC orders within the states were commonly cited as reasons for this poor record. The ICPC also suffered from intrinsic limitations in its mandate and powers.[50] By the end of March 2003, the Commission had received no less than 800 petitions requesting investigation, yet bribery and fraud continued to percolate through public and private sector alike.[51] The ICPC itself was not spared allegations both of corruption and partisanship. In particular, the Commission was the object of persistent allegations that it was being used as a weapon of the executive for use against opponents in the federal legislature.[52]

The erosion of state power and legitimacy

Nigeria's version of federalism imposes strong financial and bureaucratic restraints on the ability of states to secede. This is in strong contrast to the situation in the fifties and sixties when the much larger regions controlled most of their own resources.[53] Nigeria is nonetheless being confronted with a more insidious series of challenges, namely the debilitating defects of its consociational system, a decline in institutional capacity and in federal territorial control and the clash between secular values and religious ideologies.

Institutional decay

During Nigeria's most recent period of military rule (1983–1999), declining oil revenues and a predatory style of leadership led to arbitrary and irresponsible governance. No established structure was spared: the deterioration affected first and foremost the police and armed forces, but also spread to the judiciary and the federal, state and local government administrations, which suffered from under funding, disregard for bureaucratic procedures, cronyism and corruption. By mid 1999, the disempowerment of the legislative assemblies and the subjection of civil servants to the whims of government meant the disappearance of 'any credible system of accounting or auditing'.[54] More generally, Nigeria's administrative system seemed to have lost '... any sense of public service, accountable governance or morality other than power for personal use'.[55]

Institutional decay was also aggravated by the unrestrained powers conferred on state agents under the military: extra judicial killings, arbitrary detention and other human rights violations became common in the unstable legislative environment.[56] In 1991, the Civil Liberties Organisation (CLO) reported, after inspecting Nigeria's fifty six prisons, that at least half of the 60,000 inmates had never been seen by a judge.[57] Official sources confirmed that many of those awaiting trial had been incarcerated for periods ranging from one to ten years.[58] Rule by the military also contributed to institutional decay through the diffusion of a culture of impunity among the law enforcement agencies. The assassination of the editor of *Newswatch*, Dele Giwa, by a parcel bomb; the execution of the writer Ken Saro Wiwa and his nine co accused after a mock trial; the killing of Shehu Yar Adua by lethal injection in jail; the mysterious death of Moshood Abiola as he was about to be released; and the assassination of his wife Kudirat, gunned down by thugs near an army checkpoint, represent but a small sample of the kind of state violence unleashed on citizens during Nigeria's successive military regimes.

The inauguration of the Fourth Republic formally reinstated constitutional rule and press freedom, but could not obliterate the effects of years of institutional decay and disrespect for both justice and the due process of law. As described above, the prebendal expectations of the new civilian elite severely hampered the reinstatement of institutional procedures. The persistence of state failure and institutional decay were brought into the limelight by the explosion of insecurity across the country. The soldiers' retreat into their barracks in May 1999 was the signal for an upsurge of criminality within the urban areas, along highways and in the borderlands. Homes were broken into, banks raided, cars and at times buses were seized by gangs of thieves who were often better armed than the police.

The institutions of the Fourth Republic were also unable to cope with the multiplication of violent conflict across the country. According to official data, during the first three years of the Obasanjo administration no less than sixty outbreaks of fighting occurred. These occasioned several thousand deaths, many injuries, massive property destruction and about 1.7 million internally displaced persons.[59] The issue remained of recurrent and dramatic topicality in mid 2004, especially in Plateau state, where ethno religious violence and its spillover effects in neighboring states prompted President Olusegun Obasanjo to demote the governor and proclaim the state of emergency, on 18 May, for an initial period of six months.

The full reinstatement of consociationalism has opened new opportunities for what may be termed the politics of exclusion, namely the instrumentalisation of indigenes versus settler dichotomies by 'son of the soil' movements. Even when outbreaks of violence have been purely local, their focus on extremely sensitive issues has contributed to their transformation into events likely to have severe national repercussions. Most commonly, conflicts originate from disagreements over boundary demarcations; demands for the creation of new local governments; quarrels over land use or ownership; objections to policy discrimination between settlers and indigenes; interactions between minorities and dominant ethnic or religious groups within states and local governments; and rivalries between political parties.

For political aspirants, the return to democratic rule has meant fresh opportunities for access to office and resources. Democratisation has unleashed a fierce and often violent scramble for positions, initially within the parties and later within the federal, state and local governments. The federal government's failure to guarantee the security of citizens has further enhanced what has become viewed as a criminalisation of Nigerian politics, marked by the assassination of several prominent personalities and the paralysis of public security institutions.[60] Numerous assassinations or assassination attempts were also recorded during the March 2004 local government elections. The privatisation of security through the employment of 'area boys', ethnic militias, *yan banga* and vigilante groups also generates its own quagmire. Indeed, private security agents often seem inclined to combine the protection of their patron with criminal behaviour against his political opponents, the police force and ordinary citizens.

The ability to purchase, sell or lease private protection is becoming essential in the conduct of Nigerian politics. The classic figure of the 'big man' is challenged by the emergence of a new prototype of entrepreneur, the 'strong man'.[61] While the big man combines economic power with key political functions as broker in a neo patrimonial setting, [62] the strong man does so through his ability to control 'illicit' forms of violence, if need be through the manipulation of public means of coercion. The strong man may be a warlord or the boss of a gang; he may also be, as observed in Nigeria under the Fourth Republic, a rogue politician or his 'godfather'. The rising phenomenon of 'godfathers' and 'godfatherism', is a reflection on both the rising influence of Nigerians involved in illicit activities and their personal ability to determine 'who gets nominated to contest elections and who wins in a state'.[63]

Insecurity across Nigeria is widely perceived to have reached levels unseen since the civil war, partly owing to the behaviour of the security forces themselves. Police performance suffers from the combination of insufficient numbers, inadequate training, low salaries, harsh conditions of service, lack of accommodation and fluctuating logistical budget allocations.[64] Police officers are not simply viewed as ineffective, but as a source of material and physical insecurity. This begins with the much resented collection of petty bribes at checkpoints and continues through their providing services only on payment. Police behaviour is also associated with repeated allegations of unlawful executions and human rights violations.[65]

The response of security forces to the collective unrest has also been particularly poor, owing to the absence of coherent policy orientations:[66]

> different factions of the ruling party and component groups ... have divergent interests to protect during such conflicts ... The overriding motive of government appears to have been not the resolution of crises but their suppression by armed soldiers.

This was the case in November 1999, when the army was sent to Bayelsa state, in the Niger delta region, to restore order after the abduction and murder of twelve policemen near Odi. The small town was sealed off by soldiers who then went on the rampage, killing many of its inhabitants. No public prosecution of the perpetrators or payment of compensation to the victims ever followed. In October 2001, ruthless army behaviour was again observed in Benue state when, following the death of nineteen soldiers after they were ambushed by a Tiv militia patrol, reprisals were launched against several villages. Gbeji, Vaase and Zaki Biam were ransacked and at least 250 people killed in cold blood.[67] A year later, the 'Miss World riots', which broke out in Kaduna on 21–23 November 2002, became another instance of 'continued impunity for killings'.[68] The security forces failed to intervene at the first signs of inter communal violence, and when they did, dozens of innocent people were injured or killed. Other areas where security forces have been sent have not been spared what has been described as a conjunction of 'impunity and state sponsored violence'.[69] Not surprisingly, under Nigeria's Fourth Republic, Nigerians remain inclined to describe the security forces as corrupt, inefficient and partisan.

The debilitating defects of consociationalism

The fragmentation of Nigeria into an increasing number of dependent states and local government entities may have helped to contain centrifugal tendencies, but this has not been without cost. The financial rewards associated with the creation of new territorial units have triggered a self perpetuating stream of demands (as in the Niger delta), which often take violent forms. These have occurred in conjunction with the sharpening, or at times sheer invention, of distinct geo ethnic identities. The Irikefe panel on the creation of new states during the mid 1970s had already pointed to the risks incurred by the creation of new states and local governments, which had established the conditions for 'new majorities [to] emerge while new minorities prepare to organise to make demands for further fragmentation'.[70] The panel then remarked that 'More minorities seem to have sprung up from the creation of twelve states than during the existence of the first regions'.[71]

A legal distinction between settlers and indigenous Nigerians was formally inserted in the 1979 constitution, which alternatively refers to the 'indigenes from a state' or to the 'populations which belong to a state'. Both expressions refer to Nigerian citizens 'either of whose parents or any of whose grandparents was a member of a community indigenous to that state'.[72] These descriptions of indigenous status through *jus sanguinis* (blood ties) as opposed to *jus soli* (residency), are central to the implementation of the federal character doctrine; the dichotomy has also unwittingly created opportunities for discrimination among Nigerian citizens. The issue was readily exploited during the Second Republic (1979-83), as political competition created a fertile environment for the exacerbation of the son of the soil syndrome: non indigenes were discriminated against in appointments, the allocation of scholarships and access to education and health services.[73] The subsequent fifteen years of military rule further contributed to the consolidation of a pattern which represents the dark side of the federal character doctrine.

Nigeria's son of the soil syndrome has been denounced by several authors as 'one of the most intractable forces militating against national integration'.[74] The sponsor of Nigeria's 1979 constitution and the current president of Nigeria, Olusegun Obasanjo, himself declared on several occasions that the[75]

settler or non native syndrome ... [promotes] a theory of ethnic exclusiveness ... propagated by elite groups who are competing to advance economic and political control[,] especially during democratic regimes.

He stresses that the human implications for the Nigerian population have been dramatic:[76]

It is pathetic and most lamentable that after ten or twenty years of residence in any part of Nigeria, a 'non indigene' still regards himself as an alien in that part of the country. Worse still are the institutional and procedural mechanisms that accentuate, amplify and reinforce such a feeling of alienation... He should be free

to contest for elections and hold responsible political appointment in the area
or region.

Over the past two decades, countless numbers of civil servants have been ordered
to return to their 'home' states or local governments after the creation of new territorial
entities. Promotions within the administration have been frequently denied on the
grounds of non indigeneity. Properties have been confiscated and access to land
ownership constrained. Admission to the state funded school systems and access to
the subsidised health facilities have at times been reserved for 'indigenes', even when
these did not live in that state or pay their taxes to that state. Political competition
has further encouraged the use of indigeneity as an informal but powerful weapon
against competitors or rival applicants for party and public office.[77]

The strictures embedded in Nigeria's approach to indigeneity also act as a
constraint on both labour mobility and social interactions between communities
outside their 'home' states or local governments. In urban centres, migrants who
have sometimes been settled in a state for several decades and speak the local
languages fluently, deeply resent their treatment as second class citizens. They
tend to live in specific areas, targeted for violence whenever a conflict arises. In the
process, 'home' states are being ascribed to individuals who have never lived there,
have lost touch with relatives and do not speak the local language. This means that,
in some cases, non indigenes are stateless Nigerian citizens.

Despite the well publicised defects of Nigeria's policies on indigeneity, they
have been carried unchanged into Nigeria's 1999 constitution.[78] In consequence,
the progressive fragmentation of Nigeria's original three regions into new states
and local governments also means that the territorial space within which a Nigerian
citizen can claim full rights as a citizen and an indigene is far smaller than it
used to be. The establishment of new states and new local governments continues
formally to transform into second class citizens those Nigerians who once qualified
as indigenes within the territorial entities where they live.[79]

Another cornerstone of Nigerian consociationalism, the federal character
doctrine, has become a source of bitterness and tension because of poor monitoring
and implementation of its provisions. The adoption of increasingly precise guidelines
and the creation of a Federal Character Commission by the 1999 constitution were
meant to meet demands for equitable access to positions in the civil service. In
practice, the federal character principle remains a 'profoundly nebulous and
contentious concept'.[80] Its implementation seems to have stimulated demands for
more and more precisely defined criteria and quotas, including the monitoring

of religious affiliation and the rotation of key political functions among the geo political zones.

Competition for territorial control

Across Nigeria, the inability of the police and judiciary to protect citizens has prompted the establishment of vigilante groups and militias by ethnic or religious communities. Vigilantism gained a particularly high profile in Nigeria's south eastern states when, during the first term of Obasanjo's presidency, groups of mercenaries were formally contracted to provide private security services.[81] Insecurity in the region had reached such proportions that, by the late 1990s, traders in Onitsha had decided to sponsor a vigilante group which became known as the Bakassi boys. Their position was subsequently formalised when they were contracted to fight criminality in the Abia, Anambra and Imo states.[82] In all three, they showed little respect for court procedure and due process of law as they chased, arrested and, after closed 'trials', hacked their victims to death in public. Such acts of instant justice enjoyed wide support initially, since these methods were viewed as far more effective and no less arbitrary than police behaviour.[83] However, by the time of Nigeria's 2003 general election, perceptions of the Bakassi boys had become far more ambivalent owing to their contribution to the spreading of new forms of violence and insecurity.[84] Police attempts to crack down on their activities had been partly successful, but this did not mean that federal control of these territories was effectively restored. As in other parts of Nigeria, competition between police and vigilante groups for control has often meant opportunities 'for a third entity, the armed robbers, to operate largely unchecked'.[85]

It is against this backdrop of decaying security and judicial institutions that, in 1999, Ahmed Sani Yerima, who was a candidate for the governorship of Zamfara state, decided to campaign for the adoption of a *shari'ah* criminal code. This commitment largely contributed to his election and brought him immense popularity when the introduction of *shari'ah* law reached the stage of policy implementation.[86] The decision to proclaim Zamfara a *shari'ah* state was greeted with such enthusiasm among the predominantly Muslim states of Nigeria that, by the end of 2002, criminal codes had been drafted and were in the process of being adopted by twelve of them.[87] The ability of the *shari'ah* courts to apply decisions instantly had a wide popular appeal as a much valued alternative to the magistrates court system, which was perceived as costly and dilatory because of lengthy procedures. The *shari'ah's* harsh punishments were also welcomed as a deterrent to criminality and corruption. The state endorsed reinstatement of the social and religious precepts of Islam also aroused much greater expectations than the promises attendant on Nigeria's democratic transition. Two years later, the implementation of the *shari'ah's* harsh punishments did not seem to have been accompanied by any decline in corruption among northern politicians and other powerful persons. Amputations (the punishment for theft) were carried out only against petty thieves; sentences to death by stoning for adultery or sexual assault were proclaimed only against poor and illiterate people, with a strong gender bias against women. None of the death sentences have, however, been carried out;[88] nor has any discussion of these judgements ever been held by Nigeria's Supreme Court. The explosive question of the constitutionality of the *shari'ah* criminal codes has yet to be addressed.[89] Meanwhile, in twelve of Nigeria's thirty six states, the *shari'ah* courts coexist with the magistrates' court system, a reflection on the limitations of federal government authority. *Shari'ah* laws are formally meant to apply exclusively to Muslims, but their broader social impact has nurtured a climate of insecurity among non Muslim minorities and settlers, which has been reinforced by a legacy of violent inter religious confrontations.[90]

The establishment of *shari'ah* criminal codes in a third of Nigeria's states cannot be dissociated from the feeling of marginalisation experienced by northern Nigerian elites in the aftermath of the May 1999 election. The election of Obasanjo brought to an end two decades of military rule by northerners. This was rapidly followed by a wave of retirements and dismissals of executives from the north in the army and economic circles. Regional challenges to federal authority prompted by feelings of marginalisation have also, and most dramatically, been associated with the Niger delta region, where Ijaw claims to have control over the local oil resources have translated into demands for autonomy. These, initially formalised in the Kaiama declaration,[91] have at times expanded into extreme manifestations of the son of the soil syndrome. The frequent outbreaks of violence within the region have tended to create a permanent state of unrest, and political demands have become increasingly difficult to disentangle from general insecurity, intra community violence and organised crime, especially in relation to illegal oil bunkering.[92] In the south eastern states, an even more radical secessionist programme has been brought forward by the Movement for the Actualisation of the Sovereign State of Biafra (MASSOB), whose members have kept challenging their state's very membership of Nigeria. They use the uniforms of the former Biafra police force, hoist the former separatist flag and circulate maps showing the boundaries of Biafra.[93]

Feelings of deep frustration, this time attributable to the annulment of Chief MKO Abiola's election to the presidency on 12 June 1993, similarly prompted the establishment of the Oodua People's Congress (OPC) in the south west.[94] Founded in 1994, the OPC quickly grew into a mass movement promoting and defending Yoruba interests by means that included violence. Following the 1999 elections, and despite the election of a Yoruba to the presidency, feelings of alienation remained strong in Yorubaland. These were reflected through the adoption of the Oodua Bill of Rights, which suggested the formation of a sort of confederal arrangement within which all Yorubas would form a distinct unit[95] and requested the convocation of a sovereign national conference to discuss Nigeria's future. Within the south west, the political domination now exercised by an essentially Yoruba party, the Alliance for Democracy (AD), prompted the OPC to place particular emphasis on crime fighting and vigilantism. Protection was sold, even to non indigenous ethnic groups who, on several occasions had been the target of severe ethnic violence.[96] As with the Bakassi boys in south eastern Nigeria, although not so openly, OPC has been employed by government officials to provide security at public functions.[97] OPC activities in the south west have simultaneously involved particularly violent confrontations with the police, a pattern that has also generated tensions between the federal authorities and the AD controlled state governments.[98]

Quo vadis Nigeria?

In the 1970s, the pressure of the civil war prompted Nigerians to participate in debates and issues which were not addressed at the time by most African states. A transition towards civilian rule was organised by the military at a time when there was no international pressure to do so. As part of the quest for a new constitutional dispensation, extensive debates were also held over sensitive issues. These involved the politics of ethnicity, citizenship versus indigeneity, interactions between state and religious bodies and the establishment of checks and balances to avoid state control by a single geo ethnic group. Even though debates on certain issues were embargoed by the military (the so called 'no go areas'), the breadth of the constitutional debate eventually gave birth to a highly original combination of federalism with consociationalism.

The systemic changes of the late seventies were made to preserve Nigeria's unity. Three decades later, the Nigerian practice of consociationalism has a debilitating effect on the country's polity. In several respects, this illustrates the relevance of making a key distinction between mechanisms (such as the principles of autonomy, grand coalition, proportional electoral system and veto powers) that underwrite pluralistic polities and consociational engineering in deeply divided plural societies. In the first case, associated with the historical trajectories of Switzerland and the Netherlands, and recently adopted for the governance of the European Union,[99] consociationalism operates in conformity with its stated goals. Conversely, the prescription of consociational mechanisms in deeply segmented societies is highly dysfunctional: it politicises ethnicity and hardens existing lines of fragmentation, as exemplified by Lebanon, Yugoslavia, Malaysia and Nigeria.[100] What Simpson observed a decade ago still remains fully true: in the third world, 'the list of cases where consociational arrangements applied reads like an obituary page'.[101] In Nigeria, each wave of state and local government creation has further entrenched sectional loyalties through its reproduction of the 'settlers versus natives' dichotomy on a narrowing geo political basis. The influence of opportunistic considerations in the implementation of the federal character doctrine also strengthens sectionalism and prebendalism instead of curbing their impact. Emphasis on the state of origin of employees in federal public services, parastatals, universities, newspapers and in the larger private commercial and industrial ventures serves to 'ethnicise' issues at the expense of merit and citizenship.

Nigeria's revenue allocation formulas also stimulate a *rentier* approach to politics. The combination of significant state controlled revenues (royalties from oil or natural gas) and a complex architecture of federal, state and local government institutions has preserved in Nigeria a pattern of neo patrimonial governance, (viewed here as a generic expression of prebendalism), that has collapsed in much of the rest of post colonial Africa. Over the past three decades, the dispensation of patronage through office allocation has been insulated from the country's macro economic adjustment programmes – the share of public spending in Nigeria's GDP actually increased sharply from eighteen per cent to fifty per cent between 1970 and 2001.[102] About 600 parastatals are still directly dependent on the federal government, while an estimated 900 belong to states and local governments.[103] If Nigeria could be said to have an overarching predicament, it could well reside in the prebendal slant which the country's oil wealth nurtures at the expense of pro poor and pro growth policies. Under the Fourth Republic, competition to win a stake in state or bureaucratic resources still determines the nature of party politics and the cut throat nature of electoral competition, as witnessed during the April 2003 general elections and the March 2004 local government elections.

The availability of significant state controlled resources contributes to the material preservation of the Nigerian state, although classic attributes associated with statehood are being eroded. Decades of institutional decay and loss of territorial control signal Nigeria's steady transformation into a country without a functioning state. For a variety of reasons, the federal government cannot assert or legitimise

Nigerian timeline	
1960	Independence from Britain on 1 October
1963	Nigeria declares itself a republic.
1966	In January, Prime Minister Balewa killed in a coup. Major-General Johnson Aguiyi-Ironsi heads the military government. Ironsi killed in a counter-coup, in July, and replaced by Lieutenant-Colonel Yakubu Gowon.
1967	The Eastern Region of Nigeria secedes in May, proclaiming itself the Republic of Biafra. Country plunges into a civil war that kills an estimated one million people.
1970	The Biafra secessionists surrender on 14 January; the former eastern region is fully reintegrated into the country.
1979	Nigeria returns to civilian government rule; Shehu Shagari is elected president of the Second Republic.
1983	Shagari regime is deposed in December, as a military coup ousts the democratically-elected government.
1985	A second coup ushers in a regime headed by General Ibrahim Babangida.
1993	Nigerians elect Moshood Abiola as the new president of the country with 58% of the vote. On the eve of election results, General Babangida annuls the election. Babangida steps down in August and chooses civilian interim government. General Sani Abacha seizes power in November.
1994	Abiola arrested after declaring himself president.
1995	Playwright and activist Ken Saro-Wiwa executed with nine other Ogoni activists. EU imposes sanctions and Nigeria is suspended from the Commonwealth.
1996	Kudirat Abiola, the wife of detained Nigerian presidential claimant Moshood Abiola, is shot and killed in a Lagos street.
1998	Abacha dies and is replaced by Major-General Abdulsalam Abubakar who undertakes to transfer power to a democratically elected civilian regime. Moshood Abiola dies in jail as he is about to be released.
1999	Parliamentary and presidential elections held. Olusegun Obasanjo sworn in as president on May 29.
2000–2002	Adoption of shari'ah criminal codes by twelve northern states.
2003	President Obasanjo's People's Democratic Party wins majority in the two federal assemblies. President Obasanjo wins the presidential elections with more than 60 per cent of the vote. EU observers say polling marred by 'serious irregularities'.

Sources: *The Washington Post*, http://www.washingtonpost.com;

BBC News Country Profile: Nigeria, http://news.bbc.co.uk

its claims to monopoly over the use of coercion. The security forces' inability to restore law and order is also difficult to disentangle from demands for greater local or regional autonomy. State authority is being further eroded by the discredit cast on the Nigerian state's attempts to introduce a modernising and secular ethos. The key domestic players often appear to be ethnic militias, groups of vigilantes and neo traditional organisations such as the Arewa Consultative Forum in the north, Afenifere in the south west and Ohanze Ndigbo in the south. Federal power is also constrained by powerful geo ethnic criminal networks which have acquired a global reach in petroleum smuggling, illicit drugs trafficking, commercial fraud and identity theft.[104] The privatisation of public resources amidst poverty and, not least, the erosion of federal territorial control and legitimacy, point to an increasingly unsteady future for Nigeria. What is at stake is not the survival of Nigeria as an entity, but its transformation into a country without a state.

Endnotes

1   The author wishes to thank Boubacar Issa Abdourhamane for his assistance in collecting data for this chapter.

2   According to its regional director for west Africa, the Western Union alone channels into Nigeria remittances which represent an average $3 billion a year; these have amounted to a total of $28 billion since the transfer scheme started in 1994, *The Guardian* (Lagos), 30 September 2003. Although these figures account for only a small proportion of total private remittances and transfers, they represent a yearly inflow twice as high as Foreign Direct Investment (FDI) into Nigeria for 2001 and 2002 (see below).

3   The combined effects of droughts and irrigation projects have resulted in a dramatic shrinking of the lake's size from an estimated $30,000km^2/ 25,000km^2$ to $3,000/1,500km^2$ within the past four decades. United Nations Integrated Regional Information Networks, *Saving Lake Chad*, 21 March 2003, *www.irinews. org/wwd.asp*

4   Many of these groups outnumber the population of several independent African states.

5   Consociationalism refers to politico institutional arrangements where the co operation of different social, religious or geo ethnic groups is sought through power sharing and guarantees to minority groups.

6   Under colonial rule, federations had emerged as the standard solution for the cost effective management of resource disparities: accordingly, richer territories had to pay for those less well endowed, a source of tensions, as reflected by the debates between Felix Houphouët Boigny of Côte d'Ivoire and Léopold Senghor of Senegal over the break up of the French West Africa (FWA) federation. See Hazlewood A, *African Integration and Disintegration; Case Studies in Economic and Political Union.* London: Oxford University Press, 1967.

7   De St. Jorre J, *The Nigerian Civil War.* London: Hodder & Stoughton, 1972, pp. 69-77.

8   Resistance to the islamisation campaigns pursued by the northern premier, Ahmadu Bello and his party, was also a recurrent source of violence. Panter Brick SK & PF Dawson, 'The creation of new states in the north', in Panter Brick SK (ed.), *Nigerian Politics and Military Rule: Prelude to the Civil War.* London: University of London & Athlone Press, 1970, pp. 128-139.

9   The eastern and western regions were divided into three and two states respectively, while the midwest retained its boundaries.

10 See for instance Hicks UK, *Federalism, Failure and Success.* London: MacMillan, 1978, p. 5.

11 Suberu R, *Nigerian Federalism and Ethnic conflict in Nigeria.* Washington: United States Institute of Peace Press, 2002.

12 Gboyega A, 'The making of the Nigerian constitution', in Oyediran O (ed.), *Nigerian Government and Politics under Military Rule, 1966-1979.* London: Macmillan, 1979, p. 245.

13 Federal Republic of Nigeria, *The Constitution of the Federal Republic of Nigeria.* Lagos: Federal Ministry of Information, 1979, p. 8.

14 Ukwu UI (ed.), *Federal Character and National Integration in Nigeria.* Kuru: National Institute for Policy and Strategic Studies, 1987; Kirk Greene AHM, 'Ethnic engineering and the "federal character" of Nigeria: Boon of contentment or bone of contention?', *Ethnic and Racial Studies*, vi, 4, 1983, pp. 457-76.

15 During the aborted 1988-93 transition towards civilian rule (brought to a sudden end by Babangida's cancellation of the results of the presidential election of 13 June 1993), political parties were required to be 'well established in the federal and the state capitals and in the headquarters of *all* [emphasis mine] the local governments of the federation'. They were also to ensure that their '... organisation at each level of government reflects the federal character of Nigeria except ... in the case of local government areas'; in Federal Republic of Nigeria, *Main Guidelines*

- *Formation of Political Parties*. Lagos: National Electoral Commission, 1989, pp. 2 & 4.

16 The 1999 constitution stipulates that a candidate for the office of president will be duly elected if he obtains a majority of the votes cast and 'not less than one quarter of the votes cast. ... in each of at least two thirds of all the states in the Federation and the Federal Capital Territory'; section 133(b) in Federal Republic of Nigeria, *Constitution of the Federal Republic of Nigeria*. Lagos: Federal Government Press, 1999, p. 54. Similar dispositions apply for the election of the state governor who must secure a majority of votes, as well as one third of the votes in at least two thirds of the local governments of the state; see section 179(1) in *ibid.*, p. 71.

17 *Ibid.*, Section 14(4), p. 10.

18 Third Schedule, Part 1 C 8(l) in Federal Republic of Nigeria, *The[1979] Constitution* ..., p. 140.

19 Lijphart A, *Democracy in Plural Societies. A Comparative Exploration*. New Haven: Yale University Press, 1980, p. 27.

20 *Ibid.*

21 Zoning is explicitly endorsed by the most significant piece of legislation passed during the first term of Olusegun Obasanjo, the Corrupt Practices and Other Related Offences Act 2000. Section 3 (3) of the Act prescribes that its Commission (ICPC) must consist of a chairman and twelve other members 'two of whom shall come from each of the six geo political zones'. Online at *http://www. icpcnigeria. com/act.htm.*

22 Iwayemi A, 'Le Nigeria dans le système pétrolier international', in Bach DC, Egg J & J Philippe (eds), *Le Nigeria, un pouvoir en puissance*. Paris: Karthala, 1988, pp. 34 ff.

23 Karl TL, *The Paradox of Plenty; Oil Booms and Petro States*. Berkeley: University Press of California, 1997.

24 Thomas S & C Sudharshan, *Poverty in a Wealthy Economy: The Case of Nigeria*. Washington: IMF Working Paper, WP/02/114, 2002, p. 4.

25 UNCTAD, *World Investment Report 2003; FDI Policies for Development; National and International Perspectives*. Geneva: UNCTAD, 2003, p. 12.

26 *Ibid.*, p. 7.

27 *Vanguard*, 16 October 2003.

28 Policy capture refers to the use of inappropriate influence on the regulatory body by interest groups such as provider or professional associations.

29 In the weeks preceding the outbreak of the March 2003 war in Iraq, gas shortages multiplied. The official reason given was that international price volatility was so

high that suppliers preferred to sell cargoes to the highest bidder, *International Herald Tribune*, 11 April, 2003. A few weeks later, as the April general elections deadline came to a close, the situation worsened, as the Nigerian refineries allegedly became unable to receive their regular supply of Nigerian crude oil - the country's production went down by as much as forty per cent due to ethnic violence in the delta. Distribution companies were also stigmatised for supplying 'informal' operators within Nigeria and in neighbouring Benin, Niger and Chad.

30 Flaring is scheduled to stop by 2008. By 1981, eighty four per cent of Nigerian gas was either flared or burned off. Over a hundred flow stations had been doing so day and night for several decades, causing serious atmospheric pollution, constant heat around the flare pits and abnormal salinity of the pool water, resulting in serious disturbances to the life cycles of plants, animals and local communities; Ikeagwuani FD, *Petroleum Exploration and Exploitation: Impact on Socio Economic Life of Nigerians Living in Oil Producing Areas.* Commissioned and sponsored by Lagos: The Petroleum Inspectorate, Nigerian National Petroleum Corporation, mimeo, 1984, pp. 11-12.

31 The pollution of surface water is of particular significance to the ecosystem of the delta since 'myriads of rivers, smaller flowing streams swamps, lagoons, fish ponds, lakes, estuaries and beaches' are particularly sensitive to discharges '... through accidental or deliberate actions, [of] large quantities of spilled oil, chemicals, drilling muds and well cuttings [as well as] produced saline formation water', Ikeagwuani FD, *ibid.*, p. 12.

32 Human Rights Watch, *The Price of Oil; Corporate Responsibility and Human Rights Violations in Nigeria's Oil Producing Communities.* New York: HRW, 1999, p. 59.

33 Ikeagwuani FD, *op. cit.*, p. 36.

34 Federal Republic of Nigeria, *Report of the Panel Appointed by the Federal Military Government to Investigate the Issue of the Creation of More states and Boundary Adjustments in Nigeria.* Lagos: Federal Government Press, 1976, pp. 39 & 41-42.

35 International Monetary Fund, *Nigeria: 2002 Article IV Consultation - Staff Report; Staff Statement; and Public Information Notice on the Executive Board Discussion.* Washington: IMF Series: Country Report No. 3, 3, p. 26, fn.17.

36 Suberu R, op. cit., p. 138.

37 Nigerian National Planning Commission, *Meeting Everyone's Needs; National Economic Empowerment and Development Strategy*, Abuja: NPC, April 2004 at *http://www.nigerianeconomy.com/needs.htm*

38 Momoh A & S Adejumobi (eds), *The National Question in Nigeria: Comparative Perspectives.* Aldershot: Ashgate, 2002.

39   *This Day,* 26 January 2003.

40   Joseph R, *Democracy and Prebendal Politics in Nigeria; The Rise and Fall of the Second Republic.* Cambridge: Cambridge University Press, 1987, p. 55–57. Prebendalism is adapted from Max Weber's earlier discussion of 'prebends' as the assignment to an official of 'rent payments for life … fixed to objects or … economic usufruct from lands or other sources'. Weber M, "Bureaucracy", in Gerth HH & CW Mills, *From Max Weber, Essays in Sociology,* London: Routledge & Kegan, 1970, p. 207.

41   Adamolekun O & M Laleye, 'Effects of creating new states on the Nigerian Public Administration System', in Adejuyigbe O, Dare L & A. Adepoju (eds) *Creation of States in Nigeria, A Review of Rationale, Demands and Problems,* Lagos, Federal Government Press, 1982, p. 70.

42   Employment in the core civil service of the federal government is estimated at 250,000 employees, while 'there could be at least' another 800,000 employees in parastatals and in the military and police. International Monetary Fund, *op. cit.,* p. 26. These figures do not include public sector employees in the states and local governments.

43   Abacha intended to go a step further as he enthusiastically subscribed to a constitutionally endorsed rotation of nine key political offices among six geo ethnic zones 'for an experimental period of 30 (thirty) years'. General Abacha's speech of 1 October 1995 as quoted in Gboyega A, 'Current options for a stabilised federal system in Nigeria', in Amuwo A, Bach DC & Y Lebeau (eds), *Nigeria during the Abacha Years (1993-1998); The Domestic and International Politics of Democratisation.* Ibadan: Africa Book Builders & IFRA, 2001, p. 309.

44   Lewis P, 'From prebendalism to predation: The political economy of decline in Nigeria', *The Journal of Modern African Studies,* XXXIV, 1, 1996, pp. 79–103.

45   Human Rights Watch, *op. cit.,* p. 52.

46   These were an executive president and his vice president, two federal assemblies (106 senators and 360 representatives), the various federal committees and commissions prescribed by the constitution, the 36 governors and members of the 36 state houses of Assembly, the 774 local government chairmen and their councillors.

47   Nigeria, widely perceived as one of the most corrupt countries in the world, features next to last on the Corruption Perception Index of Transparency International for 2003. In 1980, the Irikefe Commission was set up to inquire into the disappearance of $2 billion in oil revenues, Iwayemi A, *op. cit.,* p. 29. It is estimated that during the second Republic (1979-83), the Nigerian treasury lost between $5 and $7 billion, Wright S, *Nigeria, The, Dilemmas Ahead.* London: Economist Intelligence

Unit, 1986, p. 30. By 1987, the General Accountant of the Federation considered that corruption in the civil service represented a loss of between $1.2 and $1.5 billion a year for the Treasury, *West Africa*, 10 August 1987, p. 1551. A decade later, the Okigbo commission of inquiry, appointed by general Abacha, estimated that $12.2 billion in oil earnings had disappeared between 1990-1994. General Babangida, then Nigeria's head of state, was never asked to account for this amount; *The Washington Post*, 10 June 1998.

48 In order to avoid years of litigation, an agreement was reached in which the Abacha family, the Nigerian government and various European banks agreed to the transfer of $1 billion dollars to the federal government, who agreed in exchange to return ten per cent of this amount to the Abachas. *Financial Times*, 19 June 2002.

49 According to the bill, lawmakers, rather than the president would vet the nomination of the ICPC chairman; the prosecution of senior government officials also became more difficult. The bill was then vetoed by President Obasanjo, but, in the aftermath of the general elections, the outgoing Senate and House of Representatives enacted it. The matter was taken to the Federal High Court, which ruled on 21 May 2003 that the pre existing version of the law should continue to prevail until amended by due process of law, *Guardian*, 22 May 2003.

50 The Commission is not entitled to initiate investigations without a formal complaint from a member of the public. The ICPC's powers are also restricted to offences committed after the adoption of the Corrupt Practices and Other Related Offences Act (13 June 2000).

51 In February 2003, the Acting Auditor General, Vincent Azie, released his audit report of the federal ministries and parastals for 2001. The document, made public for the first time in the country's history, noted the misappropriation of N23 billion in 10 federal ministries through financial fraud, over invoicing, double debiting, and inflated contract figures, *Newswatch*, 24 February 2003, p. 20. Also noted were abuses concerning the NNPC, the Nigeria Customs Service and the two federal assemblies. No inquiry followed these allegations. Their author was stigmatised by the federal government for 'gross insubordination and incompetence' and lost his position when it came up for confirmation six months later; Enweremadu DU, *The Struggle Against Corruption in Nigeria: The Role of the National Anti Corruption Commission in Nigeria Under the Fourth Republic.* Bordeaux: IEP, DEA thesis, mimeo, 2003, p. 109.

52 Enweremadu DU, *ibid.*, pp. 79-92.

53 Tamuno TN, 'Separatist agitation in Nigeria since 1914', *The Journal of Modern African Studies*, VIII, 4, 1970, pp. 563-584.

54 Olowu B, *Towards Resolving the Nigerian Governance Crisis*. The Hague: IDS, mimeo, 1999, p. 28.

55 *Ibid.*

56 The State Security (Detention of Persons) Decree No. 2 of 1984 and its subsequent amendments authorised the arbitrary and indefinite detention, without charge or trial, of any person deemed by the government to be a threat to the security or the economy of Nigeria; Civil Liberties Organisation, *From Khaki to Agbada; A Handbook for the February, 1999 Elections in Nigeria.* Lagos: CLO, 1999, pp. 8–9.

57 Civil Liberties Organisation, *Behind The Wall; A Report on Prison Conditions in Nigeria and the Nigerian Prison System.* Lagos: CLO, 1991, p. 63.

58 Quoted in *ibid.*

59 Statement by Nigeria's Inspector General of Police, Tafa Balogun, as quoted in *This Day* (Lagos), 12 September 2002. It is commonly estimated that over 10,000 people died from ethnic, religious or political unrest during the first two and a half years of the fourth republic. Centre for Law Enforcement Education & Organisation Mondiale Contre la Torture, *Hope Betrayed? A Report on Impunity and State Sponsored Violence in Nigeria.* Lagos & Geneva: CLEEN & OMCT, 2002. p. 187; also Fourchard L, 'Security, crime and segregation in historical perspective' in Fourchard L. and IO Albert (eds), *Security, Crime and Segregation in West African Cities since the 19th Century,* Paris: Karthala, Ibadan: IFRA, pp. 25–52.

60 The assassination of personalities has also remained largely unpunished. The most prominent victim was the Attorney General of the federation, Chief Bola Igue (December 2001). Also assassinated were the Chairman of the Nigerian Bar Association, nearly two dozen local government (LG) chairmen and state assembly legislators.; see Human Rights Watch, *Nigeria: Testing Democracy: Political Violence in Nigeria.* New York: HRW, 15, 95A, mimeo, pp. 27–32.

61 The distinction between 'strongman' and 'big man' was initially suggested by Godelier in the course of his discussion of Sahlins. Godelier M., *La production des grands hommes; pouvoir et domination masculine chez les Baruya de Nouvelle Guinée,* Paris: Fayard, 1982; Sahlins M, 'Poor Man, Rich Man, Big Man, Chief: Political Types in Melanesia and Polynesia', *Comparative Studies in Society and History,* V, 3, 1963, pp. 285–303.

62 Médard JF, 'Le 'big man' en Afrique: esquisse d'analyse du politicien entrepreneur', *Année sociologique,* vol. 42, 1, 1982, pp. 167–192.

63 Ibrahim, J, 'The rise of Nigeria's godfathers', BBC Focus on Africa magazine, 10 November 2003 at *http://news.bbc.co.uk/2/hi/africa/3156540.stm*

64 See account in *Newswatch,* 8 September 2003, pp. 36–37.

65 Since early 2002, in an attempt to curb criminality, operation 'Fire for Fire' has authorised police force members to shoot on sight; Human Rights Watch, *The O'Odua People's Congress: Fighting Violence with Violence.* New York: HRW, 15, 4(A), 2003, p. 9.

66 Ukiwo U, 'Politics, ethno religious conflicts and democratic consolidation in Nigeria, *Journal of Modern African Studies,* XIL, 1, 2003, p. 128.

67 Human Rights Watch, *Military Revenge in Benue: A Population Under Attack.* New York: HRW, 14, 2(A), April 2002.

68 . Human Rights Watch, Nigeria *'The Miss World Riots': Continued Impunity for Killings in Kaduna.* New York: HRW, 15, 3(A), 2003.

69 Centre for Law Enforcement Education & Organisation Mondiale Contre la Torture, *op. cit.*

70 Federal Republic of Nigeria, *Report of the [Irikefe]Panel ...,* p. 45.

71 *Ibid.*

72 Art. 277(1) Federal Republic of Nigeria, *The[1979] Constitution ...,* p. 90.

73 Bach DC, 'Indigeneity, ethnicity and federalism', in: Diamond L, Kirk Greene A & O Oyediran (eds), *Transition without End; Nigerian Politics and Civil Society under Babangida.* Boulder: Lynne Rienner, 1997, pp. 333-350.

74 Awa EO, *National Integration in Nigeria: Problems and Prospects.* Ibadan, NISER, Distinguished Lectures No. 5, 1983, p. 11; also Ikime O, *In Search of Nigerians: Changing Patterns of Inter Group Relations in an Evolving Nation State.* Presidential Inaugural Lecture delivered at 30th Congress of the Historical Society on 1 May 1985, Ibadan: Impact Publishers, 1985; Nigerian Political Science Association, 'Communique of the Seminar to mark the Silver Jubilee of Nigeria's Independence', in *Journal of the Nigerian Political Science Association,* 4, 1985, p. 27.

75 Obasanjo O, 'Keynote Address' in Africa Leadership Forum, Conflict Prevention and Management Centre, *Community Seminar Series on The Settler Question in Nigeria: the Case of Jos Plateau,* 15-17 December 1993. Lagos: Friedrich Naumann Foundation, 1994, p.23; also Obasanjo O, *Constitution for National Integration and Development.* Yaba: Friends Foundation, 1989, p. 116.

76 Obasanjo O, 'Keynote Address', *ibid.,* p. 24.

77 Jinadu AL, *Ethnic Conflict and Federalism in Nigeria.* Bonn: Zentrum für Entwicklungsforschung, Discussion Paper No 49, 2002, pp. 36-37.

78 Section 318(1) in Federal Republic of Nigeria, *Constitution of [1999] ...,* op. cit., p. 120.

79 Under Nigeria's Fourth Republic, one of the issues sustaining demands for a national sovereign conference is the creation of new states; by mid 2004, a legal tussle was

also opposing the federal government in four states (Lagos, Niger, Katsina and Nassarawa) over their creation of new local governments; *The Vanguard*, 26 June 2004.

80   Suberu R, *op. cit.*, p. 114-115.

81   Harnischfeger J, 'The Bakassi Boys: Fighting crime in Nigeria', *Journal of Modern African Studies*, 41, 1, 2003, pp. 23-49; also Human Rights Watch, *Nigeria; the Bakassi Boys: The Legitimisation of Murder and Torture.* New York: HRW, 14, 5(A), 2002.

82   Amnesty International, *Nigeria: Vigilante Violence in the South and South East,* AFR 44/014/2002, November 2002, mimeo, pp. 7-14.

83   By 2001, Onitsha had acquired the reputation of being one of the safest cities in Nigeria. A commission of journalists even awarded a prize to Anambra state as 'the most crime free state in Nigeria', as quoted in Harnischfeger J, *op. cit.*, p. 25.

84   Especially in Anambra states, the Bakassi boys became extensively mentioned in conjunction with the intimidation or elimination of political opponents of the governor (for details, see Amnesty International, *op. cit.*, p. 9-11). Individual members of the Bakassi militias were also hired by clients seeking to settle personal scores through violent means.

85   Akinyele RT, 'Ethnic militancy and national stability in Nigeria: A case study of the Oodua People's Congress', *African Affairs,* 100, 2001, p. 624.

86   Kalu OU, 'Safiyya and Adamah: Punishing adultery with Shari'ah stones in Twenty First Century Nigeria', *African Affairs,* 102, 2003, pp. 390.

87   Bach DC, 'Nigeria: Application et implications de la shari'ah' *Pouvoirs*, 104, January 2003, pp. 117-127.

88   As the court's written transcripts indicate, poor implementation of the *shari'ah* law by inadequately trained lawyers was a key factor in the much publicised decision of the judges of the *shar'iah* Court of Appeal, Sokoto, to acquit Safiyya Hussaini, initially sentenced to death by stoning for adultery, Kalu OU, *op. cit.*, p. 401 ff. Since the acquittal of Safiyya Hussaini two other sentences to death by stoning have been examined by *shari'ah* appeal courts. The sentences against Had Sarimu Mohammed and Amina Lawal were both quashed on legal grounds. *The Vanguard*, 20.August 2003; and *The Guardian*, 26 September 2003.

89   President Obasanjo, after initially making bold statements on this issue, refused to request an arbitration from the Supreme Court, probably because this would have meant additional problems: the judges would have been divided along religious lines, and their decision, if favourable to the federal government, would have been difficult to impose.

90 On 21 February 2000, an anti *shari'ah* demonstration in Kaduna triggered a wave of inter religious violence which spread throughout the country. Several thousand people were killed or injured in the cities of Kaduna, Katsina, Kafanchan, Zaria and Sokoto. The massive return of south easterners to their home states led in turn to a spiral of reprisals against northern Muslims settled in Aba, Umuahia, and to a lesser extent Owerri, Port Harcourt, Calabar and Uyo. On the November 2002 'Miss World' riots in Kaduna see footnote 58.

91 *The Guardian*, 28 December 1998.

92 According to a federal government fact sheet, cases of vandalisation of pipelines and other oil industry installations jumped from 131 during the 1995-1998 period to 2,374 between 1999-2002. According to the same source, by mid 2003, this represented an estimated loss of 15% of Nigeria's daily oil output; Salisu Na'inna Dambatta, Assistant Director of Information in the Presidency, 'Tackling Vandalism in Nigeria's Oil Industry', *Vanguard*, 14 October 2003.

93 Harnischfeger J, *op. cit.*, p. 43.

94 Akinyele RT, *op. cit.*, pp. 623-640; Sesay A, Ukeje C, Aina O & A Odebiyi (eds), *Ethnic Militias and the Future of Democracy in Nigeria*. Ile Ife: Obafemi Awolowo University Press, 2003, pp. 27-39.

95 *The Guardian*, 15 May 1999.

96 Human Rights Watch, Nigeria; *The O'Odua People's Congress, op. cit.*, pp. 11-14.

97 *Ibid.*, p. 10 ff.

98 Obasanjo also attempted to outlaw ethnic militias, but his April 2002 bill on the 'Prohibition of Certain Associations' was not passed into law by the two federal assemblies.

99 On the European political system, see Costa O & P Magnette, 'The European Union as a consociation? A methodological assessment', *West European Politics,* 26, 3, July 2003, pp. 1-18.

100 See my earlier discussion of Lebanon's consociational arrangements and the so called 'Tito initiative' in Yugoslavia in Bach D, 'Managing a plural society: the boomerang effects of Nigerian federalism', *Journal of Commonwealth and Comparative Politics*, XXVII, 1-2, July 1989, pp. 237 & 240-1.

101 Simpson M, 'The experience of nation building: some lessons for South Africa', *Journal of Southern African Studies,* XX, 3, 1984, pp. 468.

102 International Monetary Fund, *Nigeria: 2002, op. cit.*, p. 19.

103 Nigeria's 1,500 parastatals employ an estimated fifty-sixty per cent of the total active population of the formal sector; Ambassade de France au Nigeria, *Les Privatisations au Nigeria*, 2002, p. 1. Online at *http://www.dree.org/nigeria/*.

104 Shaw M, 'West African Criminal Networks in South and Southern *Africa', African Affairs*, 101, 2002, pp. 291–316; also Ebbe O, 'Political criminal nexus; The Nigerian case: Slicing Nigeria's "national cake"', *Trends in Organised Crime,* IV, 3, 1999, pp. 29–59; also Catan T & M Peel, 'Bogus websites, stolen corporate identities: How Nigerian fraudsters steal millions from western banks', *The Financial Times*, 3 March 2003, pp. 1 & 11. The threat of impending sanctions by the OECD based Financial Action Task Force finally prompted the adoption in December 2002 and January 2003 of Nigerian legislation against money laundering through the creation of the Economic and Financial Crimes Commission.

4

The Democratic Republic of Congo

Claude Kabemba

Introduction

The Democratic Republic of Congo (DRC) covers a total of 2,345 million square kilometres. It is the second largest country on the continent after Sudan. There is no debate about its status: a consensus has been reached among scholars that the DRC represents the stereotype of a collapsed state. No central power controls the entire Congolese territory; the state institutions have all but broken down; and the state is unable to satisfy the minimal Weberian test of exercising a monopoly of coercive force over its land and people. The DRC's disintegration started soon after independence and reached its maturity when Mobutu disappeared from the political scene in 1996, and the armies of Rwanda and Uganda invaded in 1998.

Today, the central government in Kinshasa does not have control over the entire country. The territory of the DRC remains divided, especially in the Kivu province[1] into small rival 'micro enclaves' linked to external powers. These micro enclaves are failed ruling entities in themselves. They share the same features as the original state: all lack central authorities and institutions to carry out day to day state functions. The dilemma in the DRC is not just that these enclaves are not serving the interests of the population, but that they are failing to preserve social order.

The logical next step is to ask the question, how can the state in the DRC be reconstructed? What alternatives are there to the current situation? Any attempt to address these questions would have to deal first with another question: Why did the Congolese state evolve in the manner it has? A critical approach to this question is essential before we can attempt to reply.

Two theses in the literature on state collapse in Africa need to be dismissed at the outset. The first maintains that state crisis on the continent has its roots in the artificial nature of colonial boundaries (although this factor is an important contributor to the problems faced by a number of states on the continent).

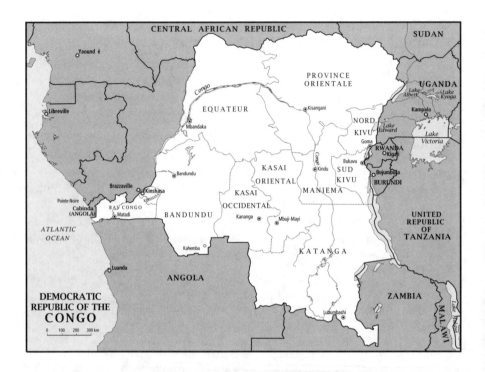

The second is the attempt to understand states in Africa through analogy, rather than through the history of each state.

What renders the DRC's position unique is that at independence it already had the characteristics of a failed state. The centralisation of power in the hands of a government based in Kinshasa has been ineffective throughout the forty four years since independence. The transitional government was inaugurated on 30 June 2003 following the signing in February 2002 in Pretoria of the Global and All inclusive Peace Accord and its adoption in April 2003. There is no doubt that as the Congolese attempt to pick up the pieces after five years of war, the structure of the state will come under further serious strain. The geographical size of the country alone poses a problem for the construction of a state that is capable of securing peace, providing for the welfare of its people, monitoring the country's extensive borders to prevent trafficking by organised crime syndicates, and deterring the illegal exploitation of resources.

Geography

The DRC, which has been described as the strategic heart of Africa, is situated at the centre of the continent. It contains roughly 56 million people (making it the fourth most populous country in Africa after Nigeria, Egypt and Ethiopia) who belong to more than 250 different African ethnic groups. The majority are Bantu.

There are four main geographic regions in the DRC, defined in terms of the terrain and patterns of natural vegetation. The core region is the Central Congo Basin, a large depression with an average elevation of about 400 metres. It is also referred to as *La Cuvette*. It covers about 800,000 square kilometres, almost one third of the total Congolese territory. Around it in the north and south we find higher plains and, occasionally, hills, covered with varying mixtures of savannah and woodland. The population here is mostly agriculturalist. The western part is shaped like a panhandle stretching to the Atlantic Ocean. The Eastern Highlands, which extend for more than 1,500 kilometres, represent the highest and most rugged portion of the country. The hills in this region range from 1,000 to more than 5,000 metres. The Great Rift Valley which constitutes the eastern border of the DRC, consists of a system of lakes separated by plains situated between high mountains. The principal rivers of the DRC are the Ubangi in the north and the Congo River, which flows into the Atlantic, in the west. The entire length of Lake Tanganyika lies along the eastern border with Tanzania and Burundi.

The Ruwenzori Mountains, which form the highest range in Africa, are located in this region. The changes in elevation of the different mountains and their location on the equator make for varied and spectacular flora. Equally important in the east are the Virunga Mountains north of Lake Kivu, where there are a number of active volcanoes.

The DRC's location on the equator influences the pattern of the rainy seasons. When it is raining in the south it is the dry season in the north, and vice versa. The connections between its rivers ensure that on both sides of the equator they are supplied with water throughout the year. In general there is no part of the DRC that suffers from lack of rain, but rainfall is highest in the central part of the *Cuvette*. The country has vast areas of arable land, especially in its eastern parts. Since independence, successive governments have relied on the exploitation of the DRC's minerals, especially diamonds, as the main source of foreign exchange to fund the functioning of the state. This has meant the DRC is a net exporter of raw materials and a net importer of most of its manufactured goods, including food stuffs.

Historical background

The Western world began to be interested in the Congo only in the nineteenth century. Not much is known of 'the human origin of present day DRC'.[2] The climate has destroyed all archaeological evidence. But what is certain is that there were groups of people living on delimited territories. The state as a form of organisation involving a group of people settled within a defined territory is not new to Africa. Although pre colonial states had no written norms, they had regulations and checks and balances to prevent the abuse of power and the violent redistribution of goods. Quoting extensively from the work of the French scholar, Fustel de Copulanges, who studied the 'Ancient City', Cheikh Anta Diop in his book *Pre colonial Black Africa* was able to demonstrate that the concepts of a state as a 'territory' comprising several cities, or that of an 'empire' and its organisation came from the African–Egyptian political experience. He described institutions that had developed in Africa before they were replicated in Europe. The most important lesson to be learned from African political experience, which the evolutionary and structural approaches did not capture, was the diversity of forms of social and political organisation and political systems to be found at each stage of the development of the state.[3]

This chapter does not intend to make an extended analysis of the concept of the state. The debate has been at the centre of theoretical and policy debate about the African political economy since the 1970s. What is important here is to recognise that before the imposition of a Western political system in what is now known as the DRC, there were groups organised as states, though lacking the fixed boundaries of modern states. A number of different ethnic groups lived within the area which today comprises the DRC[4] and had lived in small kingdoms and republics for centuries.[5] For example, by 1300 groups around Stanley Pool had already begun to form small states that were governed by chiefs.[6] The most successful was the kingdom of Kongo. Through conquest, this kingdom expanded and was divided into provinces; government income was collected in the form of taxes and labour; the king was elected from among male descendants of the conqueror of the area; and judges, who specialised in different matters, presided over courts. Other kingdoms included the Luba, Lunda, the Teke, the Kuba and the Chokwe. The Luba state used a centralised system, especially in matters concerning the military and trade. Subordinate chiefs paid tribute to the central government. The histories of most of these kingdoms show major advances from acephalous societies and chieftainships to early state formations, and from these to fully fledged states.

Like the early Christian missionaries, who misunderstood or misinterpreted African traditional religions, the colonial administrators were unable to comprehend the meaning behind African traditional political systems. Roland Oliver argues that in order to 'invent' new forms of administration (which were inconsistent with African political systems), the colonial powers in many cases crammed different kinds of African communities into an entity which they then called a 'tribe' for purposes of administration. In other cases they broke up and segmented already existing larger polities into units which they regarded as coherent tribes. When the Congress of Berlin, in 1878, conferred the entire Congolese territory on King Leopold II and recognised him as sovereign of the new state, in keeping with the requirements of the Berlin Treaty, Leopold created the Congo Free State (CFS) administration, ostensibly to facilitate international trade. 'Leopold accumulated a vast personal fortune from ivory, rubber and precious commodities'[7] by using Congolese slave labour. It is estimated that ten million people died from forced labour, starvation, and outright extermination during his rule. The Congo was the only European colony to run at a profit almost from its inception. In fifteen years, the king, who publicly claimed a cumulative loss of $5 million on his Congo enterprises, actually earned $25 million in profits.[8] Leopold, like Mobutu decades later, invested revenue from the Congo outside the country, and gave huge concessions with unlimited rights to allies and friends' companies. No wonder economic historians called Leopold's Congo economic system a '*raubwirtschaft*' or a robbery economy.[9] In an effort to extract the maximum profit, the king degraded Congolese political systems or destroyed them when they posed a real threat to his interests.

When the Belgian government took over the administration of the Congo in 1908, the transfer of power, long planned by the king, was intended to maintain Belgian control of the colony. The colonial state that replaced it was rigidly controlled by a small managerial group in Brussels representing an alliance between the government, the Catholic Church and the giant mining and business corporations whose activities were virtually exempt from outside scrutiny.[10] Belgium continued to exploit the colony through a system based on a condescending paternalism. Claiming that each ethnic group had its own distinctive custom, Belgium created a different set of customary laws, one for each ethnic group, and established a separate Native Authority to enforce each set of laws.[11] This seriously weakened the cohesion of Congolese communities. There was no rule of law, only of expediency during the time of Belgian colonisation. While Leopold had set a precedent for conflict promoting activities through large scale looting, the Belgian state administration practised exploitation in more regulated forms. It systematised the use of forced labour and cash cropping, and used coercive taxation to transform the Congolese peasantry into a wage labour force working for Belgian owned mining and agricultural firms. It was for this reason that the Belgium Congo was seen as a 'model Colony.' Under colonialism, democratic principles were not given a second thought and whatever justice may have occasionally been served was arbitrarily dispensed on an ethnic basis.

A chaotic independence

In January 1960, the Belgians abruptly announced that they were granting the Congo independence within six months. The modern Congolese state came into being on 30 June 1960. Despite its development as an economy geared to serve Belgian colonists in the Congo, the former administration had given no thought to the requirements of an independent Congolese state. The instability that plagued the new state from the eve of independence was a direct consequence of colonial policies and a lack of preparedness for independence. Like other post colonial countries, the Congo was expected to build modern state institutions from scratch, but that did not happen. From the beginning, foreign governments dispensed bribes to key political figures in the newly formed state which in many instances contributed to its fragmentation into secession movements around key economic regions (Katanga, Kasai and the Kivu provinces). Zartman makes the interesting observation that 'the genesis of the independent state in Congo was a result of state collapse'.[12] The Congo, in comparison with the other countries in this volume, is unique in that its transition to independence occurred because the colonial state had failed. (It is worth mentioning here that as soon as the nationalist movements started to challenge the Belgian interests in the Congo, the United States began to show interest in the country.)

For the first five years of its independence, the Congo remained a country without a single, effective political authority to govern it, a situation exacerbated by the lack of trained personnel to run the country. At independence there were less than a dozen Congolese university graduates. Under Belgian rule, some 10,000 Belgians handled all the important administrative and public responsibilities.

Even with this number, the colonial administration had difficulty in administrating and maintaining order because of the vastness of the country. In addition the newly independent state was under threat from tribal and ethnic conflict, and was built on laws which were not adapted to Congolese realities.

The Belgians were very much aware of the fact that, with no qualified personnel, the new government would collapse. They were expecting to continue running the country in the name of the new rulers. It is not surprising that a Belgian commander should have declared that 'After independence equals before independence.' This is why the outspoken first prime minister to be democratically elected was assassinated, in January 1961, six months after independence had been achieved. Lumumba, unlike the colonial power, 'sought to elevate national interests over the divisive interests of ethnicity, religion or class'.[13]

After five years of political instability, Colonel Joseph Desiré Mobutu took power in a coup on the 24 November 1965, with the help of the US. America, deeply involved in an ideological confrontation with the Soviet Union, was not prepared to see the Congo disintegrate. Despite a strong call from politicians for a federal state, Mobutu, like the Belgians before him, maintained a strong centralised state and an oppressive administration. The West supported Mobutu in keeping together a weak state because it served their economic and ideological interests. America was convinced that the Congo's geographic position, size and resources could be used to stem the advance of the Soviet Union in central and southern Africa. One factor that has had a long term effect on state capacity in Africa, especially in the Congo, has been the vulnerability of the polity to outside influence and interventions. The consolidation of Mobutu's regime by the US was not done to benefit the Congolese people, but to empower Mobutu as a '*bouclier*' against communist penetration. Shortly after coming to power, as part of an 'Africanisation' programme, Mobutu changed the name of the country to Zaïre.

The Mobutu regime was a kleptocracy, bent on promoting the interests of a narrow group, to the detriment of the general welfare. Mobutu had all the characteristics of what Fanon called 'the chairman of the board of a society of impatient profiteers'. Almost forty per cent of Congo/Zaïre national revenues accrued to Mobutu and his cronies, while the average Zaïrian made $190 a year. During the Cold War, especially in the mid 1970s, as Africa became more important as an arena of international rivalry, the US sustained Mobutu's regime for its own purposes. However, instead of being strengthened, Zaïre continued to weaken. The erosion of the Zaïrian state, as Richard Joseph argues, 'resulted from the combined effects of external manipulation over an extended period and internal misrule and mismanagement'.[14]

Recent history

The end of the Mobutu regime

The recent history of the DRC starts at the beginning of the 1990s. This was a period when undemocratic states on the continent were under pressure from 'above' – the international community (World Bank, IMF and bilateral donors) and 'below' (their own citizens) to democratise.[15] This pressure followed the fall of the Berlin Wall and the subsequent political liberalisation in Eastern Europe after the end of the Cold War. With communism defeated, the strategy of the US changed. An earlier generation of African dictators was abandoned in favour of a new generation of leaders who accepted the new creed of globalisation. Mobutu, who had been applauded for nationalising mining companies when he took power in 1965, was asked to embrace economic liberalisation and privatisation. He failed to read the signs of the times and was so reluctant to democratise and privatise companies that his allies started to consider bringing about a change of regime.

By 1993, the Congolese state was being forcibly prepared for privatisation. By this time Congolese day to day life was characterised by harsh security, and equally harsh political and economic conditions throughout the country. The extent of state failure was so pronounced that people ceased to think in terms of what the state could provide. Zaïre had accumulated an external state debt amounting to $8 billion. As Mobutu's fortunes declined, the Zaïrean state began to default on the payment and servicing of debt. As a result, the IMF and the World Bank refused to advance any further loans until Mobutu agreed to the privatisation of state owned mineral conglomerates. This time a big plan to dismantle the country was envisioned by Western corporations, as Mobutu could not hold the country together or protect Western interests. The new conglomerates, which wanted to redraw the African map in their own favour, independent of the Berlin arrangement, were no longer interested in large post colonial states. It seems that they preferred 'down sized', small non state entities that could be run by private mineral groups. The idea was inherent in the whole economic globalisation project. By the time of the collapse of the Mobutu regime, Zaïre's institutional apparatus had been reduced to virtual irrelevance. Municipalities had long ceased to exist; public transport had collapsed, water and energy distribution was inadequate and there was a serious shortage of houses. By 1994 life expectancy in the country had fallen to fifty three years. People responded to the challenge of daily survival by developing their own solutions. In 1996, when Mobutu realised his American friends who had for so long pushed him to work against his own people, were working against him, he, for the first time, understood their real interests. He said: 'I am not a colony of westerners. It is because of copper, cobalt, gold and diamonds that they are in the process of arming Kabila'.[16]

As Mobutu's legitimacy dwindled, he ruled increasingly through coercion, mainly via the army, until his overthrow in 1997 by forces commanded by Laurent Kabila and backed by Rwanda and Uganda. The end of Mobutu's rule found the Congolese once again unprepared to cope with the reconstruction of the state.

Laurent Desiré Kabila: unavoidable downfall[17]

The 'intervention'[18] of Rwanda and Uganda that installed Laurent Kabila as president followed a chaotic period of conflict that was compounded by continual interference by various Western groupings in the internal affairs of states on the continent. From 1992, international organisations effectively made military intervention an instrument of foreign policy. It was in this context that Rwanda and Uganda decided in 1996 to engage in military operations in the eastern province of Zaïre in pursuit of those who had taken part in the genocide in Rwanda and who had fled into Zaïre. It seems they were assured of the tacit or even perhaps active support of some Western governments.

But Kabila was an insecure man with the country totally in the hands of foreign armies. His downfall was the result of his inexperience in governing, coupled with his self destructive tendencies. He made the same mistake as Lumumba, of trying to take on the West soon after independence.[19] Instead of strengthening the foundation of his power and rebuilding the state, he weakened it. He could not adjust to the new international landscape at the end of the Cold War, the balkanisation of the Soviet Union and the modernisation of China's Cultural Revolution in the new world environment. Like Lumumba before him, Kabila's demagoguery and intransigence succeeded in alienating Western countries, especially the US. The seizure of power is one thing but its effective use is another. Domestically, instead of building an inclusive government with the democratic forces he found, he crushed them. In an effort to place people he could trust around him he disregarded merit, experience and expertise. He controlled all revenue, from customs to mining. Nothing was allowed to happen without his permission. Like Mobutu, he created an administration whose agents were either loyal to him or totally dependent upon him, and were totally dedicated to self enrichment.[20]

Kabila's nationalism also caused him to reject attempts by Rwanda and Uganda to maintain a permanent presence in the newly named DRC. His attempt to expel these former allies backfired. He did not have the capacity to assure even a minimum degree of physical security for the country. What followed was unsurprising. The Rwandan and Ugandan forces refused to withdraw, and launched an attack to overthrow his regime. The 1998 war was not initially a rebellion, but a foreign invasion that transformed itself over time into an insurrection.[21] UN resolution 1341, drafted by the French, 'condemned the Rwandan and Ugandan invasion of the Congo as akin to the 1991 Iraqi invasion of Kuwait, and in spite of his foibles, it recognised Laurent Kabila as the legitimate national leader of his country'.[22]

Although the war of August 1998 failed to unseat Kabila, the Lusaka accords were engineered to include the rebels as undisputed and equal partners in the negotiations, at the end of which Kabila was to be replaced as head of state. The format for the talks outlined in the Lusaka ceasefire agreement was expressly designed to unseat his regime. Despite having signed the accord, Kabila blocked every move to see it implemented. Finally, he was assassinated at his residence in January 2001 in circumstances which are still obscure. He left the country under foreign occupation. His refusal to recognise the country's debt obligations, his rejection of requests by the IMF and World Bank to implement their adjustment programmes and his refusal to give mining contracts to US companies were not acceptable to Western political and economic interests.

Joseph Kabila: redeeming Congolese leadership credibility?

Laurent Kabila was replaced by his son Joseph Kabila as head of state. The circumstances surrounding Joseph's appointment are still obscure and confusing. It seems external influence from Zimbabwe and Angola, played a role in his becoming president. But it is now established that Congolese leadership also played a prominent role in choosing Joseph Kabila. Since his father's friends and protégés could not agree amongst themselves, they chose Joseph as a compromise and hoped to rule the country through him. But Joseph has distanced himself from his father's friends and started to build his own political entourage. During the war he demonstrated strong leadership ability and his diplomatic successes early in his presidency created hopes that he was a real peacemaker. Under his presidency the Congolese signed the All inclusive Peace Accord which was successfully concluded in South Africa in April 2003, with the adoption of the transitional constitution and a military structure. The major success for Joseph Kabila was to have successfully persuaded Uganda and Rwanda into signing peace agreements that would ultimately force them to withdraw their troops from the DRC. He also successfully negotiated a rejection of their efforts to ensure that they, and not the Congolese, remained in control of the DRC through Congolese surrogates. The transitional government at present is headed by President Kabila, who is supported by four vice presidents, Jean Pierre Bemba of the Movement for the Liberation of the Congo (MLC), Azarias Ruberwa of the Rally for Democracy (RCD), Yerodia Ndombasi of the People's Party for Reconstruction and Democracy (PPRD) and Zahidi: Ngoma representing the Non armed Opposition. The '1+4' structure, although imperfect in many ways, has introduced the positive values of power sharing, inclusiveness and representivity into Congolese politics for the first time.

Splitters and controllers

Ethnicity

The question here is: does ethnicity in the DRC pose a threat to the reconstruction of the state? In the DRC, ethnic identity politics have been a part of intra state and inter state conflicts since independence. President Mobutu was a master at opposing one leader, tribe or ethnic group against another in order to get what he wanted.[23] This game contributed to serious ethnic tensions and conflict in the country between the Katangese and the Kasaians on the one side and the indigenous Congolese of the east and Congolese of Rwandan origin, commonly called the Banyamalunge. Despite the ethnic tensions that have emerged, it is the inter state ethnic conflict fostered by political elites, and not hatred between people, that poses a problem for state survival.

The ethnic divisions in the states of the eastern part of the country pose the greatest threat to state recovery. The Kivu province was the powder keg where ethnic massacres first exploded in 1990s. It was also the place where the regional wars of 1996, which drove Mobutu from power, and of 1998, which attempted to overthrow Laurent Kabila, began. Two inter related factors contribute to ethnic conflict in this part of the country. The first is the aftermath of the invasion of the DRC by Rwanda and Uganda. Second is the problem of citizenship for the Banyamulenge who are Congolese of Rwandan origin. There exists a link between these two factors, because one motivation for Rwanda to invade the DRC, beside economic interests and the search for *Interhamwe* (rebel Hutu militia from Rwanda), was also the wish to protect the Banyamulenge and to ensure their political survival inside the Congo. Colonial legislation was not clear on the issue of the status of this people and at independence, the legal arrangements dealt only with election related problems. The Belgian administration failed to address the citizenship question in what had become an extremely diverse population. (Citizenship remains one of the causes of the current conflict in the DRC.) Unless the Banyamulenge are recognised as citizens, the prospects for peace will remain doubtful,[24] especially in the east of the country. Although the decision on the future of this group falls within the competence of the DRC, it will have a profound effect on Rwanda and its relations with the DRC.

Leadership

Congo has a problem in terms of the quality of its leadership, both in civil society and in its political parties. These are all ethnically based, too often show a narrow self interest, and are preoccupied with short term concerns that obscure any regard for democracy, the public good or national interests. Congolese politicians seek power through whatever means they deem expedient. In general, personalities tend to dominate parties, which makes co operation among them difficult. The danger is that in the effort to secure their own political survival, would be leaders who have no political base might prefer to sacrifice the interests of the Congolese people by retreating from democracy and trying to restore the previous status quo.

Congo does not have well organised and structured membership organisations such as labour movements, professional associations and student movements which are necessary for democracy to flourish. The church remains an important role player and its leadership is needed, but it suffered as a result of Mobutu's manipulations. By the 1980s, the church had become reluctant to criticise the government and some felt that it had been infected by the system of corruption, accepting that it must pay bribes to conduct its business.[25] While the church has not yet fully recovered from this, it has a central role to play in mobilising citizens in the transitional period.

Resources

The DRC not only possesses vast water resources but is extremely rich in mineral resources. This makes it not only the envy of neighbouring states but also a country of strategic importance to powers such as the US, equivalent to that of the Persian

Gulf region. The DRC is capable of producing eighty per cent of the world's industrial diamonds, possesses eighty per cent of the world's known reserves of coltan in its eastern provinces; and is also a source of cassiterite, tin, copper, cobalt and gold.'[26]

The DRC is a leader in the potential use of hydro electric power with reserves of billions of kilowatt hours. The Congo river, second largest in the world in terms of volume of flow (30 000 to 60 000 cubic metres per second) by itself has a potential generating capacity of more than 600 billion kilowatt hours annually which represents two thirds of entire global production.[27] With this massive potential, 'the Congo River Basin is destined to become the leading industrial region of Africa, the principal centre of Africa's heavy industry.'[28]

Internally the extraction and distribution of resources has been a source of tension. In the DRC, copper and diamonds mined in the Katanga and Kasai provinces have contributed largely to government revenues. As in the colonial period, the Copperbelt in Katanga continued to be the jewel in Mobutu's state's crown. Revenue from Gecamines furnished the government with a large part of the finance required for the administration of the country. However, the distribution of the earnings from diamonds and copper has been a source of tension between the central government and the people of both Kasai and Katanga since independence. It was in these two provinces that Mobutu had least support. Resource extraction revenue affected the relationship between state and society in the DRC. The disproportional redistribution of earnings, with the lion's share going to the capital, where it was quickly distributed among Mobutu's clique, created serious discontent in those who lived in the mineral rich areas but did not benefit.

The war economy that has prevailed in the DRC over the last five years points to the weakness of the Congolese state. It has reached a point where it cannot protect itself or determine its own future. There is no doubt that conflicts are more likely to break out where governments are dysfunctional.[29] While Rwanda, Uganda, Burundi and Angola might have had genuine security concerns and Zimbabwe and Namibia initially had a straightforward desire to help protect the sovereignty of the DRC, the motives for sending forces to the DRC changed over time until the exploitation of the DRC's resources became the pre eminent intention. Each force was seeking, as René Lemarchand correctly puts it, 'to draw maximum advantage from the near collapse of the Congo state, and this with the direct or tacit complicity of local actors'.[30] Apart from the military, there have been numerous groups, private companies and individuals, who have been involved in the exploitation of the DRC's natural wealth. It is this easy usurpation of state functions and unchecked exploitation of its raw materials that demonstrates the level of state collapse in the

DRC. Hottelet describes the DRC as 'a carcass being chewed at by its elite and its neighbours'.[31]

From the time of Leopold II to the present, the problem of the Congo has remained the same. It has not been divided by ethnicity or disputes over boundaries but by the imbalance in the redistribution of the country's resources between the national interest and those of external parties, in favour of the latter. Illegal exploitation remains one of the main sources of funding for groups involved in perpetuating the conflict. There is no doubt that flows of arms, mining income and the continuation of the conflict are inextricably linked. This cycle remains the biggest threat to state building in the DRC.

When a state collapses, the structures of authority, law and order within it disintegrate. Security is no longer guaranteed, there is no rule of law, and public services decline or cease to exist. As Tshikala Biaya suggests, in 'weak states where sovereignty and territoriality are difficult to uphold, the pressure increases from internal and external actors who take the opportunity to advance their particular positions'.[32] The lack of a strong national army, the permeability of its borders, the ineffectiveness of the administration and the chaotic organisation of public affairs by successive governments and regimes have emphasised the weakness of the Congolese state in the face of internal and external pressures and ambitions. It was the fragility of the Mobutu state that persuaded Rwanda and Uganda, joined by Angola and Zimbabwe, to challenge the regime in Kinshasa and install Laurent Kabila as the new president in May 1997. But these interventions gave external forces power to dictate the operation of government activities and the exploitation of the country's natural wealth. Evidence exists that all of the foreign forces deployed in the DRC plundered the country's assets.[33] The UN report on the subject noted that the conflict in the DRC had become mainly about access to, control of, and trading in, five key mineral resources: coltan, diamonds, copper, cobalt and gold. The wealth of the country, as Greg Mills puts it, is appealing and hard to resist in the context of the lawlessness and weakness of the central authority.[34]

Regional connection

The DRC shares borders with nine countries. Its neighbours are Congo Brazzaville in the west and north west, the Central African Republic in the north, Sudan and Uganda in the north east, Rwanda, Burundi and Tanzania in the east and Zambia and Angola in the south. These countries can be divided into three geographical zones:

the Great Lakes states (Burundi, Rwanda, Tanzania and Zambia); the states of the Congo River Basin (Angola, Congo Brazzaville and Central African Republic); and finally Sudan and Uganda. All significant political events in any of these countries have a direct impact on the stability of the DRC; conversely, any unrest or conflict in the DRC is immediately felt in these neighbouring states. Our focus here will be limited to countries which have had a direct impact on the politics of the DRC in the last two decades: Rwanda, Burundi, Angola and Uganda.

The decision by countries in the region to form a coalition that was ultimately to oust Mobutu in 1996 was influenced by his foreign policy. Since 1970 Mobutu had wanted to establish Zaïre (on account of its size, mineral wealth and strategic location) as the leading African country and himself as a major African statesman. In Rwanda and Burundi, Mobutu was considered a father figure. But the situation changed with the 1994 genocide in Rwanda. When the Tutsi minority party, the Rwandan Patriotic Front (RPF) launched an insurgency in 1990, in a bid to regain power in Rwanda, French forces and Mobutu's Zaïrean Armed Forces (FAZ) helped the Hutu dominated government of President Habyarimana to stop the advance of the RPF. When, in 1994, the RPF took over Kigali, relations between Kinshasa and Kigali were strained over the issue of the DRC having armed the Rwandan government forces.

Directly or indirectly, President Mobutu also supported militarism in Burundi. The armed opposition to President Buyoya's military regime, particularly the FDD/ CDD *(Forces de défence de la démocratie/Conseil national pour la défense de la démocratie)*, had their headquarters in Zaïre. This does not mean that Mobutu actively opposed the regime of President Buyoya. Due to developments linked to the effects of the 1994 genocide in Rwanda, the *coups d'état* in Burundi and the increased ethnic conflict fomented by Mobutu's geopolitics, the Burundi regime found itself on the side of the Banyamulenge insurrection against Mobutu in 1996.

The relationship between Mobutu and Ugandan President Yoweri Museveni was very cold as a result of the competition for leadership in the region. However, the Ugandan intervention in the DRC to oust Mobutu had more to do with its support for the Tutsi led operation initiated by Paul Kagame and less to do with Uganda's own security concerns. Most of the Ugandan rebels operated inside Ugandan territory and from Southern Sudan. Museveni's support for Kagame was initially limited to destroying refugee camps used by the *interhamwe* and the ex FAR to destabilise Rwanda. The decision then to support Kagame and the advance of his forces up to Kinshasa was informed by Museveni's own experience in Uganda.

The Ugandan approach was very much influenced by the experience of direct

Tanzanian involvement in the war that removed Idi Amin in 1979. The situations were comparable. President Mobutu had acquiesced in the transformation of border camps for Rwandan refugees into armed training centres for the proponents of 'Hutu Power', while Idi Amin had invaded the Karega region of Tanzania. When Tanzanian forces pushed him out, the question of what should follow arose. Should the next step be for them to push onward to Kampala, thus overthrowing the dictatorship? Or should they leave matters to Ugandan groups opposed to Amin, giving them as much material and political assistance as the situation called for? However, this latter alternative involved a risk: if you hit a dictator but allow him to recover, would you not be inviting a second and more lethal strike from him?

In Angola, Mobutu played the roles of both the instigator of conflict that paralysed that country for more than twenty five years and the mediator between the opposing parties. He was used by the US as a conduit for arms to Jonas Savimbi and his liberation movement UNITA. In 1992 he presided over an African diplomatic effort to broker a ceasefire between UNITA and the MPLA.[35] Observers, however, dismissed his efforts as insincere. Mobutu was pursuing his own objective of making himself important in the eyes of the Americans, whose attitude towards him was changing with the end of the Cold War. There is no doubt that Mobutu used himself and the Congolese territory as pivotal factors for US control of Angola.

International connection

The DRC's relationship with the West is simplified here to a discussion of three key countries – Belgium, the US and France. With Belgium the relationship has always been that between colonisers and the colonised. Very close ties have always existed between the two countries, and the DRC is heavily dependent on Belgian foreign aid. In spite of the apparent closeness between the two countries, there have been periodic outbursts of friction. At the end of Mobutu's reign relations were at their lowest level. The elder Kabila did not do much to restore relations between the two countries, but under Joseph Kabila the relationship is better than it has been for more than twenty years.

The US DRC relationship followed from what the US perceived was the pivotal location of Zaïre in central Africa. As mentioned earlier, America's interest in the DRC coincided with the lessening of Belgian influence in the late 1950s. A special relationship was forged during the Cold War. Both the US and the Soviet Union sought to cultivate sympathetic politicians among the Congolese because each hoped to bring this huge, resource rich country into its sphere of influence. During the crisis experienced in the DRC in the early 1960s, presidents Eisenhower, Kennedy and Johnson sought to maintain the territorial integrity and pro Western orientation of the former Belgian colony. After his takeover in 1965, Mobutu's consistently pro Western stand served to underscore Zaïre's strategic importance, particularly as the US believed there was renewed Soviet interest in Africa in the 1960s and 1970s. It was hoped that under Mobutu's leadership, the DRC might be the focal point for US foreign policy objectives in sub Saharan Africa, in much the same way as Brazil was in Latin America. The consensus in the American foreign policy establishment was that the alternative to Mobutu was chaos. The foreign policy of the US focused on assuring total security, not of the Congo but of the person of Mobutu through military, political and economic support.[36] It was President Mobutu's ability to procure aid from the international community that was critical to the maintenance of this increasingly dysfunctional political entity.[37]

With the end of the Cold War, the US abandoned Mobutu. In the face of growing rebellion the US appreciated that Mobutu's undemocratic regime was adding to the instability of the region. The ambivalence and lack of policy on the issue of Mobutu's removal became a policy in itself when the US chose to remain quiet in the face of the invasion of the country by Rwanda and Uganda.

The DRC's relationship with France has developed more recently. France was the only Western power that continued to support Mobutu in the face of a fast advancing rebellion. To the French, Mobutu still appeared the essential force required to solve the regional conflicts. In other words, the cause of the problem was perceived as the solution to the problem. But France's relationship with the DRC is also cultural. The DRC is the most highly populated francophone country after France, which means that France would not like to see the DRC fall within Anglophone influence. However, over time, cultural imperatives were transformed into French political and economic interests in the country.

In recent times Belgian and French efforts have been influential in generating international assistance for Joseph Kabila's government. To an extent, they have supported the Inter Congolese Dialogue, which altered the balance of power in the negotiations in favour of Joseph Kabila. The European Union (EU) Commission formally resumed direct co operation with the DRC on 5 February 2002 after ten years of suspension.[38]

Western diplomacy in Central Africa and the DRC in particular has been to a large degree a dynamic process, which has been changing since the end of the Cold War. But one element has remained the same. For the West, any government in the

DRC must maintain the kind of friendly and constructive relations with Western powers that serves their interests, which may not necessarily be identical with those of the Congolese people. Lumumba and Laurent Kabila, who attempted to oppose Western interests, were killed.

Alternative future

The DRC is a dysfunctional state *par excellence.* It is really a stereotype of an African state, rich in natural resources but poor in governance. There is no doubt that rebuilding a functioning state on the ashes of King Leopold II's Congo, Mobutu's Zaïre, and the destruction caused by the Congo war will be a Herculean task. But it is not an impossible one. History offers worse cases of unstable states affected by epidemic civil wars and social disorder in Europe which were successfully rebuilt. There is no good reason why the Congolese cannot do the same.

However, there is no guarantee that a society undergoing transition from war will become a fully fledged democracy. A starting point for rebuilding the state has already been achieved in the successful conclusion of the Lusaka Accords. The formation of a transitional government that is to some extent acceptable in the eyes of the majority of citizens is the first prerequisite. But it would be naïve to assume that the simple fact that the Congo has a negotiated transitional government in place means that the problems of the DRC have been solved, because the point at issue has never been exclusively that of peace.

The challenge for the new Congolese leadership is how to turn this opportunity into a success story. The DRC of Mobutu was, although badly governed, relatively peaceful. The root of the DRC problems has always been the absence of an effective state that is capable of meeting the minimum social needs of its people. The level of disintegration of political power; the extent of the country's exposure to external interference, linked to the wish to exploit the country's resources; and a total absence of principled leadership are factors which made governance difficult in the past and continue to pose the greatest threat to the reconstruction of the state.

There are those who maintain that the DRC is too large a country to govern, and that in the absence of a central power capable of managing it, it is not in the interests of stability to try and keep it together. It is argued that although the Congolese have demonstrated a strong commitment to maintaining the political cohesion of the country, a long term political vacuum caused by the failure of the central government to control the entire territory would perpetuate the cycle of violence and conflict. There is no doubt that the legacy of economic predation, use of resources to fund military interests and illegal trade in the country's natural assets in which many of those who are in government today were or are still involved, will continue to hinder any attempts to establish a functional state which controls the entire territory. At present there are certain parts of the country that the central government cannot control because it has insufficient resources (both administrative and military) to do so. This school of thought argues that it will require enormous injections of financial aid to establish an efficient administration in the DRC and give it the organisational capacity to manage the entire territory. While it is much easier to conceive strategies, including foreign funding, to rebuild smaller states such as Sierra Leone and Liberia, Western countries are simply not prepared to fund the reconstruction of bigger states such as the DRC. Assumptions that what the Congolese need is to end the war, commit themselves to a democratic process and that the West will fund the country's reconstruction are not in touch with the new thinking in the Western world. This is that even though the current situation in the DRC is related to the legacy of colonialism and the support Mobutu received from the West and former colonial powers, the problems of the DRC are Africa's alone, to be solved by Africans themselves. If Congolese cannot find the necessary resources, then they might as well consider breaking the country up into more manageable territories.

This argument has serious flaws. Firstly, there is a correlation between the size of the country, the illegal exploitation of resources and the dysfunctionality of the state. Whenever states vacate social space, alternative actors can gain legitimacy by occupying it and performing the abandoned core functions of the state. In most cases these spaces are maintained by organised violence funded by the exploitation of the country's assets. Although it is true that post colonial Congo has proved impossible to manage so far, it does not necessarily mean that the Congolese are incapable of running an effective state. After the five years of instability that followed independence, the DRC achieved stable government under Mobutu, whose government was represented and recognised across the entire territory. During this period, it seems, the DRC was faced with a problem of governance that was related not to the country's size but to inadequate capacity, which made it impossible for the central government to expand the provision of social services beyond the capital and certain major cities. This is a common problem for most states, big and small, on the continent. In contrast, King Leopold II and the Belgian government maintained control of the entire territory during the colonial period. They were able to maintain security and construct a network of well built, albeit untarred roads connecting all parts of the vast country, 'which could be reached without trouble by motor car'.[39] The only time the size of the country itself is likely to pose a threat to the stability of the state is if the new dispensation is not built on sound democratic principles acceptable to all.

It is still not clear, although the belligerents, the non armed opposition and civil society are all part of the government of transition, that they will be able to create a climate within which their efforts towards democracy can be sustained. This convergence on the basic elements and needs of democratic government for the DRC might be challenged by militants, radicals or reactionaries in defence of their own interests.

What would help to build a functional state in the DRC is an approach to politics that transcends the limits of the style of governance that has so far been largely informal, personal and highly centralised. Careful decisions need to be made on constitutional and institutional arrangements to ensure that there is meaningful political representation, a consolidation of peace, and a general belief in the legitimacy of the political process. Constructive lessons are already emerging from the African continent. It is increasingly clear that the most desirable constitutional and institutional arrangements need to include: a power sharing formula, the decentralisation of state structures, a parliamentary system and an electoral system that ensures representation, inclusiveness, and reconciliation.

This can only happen through a strong and visionary leadership, which is able to rise above regional and ethnic allegiances. The DRC is in need of a leadership that is capable of reclaiming the ownership of the state and freeing it from external influences and manipulation. Rebuilding the state can begin only when an organised and determined group of indigenous political actors creates a form of government that does not replicate the failings of the old one. Political culture is one of the most powerful influences that shape a country's political system because it creates norms and beliefs about how people should behave which influence social behaviour. The Congolese since 1885 have been at the mercy of a succession of cruel and authoritarian regimes. It is now required that the Congolese should adapt to the demands of democracy, and they will have to do it fast if the country is to become a functional state.

Secondly, countries like the DRC and Angola could finance their own reconstruction, making them free of external aid. The problem of the DRC is not a lack of resources but their utilisation and management. Mobutu's kleptocratic regime was the source of most of the country's socio economic problems. Even with external aid that Mobutu received from the West, he did not manage to construct an efficient state. Rather, aid served only to undermine the Congolese nation state further. The rebuilding of the state in Congo will have to start by reinstituting the capacity of the state to collect tax, a problem in many African states. Debt to international institutions has become the only source of capital for state functions, plunging the state into perpetual dependency without assisting development. But this is not a rejection of the necessity for external funding and support (which in any case would not come as a donation). While the state rebuilds its capacity to collect tax, there will definitely be a need for external investment to help restart production in the industrial and manufacturing sectors, to get the parastatals back on the rails, and to restore the infrastructure.

The extension of state capacity over the entire territory will not happen automatically, even with a Marshall plan. Just as the decay of the Congolese state did not happen overnight, reconstruction will also happen in stages. Perhaps the most important lesson learned in other transitional situations, such as in South Africa and Mozambique, is that the well being of the economy is pivotal for the success of whatever follows a negotiated transition. Even more important is the recognition that the economy is not something that can be put on ice until the transition is over; its soundness is dependent on how the transition occurs. It is perhaps here that intervention from the international community is mostly needed.

Thirdly, any attempt to divide the DRC into manageable states would not solve the problem of the weakness of the state. There are small territories on the continent which are failed states or are too weak to perform their duties. There is equally no guarantee that the new states would not inherit the endemic weaknesses of the original state. Further, how could the whole be divided without creating imbalances between the subdivisions that might become a source of fresh conflict? Any attempt to divide the DRC would have serious repercussions, and might even destabilise the region further.

Other ways exist of resolving problems related to the country's size and the exposure of its resources to illegal exploitation, which perpetuate conflict, undermine state capacity and disrupt attempts to reconstruct it. Firstly, there is an urgent need to create a relatively strong and professional army capable of exercising power over the entire territory. A well co ordinated integration of the different armies which are now controlling different parts of the country could achieve this. The war of 1997 exposed the military weakness of the Congolese state. Mobutu's army, which had never been seriously tested on the battlefield, failed to defend the integrity of the Congo due to its lack of professionalism, preparedness and training. The 1998 war succeeded in creating distinct pieces of territory under the control of rebel groups and of their foreign allies, Rwanda and Uganda. The state then lost its monopoly of power over its territory.

Secondly, there is a need for an administration that is capable of monitoring and ensuring state presence in all parts of the territory. This means a more decentralised administration. But, while it makes sense to devolve political power to the provinces, this should not undermine the unity of the state by allowing the emergence of centrifugal forces. As the case of Nigeria clearly demonstrates, regional and ethnic leaders can use their authority to advance their personal political and, by implication, economic interests. Yet in the DRC, a decentralised state within a unitary state might be the way forward. The Congolese have repeatedly expressed their commitment to the entity called the DRC. Introducing a debate on federalism in the DRC should not focus on separation, but about finding ways of strengthening state capacities so that they are represented over the entire territory. Most of the internal problems in the DRC were caused by an excessive centralisation of power in Kinshasa that left the provinces with no decision making powers at all. There is no way that a government sitting in Kinshasa can provide services to the entire population, even within the most democratic environment. Any federal system would have to be structured in a manner that corrects imbalances based on ethnicity and resource allocation.

Thirdly, regional integration should be speeded up. The exploitation of the DRC's resources by foreign forces, multinationals and individuals is carried out in collaboration with Congolese citizens. Neighbouring states are the keys to the success of these operations. The conflict in the DRC has highlighted the need to view the political economy of the conflict in its regional context. The illegal trade in the DRC's resources, using neighbouring states as transit routes, could be resolved through the adoption of a common security mechanism. This would include proposals for economic co operation between the countries of the region and for tighter border controls. A regional organisation could alleviate the political, security and economic fears of the most vulnerable states in the Great Lakes and reduce the opportunistic exploitation of resources, especially those located on the long DRC border.

There is no doubt that relations between the DRC and its neighbours have to an appreciable extent replaced connections with the superpowers as critical determinants of state security. The adoption of the New Partnership for Africa's Development (Nepad)[40] could not have come at a better time for the DRC. Today, the critical prerequisite for both economic development and political stability on the continent is centred on democratic governance. At the continental level, the newly established African Union (AU) has committed member states to democratic governance which will be monitored from time to time through the African Peer Review Mechanism (APRM).[41] The APRM is intended to create an external source of pressure on weak states. Peace and security is one prerequisite for sustainable development in Africa. Neighbouring states will be under serious pressure to stop destabilising the DRC. But the APRM will not work unless it is reinforced by pressure 'from below', reflecting a demand from Congolese citizens for improved governance.[42] A strong, vibrant and organic civil society to oversee that the above concerns are addressed is urgently needed in the DRC.

Endnotes

1   Despite the installation of the new government, the appointment of military commanders for the country's eleven military zones in early 2004 and the nomination and inauguration of the new governors, many former rebel movements continue to maintain their command and control structures.

2   Kaplan Irving (ed.), *Zaïre: A Country Study,* US Government printing, Washington DC, 1979, p. 9.

3   Nabudere DW, 'Traditional and modern political systems in the contemporary governance in Africa'. Paper presented at the Africa Conference: Elections, Democracy and Governance. Pretoria, 7–10 April 2003.

4   Gourou P. 'The Democratic Republic of Congo: Physical and social geography', in *Africa South of the Sahara.* London: Europa Publication, 2000, p. 349.

5   Davidson B, *The Black Man's Burden: Africa and the Curse of the National State,* James Currey London, 1992, p. 255.

6   Kaplan I, *op. cit.*

7   Askin S & C Collins; 'External collusion with kleptocracy: Can Zaïre recapture its stolen wealth?', *Review of African Political Economy,* 57, 1993, pp. 72–85.

8   *Ibid.*

9   Minter WG, *King Solomon's Mines Revisited: Western Interest and the Burdened History of Southern Africa.* New York, Basic Books, 1986, p. 30.

10   Meredith M, *The State of Africa: A History of Fifty Years of Independence,* Jonathan Ball Publishers, Cape Town, 2005, p. 96.

11   Mamdani M, 'Understanding the crisis in the Kivu.' Report of the CODESRIA Mission to the Democratic Republic of Congo, September 1997.

12   Zartman WI, 'Introduction: Posing the problem of state collapse', in *Collapsed*

States: The Disintegration and Restoration of Legitimate Authority. Colorado, Lynne Rienner Publishers, 1995.

13 Nest M, *The Evolution of a Fragmented State: The Case of the Democratic Republic of Congo.* Working Paper 1, New York University: International Centre for Advanced Studies, March 2002, p. 21.

14 Joseph R, 'State, conflict and democracy in Africa'. Paper presented at the conference on African Renewal, MIT, 6–9 March 1997.

15 Although the initiative for democratisation came from the Zaïrian elites, it was the determination of the popular classes that sustained the struggle from the days of Belgian colonialism. See Nzongoloa Ntajala G, 'Zaïre: Moving beyond Mobutu', *Current History*, May 1994, pp. 219–22.

16 *The Sunday Monitor*, Kampala, Uganda, 13 April 1997.

17 Kabemba C, *Mediating Peace Where There is None*, Policy Brief. Johannesburg: Centre for Policy Studies, 1999.

18 In October 1996, the Alliance of Democratic Forces for the Liberation of Congo-Zaïre *(Alliance des forces démocratiques pour la libération* – AFDL), commanded by Tutsis and composed mainly of Tutsi military forces from Paul Kagame's Rwanda Patriotic Army (RPA), along with Tutsi refugees from Zaïre and some Congolese exiles, all under the titular leadership of Congolese exile Laurent Kabila, crossed into Zaïre from Rwanda and Burundi. While marching west across the vast Zaïre, divisions of this army wreaked terrible vengeance on the Rwandan Hutu exiles who had been encamped since 1994 in eastern Zaïre. The intervention of the South African President, Nelson Mandela, to help resolve the conflict peacefully, failed. President Mobutu was overthrown in 1997 and later died in Morocco. The war in DRC grew directly out of the regional politics of the Mobutu era.

19 Kabila was part of the Simba rebellion in the 1960s, in which the Simba professed to be Maoists. Playing on a rural anti colonial sentiment, which equated modernity with Belgian rule and favoured a return to traditional tribal forms of governance, the Simba mixed traditional African animist beliefs with the concept of an agrarian utopia. All these tendencies could be seen in Kabila's approach to governance during the short time he was in power. He was a total contrast to Mobutu. The latter made sure that he had enough leverage within most Western governments that he could set one against the other when necessary. Throughout his career Mobutu was a consummate pragmatist. He used the Congo's immense mineral wealth and strategic position in the heart of Africa, to play his cards.

20 On 20 April 1999, Kabila announced the dissolution of AFDL, which had swept him to power in 1997, accusing some members of opportunism and self enrichment.

21   The intervention of Rwanda and Uganda in the DRC, which brought about the involvement of various SADC countries, was made possible by the weakness of the state in the DRC. To hide their intervention, the two countries created small separate groups of Congolese armed factions posing as rebel movements fighting for democracy and justice.

22   International Crisis Group, *Africa Report No 27*, Nairobi, 2001.

23   Kabemba, C, *The Democratic Republic of Congo: From Independence to Africa's First World War*. Writenet (www.writenet.gn.apc.org) Paper Number 16/2000.

24   Lemarchand R, 'The tunnel at the end of the light', *Review of African Political Economy*, 93/94, 2000, pp. 389-398.

25   Leslie WJ, *Zaïre: Continuity and Political Change in an Oppressive State*. Boulder: Westview Press, 1993, p. 51.

26   The uncontrolled exploitation of minerals has also had a negative effect on the DRC's wildlife and environment. National Parks that house endangered gorillas and other animals are often overrun by factions eager to exploit the minerals and resources to be found there. This is why one newspaper in the DRC called for the presence of a gorilla at the Inter Congolese Dialogue.

27   Cheik Anta Diop, *Black Africa: The economic and cultural basis for a federal state*, Africa World Press, Laurence Hill Books, 1987 p. 38.

28   *Ibid.*

29   Amaoka KY, 'The economic consequences of civil wars and unrest in Africa'. Address to the 70th Ordinary Session of the Council of Ministers of the Organisation of African Unity (OAU), Algeria, 8 July 1999.

30   Lemarchand R, *op. cit.*

31   Hottelet R, 'The plundering of the Congo', *Christian Science Monitor*, 16 May 2001.

32   Väyrynen R, 'Regional conflict formations: An intractable problem of international relations', *Journal of Peace Research*, 21, 4, 1984, pp. 337-59.

33   See the UN's Report of the Panel of Experts on the Illegal Exploitation of Natural Resources and Other Forms of Wealth of the DRC of April 2001.

34   Mills G, *Kabila is Dead - Long Live Kabila*? Prospects for Stability and Recovery in the DRC, Country Report No 7, Johannesburg: South African Institute of International Affairs, 2002.

35   Mobutu became the first African head of state to be received by President Bush Snr. after he had presided over a *tête à tête* encounter between Dos Santos and Savimbi at his Gbadolite (Zaïre) presidential house on 22 June 1989.

36   Both the 1977 (Shaba I) and 1978 (Shaba II) insurgencies by Katangese separatists were repulsed by American, French, Belgian and Moroccan forces. These invasions

threatened the basis of the Zaïrian economy. Equally importantly, they exposed the weakness of Mobutu's army and wasted financial resources donated by the American government - over $850 million in economic and military aid between 1960-1976 was given to Mobutu.

37   Kabemba C, 'Whither the DRC? Causes of the conflict in the Democratic Republic of Congo, and the way forward', *Policy: Issues and Actors,* 12, 1. Johannesburg: Centre for Policy Studies, 1999, p. 9.

38   Co operation with Mobutu's Zaïre was suspended on 22 January 1992. The relationship between the EU and the DRC can better be understood by looking at the relationship between the EU and ACP countries. The DRC, like other ACP countries, was a recipient of EU development aid, and specifically because of its size, received considerable aid packages. The lack of any genuine progress towards democratisation and the abuse of human rights caused the EU to suspended its co operation with the Congo under the Lomé Convention, which has been replaced by the Cotonou Agreement.

39   Nzongola Ntajala G, *op. cit.*

40   Mamdani argued in *Current Affairs* of 11 October 2002 that the architects of both the African Union (AU) and Nepad seem not to have taken into consideration the failing state in Africa ... the heart of Africa's development.

41   Matlosa K, "Democratic consolidation in Africa: Focus on the Southern Africa region". Paper presented at the EISA conference on 'Strengthening Democracy Through Nepad: The Role of African Civil Society', Johannesburg, 25-27 May 2003a.

42   Gebb S, 'Effective state is Nepad goal', Occasional paper in response to Mandani's criticism of Nepad, 2002.

5

From *confusão* to *estamos juntos*?

Bigness, development and state dysfunction in Angola

Greg Mills[1]

> *The sad thing about Angolans is that they are so decisive and stubborn in war time, and yet so indecisive in peace time.*
> Abel Chivukuvuku, UNITA Parliamentarian[2]

Introduction: from *confusão*

On 22 February 2002, Dr Jonas Savimbi, head of the *Uniao Nacional de Libertação de Angola* (UNITA) rebel movement, was shot dead. This event marked a significant change in the course of Angola's more than thirty years of civil war, removing a stumbling block to negotiations and leading to the signing of a peace settlement in April 2002.[3]

The MPLA *(Movimento Popular de Libertação de Angola)* had been able to achieve what apartheid South Africa, the US, Cuba, the Soviet Union, East Germany and others had not: a military victory in Angola that brought the war to an end. Indeed, Angola has long been a military power in southern Africa, its martial abilities backed up by a willingness to utilise force both within and outside its own borders. It possesses the potential to match this capacity in the economic realm. It is the second largest oil producer in sub Saharan Africa.

The current production levels of 1.1 million barrels per day are set to increase to two million barrels by 2008, to the level that Nigeria produces today, though Angola has only one tenth of Nigeria's population. Although government (and other) statistics are notoriously unreliable, oil currently accounts for an estimated fifty per cent of GDP, eighty per cent of government earnings, and ninety per cent of export revenue. Angola is also the fourth largest producer of diamonds world wide,[4] with an estimated annual income of $700 million, a figure which could rise

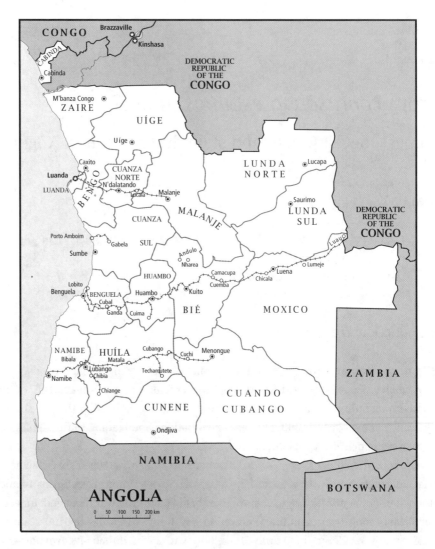

with both stability and the opening up of the industry to additional producers and marketing companies.

A corrosive cocktail of pernicious colonial inheritance, war and bad government has meant, however, that little of this wealth has reached Angola's thirteen million people. According to the International Monetary Fund (IMF) (though disputed by the Angolan government), around one quarter of the $4 billion spent by the government annually is unaccounted for.[5] Four fifths of Angola's population lives in abject poverty (on less than $1 a day), and, by the time of Savimbi's death, an estimated four million lived in refugee settlements inside Angola, with a further

450,000 accommodated in refugee camps outside its borders. The area in which Angola functions as a state is limited to a few urban centres. The country's infrastructure has been destroyed almost in its entirety.[6] The effects of civil war - UNITA's banditry, combined with the scorched earth policy pursued by the MPLA from 1999 onwards to eliminate UNITA's military assets and support, and ultimately, its leadership - has left vast regions of Angola ravaged. It has also led to largely unchecked migration to the coastal areas. Once self sufficient in meeting its food requirements,[7] Angola today has to import fifty per cent of its needs. The manufacturing sector has largely ceased to exist. Sixty percent of the population now lives in the urban areas where many of them survive by trading in imported goods in the informal sector. Many of those who remain in the rural areas are destitute, displaced, desperate and forgotten.

More positively, Savimbi's death has brought UNITA back into the formal political system once more. This should result in enormous savings in military expenditure, which has until recently consumed around fifty per cent of the government budget. It has also facilitated greater transparency and opened debate on humanitarian issues. Most important, it has meant that the war no longer serves as a 'national' issue that deflects attention away from government mismanagement and failures of performance.

Angola: from war to peace[8]

Following the granting of independence to Angola by Portugal on 11 November 1975, rival nationalist groups supported by foreign backers - the Soviet Union and Cuba in the case of the MPLA and the US and South Africa in the case of the FNLA *(Frente Nacional de Libertação de Angola)* and UNITA - vied for control. After the withdrawal of the South African military in 1976, from the late 1970s the South African Defence Force (SADF) carried out a series of incursions into southern Angola with the main aim of destroying the capacity of the South West African People's Organisation (SWAPO) to wage war against the government in what was then South West Africa (Namibia). At the same time these operations were intended to support Savimbi's UNITA and destabilise the MPLA regime.

US and South African support ensured that UNITA recovered sufficiently to become active in every province of the country by 1984, even at times threatening Luanda. From 1986, the struggle in Angola assumed the clearer dimensions of a Cold War competition. Following the rescinding of the Clark Amendment, which had outlawed direct assistance to insurgency groups, the Reagan administration began overtly supporting UNITA. This involved the supply of material via Mobutu's Zaïre, including sophisticated Stinger surface to air missiles. Soviet arms supplies to the MPLA were increased to match this threat.[9] The result was a combination of military stalemate and the devastation of infrastructure in much of the interior. Control of Luanda and the coastal strip and urban areas was key to the MPLA strategy, but it also retained its grip on most of the country's urban settlements. However, huge tracts of land remained ungovernable. At its peak, UNITA claimed it had established a sophisticated socio economic infrastructure, including schools, health services and agricultural projects in some of these areas.[10]

The collapse of the Soviet Union and the end of Cold War created a space for peace and political settlement in Angola. It permitted the superpowers to disengage from the country, and with the help of Angola's previous colonial power, Portugal, to urge the protagonists towards a peace accord. An agreement was signed in December 1988 between Angola, South Africa and Cuba which linked the staging of the 1990 elections in Namibia to both the withdrawal of Cuban troops from Angola, and the closure of African National Congress (ANC) bases there.[11] The Cuban pull out, which was monitored by the first UN verification mission to Angola, UNAVEM I, was completed by mid 1991. Talks between UNITA and the MPLA in Portugal were also completed in the course of 1991, resulting in the Bicesse Accords. A ceasefire was implemented by both parties and the UN created a new mission to Angola, UNAVEM II. However, significant mistrust remained between the parties, casting a shadow over the attempts to implement the Accords.

Amidst claims of intimidation (unsurprising, given that the rival armies remained largely intact)[12] and election irregularities related in part to an insufficiently strong UN presence, elections went ahead on 29–30 September 1992.[13] The MPLA's Dos Santos won 49.57 per cent of the vote and Savimbi 40,1 per cent.[14] Although a second round of voting should have occurred since neither candidate had obtained an absolute majority, UNITA re mobilised its forces, alleging electoral fraud (despite a UN assertion that the ballot had been largely free and fair). Between November 1992 and November 1994 an estimated 300,000 people were killed, thousands more displaced and much of the remaining infrastructure of the country was effectively destroyed. Although peace returned temporarily following the signing of the Lusaka Accords in 1994, fighting soon broke out again and continued virtually unabated until Savimbi's death in 2002.

Against this background, this chapter considers Angola in the context of a number of factors that shape the functions and cohesion of states. These are:

- the part played by external intervention, including military support and aid from governmental and non governmental sources;
- the role of ideology, personalities and leadership;
- the effects of borders, geography, religion and ethnicity;
- the impact of commodities;
- the relationship between regional networks, organisation and state functions; and
- the role of political structures.

The analysis is intended to examine a core issue of the 'Big States' project. It is central to assessing the conditions necessary for African economic recovery, most notably these questions:

- do 'big' states have characteristics which predispose them to collapse or engage in conflict?
- to what extent are these characteristics of a sort that states can do something about (as in policies or personalities)? Or are these issues beyond their control (for example, attributable to structural deficiencies)?

The chapter concludes by examining the following hypothesis: Angola's

Angola: facts and figures			
	1996	1999	2000
Population (millions)	11.7	12.8	13.1
Population growth annual %	3.1	2.9	2.9
GDP $ billion	7.5	6.2	8.8
GDP growth $ annual %	10.0	3.4	2.1
GNI per capita $	270.0	240.0	290.0
Inflation annual %	5,461.8	560.2	402.0
Total exports $ million	–	5,157.0	7,802.0
Total imports $ million	–	3,109.0	3,430.0
Trade in goods/share of GDP	95.0	134.3	127.5
Foreign direct investment Net inflows $	181 million	2.5 billion	1.7 billion
Present value of debt $	–	–	9.7 billion
Total debt service % of exports (goods & services)	18.2	18.7	15.1
Aid per capita $	40.5	30.4	23.3

dysfunctionality has been to a degree self serving, in that it has been used to prosecute the civil war and as a means of ensuring political support. Its path to state functionality (and global acceptance) will be determined by the number of milestones it succeeds in reaching. These include the establishment of an inclusive, popularly supported government; increasing congruence with the regional norms exemplified, at least on paper, by the Southern African Development Community (SADC) and New Partnership for Africa's Development (Nepad) programmes of action; an improvement in transparency and observance of the rule of law (especially as regards the role of the oil and diamond industries and related networks); and the fostering of an open society as typified by a healthy civil society and a free press.

Bigness and Angola's dysfunctionality

Angola qualifies as a 'big' African state by reason of its large geographic area (1,246,000 km²), but such a status would also be justified by its economic potential (especially, but not exclusively, in the oil sector) and its impact on the southern African region. In terms of the latter, it could be argued that Angola does not qualify as a dysfunctional state, at least not in terms of the definition provided by Marina Ottaway – 'the [lack of] capacity of the state to attain the goals set by its leadership'.[15] Indeed, in some respects, as has been intimated, it displays high levels of functional capacity, particularly in terms of its relative military prowess both internally and in the region. Indeed, as Van de Walle has argued, '[i]n virtually unprecedented fashion, Uganda, Rwanda and Angola have seen their foreign policies as instruments of national state formation and consolidation. These cases remind one of Clausewitz's dictum that war is the continuation of politics by other means'.[16]

In terms of statistical indices, however, Angola ranks as a collapsed or at least a barely functioning state, with high levels of inequality and an ongoing requirement for imported humanitarian assistance. Although the Angolan oil company, the *Sociedade Nacional de Combustiveis de Angola* (Sonangol), has an annual revenue of more than $2 billion, the average annual per capita income of Angola's thirteen million people is $260. Life expectancy is just forty six. In 2003, Angola ranked 164ᵗʰ out of 175 countries on the UN's Human Development Index, below countries such as Zambia, Benin, Malawi, Nepal, Madagascar and the Democratic Republic of Congo (DRC.)

Access to education is limited, partly because the government has had other priorities. Angola's education budget comprised 2.5 per cent of GDP versus defence expenditure of 21.7 per cent in 1999. (The latter was estimated as having increased to around fifty per cent by 2002.) In 2000 it was estimated that eighty per cent of Angola's schools had been destroyed or abandoned since 1998. Those that still function are under staffed and under resourced. Also, the low birth registration rate in Angola effectively limits the access of many to education, health facilities and employment.[17]

Angola has thus been described as a 'quasi state'[18] and a 'shadow state'.[19] The former relates to its failure to provide basic services to its people and the widespread ethnic, regional and political divisions within the population that resulted in four decades of conflict. The latter describes the nature of the relationship between the government (*Futungo*),[20] including the treasury, the oil sector (Sonangol), and the banking system as represented by the National Bank of Angola (BNA). This relationship has been described as a 'Bermuda Triangle' of actors exploiting 'sources of government income through secret and complex accounting procedures'.[21] During the peak of Savimbi's and UNITA's powers, UNITA controlled a parallel 'state within a state', described by some as 'Savimbiland', in which UNITA demonstrated to a degree, 'the extension of force, territory, national identity and internal legitimacy, capacity to generate revenue and … administration and infrastructure'.[22] This reached its apogee after the 1992 breakdown of the ceasefire, with UNITA claiming control of an estimated eighty per cent of the country by September 1993. This included the north east, a region rich in diamonds, even though in effect this area amounted to little more than a no man's land.[23]

Savimbi's military fortunes and the administrative, revenue generating and territorial integrity of Savimbiland were substantially degraded by a number of events, among them, the imposition of UN Security Council (UNSC) sanctions in September 1993 (Resolution 864, banning the sale of weapons and petrol to UNITA), in 1997 (Resolution 1127, preventing UNITA officials from travelling) and June 1998 (Resolution 1173, banning the purchase of diamonds from UNITA), all of which hampered his access to diamond income and consequently to oil and weapons. Another setback was the bolstering of the Angolan government's military capabilities through, *inter alia*, the use of foreign mercenaries, including Executive Outcomes (a private military company), along with the government's decision to suspend the Lusaka Protocol and to launch a full scale military offensive in December 1998.[24] These difficulties were compounded by poor military decisions made by Savimbi, including his attacks on Luanda, his attempts to capture towns and cities, and his strategy of waging a conventional war which included attempting to hold Bailundo and Andulo,[25] the centre of Ovimbundu nationalism and Savimbi's home town respectively.

Angola's problems of bigness and development

Does Angola's size create special problems for development?

Many of Angola's present difficulties relate to the effects of the forty year civil war. Paradoxically, the siphoning off of internal capacity – financial, material and personal – into the military struggle is evidence of the government's possession of considerable resources. The regime's insistence on controlling the Demobilisation, Disarmament and Integration (DDR) process implemented from 2002 is illustrative, too, of a certain arrogant self confidence in government capacity. It also reveals a desire to control the process and derive political and economic patronage from it, and a distrust of outsiders, especially (in this case) the UN.

Angola's large geographic extent has exacerbated the problems caused by the destruction of its infrastructure. For example, road and rail links were critical to the growth of towns in the interior, opening up the rich agricultural area of the Angolan central plateau. By 1999, an estimated 10.4 per cent of all roads (76,626 km) were paved, ranking Angola 148th out of 168 nations reviewed.[26]

There is a total of 2,648 km of 1.067 metre gauge and 123 km of 0.6 metre gauge railways in the country, but most of these are unusable. In the 1980s, three different 1.067 metre gauge rail systems ran from the hinterland to major ports on the Atlantic Ocean. The longest of these (1,394 km) was the Benguela Railway, linking the port of Lobito with the central African rail network, servicing the mining regions of Shaba (Zaïre) and the Zambian copperbelt, with a spur to Cuima, near Huambo. To the south, the 899 km Namibe Railway linked the port of Namibe to Menongue, with branches to Chiange and to the Cassinga iron ore deposits. In the north, the Luanda Railway ran from Luanda to Malanje, with rail spurs to Caxito and Dondo.

By 2003, however, as one analyst has noted:

> Investors are indeed flocking to the area – at least seventy South African companies are active here, but the infrastructure has not changed since the war: it remains shot to pieces. Everything needs reconstruction: roads, railway lines, electricity networks and water and sewage systems. Pavements are littered with rubbish, and puddles, resulting from leaking water pipes, are everywhere. At least eleven million landmines (one for each Angolan), lie buried in the fertile earth and need to be defused. In city traffic you will find a mix of old cars and modern 4x4 vehicles. Dotted between restored buildings, some dating from colonial times, are others that are clearly serious safety risks begging to be demolished. [27]

All three major railway systems have been severely incapacitated, as a result of both the guerrilla war and mismanagement. By late 1988, the Benguela corridor was operating only between Lobito and Benguela. By 2002 only a thirty kilometre section along the Angolan coast remained in service.[28] Traffic on the Namibe Railway has declined both because of damage from guerrilla attacks and the closure of the Cassinga iron mines, which had provided the line with most of its freight. By 1986 the Luanda Railway was carrying only one fifth of the amount carried in 1973, owing to raids by guerrillas and the deterioration of the line. Finally, a 123 km, narrow gauge (0.6 metre) line that had run from Porto Amboim to Gabela was closed in 1987.[29] The drop in rail traffic has led to a decrease in activity at the country's major ports at Luanda, Lobito and Namibe. By 1986, the volume of freight handled by Luanda had fallen to only thirty per cent of its 1973 level. Two years later Luanda, which had berths for eleven ships with adjacent rail sidings, and forty one cranes, had fallen into disrepair. Only two of the sidings and a small number of the cranes remained operational. The situation had improved a little by 2003 but the port was still plagued by difficulties, including broken cranes and dilapidated warehouses. An estimated $200 million is required to modernise Luanda's port facilities.[30] By 2003, *Caminho de Ferro de Luanda* (CFL) was seeking $600 million to rehabilitate the country's railway infrastructure.[31]

However, state weakness in Angola relates to the impact of the war and to the effects of Portuguese colonialism, which were exacerbated by the manner of Portugal's withdrawal in 1975. The hurried departure of the panicked Portuguese settlers, who often vandalised what they could not take, devastated both the country's economic productive capacity and robbed it of technical and managerial experience.[32] As Judith Matloff notes, 'The *retornados* left behind a country where practically no one knew how to read[,] let alone run a government'.[33]

In addition to the challenge posed by the lack of economic infrastructure, Angola inherited seven distinct legacies:

- the extraordinary demarcation of Angola's borders, particularly in the inclusion of the enclave of Cabinda, and its marked ethnic and urban rural divisions;
- a racial, ethnic and regional bias, reflected in the support bases of the political parties;
- the absence of a mature, indigenous polity that could embrace the transition to independence and democracy;
- the centralised nature of the Angolan state;

- the polarised ideological context and the political violence of the transition to independence;
- the linkage with Portuguese institutions, and dependency on Portuguese nationals for managerial and technical capacity; and
- unresolved ambiguities and difficulties in regional relationships, most notably with apartheid South Africa[34] over Namibia, and with what was then Zaïre, in terms of the personal links especially through Shaba (formerly Katanga) and the Bakongo, and the relationships between the FNLA, UNITA and Mobutu Sese Seko.[35]

Acknowledgement that Angola inherited many of its problems is not meant simply to provide an excuse for its failings after independence or to apportion blame. Instead, it provides a basis for comparison. If Angola is dysfunctional, then on what objective basis is this comparison being made – the past system of colonial government (certainly politically dysfunctional and untenable), or some hoped for model of state and societal integration?

Assessing the impact of 'splitters'

This Big African States project is, however, concerned less with the past than the present, and in particular the factors which could induce state failure or collapse – the so called 'splitters' such as religion; borders and geography; ethnicity; regional and other international relationships and potentially predatory external state units; population dispersal; ideology; resources and control over them; and ecological and environmental factors. The make up and impact of these factors are examined below.

Angola, Cabinda and self determination[36]

Considering that Angola is the size of Germany, France and Spain combined, one should not find it surprising that it is stratified by race, class, ethnic, rural urban and regional divides. These were manipulated by the colonial authorities (through the policy of providing special status for the *assimilados* – the 'assimilated ones'), by the MPLA whose support base was principally among the *mestiços* (those of mixed race) and Kimbundu; and especially by UNITA, which has portrayed itself as a non white, rurally based party located principally in the central highlands among the Ovimbundu people.[37]

While the bleak electoral choices facing Angolans in 1992 could be summarised by the popular graffiti of the time: 'The MPLA steals - UNITA kills',[38] to a great extent, the choices were made on the basis of ethnic identity and local concerns. UNITA, for example, exploited the notion of the 'real African' (versus the more urban wealthy Kimbundu and *mestiço*) and the rural urban divide, portraying itself as the party of those living close to the land.[39] As one UNITA member reportedly put it, following his party's loss in the 1992 election, 'The whites are not ready to hand over Angola to UNITA'.[40]

In 1992, both parties attempted to win over the Bakongo, who held the balance of power. Many Bakongo and other voters not belonging to one of the three major ethnic groups reportedly voted for the MPLA because of fears related to UNITA's prejudices. However, in the violence that followed the 1992 election, Bakongos and Ovimbundu were reportedly targeted by the MPLA as suspected of being UNITA supporters.[41] Notably, however, 'Rather than being based on some notion of primordial enmity, ethnic divisions have been deliberately exacerbated in order to further the political and economic aims of both the MPLA and UNITA'.[42] The war that followed the breakdown of peace in 1992 also had a regional dimension, being referred to as the 'war of the cities'.

Today, however, the most notable ethnic/regional 'splitter' is potentially that involving the oil producing enclave of Cabinda. Its population of perhaps half a million belongs to the Kongo cultural zone. Today, more than half of the Cabindans live in neighbouring countries such as the DRC and Congo Brazzaville. The enclave is central to Angola's wealth and power, reportedly accounting for more than sixty per cent of the country's oil production.[43]

The Liberation Front for the Cabinda Enclave (FLEC) was established prior to Angola's independence to fight against Portuguese rule. Currently represented by a number of factions including FLEC Renovada and FLEC FAC (the Armed Forces of Cabinda), the movement has a separatist agenda. Neither party recognises the Alvor Treaty, which signed the province over to Angola after independence from Portugal.[44] As one former commander argues, 'History shows us that Cabinda is not Angola. And because it is not Angola, we could never go and fight alongside the MPLA. The war in Cabinda continues; it's not over yet'. The fact that a high percentage of Cabindans do not see themselves as Angolans is borne out partly by the high percentage of voter absenteeism in the province (38.13 per cent), compared with the national average (8.65 per cent), in the 1992 elections.

Differences over whether FLEC is Angolan or not have been exacerbated by the revenues generated by the oil produced in Cabinda. Even though officially ten per cent of the oil income has to be spent on local development projects, on a *per capita* basis the overall income is said to equal $100,000 per Cabindan resident.[45] But the Cabindans themselves apparently recognise that while independence is a 'desirable solution', they must remain open minded over the 'future status' of the province.[46] Other potential ethnic splitters include the growing debate within the Luanda dominated Party for Social Renewal (PRS) on the question of self determination, and the calls by the king of Malanje for independence.

Angola's self determination vision is thus very much 'reduced' to the current constitution making process.[47] At this stage no regional autonomy is provided for in the draft. All provincial governors will continue to be appointed by the central government, and the provinces will have no revenue of their own, even though the Lusaka Protocol (the basis for the current settlement) stipulates that the 'provincial authorities [are to] have their own powers in the fields of administration, finance, taxation and economy, including the capacity to attract foreign investment'.[48] The constitution drafting process has not been assisted by UNITA's split (before its June 2003 congress) into two factions: that led by Paulo Lukambo 'Gato' (who has been portrayed as working more closely with the MPLA) and that headed by Isaias Samakuva, apparently intent on pursuing a more independent route. The Samakuva element foresees little likelihood of the constitutional process leading to 'serious changes and a decentralisation of power'. It is probable in these circumstances that Cabindan separatists will be given short shrift in the provisions of the new constitution.[49] The Angolan government's strategy towards the FLEC has been akin to that employed with UNITA: a military approach tempered by the offer of political dialogue. Yet without a measure of autonomy for Cabinda plus a radical socio economic reconstruction plan, the problem is likely to simmer.[50]

Fundamentally, the ability of the provinces (or the political parties) to articulate a different viewpoint and pursue a strategy independent of *Futungo* depends on the remaking of the client system of Angolan politics, in which financing and patronage is all pervasive. This is the reason behind the slow pace and shallowness of current constitutional reform planning, the lack of public institutions and widely accepted norms, the dependency of the *Futungo* on keeping the current system intact, and a weak, fragmented civil society.[51]

Resources, governance and transparency

The conflict in the period 1992-1994 marked a watershed in the history of the Angolan civil war. Stripped of superpower patronage, both sides exploited the country's natural resources to provide the funding they needed for their campaigns, making the accumulation of wealth and the war almost inseparable. In this respect, Angola, far from being a dysfunctional, failing state, showed considerable capacity for organisation and control. As Ottaway notes, the 'exploitation of commodities remained firmly under the control of the political entity, either the government or UNITA, which controlled a specific territory'. She continues:

> The Angolan government, which began by embracing Marxism Leninism and remains highly statist, set up state companies to exploit all commodities - oil (Sonangol), diamonds (Endiama), and even coffee.[52] It worked out deals with foreign corporations for the exploitation and commercialisation of its commodities, and maintained control of those commodities.[53]

While it may have been a corrupt system, it functioned. In the DRC, by comparison, she argues, 'it is difficult to see a legitimate system[,] even a corrupt one'. Thus an awareness of how each side profited: the government from oil, UNITA from diamonds, is critical to understanding both Angola's past conflict and its future path.

Today, as noted above, the oil sector accounts for around fifty per cent of Angola's GDP, is the largest contributor to state revenue (between seventy and ninety per cent from 1994-99), and represents eighty to ninety per cent of all Angolan exports. Yet the oil industry employs only an estimated two per cent of Angola's population, and is essentially an offshore, enclave economy.

Table 5.1 Exports from Angola: 1995-99 ($ millions)

	1995	1999
Crude oil	3,425	4,609
Refined petroleum products	78	75
Gas	18	10
Diamonds	168	629
Coffee	5.8	5.0
Other	27	15
Total	3,723	5,344

Source: IMF, *Angola: Recent Economic Developments*, August 2000, p. 41.

The potential of the oil sector is huge. Four of Angola's deepwater areas – Blocks 14, 15, 16 and 17 – are believed by experts to have at least ten billion barrels of oil in recoverable reserves.[54] Chevron alone plan to invest $5 billion between 2005 and 2010. Coupled with a high oil price, this factor alone is expected to drive GDP growth to over ten per cent, though the extent of the benefits within Angolan society remain questionable without improvements in human and physical infrastructure, regulatory institutions and policy, and judicial independence and oversight. For example, Angola ranks 151st out of 158 on Transparency International's 2005 Corruption Perceptions Index. By comparison, official development assistance (ODA) flows to Angola amounted to $306.7 million in 2000, or $23.30 per capita and 3.5 per cent of GDP (whereas it was 2.6 per cent ten years earlier). Net foreign direct investment – predominantly in the oil sector – amounted to 19.2 per cent of GDP in 2000, compared with –3.3 per cent in 1990.[55]

Table 5.2 Angola's oil production by operator: 1999

	Bls/day	% Total
Chevron	475,000	62.0
Elf	175,000	22.9
Texaco	85,000	11.1
Totalfina	16,000	2.1
Ranger	9,000	1.2
Sonangol	4,900	0.6
Agip	1,000	0.1
Total	765,900	100.0

Source: Frynas JG & G Wood, 'Oil and war in Angola', *Review of African Political Economy*, 90, 28, 2001, p. 591.

The offshore nature of Angola's oil resources has meant that oil production, while it helped to fund the war, remained largely untouched by it. Oil revenues were essential to fund the MPLA's war against UNITA and finance arms purchases, and largely bypassed the accounting procedures of the central bank and the finance ministry.[56] The government's war effort also involved securing lines of credit by mortgaging future oil production.

The regime's dependence on oil revenues during the war was replicated by the use of diamonds as a key source of funding for UNITA. As John Mackinlay[57] has argued, global changes have radically altered (and increased) the activities and options facing the insurgent group, and greatly complicated (and weakened) the policy responses facing some governments. Improvements in access to transport, for example, have taken a number of forms. These include the proliferation of ex Soviet aircraft capable of operating in remote areas, the widespread availability of reliable (mainly Japanese) trucks and minibuses, and the reduction in the cost of sea freight through containerisation (which had the added advantage of imposing limitations on customs checking procedures). This added mobility has had a number of effects, chief among them an improved ability to 'override the limitations imposed by terrain and poor technology' which was previously available only to international corporations and state armed forces.[58] These developments have meant that communities have been brought closer to the global economy without (or in spite of) the state's involvement, for example in the trade of portable – or 'lootable' – resources, which include diamonds, gems, hardwoods, drugs, antiques and weapons.

In line with the change in its fortunes as a result of the end of the Cold War, consequent on its loss of Russian support, and given its easy access to diamonds and international markets, UNITA naturally focused on this combination as a key means of income. The movement's occupation of the north eastern provinces of the country earned it income from mining, taxes on miners and the sale of mining licences. Violence was regularly used as a means of enforcement and control of the diggers. Global Witness has estimated that diamonds sold by UNITA raised $3.7 billion. The money was used mainly to buy arms and supplies.[59] South African industry experts have, however, suggested that the country's total diamond mining output per year was, during the war years, worth around $600 million, reducing the amount earned by UNITA to $1.4-1.8 billion,[60] although, as Shaw observes, this was still sufficient to run a damaging military campaign. International sanctions made access to the markets more difficult, though not impossible.

However, with the coming of peace, diamonds could be used for development rather than war, although this change would be conditional on the opening up of the industry and the successful (and peaceful) resolution of outstanding issues relating to diamond mining. These include the right to mine UNITA concessions such as those in Kwango Valley, Luareca, Mussendo and Mupupa, held by its proxy company *Sociedade General Mineiro* (SGM).

Today diamonds are the second largest earner in Angola (after oil). The country currently produces an estimated 2.5 million carats, worth around $700 to $900 million a year, approximately twelve per cent of world production. Angola could, under stable security conditions, double production which would make it the world's second largest producer, outranked only by Botswana.[61] Overall, the significance of the Angolan oil and diamond sectors and the role of the multinational will be critical to the future economic and political development of the country. However, business practices by most oil multinationals have not assisted in improving the ruling party's transparency or accountability as regards government expenditure. Stricter enforcement of corporate governance principles and practices is essential if economic activity by multinationals is to contribute positively towards the development of the country, instead of continuing to sustain the existing vicious cycle of corruption and patronage.

Organised criminal networks and linkages

The breakdown of state capacity, combined with wealthy enclaves, and the existence of natural resources that are easily plundered has meant that Angola has been both a target for, and source of, international criminal networks, which have supplied weapons to UNITA and accepted diamonds in exchange for these and other purchases. Although precise information is difficult to come by, reports[62] indicate that, unlike in situations elsewhere in Africa, (the Liberian/Sierra Leonean nexus, for example) Angola's neighbours have played only a limited role in the trade in diamonds. However, the war in Angola has had important consequences for criminal operations in other adjacent states, particularly Zambia and Namibia. The Fowler report of March 2000 identified Togo, Burkina Faso, Rwanda, Ivory Coast and Gabon as major buyers of UNITA diamonds.[63] As Shaw notes, the demand for supplies and the flow of illegal diamonds out of the country have given rise to opportunities for criminal behaviour and organisation. In the case of South Africa, the relationship is more complex, and has involved a legacy of networks and associations going back to the South African involvement in the Angolan-Namibian conflict and apartheid South Africa's support for UNITA. Again, many of the weapons and other links between crime syndicates and UNITA have been a result of the involvement of Ukrainian, Bulgarian and other nationals taking advantage of the breakdown of controls after the end of the Cold War.

A new problem, which some might see as presaging an increase in international attention and pressure on the Angolan government to comply with international legislation to control crime, concerns the reported use of Angola as a transit point for drug smuggling from Latin America.[64]

The risk to the consolidation of political processes in Angola posed by these relationships has been significantly reduced by the end of the conflict. The extent to which they will permeate and influence the Angolan state and society is likely in the future to reflect the extent to which the Angolan government and its international and regional partners are able to co operate to solve the country's pressing social and security problems.

International and regional relations

Angola's conflict has been global in terms of involvement, and largely local as far as its impact is concerned. As is noted above, it was a truly Cold War struggle, with the Soviet bloc and the administrations of Presidents Reagan and George Bush senior providing more than $6 billion in weapons and aid to the MPLA and UNITA respectively during the 1980s.

Today, however, the role of the international community needs to be separated into the different relationships that Angola has with the so called 'Troika' countries (the US, Portugal and Russia), other international partners, and countries in the southern African region. The Troika currently has no further specific role as defined within the framework of the peace agreement, and at most enjoys observer status, yet these three countries could play a critical role in determining government policy on a range of issues.

The US is Angola's biggest trading partner. It accounted, for example, for approximately forty per cent of Angola's oil exports in 2000. Angola currently supplies an estimated ten per cent of America's oil imports. On the other hand, Angola's bilateral debt burden is dominated by Russia, which has maintained its primary position as the country's most significant arms supplier. Oil will be the main factor influencing US and Russian policy making in relation to Angola, as has been shown by their tactics since 1996. Portugal's relationship with Luanda is both ambiguous and complex. On the one hand, there is a need to confront perceptions in Angola of Lisbon's historical role and its colonial responsibility. On the other, relations between the MPLA and UNITA elites and Portugal remain close and cordial, and are strengthened by familial, financial and emotional bonds.[65] Other, non Troika states, such as Brazil, France, Spain, Israel and Norway, play significant roles, especially through the development of oil and other commercial interests, although for different reasons. However, their political will and means to influence the socio political environment positively are apparently limited.

As I have commented in an earlier section of this chapter, Angola has been willing to project its military power beyond its borders in pursuit of the MPLA's interest in defeating UNITA. This led to Angola's involvement in the DRC conflict; first on the side of Rwanda and Uganda to defeat Mobutu (long a supporter of

UNITA), and later against its erstwhile allies in defending the regime of Laurent Kabila. Angola has also reportedly involved itself in the affairs of its neighbour, Congo Brazzaville, in helping to depose Patrick Lissouba's government, and in Sao Tomé in 2003.

The relationship between Angola and South Africa has been both ambiguous and complex. Pretoria has felt concern about Luanda's regional role, and about the Angolan government's commitment to democratisation and liberalisation. The Angolans' view is shaped by South Africa's past history of military involvement in their country, and by their suspicions that South Africa plans to play a hegemonic role in southern Africa. Yet there is significant advantage to be gained by improving Pretoria-Luanda ties. Luanda has displayed a willingness to engage regionally and use its military prowess in African peacekeeping interventions (for example in the Congo). For South Africa based businesses, closer ties between Pretoria and Luanda could assist in providing the regulatory cover currently missing from the Angolan business environment.[66] However, there are political obstacles to be overcome before such a regional partnership can eventuate. For instance, Pretoria will need to make positive, public overtures towards the MPLA. In doing so it will help to placate the many Angolans who perceive South Africa's ruling African National Congress as having shown insufficient gratitude for the years of sanctuary and military assistance Luanda provided before 1994.

Undoubtedly the end of the Angolan civil war is of enormous significance to sub Saharan Africa. The forty year conflict not only embroiled its eastern and southern neighbours, Zambia and Namibia, but spilled over into the DRC and resulted in an unconstitutional regime change in the Republic of Congo (RoC). Yet despite its past military history of intervention and its growing regional stature Luanda has managed to remain largely estranged from organised regional political and economic relationships, a position which is to a great extent a reflection of its international economic (oil) relationships. There has been no significant rapprochement with more reformist regional governments so far, and Angola's traditional partners have remained firmly within the ranks of the SADC old guard, notably Namibia's Sam Nujoma and Zimbabwe's Robert Mugabe.

Among the 'non state' actors, international humanitarian organisations tread a difficult path. They are not only confronted by the dire humanitarian situation in Angola, but have to deal with a huge shortfall in funding. This is largely attributable to a perception among donors that the Angolan government is not doing enough to address the survival needs of its citizens, and that official corruption is so pervasive that relief aid that is channelled through government departments does not reach those for whom it is intended. This could prove to be a critical factor in Angola's future, as the humanitarian crisis may well worsen and in turn heighten the risk of continuing instability for an indefinite period. It is however incumbent on humanitarian organisations to move beyond their strictly circumscribed aid role and to develop active partnerships within Angolan civil society that can assist in rebuilding the shattered fabric of society and the economy. Although the government has been extremely resistant to allowing human rights education, peace activism, an independent media or an open discussion of the ills of the current state apparatus, such partnerships represent the way to ensure that Angola as a society can move beyond its current crisis mode towards sustainable development and peace.

Political pathology and organisation

Both UNITA and the MPLA face considerable restructuring challenges following the end of the conflict. UNITA has to unify its various factions and transform itself from a military movement into a political party, giving itself both an organisational focus and a new political profile, since it was shaped in the past by the dominant personality of Savimbi. The MPLA has to face up to the realisation that the end of the conflict requires a policy and leadership change within the party. Other social movements and groupings have to find their niche, either as political parties or as part of civil society.[67]

UNITA

There are three core challenges facing UNITA in the post Savimbi normalisation phase:

· first, there is a need to unify the organisation, to reorganise and to modernise. This includes the completion of the merger with UNITA *Renovado*, the development of a transitional strategic plan for the party, and the election of a new leader. The latter was partly accomplished when Isaias Samakuva was made head of UNITA at the June 2003 party congress, but the transition from being a guerrilla movement to a fully fledged political party remains some way off, partly because the process is not entirely in the hands of UNITA;

- secondly, its international relations and business links within Angola need to be normalised. This includes the relaxation of international sanctions, the recovery of funds, and the regaining of mineral rights;
- thirdly, UNITA needs to develop a national political party, extending its power base beyond the Ovimbundu. This is most likely to be pursued by reaching out to the Bakongo.

The MPLA

Like UNITA, the ruling party faces three main challenges:

- first, a decision needs to be made on who will replace President Dos Santos as leader, should he choose to step down;
- secondly, the government needs to engineer a marked improvement in the socio economic environment to avoid a humiliating loss of support at the polls;
- thirdly, a strong support base needs to be created that extends beyond Luanda and the Kimbundu ethnic group.

The main issue within the MPLA is the future of its president, José Eduardo dos Santos. This has been the subject of ongoing speculation after the commitment he made in 2001 to step down after his current term of office. Yet there is a firm belief that he is not ready to relinquish the presidency, especially as the MPLA is currently the only party with the organisational capacity to participate fully in national elections. It is considered highly likely that the MPLA will remain in government after the next elections. The composition and character of the MPLA leadership in the coming years will be extremely important determinants of Angola's future. In particular, its economic reforms and government policies will require close scrutiny. Thus the main question is not necessarily who will be running the country in the years to come, but rather how the post conflict MPLA government will both address the problems facing Angola and engage with other political actors in the process of reform.

The restructuring (and realignment) of the leadership that seems likely to occur within both parties augurs well for the political dispensation in Angola. It presents the first opportunity in ten years for Angolans to campaign actively for new leadership. However, it remains an open question to what extent a 'new' leadership in both parties will usher in the beginning of a greater liberalisation of the political realm. It may serve only to safeguard the interests of the outgoing elite.

In summary, before Angola's electoral process can be considered to have 'normalised', at least the following steps will need to have been taken:

· the transformation of both UNITA and the MPLA from stratocracies to political parties;
· the rehabilitation of essential infrastructure to make free and fair elections possible;
· the conduct of a nation wide census;
· the registration of voters (in a country where very few have any identifying documentation and only five to ten per cent of births are registered);
· the passing of electoral laws regulating the duties of national and local governments;
· the publication of Angola's new constitution,[68] in which the division of power between the executive, legislative and judicial branches at each of the national and regional/provincial levels; and
· the establishment of the necessary electoral and support infrastructure.

Any failure by UNITA to transform itself into a non violent national political force could have serious implications, not least the threat of a reduction in legitimacy for both parties. The degree to which UNITA decides to co operate with government in its own interests as well as those of national unity could determine the extent of public faith in the political process, at least in the short term. There is little likelihood of a new, mainstream political grouping emerging. There is a greater chance that the conservative, Africanist discourse of UNITA might be abandoned, however, as the party is absorbed by the urban based political process.

Civil society and the church

While the religious denominations – particularly the Catholic church[69] – are an established part of Angolan social life, the emergence of organised non governmental organisations (NGOs) in Angola is of relatively recent occurrence. It was only after the MPLA Central Committee had abandoned the one party system in June 1990 and the 1992 elections and peace process had failed that this element of civil society began to emerge as another actor in the Angolan political arena, which had been so long dominated by UNITA and the MPLA.

A decade later, following the death of Savimbi and the cessation of official hostilities, civil society faces a unique range of challenges. Despite being caught off guard by the speed of military developments, civil society now had to rally to undertake vast new responsibilities. These range from ensuring the provision of basic services to the people of Angola to shaping the debate about the future institutions and to lobbying for greater transparency and accountability in governance. With elections due in 2006 or 2007 and constitutional reform already under way, civil society can bridge the gap between the formal political process and the citizenry. However, until now, the MPLA has attempted (largely successfully) to control the NGO process, through co option and the establishment of its 'own' NGOs.

The church, in particular, has a central part to play. While some NGOs have an overtly political character (and thus are distrusted by government), the churches maintain a focus on the humanitarian situation and have much greater access to communities in the countryside, which they enjoyed even during the worst times of the war. The Archbishop of Luanda, Damiao Franklin, has named the need for 'social justice' and the fight against poverty as the principal challenges facing the church and country alike. He has also identified the need both to consolidate democracy so that 'the leader does not feel the country is his private property' and to improve education opportunities 'so as to provide some basis for life'.[70] It remains imperative for other representatives of civil society to extend their activities beyond the borders of Luanda. Most of these organisations are based in the capital, whereas the greatest need for civic education programmes is in the rural areas.

The role that a restructured UNITA, as well as other political parties and civil society organisations can play in pressurising the MPLA to engage in a more inclusive debate and restructuring process is crucial for the immediate future. There are various areas that require attention. The establishment of the rule of law; the reinforcement of judicial institutions; a national, comprehensive campaign for disarmament; and the restoration of public faith in the state's ability to protect and respond to the needs of its citizens are all essential, and are all matters in which civil society and opposition party contributions and involvement can make a difference.

Social exclusion and integration

From the mud and wattle *musseques* (sand slums) of Luanda to the informal marketplace of the Roque Santiero above the city, arguably the greatest challenges facing Angola today are social integration, the reduction of disparities in wealth, the provision of basic services, and giving the average citizen a stake in the system.

To an extent, achieving this hinges on the ability of the government to reintegrate former guerrillas into society, providing them with alternative means of income and resettling them, and disarming civilians. This raises the issue of land reform and the need to address the subject of transparency. Unless this is done, the seeds of conflict may be sown anew.[71]

Recovery also depends on the pace of economic growth and the extent to which this will touch the lives of ordinary citizens. With eighty per cent of Angola's population living in either absolute or relative poverty, and with limited or no access to health care, 'the government's failure adequately to address serious economic disparities among the population could threaten growth and spark localised violence'.[72] The avoidance of such disasters must be linked to significant interrelated challenges in the socio economic environment. These include the need for improvement in the state's capacity to deliver goods and services (particularly increased investment in basic infrastructure and amenities). There must be a demonstration of greater ability and willingness to implement reforms which might allow more space to the private sector, adoption of greater transparency and a more open political process that entails improved public accounting and government accountability. Agricultural assistance must also be provided to the rural population, particularly those recently resettled, and poverty reduction programmes must be linked to structural adjustments that may enable ordinary Angolan citizens to benefit from Angola's formal economy. Without action in these areas, as the International Crisis Group (ICG) notes, '[r]egional and ethnic inequalities that intersect with an inadequate governmental response to the needs of the displaced and the former UNITA insurgents can sow the seeds for future instability and warlordism'.[73] One UNITA official has warned:

> How these people are treated will determine the stability or instability of the country. The government must be willing to pay the price of peace and stability. These men are still soldiers without guns. If the government fails in its reintegration programme, everything in life has its price. The causes of social conflict are still alive. [74]

However, addressing these issues demands fundamental reform of the patronage system and the networks that 'comprise the foundation of the state and control the resources and major governmental decisions'.[75] Unless these are dismantled, levels of societal resentment and embitterment are likely to increase among those excluded from the system, exacerbating the national divisions created by a war which left a million dead and a third of the population displaced.[76] Herein lies *Futungo's* dilemma: reform and transparency are necessary to reduce longer term societal instability and to cement improving international relationships; but they may prove counter productive in the shorter term because they entail undermining the patronage based system in which power and wealth are located and dispensed. The means of reducing this tension is national reconciliation; the commencement of a national debate through the staging of elections, the extension of basic rights, freedoms and services; and normalisation of the political process.

Put differently, the MPLA faces, not a serious political or military threat, but a widespread social crisis. To address this, it will have to:

· continue to deal proactively with the social needs of former combatants;
· address funding and policy shortfalls in dealing with internationally displaced persons (IDPs);
· assist (or at least be seen to be assisting) in the breaking of the cycle of political and economic impunity currently enjoyed by both the government and UNITA;
· build state networks, provide social services, and develop the capacity to absorb donor funds;
· construct public security institutions and build public trust in them;
· improve transparency in line with IMF precepts, opening up international credit lines beyond those available from the Chinese;
· embark on a physical infrastructure building programme;[77] and
· bring under control the fiscal deficit (about five per cent) and inflation (around forty per cent in 2005).

Conclusions: ... to *estamos juntos*?

In the absence of the ideological contest between the Marxist Leninism of the MPLA and UNITA's cocktail of pro Western pragmatism and Maoist populism which motivated both parties during the Cold War, Angolan politics now operates in a comparative conceptual vacuum. It is currently characterised by unrestrained capitalism, a Darwinian struggle for survival and a quest for personal aggrandisement.

Within this context, the likelihood of continued peace and development in Angola is dependent on the roles to be played by a wide range of actors. These are the MPLA, UNITA and other political parties; civil society and church groups; local and international business interests; external political actors including the UN, the Troika, South Africa, France, Spain, China, Norway and Brazil; international financial institutions, including the IMF and the World Bank, and the regional associations of SADC and the Common Market for Eastern and Southern Africa (Comesa). Many specific short, medium and longer term challenges lie ahead. The evolving relationship between the government (as the *de facto* victors of the war) and UNITA will influence the peace process, as will the interaction between the government and its donors and oil partners. Indeed, the capacity of the government to fulfil its responsibilities during the process of demilitarisation, to engage domestic and international actors in supporting the reconstruction of Angola's economy and to establish its authority over the whole territory of Angola, so as to ensure full service delivery and participation in any future elections, is critical if the peace is to hold.

Global developments have assisted Angola in its search for peace and stability, at least in the short term. It is likely that Luanda's international relationships benefited from the events of 11 September 2001 and the war in Iraq for three reasons:

· first, the attacks of 11 September on US targets focused attention on the cost of a failure to deal with traditional and dysfunctional states;
· second, in the short term, the manner in which Luanda, as a member of the UN Security Council, played its hand over the Iraq issue could only have cemented its relationship with the Republican administration in Washington. It did this without setting its wider African ties at risk, because it allowed both sides to believe that it would vote for (and against) a second resolution without, of course, ever having to commit itself. Angola's elevation to the status of a 'pivotal' state in international eyes, will depend on the pace of its own internal reforms and the manner in which it is prepared to engage with certain outstanding regional problems, such as Zimbabwe;
· third, the West (and China) has become aware of a strategic need to locate and secure oil supplies outside the Middle East.

There is thus little likelihood of pressure for internal change being brought to bear in the current international context, especially given Angola's increasing importance as a source of oil production. It is more probable that change will come from within the MPLA, and possibly also from the cadre of now under employed generals. The war is won, but the country's challenges remain the same. The claim that a more effective state could emerge from military victory has yet to be made good. The state remains weak, with its political and bureaucratic systems structured around patronage, which remains a formidable barrier to the entry of liberalising investors and political forces alike.

Angola is, in conclusion, not a dysfunctional state in the sense that it faces insurmountable structural difficulties in making its transition from war to peace. It functions rather well, albeit for only a small minority. Extending this 'functionality' to all of Angola's thirteen million people is going to prove extremely problematic, given the destruction of so much of the country's infrastructure and the social mistrust caused by years of conflict. Here its 'bigness' undoubtedly makes it much more difficult to provide government services to the population; yet, paradoxically, the country's size means that poverty in the region is unlikely to make Luanda vulnerable.

Angola has a number of advantages that should help it to make this transition from limited functionality, not least its growing market for oil and minerals. But it also requires international and regional partnerships and improved confidence within Angolan communities to ensure its path towards recovery. In the long run, Luanda will have to build better, more inclusive systems of governance, embrace notions of transparency and accountability and acknowledge political opposition and civil society as necessary elements in this process.

Reform and stability in Angola is thus not a certainty. The veneer of genuinely democratic processes and socio economic stability is paper thin, and the path ahead is littered with structural, personal, ideological and policy obstacles. To realise the fruits of military victory, the government will have to remain steadfast in commitment to economic diversification and openness, remedy its human rights shortcomings, promote individual and group freedoms, and reduce social disparities and poverty. It must also address urgent humanitarian issues, including the resettlement and reintegration of former IDPs and combatants.[78] Pluralism, transparency and meritocracy are a tall order for a country with a barely functioning state, weak institutions and a tradition of violent internal political division, party patronage and corruption.

Thus to end where this paper started: *Estamos juntos?* The answer is probably: *Vamos vêr.*[79]

Endnotes

1   This chapter draws in part on research conducted for Neuma Grobelaar, Greg Mills and Elizabeth Sidiropoulos, *Angola: Prospects for Peace and Stability*, Johannesburg:

SAIIA, 2003. Grateful thanks are extended to Manuel Ennes Ferreira for his comments on the chapter.

2   Round table discussion, SAIIA, Johannesburg, 2003.

3   Under the terms of the latter, the following stages were to be carried out. The first was UNITA's military demobilisation and reporting to quartering areas. The demobilisation process was to be managed by a joint military commission, under the presidency of the MPLA, with the UN having observer status. Second, 5,000 former UNITA soldiers were to be integrated into the Angolan Armed Forces (FAA) and the national police force, to fill current vacancies. There would, however, be no change in the structure of the FAA and the police, and FAA troops would not be demobilised. The third stage would be the social and vocational re integration of former UNITA soldiers. At the time of signing the peace deal, Luanda committed itself to providing vocational training to demobilised UNITA soldiers and to assisting their families. (The number of UNITA troops in these areas has steadily risen. Initial estimates of UNITA troops were 50-55,000, plus 300,000 family members. At the end of September 2002, this number had become 80,000 former UNITA soldiers and 260,000 family members.) See 'Interview with UN Representative Erick de Mul', *UN IRIN*, 4 April 2003. By the end of January 2003, about 90,000 ex combatants had undergone the registration process. See 'World Bank boost to reintegration programme', *UN IRIN*, 31 March 2003.

4   Some seventy per cent of these diamonds are reportedly considered gem quality. See Cortright D, Lopez G & R Conroy, 'Angola's agony' In: Cortright D and G Lopez (eds), *The Sanctions Debate: Assessing UN Strategies in the 1990s*. Boulder: Lynne Rienner, 2000, p. 151. In 1974, Angola reportedly produced 2.3 million carats of diamonds.

5   The total is an alleged $4 billion over the last five years.

6   As one illustration, the 1,300 kilometre Benguela railroad stretching from Lobito to Zambia, constructed between 1903-1929 and at its peak moving three million tonnes of freight in 1974, had been reduced to an operational strip of only forty kilometres by the end of the 1980s.

7   Agricultural production overall fell from twenty nine per cent of GDP in 1991 to under six per cent in 2000. The country had to import 725,000 tons of cereals in 2003. See 'Angola Country Report', *Economist Intelligence Unit*, November 2002 cited in International Crisis Group (ICG), 'Angola's Choice: Reform or Regress', p. 5, on *http://icg@crisisweb.org*.

8   For a good summary of the transition from colonialism to contemporary politics, see Ferreira M, 'Angola: From Conflict to Development, 1961-2002', *The ECAAR Review*, 1, January 2003, pp. 57-70.

9   Turner J. *Continent Ablaze: The Insurgency Wars in Africa 1960 to the Present*. Johannesburg: Jonathan Ball, 1998, pp. 100-125. The total volume of Soviet aid was estimated at $6 billion, and of US support to UNITA at between $15-60 million annually from 1986-91. See Matloff J. *Fragments of a Forgotten War*. Parktown: Penguin, 1997, p. 36. See also Malaquais A. 'Reformulating International Relations Theory: African Insights and Challenges.' In: Dunn K & T Shaw (eds). *Africa's Challenge to International Relations Theory*. New York: Palgrave, 2001. By the late 1980s the direct annual South African financial contribution to UNITA is estimated to have been greater than the allocation to the SA Navy at the same time, around $1 billion at 1995 values.

10 This included several hospitals, limited agricultural production, a rudimentary arms (mine) industry, schools and an extensive propaganda network including Radio VORGAN (Voice of the Resistance of the Black Cockerel).

11 For details on the military actions that led to this negotiation process, see Bridgland F. *The War for Africa: Twelve Months that Transformed a Continent*. Gibraltar: Ashanti, 1992; and on the diplomatic process, Crocker C. *High Noon in Southern Africa: Making Peace in a Rough Neighbourhood*. New York: Norton, 1992.

12 Approximately fifty five per cent of government's estimated 150,000 troops and seventy five per cent of UNITA's 50,000 strong forces remained mobilised at the time the elections were held, and only 1,500 of the 50,000 united armed force had been sworn in. Matfloff, op cit, p. 100.

13 See Jett D. *Why Peacekeeping Fails*. New York: St Martins Press, 1999.

14 The MPLA won an absolute majority in parliament, with 53.74 per cent of the votes, while UNITA won 34.10 per cent, giving the latter seventy seats. Holden Roberto's FNLA came in third in the legislative vote, with 2.4 per cent. About 4.4 million of the registered 4.8 million Angolans voted.

15 'Dysfunctional states, Dysfunctional Armed Movements, and Lootable Commodities'. Draft paper for SAIIA-SWP-Princeton conference, Cadenabbia, November 2002.

16 'External Relations and State Formation in Sub Saharan Africa.' Draft paper for SAIIA SWP Princeton conference, Cadenabbia, November 2002.

17 McGregor J. *Angola's Children: Bearing the Greatest Cost of War*. Pretoria: Institute for Security Studies (unpublished report), 21 May 2002. The UN has reported that 750,000 children aged 0-14 have lost one or both parents, only one third of infants get their required vaccinations and half of all Angolan children do not attend school. See *UN IRIN*, 31 May 2002. The importance of education for the future prospects of Angola is underlined by the fact that nearly 60 per cent of the population is under fifteen years of age. The ratio of troops to primary school teachers is 2.5 to

one, and there are 7.5 troops per 1,000 people, compared with two per 1,000 in Mozambique, 0.7 in Nigeria and 3.5 in South Africa. See Hodges T, *Angola: From Afro Stalinism to Petro Diamond Capitalism.* Oxford: James Currey and Indiana University Press, 2001, p. 64.

18 See Jackson RH. *Quasi States: Sovereignty, International Relations and the Third World.* Cambridge: CUP, 1990.

19 See Reno W. 'Shadow States and the Political Economy of Civil Wars.' In: Berdal M & D Malone (eds). *Greed and Grievance: Economic Agendas in Civil Wars.* Boulder: Lynne Reiner, 2000, pp. 43-68.

20 So named after the President's private residence, *Futungo de Belas.*

21 See Grant JA. 'The End of Savimbiland? The Rise and Decline of UNITA's "State within a State" in Angola.' Paper presented at the workshop on 'States within States: Incipient Political Entities in the Post Cold War Era', University of Toronto, 19-20 October 2001.

22 Ian Spears, cited in Grant JA, *ibid.*

23 From 1992-98, UNITA accounted for an estimated seventy five per cent of all Angolan diamond exports. See Cortright D, Lopez G & R Conroy. *op. cit.*, p. 151.

24 Executive Outcomes was paid between $60-80 million for services between 1993-96.

25 Both of these towns fell in October 1999.

26 On *http://www.nationmaster.com/country/ao/Transportation.*

27 Ferreira J. 'Angola: Painful Destruction.', at *http://www.news24.com/ News24/ Africa/ Features/0,6119,2 11 37_1441556,00.html.*

28 On *http://news.bbc.co.uk/1/hi/world/africa/2061108.stm.*

29 On *http://reference.allrefer.com/country guide study/angola/angola119.html.*

30 On *http://www.worldreport ind.com/angola/infras.htm.*

31 On *http://www.worldreport ind.com/angola/infras.htm.*

32 An estimated 335,000 Portuguese colonists (so called *retornados*) left Angola around independence.

33 See Matloff J, *Fragments of a Forgotten War.* Parktown: Penguin, 1997, p. 35.

34 South Africa had supported Portuguese colonial authority.

35 The leader of the FNLA, Holden Roberto, was Mobutu's brother in law.

36 For background on this issue, go to *http://www.fhsmun.org/docs/GA3_self_determination.doc.*

37 Angola's population of approximately 13 million can be broken down as follows: Ovimbundu 37 per cent; Kimbundu 25 per cent; Bakongo 13 per cent; Mestiço (mixed European African) 2 per cent; European 1 per cent; Other: 20 per cent (including

Chokwe, Luena, and Ovambo). See *http://www.selfdetermine.org/conflicts/angola_body.html.*

38   See Meier K, *Angola: Promises and Lies.* London: Serif, 1996, p. 69.

39   Grant, *op. cit.*

40   Abel Chivukuvuku, cited in Matloff, *op. cit.*, p. 124.

41   As one journalist then noted: 'They're targeting the Bakongos and the Ovimbundu. At first they killed everyone whom they knew were UNITA. But then it got out of control and they went after anyone suspected of being UNITA. Anyone who had the wrong accent for this [making a gesture like a cleaver coming down on a neck]'. Cited in Matloff, *ibid*, p. 150.

42   Grant, *op cit.*

43   'Cabinda Separatists Call for an End to Hostilities', *UN IRIN*, 21 August 2002.

44   For details on the Cabindan position (and those of other so called 'unrepresented nations and peoples'), go to *http://www.unpo.org.*

45   See 'Focus on Cabinda Conflict', *UN IRIN*, 13 April 2003.

46   'Separatists to Stay Open to Talks over Cabinda.' *UN IRIN*, 13 April 2003.

47   A 44 member Constitutional Commission elected by the National Assembly according to proportional support in parliament was established in 1998 under the Lusaka Protocol to draft the constitution.

48   Lusaka Protocol, 15 November 1994.

49   The constitution writing process has been entrusted to a lawyer, Bornito de Sousa, who is chairman of the MPLA parliamentary group. See the web page of the Constitutional Committee *http://www.comissao constitucional.gv.ao/* and the web page of the Friedrich Ebert Foundation in Luanda *http://angola.fes international. de/* for further details.

50   This is the view of a number of Angolan specialists who convened at a SAIIA seminar held on the 3 June 2003.

51   The client based nature of the political system is indicated by the reliance of ministers and senior officials on patronage to survive, and a related lack of reform of the salary structures to break this dependency and means of operation. For example, the President officially earns $1,500 per month; the president of the National Assembly $1,200; and ministers and MPs around $900. These amounts are supplemented by handouts of houses, cars and financial 'gifts'.

52   At the time of independence, Angola was the world's largest producer of coffee, totalling 210,000 tonnes annually.

53   *Op. cit.*

54   See *http://www.angola.org/fasfacts/economic.html.*

55   Human Development Report 2002, *op. cit.*, p. 205.

56   Hodges, *op. cit.*, pp. 139-146.

57   Mackinlay J, *Globalisation and Insurgency.* Adelphi Paper 352, Oxford and London: OUP and IISS, 2002.

58   *Ibid*, p. 18.

59   Global Witness press release, 'Is the Price of Diamonds too High? How Angola's Return to War Has Been Financed by the International Diamond Trade', 14 December 1998.

60   Hodges, using a slightly different method to calculate, comes to a figure of $2 billion. Hodges, *op. cit.*, p. 152.

61   Currently the Angolan diamond business is monopolised by Ascorp, a joint venture between Sodiam and the Omega concern headed by Lev Leviev. Sodiam is, in turn, a wholly owned subsidiary of the State Diamond Agency, Endiama. The reported ending of the sole marketing and purchasing rights currently held by Ascorp, coupled with the successful conclusion of the outstanding court case involving a claim by De Beers against the Angolan state, would, in the opinion of industry experts, 'straighten out the Angolan diamond market'. However, there have been key vested institutional interests in retaining the current relationship, which has its origins in the leveraging of Angola's $6 billion debt to the Soviet Union (mainly for arms) which has reportedly been bought by diamond linked interests led by the Israeli based arms dealer Arkady Gaydamak for $800 million. See, for example, 'Whose Peace Anyway?', *Africa Confidential,* 43, 12, 14 June 2002; "Russian Roulette", *Africa Confidential,* 43, 2, 5 January 2002.

62   See, for example, Shaw M. 'The Middleman: War Supply Networks in Sierra Leone and Angola.' Unpublished SAIIA report for Clingendael, 2001.

63   United Nations, 'Report of the Panel of Experts on Violations of Security Council Sanctions Against UNITA' (S/2000/203), 10 March 2000.

64   In October 2003, Portuguese police seized a shipment of 338 kgs of cocaine which had been sent from Colombia via Luanda. See 'A Apreensao: Rede Planeava Introduzir 338 Quilos de Cocaína em Portugal', *Publico,* 3 October 2003 on *http:// jornal.publico.pt/ publico/2003/10/03/Sociedade/SO2.html.*

65   For a discussion of contemporary relations with Portugal, see Manuel Ferreira. 'Portugal and the Lusophone African Countries: Economic Discontinuities and Disruptions', *Portuguese Studies Review,* 10 (1) 2002, pp. 85-107.

66   These efforts were boosted by the launch in March 2003 of the SA Angola Chamber of Commerce, which aims to 'smooth the way for investment opportunities' between the two states, particularly in the areas of agriculture, retail and construction. Besides international investors in the mining and oil fields, SA business names

which have invested in Angola include SA Breweries, Grinaker LTA, Investec Bank, Securicor Gray and Shoprite. See 'Efforts to Rebuild Economy Receive a Boost', *UN IRIN*, 18 March 2003.

67 Today, Angola has more than 130 political parties, a result of an official policy by the Angolan government to finance the establishment of political parties. Only a few of these would pass the stringent test of the ballot box, and most exist only in name. However, this policy was overhauled in 1997 when the law governing the establishment of political parties was revised and a moratorium introduced on the registration of new organisations. Unfortunately, this hampers the establishment and organisation of legitimate civil society organisations. See *Angola Pre Election Assessment Report,* International Foundation for Election Systems, International Republican Institute & National Democratic Institute, March 2002, pp. 4, 12.

68 The Constitutional Commission was established in 1998, but has been suspended due to the delay in the election process, and due to UNITA's insistence on 'elections before a constitution'.

69 An estimated forty per cent of Angolans are Catholic, twelve per cent Protestant and the remainder 'animist' or adherents to local religious customs.

70 Discussion, Luanda, 5 September 2002.

71 See 'Angola's Choice', *op cit*, p. 11.

72 'Transparency Key to Long term Stability, ICG', *UN IRIN*, 8 April 2003. For details on the humanitarian and social challenges to peacebuilding see International Crisis Group (ICG), 'Dealing with Savimbi's Ghost: Angola's Peace Process at the Crossroads', 26 February 2003 on *http://icg@crisisweb.org*; and on the economic and political issues see ICG, 'Angola's Choice', *op. cit.*

73 'Angola's Choice', *ibid.*

74 'Savimbi's Ghost', *op. cit.*, p. 5.

75 'Angola's Choice', *op. cit.*, p. 1.

76 *Ibid*, p. 2.

77 The government has announced (though not implemented) a $20 million infrastructure programme for each of Angola's eighteen provinces (Cabinda, Zaïre, Uige, Lunda Norte, Lunda Sul, Moxico, Luanda, Bengo, Cuanza Norte, Cuanza Sul, Malanje, Bie, Huambo, Benguela, Namibe, Huila, Cuando Cubango and Cunene).

78 'Angola's Choice', *op. cit.*, p. 3.

79 Literally, 'We'll see'.

6

South Africa: the contrarian big African state

Tim Hughes

The inclusion of South Africa in a research project examining Africa's big dysfunctional states appears incongruous and misplaced. The contrast between South Africa and a number of the other states in this study could not be more pronounced. For example, in sharp contrast to the efforts of the governmental and state structures in the Democratic Republic of the Congo (DRC), Nigeria and Sudan to hold together the geographic integrity of the nation state, the 'grand apartheid' policy of the National Party government from the 1950s until the 1980s was to split the South African land mass into discrete geographic areas aimed at achieving a white dominated South Africa and ten 'independent' ethnic states. This was nominally achieved in four, namely Transkei, Bophuthatswana, Venda and Ciskei. Yet unlike the DRC, Nigeria and Sudan, contemporary South Africa is a largely coherent nation state exhibiting very little threat of balkanisation, or even formal federalist impulses.

Indeed, when viewed against the other countries in this study, South Africa is nowhere near a dysfunctional state even in global terms, let alone African ones. With forty five million citizens, the country certainly qualifies as a big African state as regards population, but it is also an incomparable economic giant. At 1,219,912 km², South Africa is a large geographic state, though far smaller in land mass than Algeria or Libya and only slightly larger than sparsely populated Namibia and Botswana. The country has a nominal GDP in excess of $213 billion, with an external debt of only some $46 billion. The per capita income of $2,974 is less impressive and the country remains one of the most unequal in the world with a Gini co efficient of 0.64[1]. GDP growth between 1994-2002 was a pedestrian 2.7 per cent annually. Recent trends have been more encouraging, however, with the country achieving 4.5 per cent growth in 2004 and touching 5.5 per cent in the second quarter of 2005.[2] Conversely, of acute concern is that South Africa has

dropped thirty five places on the UNDP Human Development Index since 1990 and is now ranked 119th out of 177 countries.

The political, business and economic ratings of South Africa compared to its African emerging market and global market peers in the tables below illustrate that South Africa has achieved relative success rather than dysfunctionality. Indeed South Africa accounts for some thirty two per cent of Africa's GDP measured on a purchasing power parity basis and thirty eight per cent at market exchange rates. Placed into perspective, its GDP is nearly four times that of the second largest African economy, Egypt. South Africa ranks 46th out of 158 countries on the 2005 Transparency International Corruption Perceptions Index. Botswana (32nd) Tunisia (43rd) and are the two highest ranking African countries.[3]

Table 6.1   Political, business and economic ratings of South Africa compared to
other African states

Long-term political rating

	Long-term political	Rank*	Trend
Mauritius	88.0	10	< >
South Africa	68.3	35	< >
Libya	63.0	46	< >
Tunisia	60.0	49	< >
Morocco	58.3	50	< >
Zambia	55.0	54	< >
Kenya	50.0	64	< >
Algeria	45.8	73	< >
Nigeria	32.5	85	< >
Côte d'Ivoire	30.8	86	–
Zimbabwe	21.7	87	< >
Regional Average	52.1		
Emerging Market Average	57.1		
Global Market Average	64.3		

Business environment rating

	Business environment	Rank*	Trend
South Africa	67.1	28	–
Tunisia	64.0	34	< >
Morocco	60.4	45	< >
Algeria	46.3	69	< >
Nigeria	45.5	72	< >
Zambia	44.5	75	< >
Kenya	43.7	78	< >
Côte d'Ivoire	25.3	83	–
Zimbabwe	19.5	84	< >
Regional Average	46.3		
Emerging Market Average	55.8		
Global Market Average	61.9		

Not ranked: Libya and Mauritius

Long-term economic rating

	Long-term economic	Rank*	Trend
South Africa	60.6	32	< >
Morocco	56.8	40	< >
Tunisia	54.8	46	< >
Algeria	52.9	53	< >
Kenya	47.1	67	< >
Côte d'Ivoire	45.2	71	–
Nigeria	36.8	79	< >
Zimbabwe	17.4	82	< >
Regional Average	46.5		
Emerging Market Average	53.3		
Global Market Average	58.4		
Not ranked: Libya, Mauritius and Zambia			

Trend arrows reflect two consecutive months of significant movement in the same direction.
* out of 94 global markets rated.
Sources: Business Monitor International Limited, *South Africa Quarterly Forecast Report, Report on Political Risk, Economic Performance and Outlook, and Key Economic Sectors, Q3 2003*, London.

These tables indicate a well performing state in the three key areas shown above, not only in relative African terms, but also when measured against South Africa's emerging market peer group. Furthermore, the post apartheid state can claim considerable success in a number of the key developmental areas.

Table 6.2 Post-1994: provision of services

Services	Period	Quantity
Households with clean water	1996	60%
	2001	85%
Access to sanitation	1994	49%
	2003	63%
Electricity connections	1996	32%
	2001	70%
Subsidised houses built	1994	
	2005	1,831,860

The above housing statistic needs to be placed in the context of the on going shortage of some 2.2 million low cost housing units and the recent outbreaks of urban unrest in the Western Cape and Gauteng in protest at slow housing and service delivery.

Primary school enrolment is now over ninety five per cent and secondary school enrolment has risen more than fifteen per cent to eighty five per cent of eligible children. Under a democratic government adult literacy has risen to eighty nine per cent and the pass rate for the school leaving matriculation certificate has risen to 68.3 per cent in 2005 (although this was down from the 73.3 per cent in 2003 and 70.7 per cent in 2004)[4]

Despite this progress, 5.3 million South African children are still severely deprived and frequently hungry, according to a written reply in the National Council of Provinces by the Minister of Social Welfare in September 2003. Of eighteen million children living in South Africa, 10.5 million are poor and suffer from severe deprivation.[5]

What then is the purpose and value of incorporating South Africa into the study? The principal reason is that South Africa exhibits a number of the variables characteristic of the dysfunctional big states analysed in the rest of this volume; yet it is a relatively successful big state. South Africa is a heterogeneous society with deep racial, ethnic and class cleavages. It has historically been a mineral/resource/ commodity dependent country. Its late twentieth century history was marked by acute political conflict and regional, low intensity civil war. The country experienced successive crises of popular leadership, principally owing to the fact that legitimate leaders of the black community were either incarcerated or in exile. The country was also subject to the most comprehensive international sanctions (including UN Charter Chapter 7 measures) and is still marked by the effects of the most thoroughgoing policies of social, political and economic engineering the continent has witnessed. Furthermore, South Africa may be regarded as approximating in some respects a post colonial society. More accurately, it may be regarded as now emerging from colonialism of a special type, although perhaps not for the analytic reasons given by the African National Congress (ANC) when in exile.[6]

Thus the value of including South Africa in the research programme is threefold. First, it serves to test the explanatory value of the variable and analysis of bigness used in the other country reports. Second, it offers some explanation of South Africa's relative success despite profound impediments. Third, an analysis of the performance of the South African state may lead to a re evaluation or refinement of the working hypothesis of the Big African States project.

Why is South Africa a relatively successful big African state?

The explanations suggested are perforce at a high level of generalisation, but still serve to highlight the contrast between South Africa and the other states examined in the study.

The effect of grand apartheid was disastrous from a human and economic perspective, yet in terms of the efficacy of the state apparatus, it was highly organised. The security, control and social engineering imperatives of the logic of apartheid resulted in and indeed necessitated a highly bureaucratised country, effectively administered in most respects of public and private life. That this policy eventually failed to achieve its objectives should not mask the fact that the country was intensively controlled by the successive incarnations of the Native Administration, Bantu Administration, Plural Administration and Urban Administration Boards. Under apartheid there was no township, no city, no border area and indeed very few rural areas where the state was not manifestly present. The social artificiality of apartheid demanded that the state administer and police its discriminatory legislation to ensure its implementation and adherence.

Thus, in a perverse manner, the apartheid state was effectively an administered state, not unlike a fascist state. Efforts in the 1980s to reform Black Local Authorities, and constitutional reform in 1983 and 1984 gave rise to a more active popular opposition movement which *inter alia* sought to make the townships 'ungovernable'. Yet despite the rapidly escalating cost of policing black townships and the watershed decision to bring the South African Defence Force (SADF) into a policing and domestic security role in 1984, at no point was South Africa 'ungoverned'. The South African state was never in danger of falling apart; nor was it defeated. The integrity of the geographically bounded area of South Africa was never threatened, internally or externally.

Furthermore South Africa does not fit the mould of a typical post colonial state. Despite declaring its constitutional and sovereign independence as a Republic only in 1961, the country had been effectively functioning as an independent state since 1910. It occupied a particularly ambiguous and uncomfortable position with regard to Britain and the Commonwealth after the National Party took office in 1948.

Importantly, South Africa has a domiciled European settler community that finds its roots in the seventeenth, eighteenth and nineteenth centuries. International repulsion and opprobrium caused by South Africa's domestic policies also limited opportunities for emigration and secondary citizenship of the 'settler' community. South Africa has significant, if proportionally reducing, European and Asian settler communities.

This proportionate population decrease can be ascribed to a lower birth rate than in black and coloured populations, and a consistent net emigration of whites. Nevertheless South Africa remains atypical as a post colonial society in that a significant proportion of its population is non African in origin, yet remains domiciled. Furthermore, the South African 'settler' community did not follow the typical post colonial emigration pattern of asset stripping and razing before returning to the colonial metropole. On the contrary, the overwhelming majority of whites, Asians and Coloureds have remained in the country since the transition commenced in 1990. Despite greater access to international employment opportunities since 1994, Afrikaners still have no other claim to statehood and citizenship than South Africa. The English speaking, Portuguese and Indian communities have a more ambiguous national identity, yet have largely remained (and indeed often prospered) in South Africa.

A further departure from the colonial model is that the economic formation of South Africa did not follow the purely 'extraction of raw materials' patterns common in the other cases. Particularly during the 1970s (with the assistance of extensive international bank loans), South Africa successfully built up an infrastructure that has facilitated both industrial development and relatively effective spatial and financial administration. At times this was driven by perceived or real security and strategic concerns: the extensive infrastructural programmes of the 1970s included the building of highways, docks and airports to support military imperatives. The development of the heavy iron and steel manufacturing facility ISCOR; of oil from coal technology through SASOL; the controversial MOSSGAS project off the southern Cape coast; and the Atlantis Diesel Engine Facility on the Cape West Coast were all examples of attempts at import substitution and state driven industrial growth. The imposition of sanctions, particularly military ones, against South Africa gave rise to an industrial sector that attempted increasing self sufficiency. Perhaps as important, sanctions spurred a growth in tertiary study of engineering, applied mathematics, chemistry and physics. The development of a small nuclear weapon capability was the symbolic peak of this programme of strategic and military self reliance.

For both ideological and pragmatic reasons the apartheid state also identified itself with, and measured itself against, the 'West', and in particular the United States, Europe and (to a lesser degree) Australasia. Thus excellence was often taken to mean a degree of technological, banking, or insurance sophistication, the possession of a fleet of modern aircraft, or the building of high rise office blocks. This mirrored the achievements of Western allied states and reinforced both the reality and the myth of South Africa's relative sophistication. Indeed for much of the post 1974 period, the major task the apartheid state set itself with respect to the international community was to convince it of the strategic and ideological importance of supporting the 'God fearing and anti communist' South African state. Successive apartheid regimes can claim the success of this strategy with some justification until the end of the Reagan and Thatcher eras.

Why didn't South Africa fall apart during its transition?

The first reason South Africa weathered its political transformation successfully is the irony that, despite decades of forced separation, the country had begun to show signs of weaving a progressively more integrated social and economic fabric. Simply put, race based legislation that ran counter to powerful economic and social imperatives became unsustainable. During the late 1970s and 1980s, for example, the pressure of urbanisation and the demands of the contemporary economy caused the progressive erosion and undermining of the Group Areas Act. Finally, such policy became unsustainable and un policeable, and thus fell apart, ending decades of urban influx control legislation. Furthermore, commencing in 1976 but intensifying markedly from 1983 onwards, the state security apparatuses were forced to expend greater sums on controlling internal social and political rebellion for ever diminishing political returns. By the late 1980s the ruling National Party had lost any claim to moral leadership and legitimacy, lacked ideological vision and had reached a position of policy uncertainty and increasing dysfunctionality.

The second reason for South Africa's survival of its transition was that both the domestic and the exiled political leadership recognised that South Africa was in danger of decaying into a state of internecine conflict from which it would not recover, and that the alternatives, such as a negotiated peace, although politically costly, were potentially more beneficial for the country in the long run. A negotiated settlement held the potential reward of a country whose social fabric and economy, although profoundly damaged, could be resuscitated in the medium term. In short, the risks of not reforming and democratising began to outweigh those of doing so. To be sure, unique and conjunctional forces, including the global failure of state socialism and the stroke suffered by PW Botha in January 1989, were crucial in creating a space within which the political protagonists could conceive of new opportunities and prepare to take risks. A key element in South Africa's trajectory towards transition was pragmatic and prescient leaders on both sides, who seized the opportunities presented.

After the period of negotiations and particularly after the launching of the

Convention for a Democratic South Africa (CODESA) in 1991, all mainstream political leaders were successful in persuading their constituencies to follow them to the ballot box three years later. This despite the often tendentious position adopted by Chief Mangosuthu Buthelezi of the Inkatha Freedom Party (IFP), until the success of eleventh hour negotiations brokered, *inter alia*, by Thabo Mbeki and the promise of international arbitration brought the KwaZulu Natal based party to the elections in 1994. Furthermore, black leaders, particularly from the ANC, exhibited remarkable restraint and pragmatism in times of crisis and provocation, such as the spate of train and township attacks led by state sponsored third forces. At the time of the assassination of South African Communist Party (SACP) leader, Chris Hani, in 1993, the qualities of charismatic leaders such as Nelson Mandela and Tokyo Sexwale brought the country back from the brink of political collapse. Religious leaders such as Archbishop Desmond Tutu and Dr Beyers Naude also played a crucial role during the period of heightened tension in the early 1990s.

At the leadership level, however it was the nation building achievements of Nelson Mandela during the political transition that were decisive. Until 1990, for most people in South Africa, Mandela was either a demon or a mythical figure. Yet by the end of the 1990s, he had become an iconic and unifying figure for all but the most reactionary. An astute politician imbued with vast charisma, Mandela more than any other political leader succeeded in conveying a message of tolerance, forbearance, forgiveness and reconciliation, whilst at the same time holding together a fractious party and a deeply divided country. During the 1990s Mandela was as comfortable addressing a gathering of Afrikaners as he was in addressing a COSATU congress. His personal charm, sincerity, integrity and exemplary behaviour also ensured that big business in South Africa (relieved that the banks, mining and industry had not been nationalised) responded to Mandela's injunctions with public gestures of funding for foundations, charities, schools and clinics.

The third significant reason for national cohesion was successful indigenous institution building and transformation. The common factors in the transformation of institutions were inclusiveness and negotiation. These principles led to the eventual success of CODESA and the Transitional Executive Council, which ran parallel to the tricameral government prior to 1994. Even the interim constitution, which applied until May 1996, was imbued with the ethics of reconciliation, nation building, inclusiveness and tolerance. The constitutionally entrenched Chapter 9 institutions such as the Human Rights Commission have been alluded to earlier, but other institutions, not constitutionally entrenched, have also played a central role in ensuring that South Africa held together and retained functionality. At the political level the operation of a Government of National Unity, no matter how flawed, served as an important bridging mechanism for the country's politicians and policymakers. At the level of social justice, the role of Truth and Reconciliation Commission (TRC) was vital. Whilst the TRC did not expose all apartheid's atrocious truths, it did provide a forum for truth telling, for healing and for an element of restorative justice. At the economic level the establishment of the National Economic Development and Labour Council (NEDLAC) provided an important corporatist forum in which business, labour, civil society and the government could hammer out economic policy principles. The most tense and vexed of the institutional transformations has been the amalgamation of the disparate forces of South Africa's national defence force, those of the so called independent homelands, and those of the liberation movements. Transformation in the security forces effectively eliminated the threat of a military coup and of so called counter revolutionary activity against the democratically elected government of the day.

Areas of policy dysfunctionality

A distinction has to be made between state dysfunctionality and governmental policies that may lead to poorer performance, or a failure to carry out duties. In no sense can South Africa be regarded as a dysfunctional state in the mould of the DRC, Angola or Sudan. However, if the interpretation of dysfunctionality is extended to degrees of poor performance and implementation of state policy, South Africa has a mixed, and at times a paradoxical record. Four areas of public policy - the economy/employment, land affairs, health and crime - will be briefly examined in this chapter. These areas are, by definition, cardinal to the country's development; but they also serve to illustrate a number of the functional/ dysfunctional dichotomies that permeate contemporary South Africa.

The economy

In no other sphere is the dichotomy of South Africa's mixed performance more acutely manifest than in economic policy. However, before embarking on an analysis of the functioning of the South African economy and related public policy, it is important to recap what the post 1990 economy inherited. The newly elected government did not start with a blank sheet; rather, it took over an economy riven by acute structural constraints, dysfunctionalities and asymmetries.[7]

In broad terms, the pre 1994 white government had pursued an economic policy that had favoured commodity exports (particularly minerals) and a programme of import substitution. Comprehensive tariff barriers and import quotas had protected local industry. This, together with the forced isolation of the South African economy by sanctions which denied it free access to global markets, had spawned a heavy manufacturing industry which specialised in such fields as mining engineering, iron and steel, chemicals and motor manufacturing.

Economic self sufficiency was an objective forced on South African industry as a result of sanctions and boycotts. By the mid 1960s the South African economy had begun to show signs of declining momentum, and the benefits of import substitution had been all but played out. The effective foreclosures of, or moratoria on, South Africa's international bank loans from 1985 onwards effectively set a limit on South Africa's growth and severely constrained its balance of payments flexibility.

The progressive decline in South African economic growth and subsequent recovery under a democratic dispensation is indicated below.

Table 6.3 South Africa's average annual GDP growth (%)

1960s	5.7
1970s	3.3
1980s	1.5
1990–1993	-0.4
1994–2002	2.8
2003-2005	3.8

Source: Bruggemans C, Change of Pace: South Africa's Economic Revival. Johannesburg: Wits University Press, 2003, p.22. and South African Reserve Bank Quarterly Bulletins

The legacy of inequality was, however, the most threatening long term problem for the newly elected government. This is illustrated below.

Table 6.4 Composition of income quintiles by race, 1990

	Q1% (High)	Q2%	Q3%	Q4%	Q5% (Low)	Total %
Black	2	10	23	31	34	100
Coloured	8	28	33	20	12	100
Asian	17	36	27	12	8	100
White	51	30	12	5	3	101

Source: Bruggemans C, *Change of Pace: South Africa's Economic Revival.* Johannesburg: Wits University Press, 2003, p.26.

As Marais has noted, when the ANC was unbanned in 1990, it had no coherently defined economic policy.[8] Later in 1990, the newly formed ANC Department of Economic Policy developed a 'Discussion Document on Economic Policy', which identified a need for the 'restructuring of the economy' and saw the state as playing a central role in planning industrial development that would overcome historical racial, gender and geographical imbalances. The financial services sector came in for special scrutiny, as it was perceived as fostering and encouraging short term speculation and profiteering at the expense of infrastructural investment. The overarching impulse of the document can be described as one of 'growth through redistribution'. There followed a robust and intensive debate amongst economists, business unions and activists about the document and, more broadly, about what the appropriate economic development model for South Africa should be. In essence the only agreement that could be found was the need for fundamental rethinking of the system adopted during the preceding decade. The growth through redistribution formulation eventually found expression in the ANC's RDP (Reconstruction and Development Programme) and was both popular and populist. Yet even under the Mandela presidency the office of the RDP and its minister, former COSATU leader Jay Naidoo, did not prosper and was eventually disbanded.

In 1996, under considerable international pressure, the government inverted its economic strategy moving from growth through redistribution to 'redistribution through growth' in launching its Growth Employment and Redistribution (GEAR) strategy. It is against GEAR that current government economic policy and performance should be measured.

The broad policy objectives of GEAR were to achieve higher economic growth and job creation, whilst enhancing redistribution in favour of the poor through improved provision of social services and infrastructure. This required the economy to become more competitive and outward orientated, which, in turn, was to be achieved through a growth in exports other than gold and in private and public fixed investment. The need for greater labour absorption was also identified. In order to bring about the necessary structural changes, South Africa had to become more competitive in the export sector, exhibit greater labour market fluidity, and develop its supply of skilled labour. Accordingly, a number of different policy proposals were made. These included a speeding up of the budget deficit reduction rate, a more distributive direction of state spending and a gradual relaxation of exchange controls. Furthermore, and controversially, there was to be consistent monetary policy to contain inflation, with the rand being kept to a relatively low trade weighted rate. Trade reform measures included a reduction in tariffs; tax incentives to stimulate investment; increased privatisation; the imposition of training levies; and the forging of a social agreement to moderate prices and wages.

Significantly, GEAR set itself a number of targets for the period 1996-2000, which allow us to measure the government's relative success or failure. They are summarised below.

Table 6.5 GEAR objectives: Prior, targeted and actual, 1996–2000

Policy objective (annual average)	Prior to GEAR	Target GEAR	Actual
Export growth	6.9%	8.4%	6.6%
Real private investment	5.6%	11.7%	2.4%
Real public investment	2.7%	7.6%	3.8%
Real GDP growth	2.8%	4.2%	2.5%
CPI Inflation	9.5%	8.2%	6.7%
Current account deficit (% of GDP)	1.4%	2.4%	1.0%
Private wage growth	1.4%	0.8%	2.5%
Formal job growth	1.0%	2.9%	-0.3%
New formal jobs (in thousands)	104.0	270.0	-30.0

Source: Bruggemans C, *Change of Pace: South Africa's Economic Revival*. Johannesburg: Wits University Press, 2003, p.63.

As can be seen from the above, almost all targets were missed, some badly. Those that were achieved, such as a reduction in the current account deficit and inflation targeting, were economically conservative in nature, and went hand in hand with the relatively low growth rates achieved. Most tellingly however, real private investment was one quarter of the targeted range, and formal job growth numbers shrank. Despite the value of the currency reducing by a full twenty per cent between 1995 and 2000, South African exporters were unable to exploit the attendant opportunities to the full. Poor export performance was further affected by the 1997-1998 Asian economic crisis.

The unwelcome outcome of the GEAR programme gave rise to the term 'jobless growth'. The medium term scenario painted by GEAR envisioned faster GDP growth that would create 1.4 million jobs, an increase from some 6.8 million to 8.2 million, during the period 1996 2000. In the event, the number of formally employed people dropped to 6.7 million during the same period because some 1.5 million jobs were shed during that time. This reduction can be explained by a number of factors, including the natural attrition of previously sheltered positions, greater productive efficiency driven by capital intensive investment, and (perhaps most threatening), the effect of greater international competition driven by globalisation and the impact of South Africa's re entry into the international economic, financial and trading community.

The social consequences of the decline in formal employment are likely to be serious, and therefore play a significant role in any assessment of South Africa's functionality and policy effectiveness.

During the period under review, relatively high wage gains were recorded by the formally employed sector, which meant that fewer people were earning more. In contrast, between 1990 and 2001 non agricultural employment fell by twenty per cent to a point lower than it was twenty years ago. The formal commercial agriculture sector lost 750,000 jobs between 1994-1996. Furthermore, real GNP was lower in 2001 than it was in 1973.

Table 6.6 Unemployment trends (percentages)

	1994	1995	1996	1997	1998	1999	2000	2001	2002
Strict definition	20.0	16.9	19.3	21.0	25.2	23.3	25.8	29.5	30.5
Broad definition	28.6	26.5	34.9	38.9	37.5	36.2	35.9	41.5	41.8

Source: Altman M, 'The state of employment', in Daniel J, Habib A & R Southall (Eds), *State of the Nation – South Africa 2004–2005*. Pretoria: HSRC Press, 2005, p. 425.

In 2002, 36.8 per cent of the African population was unemployed, as compared with just over twenty one per cent of Coloureds and Asians. Some six per cent of whites were unemployed. In terms of the broad definition, some fifty eight per cent of rural women were unemployed. Joblessness is particularly acute amongst the younger generations: seventy five per cent of the unemployed are under thirty five, and of those under the age of thirty, some seventy three per cent have never worked.

This does not show the full picture, however. Growth in the informal employment sector has been dramatic, up from 450,000 in 1997 to 2.2 million by 2002. This includes an increase of some 200,000 domestic workers. However, some problems in obtaining data on informal employment must be acknowledged. For example, the Labour Force Survey of 2000 recorded 960,000 subsistence agricultural workers, but then reported a plunge to 360,000 the following year.

Land reform

At the time of the Lancaster House agreement on Zimbabwe's independence, some twenty three per cent of land in Zimbabwe was owned by whites. The figure for current white land ownership in South Africa is between sixty and seventy per cent. Even the president of the white dominated AgriSA has added his voice to those who emphasise the untenable nature of the current dispensation.[9] A keystone of grand apartheid (although it preceded National Party rule by some thirty five years) was race based land reservation. This was accompanied by segregation. Under successive provisions of discriminatory land legislation, some 470,000 people were removed from so called 'black spots' into the thirteen per cent of the South African land mass reserved for blacks. Even today some thirty two per cent of the South African population lives in that portion of land specifically set aside by successive white governments exclusively for black usage. Another statistic of importance is that some seventy per cent of South Africa's poor still live in rural areas.

Land reform commenced shortly after the unbanning of the anti apartheid movements in 1990. There are three major elements to land reform in South Africa. First, land restitution is designed to restore land ownership (or provide compensation) to those who were dispossessed without adequate repayment by racially discriminatory practices after 1913. Second, land redistribution seeks to provide the disadvantaged and poor with access to land for residential and productive purposes. Third, land tenure reform covers two main areas: the tenure of more than seven million farm dwellers living on 65,000 (mainly white) commercial farms, and the rights of some twelve million people living in the former Bantustans nominally owned by the state.[10] A raft of reformist legislation followed the political liberalisation of 1990, including the 1991 Abolition of Racially Based Land Measures Act, repealing the 1913 and 1936 Land Acts, and the 1966 Group Areas Act. A Commission on Land Allocation was established to examine the treatment and handling of land restitution.

Significantly too, the 1993 Interim Constitution recognised entitlement to land as a constitutional right. Even more significant than the scrapping of discriminatory land ownership and usage practices was the vital debate that took place during the 1990s on the nature of land restitution. 'A major transformation of the whole legal system' was required to restore land ownership where possible.[11] With considerable assistance and advice from the World Bank, South Africa developed a land reform programme. Its main objectives are to:

- redress the injustices of apartheid;
- foster national reconciliation;
- support economic growth; and
- improve household welfare and alleviate poverty.[12]

Moreover, the 1996 South African Constitution entrenches three fundamental rights relevant to land reform:

- Section 25 (5): 'The state must take reasonable legislative and other measures within its available resources to foster conditions which enable citizens to gain access to land on an equitable basis';
- Section 25 (6): 'A person or community whose tenure of lend is legally insecure as a result of past racially discriminatory laws or practices is entitled, to the extent provided by an Act of Parliament, either to tenure which is legally secure or to comparable redress'; and
- Section 25 (7): 'A person or community dispossessed of property after 19 June 1913 as a result of past racially discriminatory laws is entitled, to the extent proved by an Act of Parliament, either to restitution of that property or to equitable redress'.

Despite these progressive constitutional provisions and legislation to support them, the implementation of land reform under the democratic state has been relatively poor. Whereas the RDP promised the redistribution of thirty per cent of South African land, the reality is that, by the end of 2001, only some two per cent of land had been transferred from white to black ownership. By 2004, of 68,878 restitution claims received, only 43,000 had been settled. The majority of the restitution claims met were for urban dwellers, with more than forty per cent receiving cash compensation rather than land. This benefited a mere 40,000 people. Of a targeted 25.5 million hectares, by 2004 less than half a million had been transferred. Despite the government's avowed commitment to transfer thirty per cent of land to black ownership by 2015 mentioned above, at current rates it will take 150 years to complete the restitution process and 125 to redistribute thirty per cent of land from white to black ownership.

A number of issues have hampered the land reform programme. The first is budgetary. Despite a marked increase in the amount allocated for land reform in 2003, the less than two per cent of the national budget allocated by the treasury to land acquisition is inadequate to meet the demand. Another critical and related area undermining the capacity of the state to act on its promise of land reform within the target dates is the 'willing seller–willing buyer' principle. In reality, whilst this protects the rights of the seller, it also allows for widespread abuse. Sellers are sometimes inclined to massage and inflate the price of their land once it is known that it has been designated for restitution. Such recalcitrance and abuse of the willing seller willing buyer principle led the government to announce its first land expropriations in 2005. Furthermore, post settlement aid provided to landless people who have been resettled is simply inadequate. The levels at which grants are provided are too low. On a more technical issue, the Department of Land Affairs has been short sighted in not providing adequate agricultural support (tractors, harvesters, ploughs, seed, and threshers) to ensure that the land acquired can be farmed in a sustainable manner. There are also acute disjunctures between the land usage patterns of commercial farmers (the previous owners) and those of peasant and communal farmers.

Whilst this failure of policy implementation has not resulted in anything like the state sponsored land invasions of Zimbabwe, the warning signs persist. For example, in June and July 2001 informal settlers from the Bredell camp invaded adjoining farmland. Members of the Pan Africanist Congress opportunistically set up tables at entry points to the land and 'sold' parcels of land to squatters at a nominal fee. The Secretary General of the PAC took this opportunity to publicise the plight of the squatters and to illustrate the dangers of ignoring the ticking time bomb represented by the landless in South Africa. The message conveyed to the South African authorities could not have been clearer or more public, and the spectacle of the new democratic South African government seeking recourse from the law courts to remove the illegal squatters was replete with historical and political irony. Later the same year squatters and other landless people took the opportunity to publicise their plight at the World Summit against Racism.

Responding to this crisis in land restitution claims, the Department of Land Affairs instituted a 2001-2002 Strategic Plan, which has resulted in an increased budgetary allocation and a number of shifts in policy. Yet recent research suggests continued underperformance and policy failure.[13] In short, South Africa's land reform policy remains essentially dysfunctional.

Crime

If South Africa ranks incomparably higher than most African countries on all developmental indices and better than most emerging economies, the criterion for which it has developed an unenviable reputation is that of being one of the countries of the world most prone to violent crime. Between 1994 and 2000 violent crime increased by thirty four per cent, property crime by twenty three per cent and commercial crime by nine per cent. South Africa has the highest per capita rate of murder with a firearm in the world, the second highest number of manslaughters, the second highest rape rate, the fourth highest murder rate, the second highest assault rate, the fourth highest burglary rate and the fourth highest robbery rate. Overall, South Africa is the fifth most crime ridden country in the world.[14]

Figure 6.1 Comparative international murder rates

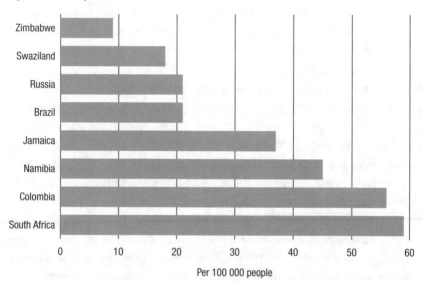

Per 100 000 people

Source: Institute for Security Studies, 'What is the state of crime in South Africa?', *Criminal Justice Monitor*. Online at http://www.iss.co.za/CJM/ CrimeinSA.html.

The purpose of this study is not to explain why South Africa has such high crime rates. But a number of associated factors bear mention, as they are salient to the question of dysfunctionality in state policy. First, however, the question of crime statistics requires clarification. It has been argued by analysts that crime statistics in South Africa since 1994 provide a clearer picture than was the case under the apartheid state, and thus the true situation 'on the ground' has not deteriorated as sharply as the raw statistics would suggest. The perception that since the demise of the apartheid state there has been an explosion of violent crime may therefore not be accurate. Crime, it is argued, is simply now more widely reported by the victims.

The most obvious factor explaining violent crime in South Africa is the legacy of institutional, political and gangster violence that characterised the apartheid years. The brutality of the apartheid police force was increasingly met in the 1970s and 1980s by equally unbridled anti state behaviour, as well as violence carried out by and against township dwellers. A generation of young South Africans have grown up on a cocktail of social and political turmoil, poor education, civil disobedience, chronic unemployment and structural poverty. Firearms are easily obtained in South African townships, and ever since the more permissive dispensation of the early 1990s, drug cartels that were previously excluded have found South African cities and townships fertile ground for their trade. Additionally, organised crime syndicates have flourished in towns and cities. A full twenty to twenty five per cent of them have regional connections that feed into the burgeoning car hijacking syndicates. Apart from criminal activity, the newly democratic South Africa experienced a wave of urban terrorism perpetrated by the former vigilante movement, People Against Gangsters and Drugs (PAGAD), from 1996 onwards. PAGAD was successfully tackled only in 2000.[15] Indeed the growth of vigilantism in South Africa is a clear manifestation of social frustration at the failure of the government's anti crime policy. A confluence of South Africa's crime, social and health crises is shockingly manifest in the increasingly common phenomenon of child rape perpetrated by HIV carriers in the belief that having sex with a virgin will cure them of the disease.

Regardless of whether or not there has been better, or more widespread, crime reporting, the state has failed to curb serious crime in South Africa. Trust and confidence in the state and security apparatuses have been further eroded by the failure of the Department of Safety and Security to release crime statistics for a full twelve month period, on the grounds that they were unreliable. If it is axiomatic that the first responsibility of the state is to protect the lives, well being and property of its citizens, then in this regard South African state policy is at least dysfunctional.

Furthermore, there is a strongly held view that the public and criminal prosecutorial system is in decay, resulting in low levels of convictions, sinking morale and high levels of corruption. The relatively poor rate of convictions is demonstrated in figure 6.2 (page 174).

A number of key statistics highlight the problem. Between 2001 and 2002 there was a forty seven per cent increase in the number of criminal cases referred to court. During 2002 some 1.1 million cases were referred to court yet only 403,000 cases were finalised with a verdict. Between 1996 and 2002 some two million cases

Figure 6.2   Number of prosecutions, convictions, cases to court and crime recorded (1992–2000)

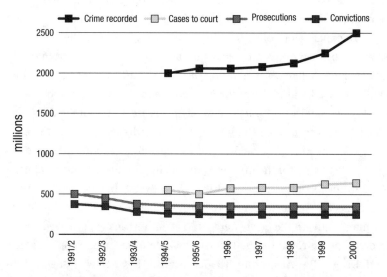

Source: Institute for Security Studies, 'National Prosecuting Authority Statistics, *Criminal Justice Monitor*. Online at http://www.iss.co.za/CJM/Justice.html

referred to court were withdrawn by prosecutors, translating into a massive waste of time and scarce resources. The major reason for cases being withdrawn is the delay in bringing the cases to trial. The constitution provides that accused are entitled to have their case heard without undue delay. The backlog of outstanding lower court cases stood at some 200,000 in 2002. The former Director of Public Prosecutions, Bulelani Ngcuka stated that already in 2000 the backlog of cases would take two years to clear, excluding new cases.[16]

Whilst insignificant in statistical terms, farm murders have been regarded as a particular litmus test for understanding crime and racial conflict in South Africa. Farm killings are a particularly vexed and potentially divisive crime because they have often been conflated with racist attacks on whites, and have therefore had particular resonance. The common argument is that South Africa is 'heading the way of Zimbabwe'. It is thus worth reflecting on the latest report into farm killings in South Africa. In the period 1991-2001 some 6,122 attacks were carried out on South African farms, resulting in the deaths of 1,254 people. During 2001, 1,011 attacks were carried out, resulting in the deaths of 147 people. In that year some sixty two per cent of victims were white and thirty three per cent black. Given the high proportion of farms owned by whites this ratio is not extraordinary. In the same year twelve per cent of all female victims of farm attacks were raped: seventy one per cent of these were black. Firearms were used in some sixty four per cent of cases. Most of the perpetrators of farm attacks were black, unemployed and aged between 18 and 35.

After a spate of complaints and protests by agricultural unions, the National Commissioner of Police instituted a Committee of Inquiry into farm attacks. The findings of the Committee were far from conclusive, but they did serve to challenge some conventionally held views that these were politically motivated or race based, and that they were part of a planned assault on white land ownership in response to the desperate shortage of black owned farm land. Where the evidence was clear, in eighty nine per cent of cases robbery constituted the main motive for the attack. In seven per cent of cases intimidation was the aim, and in only two per cent of cases did the attacks have a political objective. Thus, whilst the victims of farm attacks are overwhelmingly white, there is little *prima facie* evidence that such violence forms part of a more premeditated or political strategy.

Recent crime statistics released by the Department of Safety and Security paint a less catastrophic picture in areas of crime, leading to suggestions that South Africa may have 'turned the corner' in the fight against crime. This is illustrated below:

Figure 6.3 Total recorded crime rate in SA, 1994/95

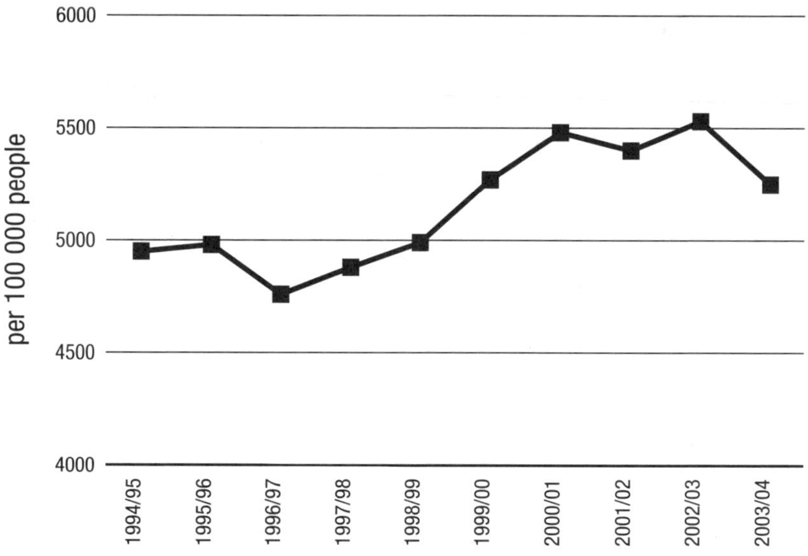

Source: SAPS Annual Report 2003/04

Figure 6.4 Changes in recorded violent crime rates, 2002/03–2003/04

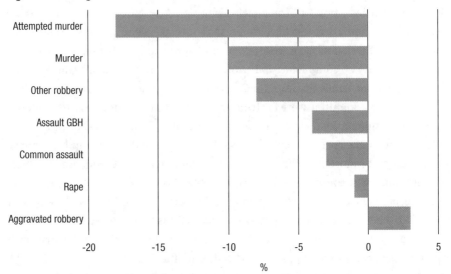

Source: SAPS Annual Report 2003/04

Furthermore there has been success in specialised courts such as those dealing with commercial and white collar crime. A number of high profile fraud and corruption prosecutions in 2005 strengthened the conviction of the prosecutorial authorities and assisted in restoring public trust in the criminal justice system. Particular success has been achieved by the Directorate of Special Operations and in particular the so called Scorpions Unit. However, the very success of this unit and the manner in which it has sometimes conducted its business (as well as political pressure, institutional clashes and jealousies within the South African Police Service) prompted the State President to establish a commission of enquiry (Khampepe Commission) into the mandate and location of the DSO. The specific issue under examination is whether the DSO and Scorpions ought to retain its independent investigative and prosecutorial role or to be incorporated within the South African Police Service.[17]

Health policy

The provision of basic health care is a key criterion both of a country's level of development and of state performance. Once again in the South African case, the record of implementation is mixed. At one end of the spectrum, in the case of

HIV/Aids treatment policy, state performance is not only dysfunctional, but catastrophic. Whilst South Africans have been getting healthier and living longer since 1960 and infant mortality rates have dropped from eighty nine per thousand to fifty six per thousand, racial inequalities in health care are entrenched. Furthermore, South Africans are particularly affected by a number of health epidemics. The South African tuberculosis (TB) rate remains one of the highest in the world, and the population of the country's northern regions is persistently plagued by malaria.

Almost half of southern Africa's 275,000 TB cases are found in South Africa. TB infection is increasingly linked to HIV status in the sub region: South Africa has a TB infection rate of 419 per 100,000 people, with thirty three per cent of these likely to be HIV positive. South Africa is also confronted by the emergence of drug resistant strains of TB. Chemotherapy treatment for patients with drug resistant TB costs some hundred times more than chemotherapy for the more benign strains. The state's response to the TB epidemic remains both inadequate and ineffective. The Medical Research Council (MRC) estimates that, should spending on TB treatment not increase significantly, the epidemic will continue unabated. This will translate into 3.5 million new cases over the next decade, and some 90,000 patients dying from the disease. The financial implications of ineffective or no treatment are profound. Although some R700 million ($100 million) is currently being spent on TB treatment in South Africa annually, should current infection rates continue, an estimated $3 billion would be required to treat the number of infected patients over the next decade. Given the link between TB and HIV/Aids, it is estimated that the roll out of an effective HIV/Aids treatment campaign could reduce TB infections by 1.7 million cases, and save the state some $400 million in treatment costs.[18]

It is the government's policy on HIV/Aids, however, that is by any measure the most dysfunctional. The social implications of ineffective policy in this context are unnecessary pain, suffering, poverty, social and economic dislocation, resort to crime and finally, death. There could be no more profound failure of policy.

As former president Nelson Mandela recently noted,

> South Africans are beyond arguments about statistics or debates about causality and controversies about the relative efficacy of medication ... Aids is clearly a disaster, effectively wiping out the development gains of the past decades and sabotaging the future ... The fight against Aids will indeed require another social revolution.[19]

Prior to September 2001, South African HIV/Aids infection statistics were notoriously unreliable. However, the publication of the Technical Report of the Burden of Disease Research Unit of the Medical Research Council on *The Impact of HIV/Aids on Adult Mortality in South Africa* provided an unequivocal assessment. In summary the report found that:

> While there is inevitably some degree of uncertainty because of the assumptions underlying both the model and the interpretation of the empirical data, we estimate that about 40% of the adult deaths aged 15-49 that occurred in the year 2000 were due to HIV/Aids and that about 20% of all adult deaths in that year were due to Aids. When this is combined with the excess deaths in childhood, it is estimated that Aids accounted for about 25% of all deaths in the year 2000 and has become the single biggest cause of death. The projections show that, without treatment to prevent Aids, the number of Aids deaths can be expected to grow, within the next 10 years, to more than double the number of deaths due to all other causes, resulting in 5 to 7 million cumulative Aids deaths in South Africa by 2010. [20]

Aids is South Africa's most common cause of death, even in a country with the world's highest homicide rate. Too often the HIV/Aids catastrophe is depicted in clinical statistical terms, without attention being paid to the social and economic consequences of the pandemic. Yet a handful of statistics bears reiteration. South Africa has 5.3 million HIV positive citizens. Six hundred South Africans die every day from Aids. Some twenty eight per cent of 25-29 year olds in South Africa are HIV positive. Amongst women this rate is thirty two per cent, that is, more than one quarter to a third of the country's most productive population cohort. Amongst 30-34 year olds the HIV infection rate is twenty four per cent. Some six per cent of 2-14 year olds are HIV positive, with a significant number of these vertically infected, that is from mother to child. In South Africa infection rates are higher amongst women than men, and women remain most at risk. Racial variations show that infection amongst Africans (18.4%) is far higher than whites and Coloureds (6%). Asian infection rates are less than two per cent. Whilst little correlation has been found between HIV infection rates and employment/unemployment levels,[21] infection rates are much lower in the higher socio economic classes.

Despite this and the fact that his own spokesperson died of Aids, President Mbeki stated in an interview with *The Washington Post* in September 2003 that he knew of nobody who had died of Aids. On the same occasion Mbeki claimed that the country 'does not have the health infrastructure to make these (antiretroviral) drugs available to whoever needs them'.[22] This economy with the truth is an attempt to avoid facing the country's greatest challenge for the future. The essence of the government's argument against the use of antiretroviral therapy is based on three premises. First, antiretrovals are both toxic and ineffective. Second, the country lacks the medical infrastructure to administer such drugs in a sustainable manner. Third, such treatment is too costly. The failure of the state to provide antiretroviral drugs and indeed its active prevention of their distribution has been at the heart of many of the battles fought between it and civil society groups.

The Centre for Social Research at the University of Cape Town has recently published the findings of a research programme which examined the government's failure to provide a comprehensive programme for the treatment of HIV/Aids, including the use of antiretroviral drugs. The research method used constructs models for the treatment of HIV/Aids using three scenarios, and estimates the financial/economic costs (rather than human costs) for each.[23] Scenario one outlines the cost of state treatment of opportunistic infections only. Scenario two includes both prevention interventions and treatment of opportunistic infections. Scenario three adds the use of antiretroviral drugs to the scenario two programme. A summary of the findings of the research project is provided below.

Table 6.7 Cost of public hospitalisation for people with HIV under the three scenarios (R bn)

	2002	2003	2004	2005	2006	2007	2010	2015
Scenario 1	24	28	31	34	36	37	36	32
Scenario 2	24	27	31	34	35	36	35	27
Scenario 3	24	27	29	30	30	30	29	26

Table 6.8 Total cost of Scenario 3 (including infrastructure and education) and as a percentage of GNP (R bn)

Year	2002	2003	2004	2005	2006	2007	2010	2015
Scenario 3	0.6	1.6	3.3	5.6	8.4	11.0	17.1	20.3
GNP	1,012	1,033	1,053	1,074	1,096	1,118	1,140	1,163
Scenario 3 as % of GNP	0.1	0.2	0.3	0.5	0.8	1.0	1.5	1.7

The research findings suggest that far from being unable to afford the provision of a comprehensive HIV/Aids treatment programme with the use of antiretrovirals, the state would find the third option the most economical of all the scenarios, not to mention the most humane. Whilst an increase in health expenditure is required for scenario three, a report recently commissioned by the World Health Organisation (WHO) has concluded that it is realistic for low to middle income countries to increase their health expenditure by one per cent of GDP by 2007 and by two per cent by 2015.

More positively, however, in April 2003, despite the chaotic state of elements of the health services, the government announced that it would implement a national programme for the free supply of antiretrovirals. The 'Operational Plan for Comprehensive Treatment and Care for HIV/Aids' was approved by Cabinet in November. It envisaged that within a year, there would be at least one antiretroviral service point in every health district across the country, and within five years, one service point in every local municipality. It aims to have 1.4 million people on treatment within five years. The programme finally, and slowly rolled out in Gauteng Province on 1 April 2004. To date the ARV plan has fallen far short of its targeted figures. Whilst the government had aimed to have 53,000 people on ARV treatment by 2004, this became the government's target for 2005. By January 2005 a mere 32,302 patients were being treated on the programme. This in a country with up to 5.3 million HIV positive citizens. Many of these are being treated by donor funded programmes.[24]

The social, economic and political effects of HIV/Aids is a broad and complex topic and beyond the scope of this chapter, but a number of points have relevance in evaluating state functionality.

The state's reluctance to effectively tackle the HIV/Aids pandemic is both a policy dysfunctionality and a profound failure of leadership. More than any other issue (with the possible exception of unemployment), the government's position on HIV/Aids has spawned widespread social discontent. The significant difference in HIV/Aids protest, however, is that it has not been class or race based in general. Street protests led by the Treatment Action Campaign marked the opening of Parliament in 2003. The South African mining industry has taken the remarkable step of providing counselling, free testing and free antiretroviral treatment to miners.[25] On the other side of the employment spectrum, COSATU has repeatedly voiced its disagreement with the government's position on HIV/Aids. There has also been political fallout between the government and its former cabinet partners, the Inkatha Freedom Party, over HIV/Aids policy. A vituperative exchange of letters between Mbeki and the leader of the official opposition, Tony Leon of the Democratic Alliance, has been published in the press. The medical academic community has spoken out repeatedly against official government policy, and has done so with the support of a number of international agencies, including the WHO. Such widespread opposition to, and protest against, government policy, while highlighting dysfunctionality, also serves to place South Africa's social formation in perspective. Mbeki's personal approval ratings across the spectrum in South Africa fell steadily on the back of his government's position on HIV/Aids and only showed signs of improvement once he had disengaged from the debate and the government had announced its intention to provide antiretrovirals as part of the national health service.[26]

Far from suggesting societal (as opposed to state) dysfunctionality, the popular social resistance and protest against government policy demonstrates the existence of a vibrant civil society which is capable of holding the government to some degree to account. Moreover the state's climb down on the provision of antiretrovirals reinforces the distinction between South Africa and other countries in this study. The South African state has relatively effective self correcting mechanisms that operate within the context of a relatively vibrant democracy.

Nevertheless, the full social, economic, security and political impact of the state's failure of policy on HIV/Aids has yet to be experienced. The cumulative impact of increasing numbers of full blown Aids patients will stretch hospital and welfare services to breaking point in the near future. A burgeoning generation of Aids orphans is emerging without the guidance and support of familial, normative and social support infrastructure. This will deepen social alienation and antisocial behaviour patterns likely to result in higher crime rates among young people. The economic impact of Aids will be felt in a lower GDP, perhaps a reduction of between 0.5 and one per cent with the greatest impact felt in the loss of productivity and productive capacity of the 15–35 year population cohort.

Conclusion

The above discussion of four key policy areas conveys a mixed picture of state performance, delivery and efficacy. Macro economic performance has been solid if unspectacular. Inroads have been made into the backlog of social welfare delivery. Yet in important respects, particularly in the area of social development, the performance of the South African state has been unsatisfactory. The second state of the nation speech delivered by President Mbeki in May 2004 after the ANC won seventy per cent of the popular vote in the general election was a watershed. In it, Mbeki implicitly and explicitly acknowledged extensive policy deficiencies and announced far reaching programmes and targets for the improvement of social delivery. This included expenditure of some $15 billion on a ten year expanded public works programme with the objective of creating one million new jobs. Moreover Mbeki's speech marked a public shift in the conceptualisation of the appropriate role of the state, not only in policy formulation, but significantly in delivery. The 2004 speech heralded the emergence of a significantly more interventionist state playing the key developmental role through massive public investment. This shift towards a more developmental state model is not simply an ideological rejection of broad Washington Consensus orthodoxies; it is a tacit acknowledgement of an unsatisfactory public policy record over the first ten years of democracy. In his February 2005 state of the nation speech Mbeki reinforced this theme by emphasising the need to 'massively improve the management, organisational, technical and other capacities of government so that it meets its objectives'.[27] In February 2006, the government launched a R370 billion infrastructure and development programme, the Accelerated and Shared Growth Initiative for South Africa (ASGISA). Equally significantly, however, this shift in approach conveyed the growing confidence and maturity of the South African government and polity to radically re think the role of the state in achieving critical developmental goals.

But despite sharing a number of the variables common to 'Big Dysfunctional African States', such as acute socio economic inequalities, high unemployment and crime rates and critical health challenges, South Africa is a geographically coherent, politically stable, industrially developed and economically sophisticated country. There is no threat to the integrity of the state, nor is there any area of the country which is not effectively administered by the government. Perhaps the closest the South African government has come to acknowledging the importance of geographic size or bigness with respect to governance was in December 2005 when the Minister for Provincial and Local government floated the possibility of a reduction in the number of Provinces in order to achieve effective policy delivery. This sentiment was spurred by legislation reducing the number of cross (provincial) border municipalities, which requires an amendment to the constitution. This in turn was driven by a concern over the poor performance of many local authorities in South Africa and particularly those in distant rural areas. Once again, however, the South African state moved to address these challenges through the introduction of 'Project Consolidate' in which central government provides material, managerial and infrastructural support to local governments suffering from acute capacity deficiencies.

The reasons for South Africa's relative success, even as a big African state, are difficult to reduce to a clear set of variables, but include its unique colonial history; the administrative capacity of the state apparatuses; its historical industrial development policies; the existence of a sophisticated road, rail, harbour and tele communications infrastructure; remarkably high levels of social co operation, even across races (despite centuries of racially discriminatory practices and policies); and the quality of its political leadership.

Even where contemporary governmental policy may be regarded as failing or dysfunctional, it is clear that through an effectively functioning polity, represented by the pressure that a vital civil society can bring to bear through the normal dynamics of a healthy plural democracy, government policy can be influenced and policy adjustments made. As recent announcements regarding the launch of the extended national public works programmes and the national roll out of antiretrovirals demonstrate, the state can and does respond to policy deficiencies even in the most disappointing areas of public policy such as employment and health.

Whilst the South African case does not undermine the significance or analytical usefulness to scholars of 'bigness' as a variable in understanding dysfunctionality, it suggests that, at the very least a host of factors additional to size and in particular the form, composition and effectiveness of the state apparatus are far more crucial to such an understanding .

Endnotes

1   Gini co efficients measure income inequality with a score of 1 representing complete inequality of income and 0 representing complete income equality.

2   South African Reserve Bank Quarterly Bulletin No 238 December 2005. It should be noted that at the end of 2005 the SARB announced that the growth in the South African economy had been under estimated for some time. This also highlights a recent problem with inaccurate data emerging from Statistics South Africa, leaving the credibility of historic data questioned.

3   See http://ww1.transparency.org/cpi/2005/2005.10.18.cpi.en.html

4   The 2003 matriculation certificate results were highly controversial as upward mark adjustments were made. The matriculation pass rate for private schools in 2005 was close to 100% nationally.

5   *Cape Argus*, 24 September 2003.

6   See http://www.anc.org.za/ancdocs/history/special.html

7   It may be apocryphally reported that the major impulse for FW de Klerk's tectonic reforms in 1990 was that, after his election as President in September 1989, he was advised of the parlous state of the country's financial affairs. This was the result of the economic malaise into which South Africa had fallen under the securocratic rule of his predecessor PW Botha.

8   Marais H. *South Africa: Limits to Change – The Political Economy of Transition.* Cape Town: UCT Press, 2001, p. 124.

9   'AgriSA says land reform should be the big issue.' *Business Day,* 24 July 2003.

10   See *Land and Agrarian Reform in South Africa.* Land Research Action Network, January 2003.

11   De Villiers B. 'Land reform: Issues and challenges', *Occasional Papers.* Johannesburg: Konrad Adenauer Stiftung, April 2003, p. 47.

12   Department of Land Affairs, White Paper on South African Land Policy, 1997.

13   Programme for Land and Agrarian Studies, University of the Western Cape, August 2003.

14   The top four countries in terms of crimes committed in 2000 were the US, Germany, the UK and France. See *www.nationmaster.com.*

15   There is persuasive evidence that the leadership of PAGAD was taken over by the radical Muslim group Qibla in 1996. Bombings and assassinations against drug lords, pimps and indeed state agencies intensified during the following two years. See for example, *Terror in the Cities.* Pretoria: Institute for Security Studies, 2000.

16   Schonteich, ibid, http://www.issafrica.org/Pubs/Monographs/No93/Chap5.htm

17   See government notice No. R317 dated 1 April 2005 published in the Government Gazette No. 27446.

18   Fourie B. 'The Burden of Tuberculosis in South Africa', MRC National Tuberculosis Research Programme, South Africa, SA Health Info Consortium, February 2003.

19   'AIDS will wipe out all of our gains – Mandela', as reported by the South African Press Association, 22 September 2003.

20   For a summary of the report's major findings see *http://www.mrc.ac.za/mrcnews/dec2001/hivaids.htm.*

21   Obviously full blown Aids and unemployment due to disability are causally related.

22   As reported in *The Mercury,* 26 September 2003.

23   'The Cost of HIV Prevention and Treatment Interventions in South Africa.' *CSSR Working Paper 28.* Cape Town: Centre for Social Science Research, University of Cape Town, January 2003.

24 See Treatment Action Campaign (TAC) & AIDS Law Project (ALP) 'Updated first report on the implementation of the operational plan for comprehensive HIV/AIDS care, management and treatment for South Africa (Operational Plan)', July 2004 and National ARV rollout statistics on http://www.tac.org.za

25 Some $3 of the production price of gold in South Africa is now accounted for by the cost of HIV/Aids in the gold mining industry.

26 See the results of the AC Nielsen survey conducted on behalf of *Business Day*, 29 September 2003.

27 Address of the President of the Republic of South Africa, Thabo Mbeki, at the second joint sitting of the third democratic parliament, Cape Town, 11 February 2005.

7

Dysfunctional states, dysfunctional armed movements, and lootable commodities

Marina Ottaway

The idea that commodities and particularly easily 'lootable' resources such as diamonds, are at the heart of Africa's most intractable conflicts has recently gained currency. The conclusion is based on strong evidence that the sale of diamonds and other such easily plundered commodities has helped finance armed movements in countries such as Sierra Leone, Liberia, Angola and the Democratic Republic of Congo (DRC).[1] Unfortunately, many analysts and commentators have also jumped to broader conclusions poorly supported by this evidence. Among these are three particularly worthy of notice: first, that the main cause of conflict in African states is greed; second, that the possession of lootable commodities increases the likelihood of greed based conflict; and, finally, that the presence of such assets thus increases the probability of state collapse and dysfunctionality. A corollary of this line of thinking is that steps aiming at controlling the illegal trade in such goods would make an important contribution to the rehabilitation of African states.

Undoubtedly, lootable commodities play an important role in African conflicts today, and are thus part of the set of factors that make many African states dysfunctional. But the linkage between state dysfunctionality and a country's natural resource endowment is far from straightforward.[2] First, there are commodity rich states that are quite functional, for example Botswana, and commodity poor countries that are extremely dysfunctional, for example Somalia. The presence of natural assets that can be appropriated is neither a necessary nor a sufficient component of state dysfunctionality and civil conflict. Secondly, if a dysfunctional state is rich in lootable commodities, these will inevitably be exploited by the parties to the conflict. However, the manner in which it is done, and the effect of that exploitation will depend, to a large extent, on the level of dysfunctionality, both of the state and of the armed opposition. In countries where the government is capable of exercising relatively strong control over at least part of its territory and the military remains cohesive and disciplined, and where the opposition is well organised and united, the appropriation and use of commodities will lead neither to state collapse nor to the fragmentation of the opposition. On the contrary, it is likely to make both sides stronger and more centralised. Conflict will be fierce, but will not lead to state collapse. However, if the state is weak and the armed opposition is fragmented, the plundering of a country's lootable commodities will tend further to fragment the state and opposition. Indeed, in extreme cases, as in the DRC, the state and opposition may become so weak that control of the exploitation of resources passes to better organised outsiders.

Even the concept of what constitutes a lootable commodity can be understood properly only in the context of the existence or absence of organisation. It is true that some products, diamonds for example, are easily accessible even to small scale operators. But the trade that has an impact on conflict is not the smuggling of small and valuable objects by freelance prospectors. Rather, conflict is fuelled by large scale, highly organised trade in commodities, including many that can be extracted and transported only by highly sophisticated organisations. A UN study of the illegal exploitation of natural resources in the DRC lists diamonds, gold, coltan, copper, cobalt, timber, wildlife, fiscal resources, and exploitative trade in consumer goods as most important.[3] This commodity trade is carried out by commercial enterprises that differ from legitimate multinational corporations only in that they operate outside the control and regulation of government institutions, although most often with the full knowledge and participation of highly placed government officials in the countries of origin, transit and even of sale. Indeed, the trade that has relevance to conflict bears as much similarity to small scale smuggling by individuals as the heroin trade from Afghanistan or the cocaine trade from Columbia have to the growing of a few marijuana plants in an amateur's basement.

In the rest of this chapter, I shall explore these ideas in greater detail, applying them to a discussion of two African countries, Angola and the DRC. These two countries have been chosen because both are rich in natural assets that are being exploited outside legal channels, on a large scale, and are being used to finance conflict. Yet while the Congo is a completely dysfunctional state, indeed essentially a collapsed one, Angola is a country where both government and armed opposition have continued to display some capacity for organisation and control. As a result, there is some possibility that the conflict in Angola will come to an end, and that the extraction and sale of commodities will revert to official and legal channels.

In the DRC, the possibility of such positive developments appears, at best, very remote.

Dysfunctional states and dysfunctional opposition

A dysfunctional state is one that cannot generate sufficient administrative capacity to make it possible for decisions taken by the leadership actually to be implemented (positive dysfunctionality), or to prevent other organisations from taking over part of its territory (negative dysfunctionality). In other words, a dysfunctional state is one where the government can neither administer the country nor protect either the nation or the regime against armed opposition. All states are dysfunctional to some extent, but there are widely different degrees, starting with mild inefficiency and culminating in state collapse. All of the states discussed in this volume are highly dysfunctional, but not to the same degree or in the same fashion.

The dysfunctionality of a state can be evaluated by using either absolute parameters – measuring the capacity of that state against an ideal model of how a state should function, or relative parameters – judging the degree of functionality on the basis of the state's capacity to attain its own goals. For the purposes of this paper, the focus, above all, is on relative dysfunctionality: the capacity of the state to attain the goals set by its leadership. It is for this reason that Angola can be considered a somewhat functional state, although it clearly falls far short of any absolute standards relating to how a state should function.

Like states, armed or unarmed opposition movements can also display varying degrees of functionality, and even reach collapse. The functionality of an opposition movement, like that of a state, should be judged in terms of its capacity to attain its own goals. In Angola, the *Movimento Popular de Libertaçao de Angola* (MPLA), then still an anti colonial liberation movement, became so debilitated in the late 1960s that its Soviet backers for a time stopped supporting it. The organisation was plagued by poor leadership and by factionalism, and as a result spent more time on internecine conflict than on fighting the Portuguese. Only later did the MPLA regroup; and after independence in 1975 it became the ruling party of Angola. Another anti Portuguese liberation movement, *União Naçional para a Independêncía Total d'Angola* (UNITA), which had almost no resources and very little external support, succeeded in establishing a strong internal structure in the early 1970s. It was this functionality of UNITA that struck John Stockwell, an agent of the Central Intelligence Agency dispatched to Angola to find ways to counteract the domination by the Soviet backed MPLA at the time of independence. He concluded that it was worthwhile for the US to support and build up UNITA, although according to his own estimate the group had only a few hundred men under arms.[4]

States and commodities

One of the most important components of state functionality is the capacity to raise the revenue necessary to finance the government, the administration, and the military. Revenue raising ability is also at the core of the effectiveness of an armed opposition.

States can secure income in a variety of different ways. Taxation, the imposition of users' fees on government provided services, royalties on the extraction of minerals and, increasingly, foreign assistance grants and loans are all legitimate forms of revenue for African states. But dysfunctional states also raise funds in less legitimate ways, through corruption, illegitimate production and sale of commodities, and even looting the property of their citizens and those of neighbouring countries. A common practice in Mobutu's Zaïre was to give the military *carte blanche* to exact payments from citizens to supplement their salaries, which were paid only irregularly.

In dysfunctional states it is difficult to distinguish clearly between revenue raising that benefits the state and the kind that enriches government officials. First of all, even large amounts of official, legitimate revenue can disappear from the government's books. In Angola an estimated $1 billion in legal oil royalties were unaccounted for in 2000.[5] Secondly, the revenue that flows into the private coffers of predatory government officials is not always devoted entirely to private use. In Zaïre, Mobutu Sese Seko's enormous wealth did not just purchase lavish houses in Europe for him and his family, but was also spent for purposes (such as equipping the military) that would have been legitimate if the income and expenditure had passed through official channels and been accounted for in the budget process.

The type of revenue on which a country depends also affects the character and functioning of the state. Those that are dependent above all on taxation and other domestic revenue sources need to develop organisational capacity in order to collect taxes and fees, whether through the creation of an efficient bureaucracy, a tax farming system, or other systematic methods of persuading or coercing citizens and businesses into parting with some of their assets. No matter what form it takes, collecting revenue from domestic sources requires a state to develop organisational ability and thus to improve its functionality. Domestic revenue collection is thus a state building activity, not only because it provides the resources to finance all its other activities, but also because it builds institutional capacity.

Dependence on external sources of revenue does not have the same impact. Even a dysfunctional state can raise income through foreign aid or imposing royalties on mineral exploitation by foreign firms. It is true that in the most extreme cases states may become so dysfunctional that they no longer receive revenue from commodities because nobody wants to take the risks connected with exploiting them. However, such an outcome is rare when valuable assets such as oil and minerals are involved. In the 1980s and early 1990s American oil companies decided not to exploit the Sudan oil fields because of the explosive political situation; but more daring and less scrupulous corporations soon replaced them. In Angola, oil revenues from legitimate undertakings by large oil companies increased steadily throughout twenty five years of civil war.

Many studies have pointed out that states highly dependent on income from commodities, particularly 'petrostates' dependent on oil, develop a particular set of characteristics and problems.[6] These states have lopsided economies, with a particular commodity sector overshadowing and often depressing all others. They are also 'citizen detached', in that governments that do not depend on taxes do not feel particularly moved to listen to their citizens or respond to their demands. These problems are not, however, unavoidable. States that are already well functioning and democratic when oil starts to be produced remain efficient and democratic.

Like commodities, foreign aid *per se* does not make states dysfunctional. Rather, collapsing states are often so needy that they require and receive large amounts of aid. But foreign aid does not necessarily help to make states more functional. While at present foreign assistance is usually accompanied by a package of conditions that aim to make the state more efficient, the results tend to be at best modest. However, in extreme cases, foreign aid creates a vicious circle of dysfunctionality. Donors despair of the capacity of the state to perform and therefore channel aid through NGOs, thus decreasing further the possibility that the state will develop some competence. The case of Chad bears watching: lack of confidence in the government's effectiveness (and its honesty) has led to the creation of an NGO consortium to administer oil revenue, and consequently to the sidelining of state institutions.[7]

Natural assets in fact provide a source of income that is available even to dysfunctional states. This does not mean that commodity dependence makes states dysfunctional. Rather, it means that it is possible for a state to enjoy considerable revenue from commodities even though it is dysfunctional. No matter what its sources, furthermore, all revenue can help the functioning of a state. It makes it possible, for example, to build a transport infrastructure, communication networks, administrative capacity and schools. It is difficult to conclude that revenue derived from commodities is a problem by definition.

The potentially beneficial impact of revenue earned from the exploitation of a country's natural wealth is decreased, of course, if the money is siphoned off into their private accounts by greedy rulers, or systematically looted at each level of disbursement by corrupt government officials who skim off their share before the money is spent on public services. Even in those cases, however, it is difficult to see the commodities as the cause of the problem. Officials can divert revenue from taxes just as easily as they can the earnings from commodity exports, although the scale of the diversion may be lower because there is less to steal. Indeed, corruption is an endemic problem in all countries with weak institutions and poor governance, no matter what the source of state income.

Many analysts assume that different types of commodities have a different impact on state functionality. Diamonds in particular have earned a bad name as a resource that is easily appropriated and therefore tends to undermine the state, while oil is commonly regarded as a non lootable asset that increases state centralisation because it can be exploited only by large corporations that pour money directly into the state's coffers. This distinction, however, does not stand up well to closer analysis. Oil has indeed made the Venezuelan state highly centralised and strong. In Nigeria, however, oil revenue has not had the same effect; rather, it has created a corrupt, predatory elite on the one hand, and fuelled resentment that often explodes into violent resistance at a local level on the other. Nigeria is a deeply troubled and divided state on the brink of civil war. The same differences are found in the case of more easily plundered commodities. Diamonds have financed solidly established, orderly states like Botswana and giant multi national corporations such as De Beers. They have also been used to fund internal wars, as in Angola, or state disintegration, as in Sierra Leone. Indeed, the distinction between lootable and non lootable commodities does not appear useful in analysing their impact on state functionality, although it is more applicable to opposition movements, as discussed below.

Armed opposition movements and commodities

Like governments, opposition movements can function only if they can raise sufficient revenue. Armed factions need revenue to purchase weapons, although successful armed movements also end up by capturing at least part of the material they need. The sources of income available to armed insurgencies are similar to those used by governments: extraction of money from the population (which is the equivalent of taxation), foreign aid, and the exploitation of natural resources.

Armed movements always exact some form of contribution from the population. These contributions are not always surrendered voluntarily, but rather at gunpoint. They are a primitive form of tax collection, which starts becoming more systematic and professional, and thus less predatory, if a group establishes control over a certain area for a protracted period, as the *Frente de Libertação de Moçambique* (Frelimo) did in Northern Mozambique or the Eritrean People's Liberation Front (EPLF) in some lowland parts of Eritrea. But such revenue is usually quite limited, even when a movement can systematise collection, not only because such forces are more likely to operate in pre industrial, low income countries, but also because they usually succeed in establishing their control first in the more remote and often poor areas. Foreign assistance has thus been, historically, the most important way in which armed movements can satisfy their needs for funding. The US, the Soviet Union, and, in the Horn of Africa, Arab countries, have been the main financiers of African insurgents. The investment in African rebel or resistance forces by foreign countries has been based on the assumption that these were 'liberation' movements motivated by ideological convictions and political grievances. In many but not all cases this has been an accurate assumption.

Because there has been a decrease in international involvement in African conflict since the end of the Cold War, movements have been forced to generate more income themselves. The exploitation of natural assets has become a major source of finance for many such factions. This has led to the perception that the character of armed resistance in Africa has changed, that ideology or grievances are not (or are no longer) a significant cause of such movements, and that greed is now the main motive. The exploitation of valuable resources is seen not as a means to an end, but as the very goal of conflict.

This view needs critical reappraisal. The studies on which such conclusions are based, above all the studies by Paul Collier and his colleagues at the World Bank, and the innumerable NGO reports on 'conflict diamonds', oil and other commodities, do not provide sufficient evidence to support that conclusion. Collier's studies, which purport to show that civil conflict in African countries is based on greed more than on grievance, are based on strong statistical evidence but provide weak, indeed arbitrary, indicators of what constitutes 'greed' and what constitutes 'grievance'.[8] Furthermore, the studies do not even take into consideration the possibility that conflicts could be fought over questions of power or ideology, let alone that all conflicts have a mixture of causes, that different actors are motivated by a variety of factors, and that the character of conflicts often changes over time.

Historical evidence, furthermore, does not support the claim that African civil conflict is invariably or even predominantly driven by the enrichment opportunities offered by a country's natural resources. I find no indication that the ethnic conflicts which racked Ethiopia for fifteen years, led to the independence of Eritrea and continue to destabilise the area to this day, were fought over commodities. It is also doubtful whether the country's oil and diamonds determined the entire course of the Angolan civil war. Although the exploitation of these resources eventually became a major source of financing for both sides, the conflict had lasted for over ten years before UNITA started exporting any commodities, and close to twenty by the time it started exporting diamonds.[9] It is possible that some recent conflicts in Africa, above all in Sierra Leone and Liberia, have been driven predominantly or even entirely by a determination to control and exploit the country's mineral assets, although even in these cases it may be hard to prove that greed was the original or even the dominant factor.

Whatever the causes of conflict, commodities have become a major source of financing for armed movements in a number of African countries. As such they have an impact on the evolution of conflict and the possibilities for resolution. The distinction between lootable and non lootable (or more precisely, less easily lootable) assets, which was rejected as unhelpful in relation to states, is valid where armed opposition groups are concerned. Easily extractable commodities are a source of revenue available even to movements that are not particularly well organised, while less accessible ones are a resource only for more mature and strong movements, particularly those tied to foreign governments. The presence in a country of resources that can be plundered can quickly lead to escalation in the types and quantities of weapons that are employed in the conflicts: soldiers from rich movements drive armed personnel carriers, while those from poor ones trudge along on foot with AK 47s and *pangas*. And too easy access to exploitable commodities can lead to the fragmentation of armed movements and can therefore have a profound effect on the possibility of political or even military solutions to conflicts.

The escalation in the level of fighting and types of armament is probably inevitable in countries rich in natural assets, although how effectively such weapons will be used depends also on the degree of organisation of the armed opposition and the government. However, the mere availability of resources that can be plundered does not cause movements to fragment any more than it causes states to become dysfunctional. On the contrary, the impact of such exploitable assets on the armed opposition depends very much on its leadership and its organisational ability.

State, opposition and commodities in Angola and the DRC

A comparison of conflicts in two big dysfunctional African states – Angola and the DRC – provides more detailed information on the issues that have so far been discussed in general terms. Both countries are highly commodity dependent, and both have been in the throes of civil war for a long time. But the similarities end there. The DRC is not only a dysfunctional state; it is a collapsed one. For all practical purposes, the Congolese state exists only as a juridical fiction. It may never be restored, given the difficulty and the scope of the reconstruction effort that would be required to achieve functionality. The Angolan state, on the other hand, has struggled since independence to control its entire territory and to impose its monopoly over the means of coercion, but it has never lost the capacity to control most of the country, nor to exert its authority in a systematic, organised fashion. Furthermore, after the death of Jonas Savimbi in February 2002, the government has regained control over virtually all its provinces, and, through a disarmament and demobilisation process backed by the international community, it is establishing overwhelming military superiority, if not a complete monopoly, over the means of coercion.

The opposition in Angola was united under a strong, autocratic leader; it was disciplined and cohesive, and it appears to have remained so even after the death of Savimbi and his second in command. In contrast, the opposition in the DRC is as dysfunctional as the government. It is divided between political and armed groupings. Members of the former vie with each other and with the incumbent president for control of a government that cannot administer the country. Political organisations are highly unstable, and opposition politicians have proved highly susceptible to co option by the incumbent. The armed opposition is divided into rival movements, of which only one, the *Mouvement de Libération Congolais* (MLC), appears to be relatively strongly led and cohesive. *The Rassemblement Congolais pour la Démocratie,* based in Goma (RCD-Goma), and the *Rassemblement Congolais pour la Démocratie-Mouvement de Libération* (RCD-ML) have instead tended to fragment.[10] Alongside those groups clearly fighting the government are others, most notably the Mai Mai, who have been battling against the government's opponents but also seek to acquire control over territory in their own name, not the government's.

The patterns of commodity exploitation in Angola and the DRC reflect the differences between the two countries and illustrate the importance of capacity and organisation. In the DRC, successive UN reports show that there is essentially no legal exploitation of the country's resources, even in the areas that are controlled by the government. Furthermore, both the government and the armed opposition are heavily dependent on foreign actors for the production of these commodities. Both the Congolese government and the insurgent forces extract the country's resources through 'elite networks', which are largely controlled by the governments or government officials of Zimbabwe, Uganda, and Rwanda and by the private companies, mostly foreign controlled, with which they have made deals. The exact functioning of these networks varies, depending on whether the main actor is Zimbabwe, Uganda or Rwanda. The pattern of dominance by outsiders, however, is the same.

In government controlled areas, the latest UN report found that some $5 billion in assets were transferred from the state mining sector to private companies between 1999 and 2002. The government of Zimbabwe, through its officials and military officers, was a senior partner in most of these ventures. A number of high level DRC government officials named in the report benefited personally from this transfer. But the state itself played a role of decreasing importance in the exploitation of the country's mineral wealth. This is particularly noteworthy given that even during Mobutu's regime the state had played a relatively minor role in mineral extraction.[11]

UN studies, furthermore, show that even the armed groups have been relinquishing their role in the exploitation of commodities to foreign patrons who have superior ability to organise the complex networks needed for the wholesale exploitation of resources. In April 2001, the UN panel found that the armed movements and local population had been participants, to some extent, in the first, 'looting' phase of the exploitation of Congolese natural wealth. This phase started in September 1996 with the invasion by Laurent Kabila's Alliance of Democratic Forces for the Liberation of Congo Zaïre (ADFL) and its Ugandan and Rwandan supporters. Furthermore, the report concluded that the two major movements, the

RCD Goma and the MLC FLC, were becoming capable of financing themselves by imposing taxes on the exploitation of commodities in the territories they controlled, and by engaging directly in the systematic exportation of some products.[12] Later UN reports, however, depict these groups as completely dependent on their foreign patrons, suggesting, though not stating explicitly, that they could not compete with the better organised foreign governments and networks involved in the extraction and sale of minerals. Revenue from the exploitation of Congolese commodities continued to help finance the conflict in the Congo, but control of resources, and to some extent the conflict, was in the hands of external parties.

Angola presents a completely different picture. Exploitation of the country's assets remained firmly under the control of the political entity (either the government or UNITA) which controlled the specific territory in which the resource concerned was to be found. This does not mean that there was never any small scale smuggling. This would be extremely unlikely and, in any case, virtually impossible to prove. But systematic, wholesale use of these commodities never left the control of the two sides to the conflict. Foreigners were involved in the trade in these products only at the behest of the Angolan actors - for example, the DRC helped UNITA sell its diamonds on the international market to circumvent the international embargo imposed on illegally extracted Angolan diamonds in 1998.

The Angolan government, which began by embracing Marxism-Leninism and remains highly statist, set up state companies to exploit all of the country's products - oil (Sonangol), diamonds (Endiama), and even coffee. It worked out deals with foreign corporations for the exploitation and commercialisation of its commodities, and maintained control over them. When pressure from international NGOs to halt the trade in illegally mined diamonds mounted, the Angolan government was able to set up a certification programme. It is important to note, however, that this programme does not work very well and that there is enormous corruption, with government officials reaping large personal gains from diamond sales. Global Witness, a British NGO that has produced numerous reports on the Angolan oil industry, estimates that in 2001, some $1.4 billion in oil revenue, about one third of the total, found its way into the hands of corrupt government officials.[13] Nevertheless, there is a system (albeit one that is wide open to subornment) in Angola that gives the government a high degree of control over the extraction and sale of commodities. In the DRC, by contrast, it is difficult to detect a legitimate system, even a corrupt one.

UNITA also retained firm control of commodity exports from the territories it occupied. Beginning in the late 1980s, UNITA was forced to face the fact that, with the Cold War coming to an end and South Africa beginning its transition from apartheid, its sources of outside support would dry up. No longer receiving funding from the US and South Africa for its fight against a Marxist regime, UNITA had to become self reliant. By the late 1980s, the movement was beginning to export products, although on a limited scale.[14] However, a significant change came about after 1992. In that year, Angola held its first multi party elections, as laid down in the 1991 Bicesse agreement. Despite international assistance, the elections were a failure, because Savimbi rejected the results and returned to war.[15] Moving suddenly against a government that was not prepared for a resumption of hostilities, UNITA scored a series of impressive victories and was able to occupy important diamond producing areas. In the period 1992-1994 UNITA controlled an estimated ninety per cent of Angola's diamond exports. From 1996-1997, after the loss of some territory, UNITA's share amounted to about two thirds.[16] This percentage declined further in later years. Nevertheless, despite sanctions on the sale of illegal diamonds imposed against UNITA in 1998, the organisation reportedly continued its trade in gems. UNITA accounted for as much as thirty per cent of the world's illegally exported diamonds in 2001.[17]

Reports on UNITA's participation in the diamond trade paint a picture of a highly organised, centrally controlled mechanism. A UN body responsible for monitoring the effectiveness of sanctions against UNITA concluded in its assessment that all diamonds mined by the organisation were passed through the military operational command structures to Jonas Savimbi, and sold through various channels under central supervision.[18] UNITA's historical pattern of strong, centralised leadership and tight control prevailed even in the commodity trade.

Conclusions

The illegal exploitation of commodities does play a role in African conflicts by replacing the assistance previously provided by external supporters to both governments and the armed opposition. However, the financing of conflicts through the illegal sale of these products does not in itself mean that the motivation behind the conflict is greed rather than grievance, as some studies assert. For example, the appropriation and sale of resources is also found in conflicts that are not based purely on greed, such as the conflict between UNITA and the MPLA government in Angola, which started long before the trade in commodities became an issue. The nature of that conflict did not change from the days when the US and the Soviet

Union, as part of their African proxy wars, originally financed the opposing sides. Only in the 1990s, when outside patrons withdrew, did resource extraction become the major source of financing for both government and rebel movements.

The fact that a country is rich in natural resources does not mean that it is bound to become a dysfunctional state or to sink into conflict. A state is dysfunctional and conflict prone because of poor leadership and a lack of state administrative and organisational capacity, both in the civilian and military fields. Countries with strong leadership, good administration and disciplined military establishments prosper and become even stronger as a result of the revenue they derive from trade in commodities. Undoubtedly such countries are prone to some of the problems that are typically identified with petrostates. But such factors also affect countries that are not oil producers, but where the government derives much of its revenue from commodity trade instead of taxes. However, such dysfunction is nothing compared to what afflicts countries where governments do not even have the revenue to pay salaries and to finance the most basic services.

It is organisational capacity rather than access to commodities that determines how successful armed movements will be. Even though they operate in a region extremely rich in many kinds of natural resources, the rebel factions of the Congo remain weak and essentially dependent on outside patrons. In contrast, the better organised, centrally controlled UNITA was able to exploit the assets in territories it controlled to purchase arms and wage a successful war.

In recent years, in large part because of the efforts of international NGOs, curbs on the illegal trade in commodities, particularly so called 'blood diamonds', are advocated as a means of curbing African conflicts and restoring the integrity of certain African states. These efforts have not been very successful so far, and are unlikely to become more so for two major reasons. First, we know from long experience with the drug trade how difficult controlling contraband is. Second, the real problem in all these conflicts is not the exploitation of commodities but the dysfunctionality of the state, and often of the armed movements, and the consequent vacuum of power.

A contrarian postscript

In this analysis so far, I have taken existing states as the starting point of my analysis, and discussed the relationship between the illegal exploitation of commodities and state dysfunctionality. Here, I want to offer a contrarian interpretation, namely the possibility that this type of exploitation outside the parameters of government control may signal the beginning of a state building process, and thus be a positive rather than a negative phenomenon. From this point of view, illegal trade in a country's products is the result of state dysfunctionality rather than its cause. The wealth it generates could be the tool needed for the development of new and more successful states.

There are two possible readings of the voluminous reports on the illegal traffic in commodities in the DRC. The first reflects the intent of the authors: the reports represent the documentation of a colossal scale of illegal trade that deprives the government of the DRC – and thus the people of the DRC – of the revenue needed to promote a better life. The problem with this reading is that it is based on a juridical fiction: that there still is a legitimate state that could and should exploit national resources for the benefit of its citizens. In reality, this state does not exist now, and has never existed. Since independence, the DRC has never been capable of controlling and administering its territory, let alone of delivering services to its citizens and promoting economic development. Commodities are bound to be exploited illegally because the state charged with providing the framework within which they could be exploited legally simply does not exist. Legal exploitation is a mirage.

The second reading is that, unintentionally, the reports document the possible beginning of a new process of state building, which might eventually lead to the emergence of new countries that are less dysfunctional than today's DRC. This process starts both with the growth against tremendous odds of commercial networks, and with the early stages of emergence of new political organisations that aim to fulfill the needs of those operations.

The above statement is preposterous only if we cling to the juridical fiction that the DRC is a real state, that is, that it possesses the basic attributes of modern statehood, above all control over a territory clearly delineated by fixed borders. If we accept the actual situation, namely that much of the country consists of territories over which no government has jurisdiction, then the idea that the illegal commodity trade represents the emergence of commercial enterprises that are integrated into the global economy and may form the basis for the emergence of new state formations is at least plausible.

Such a process of state building would not lead to the restoration of the DRC. Indeed, the idea of commercially led political reformation favours the stronger, more organised states in the area, Rwanda in particular, and would eventually lead to new borders and possibly new countries. Such a process would not follow the juridical pattern of post independent Africa, but rather the historical patterns of state formation. In other words, it is a process that can be better understood by reading Charles Tilly than UN reports.

There is no guarantee, of course, that the growth of these significant trading networks will lead to the emergence of new, more functional states. First, there are the uncertainties that surround any state shaping project. It is doubtful whether it is possible to calculate historically the ratio of successful to unsuccessful attempts to create new states, but it is a safe assumption that the failures far outnumber the successes. Although trade can provide the financial resources for such a project, such resources do not guarantee that the new political structures arising will have the necessary leadership qualities, organisational capacity or military power.

Secondly, today's world is politically hostile to the collapse of old states and the formation of new ones. While the international community was not able to prevent the formation of new states during the 1990s, it continues to consider the phenomenon as problematic and to favour the status quo, even if this means supporting old states that have ceased to function over new ones that might possess to a greater degree the attributes of statehood. The largely fictional entity that is Somalia is still considered a state, albeit a collapsed one, while the existent Somaliland is not. Finally, it is unclear whether even successful trading networks, such as those developing illegally in the DRC, could provide the foundations for new states. They may be simply a segment of the global economy and thus unable to provide the impulse, or even the financing, for state building.

It would be premature to attempt to answer any of these questions at this point. But it is quite possible that by focusing attention only on the relation between the illegal commodity trade and the dysfunctionality of existing states, we could miss an unfolding process of state reconfiguration and state building that is likely to be of great long term importance.

Endnotes

1   See Campbell G. *Blood Diamonds: Tracing the Deadly Path of the World's Most Precious Stones*. Boulder: Westview Press, September 2002; 'Conflict diamonds: Possibilities for the Identification, Certification and Control of Diamonds', *Global Witness*, June 2002; 'All the Presidents' Men', *Global Witness*, March 2002; The International Consortium of Investigative Journalists, 'Greasing the Skids of Corruption', The Centre for Public Integrity, 2002; see also *The Economies of Conflict - Private Sector*

Activities and Armed Conflict. Reports compiled in 2002 by the Programme for International Co operation and Conflict Resolution (PICCR) for a series of reports on conflict and various commodity markets compiled by the international NGO community.

2   See Snyder R. 'Does Lootable Wealth Breed Disorder? States, Regimes, and the Political Economy of Extraction'. Paper presented at the session on 'Explaining Democratisation', Annual meeting of the American Political Science Association, San Francisco, September 2001.

3   UN, 'Final Report of the Panel of Experts on the Illegal Exploitation of Natural Resources and Other Forms of Wealth of the Democratic Republic of the Congo', (S/2002/1146), 15 October 2002, p. 4.

4   Stockwell J. *In Search of Enemies: A CIA Story.* New York: Norton, 1978.

5   The International Consortium of Investigative Journalists, *op. cit.*, p. 1.

6   Karl TL. *The Paradox of Plenty: Oil Booms and Petrostates.* Berkeley: University of California Press, 1997. Insights on the impact of oil are also provided by Human rights reports such as Human Rights Watch, 'The Price of Oil'. New York, 1999.

7   Complete information about the Chad project is to be found on the website of the International Advisory Group on the Chad Cameroon Pipeline Project (*http://www. gic iag.org/eback.htm*). The site contains all the original documents and the reports of all fact finding missions, which illustrate the degree of international involvement in the managing of oil revenue in those countries.

8   Collier P & A Hoeffler. 'Greed and Grievance in Civil War', World Bank Research Working Paper 2355, Washington, DC, 2000. By the same authors, see also 'On the Incidence of Civil War in Africa', *Journal of Conflict Resolution*, 46 (1) February 2002, pp. 13-28.

9   'A Rough Trade: The Role of Companies and Governments in the Angolan Conflict', *Global Witness,* December 1998, p. 16.

10   RCD-Goma is a creation of, and depends financially, militarily and politically on, Rwanda. The RCD-ML split from RCD-Goma and Rwanda and was plagued by internal discord. It eventually merged with the MLC to form the *Mouvement de Libération Congolais/Front de Libération du Congo* (MLC/FLC). The MLC, later the MLC/FLC, is dependent on Uganda. Some smaller RCD fragments have also become autonomous movements, although they remain politically inconsequential. See UN, 'Addendum to the Report of the Panel of Experts on the Illegal Exploitation of Natural Resources and Other Forms of Wealth of the Democratic Republic of the Congo', 10 November 2001, pp. 123-142.

11 UN Final Report of the Panel of Experts on the Illegal Exploitation of Natural Resources and Other Forms of Wealth of the Democratic Republic of the Congo, 15 October 2002, pp. 22-34. See also previous UN reports by the same panel dated 12 April 2001 and 10 November 2001.

12 UN Report of the Panel of Experts on the Illegal Exploitation of Natural Resources and Other Forms of Wealth of the Democratic Republic of the Congo, 12 April 2001, pp. 143-147.

13 'All the Presidents' Men', *Global Witness*, March 2002, p. 6.

14 'A Rough Trade: The Role of Companies and Governments in the Angolan Conflict', *Global Witness*, December 1998, p. 16.

15 Ottaway M, 'Angola's Failed Elections' In: Kumar K (ed.), *Postconflict Elections: Democratisation and International Assistance*. Boulder: Lynne Rienner Publishers, 1998.

16 'A Rough Trade: The Role of Companies and Governments in the Angolan Conflict', *Global Witness*, December 1998, p. 16.

17 UN Supplementary Report of the Monitoring Mechanism on Sanctions against Unita, 12 October 2001, p. 176.

18 *Ibid.*, pp. 181-182.

8

International responses to state dysfunctionality

Nicolas van de Walle

Introduction

Observers have long argued that the weak states of sub Saharan Africa used the international arena to buttress their legitimacy and power in the decades after independence. Thus, to answer the question 'how do the weak regimes of Africa persist?' Jackson and Rosberg[1] argued that the states in the regions managed to compensate for their low levels of 'empirical statehood' with much higher levels of 'juridical statehood', the latter largely conferred on these states by the international community. For his part, Bayart[2] argued that African states pursued a strategy of 'extraversion', in which they used their domestic weakness strategically to derive advantages from the developed countries of the West.

Certainly, for much of the last three decades, this analysis appeared compelling. For the most part, the Western military presence in Africa sought to protect the sovereignty of all African countries and to buttress the regional system of states. Sub Saharan Africa's governments received a historically unprecedented level of foreign aid. Despite the rhetoric to the contrary, the level of conditionality imposed in exchange for this level of funding was quite low, so that it is not an exaggeration to say that several dozen extremely corrupt and often incompetent state leaders with relatively little domestic legitimacy benefited greatly from international support that assisted them to maintain political stability. This aid from foreign countries did not result in stronger or more legitimate state structures, however, and may in some instances have arrested the process of regional state formation by allowing extremely weak states to survive.[3]

The post colonial order has evolved in subtle but important ways over the course of the last decade, and African international relations are today in a state of flux. Between the end of the Cold War, the progressive withdrawal of France (the one overtly neo colonial power in the region) and the growing dissatisfaction felt by the West with the poor results of foreign aid, previous constraints on regional state making and unmaking have diminished. New public, as well as private, actors have emerged to take advantage of the space created by the relative withdrawal of traditional powers from the region. The old norms emphasising state sovereignty at all costs have clearly receded in importance, as suggested by the West's tacit acquiescence in the mercenary dismemberment of the Democratic Republic of the Congo (DRC) by its neighbours.

Some features of the old order persist, however, and current efforts such as Nepad suggest that post colonial thinking retains substantial legitimacy, both within Africa and in the West. Somewhat ironically, the Republic of South Africa (RSA), once perhaps the leading revisionist state in the region, has emerged in recent years as one of its most conservative. Otherwise, a striking characteristic of the region over the course of the last two decades has been the inability of its big states to dominate the regional state formation process. Undermining efforts to establish a stable inter national regime in Africa is the fact that Ethiopia, Nigeria, the Democratic Republic of Congo (DRC), Sudan and Angola have all been sources of instability and state decay in sub Saharan Africa.

In this brief review, I shall argue that the present circumstances are likely to generate greater instability than in the past, but are also capable of producing isolated instances of more effective state building. Of critical importance for the themes of this project is my argument that the emergence of regional powers as key strategic actors will determine the form of the new transnational system which will develop over time. Will these big states gain the capacity and capability to project power in the name of regional state building, both as intermediaries for the Western powers (who wish to retain or gain influence in the region even as their appetite for direct intervention diminishes) or as actors in their own right? That is the critical issue for the next two decades.

The chapter is divided into two broad sections. The section that follows reviews the broad contours of what I call the post colonial order, and emphasises its distinct influence on regional state formation. The second section discusses the reasons for the evolution towards a new regime in Africa in the mid 1990s, and its likely impact on state formation in the near future.

The post colonial international regime

Most of the states in Africa can be viewed as creations of a distinct post World War II international system.[4] The poor and weak states of the region, with arbitrary borders inherited from colonialism and governments with little popular legitimacy, looked to the international community to strengthen their sovereignty and ensure their political stability. To a remarkable extent, these states managed to compensate for their very weak *de facto* sovereignty by strengthening their *de jure* powers,[5] relying on international law as maintained by an array of international organisations - the United Nations (UN) and the Organisation of African Unity (OAU) - to legitimate their tenuous hold on authority. Even governments which could not fully control their own territory, or which might not have received significant support from their own citizens in a free and fair election, could nonetheless count on the support of the international community.

For instance, the states in the region received a large amount of financial backing from foreign countries.[6] Between independence and the early 1990s, states in sub Saharan Africa received a steady and increasing inflow of foreign aid. This peaked in 1992-1993 with over $19 billion of international funding, equivalent to around twelve per cent of the average African country's GDP. This high and sustained level of external public finance is historically unprecedented. In comparison, it might be noted, the average European recipient of Marshall Plan support received no more than two and a half per cent of GDP in funding,[7] assistance that, moreover, lasted only a few years.

In the post colonial international regime, African governments used foreign assistance provided by donors to finance the growth of the state apparatus, and to secure political stability. Although the region had a more or less disastrous economic performance record during the 1970s and 1980s, incumbent governments enjoyed relative security. Even if these governments had adopted ruinous economic policies and were obviously guilty of corruption and incompetence, this appeared to make no difference to the amount of aid donated, and financial support was invariably directed to governments. Even Western NGOs that were active in the region invariably worked through state structures and sought state approval for their operations.

As the economic crisis grew worse in the 1980s, foreign funding from the West was often the only link between African economies and the global economy. Governance problems and economic uncertainty deterred foreign direct investment except in a small minority of resource rich states, while the continent's contribution to world trade declined steadily. African countries lost market share in their traditional export markets without gaining significant new markets. The high and seemingly ever increasing levels of foreign aid provided a cushion to lessen the impact of the crisis, but also undermined the incentive of governments to undertake the wholesale economic reforms needed to renew economic growth.

At the regional level, the OAU sought to protect the sovereignty of its member states. Powerful regional norms emerged in the 1960s to promote political stability. Two of these are particularly important for the purposes of this essay. First, the OAU maintained an inflexible belief that the borders which had been fixed by the colonial powers subsequent to the Berlin Conference of 1884-1885 should not be altered. In the post colonial era, this was translated into the principle that African states should accept both their own existing borders and the inviolability of all states in the region. Irredentist and secessionist claims could have no legitimacy. This precept was remarkably successful in protecting colonial borders. It was tested repeatedly, starting with the 1967-1970 Nigerian civil war and Biafra's attempt to secede from the Nigerian Federation.[8] In these cases, as in succeeding ones, almost all the states in the region supported the government in power, which was a member in good standing of the OAU. Secessionist or irredentist insurgencies typically could not get substantial support from other states in sub Saharan Africa and, in the overwhelming majority of cases, found themselves at a severe resource disadvantage. At least in part as a result, only one insurgency has ever succeeded in realising territorial claims vis à vis an incumbent post colonial government in the region. The Eritrean secession from Ethiopia in 1993 and its recognition by the OAU after three decades of unabated civil war remains the only instance in which the regional norm has been officially set aside.

This OAU precept was of course not always perfectly respected,[9] but it remained remarkably strong, with even minor transgressions criticised within Africa. For instance, when Tanzania intervened in Uganda in 1979 to help topple the increasingly chaotic and bloody tyranny of Idi Amin, long an embarrassment to the region, Tanzania was publicly rebuked at the next OAU summit by the president of Nigeria. Olesegun Obasanjo argued that interference in a neighbour's affairs represented 'a dangerous precedent of unimaginable consequences'.[10]

On the whole, this emphasis on state sovereignty was accepted by the international community. Western intervention in the region overwhelmingly supported existing governments and the international boundaries created by colonialism. These included the several Western interventions in Congo/Zaïre, support for the federal government of Nigeria during the civil war and several incidences of attempted mediation in the Sudan civil war. This uncritical acceptance of the inviolability of colonial borders was not inevitable. Ethnically driven fissiparous tendencies in each of these countries could have driven the West to see the logic of secession. But the international community respected the regional diplomatic principle, at least in part because of the compelling argument that undermining the norm in instances where it made least sense would weaken it where it mattered most.

Ex colonial powers were typically the most respectful of the sovereignty criterion as it related to their ex colonies.[11] Following the disastrous Katanga episode, Belgium remained deferential towards Zaïre, long after Mobutu's thuggish ways had become apparent. The UK devoted considerable diplomatic energy to bringing about majority rule in Rhodesia, and the French military harshly repressed the Bamileke rebellion in Cameroon. Even when outside powers opposed an incumbent regime in the region, they did so in a limited and often covert manner. Thus, France supported Biafra during the Nigerian civil war, but publicly denied it was doing so. Much of its aid to Biafrans was funnelled indirectly through Gabon and Côte d'Ivoire. The French position was roundly condemned as cynical and self serving by most Western observers.

The communist countries showed equal deference to regional norms. Their support to the region was almost entirely limited to the insurgencies that were fighting minority white governments in southern Africa. The US, on the other hand, became considerably less accepting of the OAU principle, particularly in the 1980s, when under the so called Reagan Doctrine it channelled support to insurgencies fighting against Soviet backed states in Mozambique, Ethiopia and Angola.

In contrast, under apartheid, South Africa (the RSA) worked to undermine the norms, and was perhaps the leading revisionist state in the region. It played a key role in all the civil wars that plagued southern Africa in the 1970s and 1980s. The RSA supported the Smith regime in Rhodesia as it fought against ZANU, and assisted the white minority government in Namibia with troops and finance. It subverted regimes which it opposed in the region, notably Mozambique and Angola, by providing generous resources to armed opposition groups. The RSA more or less created and then financed the *Resistência Nacional Moçambicana* (RENAMO) in Mozambique, and long supported *União Nacional para a Independência Total d'Angola* (UNITA) in Angola. Similarly, it was South Africa's changed policy towards these regimes that helped facilitate negotiations and eventually settlements between government and 'rebel' groups, even if it was not officially 'at the table' for any of the bargaining.

Besides the RSA, Libya was the only other African country that openly contested the OAU maxim by supporting insurgencies in north western and north eastern

Africa. Throughout the late 1970s and early 1980s it pursued its ideological objectives, offering support to groups in Chad, the Western Sahara and Sudan, as well as offering safe haven and support to opposition groups from countries like Egypt.[12]

With these partial exceptions, however, the post colonial order in Africa has been a remarkably stable and predictable one. The sovereignty norm has had several important implications. First, the consensual support for this principle shaped the patterns of external funding for the warring parties in the internal conflicts of the region. Without sustained external assistance, insurgencies were much less likely to succeed (except in southern Africa, where the near universal hostility to minority white regimes virtually ensured the ultimate success of the opposition, regardless of its military prowess). In general, though the foreign aid available to armed insurgencies was severely limited, while governments could, by and large, count on both the military and economic assistance of the West, and at least the passive acquiescence of their neighbours in helping them to retain power.

Secondly, the OAU conferred legitimacy on all anti colonial activities. Created by newly independent states even as other African territories remained under colonial control, the OAU has always held as central principles the anti colonial struggle and the objective of eventual African majority control over the entire continent. Thus, though regional norms were quite hostile to insurgencies when they were directed at undermining OAU member states, they were generally supportive of insurgencies directed at toppling white minority governments in southern Africa. Indeed, organisations like South West African People's Organisation (SWAPO) in Namibia, or the Zimbabwe African National Union (ZANU) in what became Zimbabwe, enjoyed such international legitimacy and high diplomatic standing that they did not need to gain military victories in the field in order to eventually achieve power.

What, finally, was the impact of these determinant values on state formation? It seems clear that the combination of strong external support and highly legitimist international norms helped the governments of the region to survive without necessarily developing either institutional capacity, credibility or infrastructural power. Instead, because they were never tested and were protected from all potential threats, the governments in the region tended to become 'lame leviathans'[13] who were condemned to being 'permanently weak'.[14]

The role of regional powers

Does this model provide analytical traction for the five 'big dysfunctional' states on which this project focuses? These five states exemplify the patterns just described, even if they demonstrate varying levels of 'statehood', and have had different relationships with the international community of states. On the diplomatic front, all five states, with the partial exception of Sudan, have had periods during which they were key diplomatic players, at the centre of regional diplomacy. But all these states have also had periods in which they were pariahs, with little international support. Thus, Mobutu parlayed his reputation as a reliable Cold War ally to attract substantial economic and military aid throughout the 1965-1990 period.[15] Over the course of the last decade however, the failure of attempts to democratise, the subsequent collapse of the Mobutu regime and the inability of the Kabila governments (both senior and junior) fully to consolidate or control their territory has isolated the country and torn it apart. The DRC's collapse and multiple civil wars have posed one of the biggest threats on the continent to the maintenance of the sovereignty principle.

Similarly, Sudan was a key player in the regional diplomacy of the 1970s and early 1980s, before the demise of the Nimeiry regime, the emergence of a fundamentalist Islamist government and the resumption of civil war all served to marginalise the country. The present regime maintains an active regional diplomacy, but has had a difficult relationship with the West. The country's extensive Middle Eastern links have provided it with significant resources, even as Western aid has been cut back to humanitarian and relief operations only.

On the economic front as well, the five countries in question demonstrate somewhat different profiles which help to differentiate between their relationships with the international community. Table 1 (page 233) provides data on the evolution of foreign aid levels, foreign direct investment, and international trade levels during the 1990s. To summarise, three of these countries, Angola, the DRC and Nigeria, are resource rich and thus have had a significant trade relationship with the rest of the world. On the other hand, Ethiopia is resource poor and although Sudan has substantial oil reserves, they are only now beginning to be exploited. All five states have received substantial amounts of foreign aid at one time or another, and all have accumulated massive international debt, given their inability to overcome fiscal and balance of payments deficits.

As in other cases, international resources probably helped these countries to maintain the borders inherited from colonial partition. Zaïre's territorial integrity was maintained during this period in some part because of Western support, and because the OAU bestowed legitimacy on it. Nigeria's and Sudan's ability to survive civil wars was probably reinforced by these same sources of support. Ethiopia appears to be the one exception to this rule because of its inability to prevent Eritrean independence, but the latter's historical claims to statehood and Ethiopia's marginal position in the post colonial situation probably go a long way towards explaining the anomaly. The current regime in Ethiopia has, moreover, received substantial donor support, despite its unimpressive human rights and governance record.

Moving towards a new regime in the 21st century

The context provided by the Cold War, the humanitarian concerns of the West, and the specific regional norms favouring sovereignty established after African independence has provided Africa with a very specific relationship with the international community. Resources provided by foreign donors to the region's governments assured relative stability, even if the regimes in question typically lacked a realistic state formation project. However, in the 1990s, new principles concerned with the development of states began to evolve, slowly but surely.

First, with the installation of Nelson Mandela as the president of South Africa, African majority rule has been achieved throughout the whole continent. In consequence, the ideology of anti colonial struggle is no longer a unifying force at the regional level.

Secondly, Western governments began to make their support of regimes conditional on the adoption of economic and political policy criteria. This came about for a variety of reasons, including the end of the Cold War, the subsequent decline of Africa's geo strategic importance, and the rise of ideological support in the West for electoral democracy and capitalist economics. Donors began to demonstrate growing impatience with the dismal performance of aid recipients in the sub Saharan region and an increasing tendency to withdraw support. The US is exhibit number one in displaying this changed attitude. From 1962 until 1988, its leading aid recipients in the region were Sudan, Zaïre, Kenya, Somalia, Liberia and Ethiopia.[16] During the 1990s, only Ethiopia and Kenya were still receiving American support, and even this was highly conditional on political and economic reform. The Mobutu regime in Zaïre, saved several times in the 1970s from insurgencies by Western military support, and a major recipient of foreign aid throughout the 1980s, had by the mid 1990s lost virtually all of its international funding.

Zaïre was allowed to fall to a not particularly impressive guerilla army in 1997, which had itself received support from both regional powers such as Uganda and Western nations such as the US.

Financial assistance has, in any event, become somewhat less generous as the effectiveness of funding practices has come under increasing scrutiny. In addition, persistent fiscal pressures have led virtually all donors to cut back on their contributions to African development. Aid today remains substantial by historical standards, but it has declined by roughly a third in real terms since the early 1990s. The recent popularity of the Jubilee Debt Campaign in the West,[17] and the reception of the Nepad proposals by African governments both suggest that the old dynamics are not entirely defunct.[18] The period of sustained increases in donor support, however, appears to be over.

Thirdly, persistent economic failure and advanced decay in state functionality in a number of countries has diminished the region's diplomatic leverage. Certainly, it has helped to change attitudes towards insurgencies. Most African countries have performed very poorly in economic terms, and the endemic balance of payments problems and fiscal deficits they have incurred since the first oil crisis have weakened state structures in the region further. Tendencies towards rent seeking and patronage based politics have been enhanced by economic problems, so that most countries in the region are characterised by extremely high levels of corruption and increasingly poor state services. In the worst examples, governments had stopped functioning by the 1990s and only a small proportion of the national territory remained under state control.[19] Failure of governance was so evident that external support for such regimes could not easily be justified in principled terms. In Zaïre, for instance, it was easy to argue that directing aid to the Kabila insurgency might actually result in improvements in law, order and some semblance of economic development.

In addition, the traditional distinction between lawful leaders of governments and warlords has begun to fade. Regimes recognised by international law have engaged in obviously illegal activities: the governments in Nigeria, Zambia and Cameroon, for example, have been linked to international drug trading.[20] On the other hand, warlords have engaged in legal trade and signed deals with multi national corporations – as did Charles Taylor in Liberia and Kabila in Zaïre.

The progressive withdrawal of external powers

The argument has been made that the end of the Cold War has affected internal conflicts in unstable regions such as Africa. The academic and policy community consensus on the impact of the end of the Cold War is well summed up by Lake and Rothchild, who claim that,

> the promise of the post Cold War world is that the great powers, freed from the shackles of superpower competition, can now intervene to mitigate ethnic conflicts by providing external guarantees of social order … [T]he paradox of the post Cold War world, however, is in the absence of the bipolar competition that drove them into the far reaches of the globe, the United States and other powers now lack the political will necessary to make a sustained commitment to this role.[21]

I believe we are witnessing a relative withdrawal of outside powers from Africa, only partly related to the end of the Cold War. There can be little doubt that the current period has witnessed the end of both Chinese and Russian intervention in sub Saharan Africa. This has brought about a striking and remarkably rapid change. Both had earlier competed with the West in terms of supplying aid and resources to a number of African countries. The Soviet Union provided extensive military and economic support to regimes in Mozambique, Ethiopia and Angola, among others, until the second half of the 1980s.[22] Today, not only have the Russian and Chinese aid programmes been largely shut down, but they are themselves recipients of substantial assistance from the Western aid agencies and are thus competitors for funding with their ex client states. Moreover, neither power can any longer claim a prominent diplomatic presence in the region.

More than any other external power, the US viewed African politics through the prism of the Cold War. In the 1990s, with the main motivation for its focus on the region gone, US foreign policy was focused elsewhere. Africa became a backwater in America's eyes. Support for both bilateral and multilateral aid programmes declined sharply, and consulates and aid missions were closed. Good intentions in Somalia did not survive the onset of American casualties because, at least since the Vietnam War, the foreign policy establishment has been unwilling to countenance the deaths of American soldiers, a reluctance that has marked military forays into other regions of the world as well. The reaction of the US to the Rwandan genocide in 1994 was limited to trying to persuade the international community that it was not taking place. However, even for US policy to Africa, the end of the Cold War did not represent the kind of sharp discontinuity implied by observers like Lake and Rothchild. American funding for sub Saharan Africa has been steadily declining for several decades, as a result of fiscal politics within the US rather than its foreign policy objectives.

The exception to the pattern of benign neglect that has long marked American policy towards sub Saharan Africa was the Reagan Doctrine. Support for anti communist insurgencies in the Horn of Africa and in southern Africa was clearly motivated by Cold War thinking. Nonetheless, it must be noted that such backing affected only a handful of countries in two sub regions of the continent. Elsewhere, the US was not nearly as important a presence, and therefore post Cold War changes in Africa were less likely.

French attitudes towards Africa are also undergoing a dramatic change, which may have more significant implications for the region. Once labelled the 'policeman of the West' in Africa for its multiple military interventions under Giscard d'Estaing,[23] France has been closing or downsizing its military bases throughout the region and French policy statements have suggested a growing reluctance to intervene in Africa's affairs. Since 1998, France has undertaken substantial reductions in the number of its troops in the region, today at levels forty per cent below those of a decade ago.[24] Even French support to key allies in the region such as Côte d'Ivoire and Senegal cannot be taken for granted. We are certainly witnessing an abandonment of the ambition France expressed earlier to expand French influence to eastern and central Africa.

This shift in French policy is however probably only partly related to the end of the Cold War. The recent change in policy is only the latest chapter in the long and tortuous process of decolonisation, or, perhaps more accurately, of *de neocolonisation*. French economic interests in the region have declined to almost negligible levels, and the once very influential pro Africa lobby in Paris has lost its audience, as policymakers have turned their attention to more dynamic regions of the world.[25] Also, ill advised French support for discredited regimes in the region, notably those in Zaïre and Rwanda, has led the public to scrutinise the country's policies for Africa more critically than in the past. In particular, the backing France provided for the Habyarimana regime in Rwanda, and the subsequent rumours of French military aid to the Hutu extremists during the genocide of 1994 generated intense national debate about French policy in Africa, and considerably weakened the pro Africa lobby in Paris. It also contributed to a growing reluctance on the part of the French government to project military power in the region.

Changing views of the state

The decline in the West's interest in Africa has been accompanied by an important policy shift regarding the proper economic and political role of the state. I do not believe that the geo strategic shift and the policy shift are causally related, at least in a directly meaningful manner, but it is true that changing views of the nature of the African state have further contributed to weakening the sovereignty paradigm described earlier.

The 1980s witnessed the renaissance of neo liberal economic doctrines in the West. Economic planning and state intervention had been emphasised in prevailing economic doctrines of the 1950 and 1960s, and provided justification for the West's attempts to buttress African states with development assistance entirely directed towards central state structures. By the early 1980s, however, many observers in the West had reached the conclusion that these economic and political interventions into African states had made development less rather than more likely. Indeed, the failure of governments provided a particularly effective prism through which to understand the African economic crisis. This resulted in two distinct institutional innovations. First, the West began actively to seek alternatives to dealing with the central state. The private sector, non governmental organisations (NGOs) and decentralised local government were all viewed as viable alternatives, and the West devoted considerable efforts to promoting them. Western donors began to demand the adoption by African governments of privatisation and liberalisation measures, to increase the economic power of private actors in the economy. These efforts, long resisted by African regimes which understood they would weaken a key instrument of their power,[26] nonetheless began to pay off in the 1990s. For instance, roughly half of the major public enterprises that existed in 1980 have been sold off to the private sector in the last twenty years,[27] substantially diminishing the patronage resources available to states in sub Saharan Africa.

Similarly, the emergence of NGOs was encouraged by generous donor support which had once been entirely monopolised by governments. Today, local and foreign NGOs capture roughly a quarter to a third of donor resources. African NGOs have forged alliances with Western ones, which allow them to gain access to the funding of the latter, resulting in a volume of resources that may dwarf what is available in terms of official development assistance. In the social sectors, NGOs are in the process of supplanting governments as the default service provider. Does this weaken states? This is not clear, but what is not debatable is that it is changing the relation between states and citizens in the region. Particularly in the countryside and far away from the capital, African citizens increasingly do not look to the state for the key public goods they wish to have. Their expectations of the state are at an all time low and, presumably, their support of that state is equally minimal.

Western donors have also aggressively promoted decentralisation efforts in the region. These shift power from the capital to newly formed local governments, and provide them with growing authority and revenues. In donor doctrine, decentralisation promotes both democracy and greater efficiency by bringing the government closer to the citizen, and making it more responsive.[28] The effects on central states are ambiguous. Having devolved many secondary functions, central states might profitably come to focus on core functions and gain strength. Many decentralisation processes have been manipulated by central governments which have turned them into exercises in de concentration, although the real power, most notably over revenues, remains safely in the hands of central governments. On the other hand, local elections and the emergence of a regional political identity may reinforce local particularisms that will, over time, weaken the legitimacy of the central state.

Another change promoted by the West was an agenda of governance reforms in the region. Having come to the conclusion that poor governance lay at the root of the African crisis, donors demanded both improvements in economic management and the democratisation of African politics. Aid has been made conditional on the introduction of anti corruption measures and the holding of regular multi party elections. Support has been provided to reinforce the independence of the judiciary, the capacity of the legislature, and even NGOs that promote state accountability. Many of these efforts are superficial, and the West's commitment to African democracy has been at best inconsistent, but the shift away from the unconditional support of the central state, regardless of its performance, has been significant.

What, more generally, have been the effects of these trends on African state formation? Clearly all of them weaken the political projects of African states, which can no longer expect the blank cheques of the past and must now contend with new actors and challenges. On the other hand, the flow of unconditional aid to African states remains high by historical standards. Contributions have become more conditional, to be sure, but African governments have become adept at manipulating and sidestepping the rules.[29] Much of the finance directed to NGOs still finds its way into the hands of politicians. The remarkable ability of the region's dictators to survive the move to multi party electoral politics should alert us to the limitations of the new dispensation. After all, as the 21st century began, nineteen of the region's forty eight leaders who had been in power before democratisation in 1989 were still in power.

Not all of the donors are equally committed to the agenda of reform in governance. The US and the northern European donors are comparatively assiduous, but France and Japan continue to favour commercial objectives over all else, while the World Bank and IMF view the governance agenda as little more than an instrument to recoup their old loans in the region and promote economic development. The only issue all the donors agree on is Africa's reduced global importance.

Attempts to promote surrogate institutions

Even as their interest in the region has waned, the Western powers have sought to maintain some control over events in sub Saharan Africa, but at a reduced cost. West Africa has often resorted to asking for the European Union's assistance in rescuing the cash strapped parastatal enterprises established by France and beholden to French commercial interests. In turn, France has long sought to use the EU to help shoulder some of the costs of maintaining French influence in its ex colonies. It was however unable to raise European support for its Franc Zone obligations in the context of EU negotiations for a common currency.

Cost sharing and the creation of surrogate institutions has been more successful in the security field. The reluctance of America to put its own troops in harm's way has led the US government to support UN peacekeeping operations in a number of African states. More recently, the Western powers have sought to build up the capacity of African states to undertake peacekeeping functions. Under the African Crisis Response Initiative (ACRI), US army instructors have been providing training programmes for troops from seven African countries since 1997, with the objective of deploying troops to crises on the continent. France and the UK have engaged in similar training exercises under the *Renforcement des Capacités de Maintien de la Paix* (RECAMP) initiative. The desirability of helping African governments to promote and defend regional security without foreign assistance is incontestable. However, the American and French motive in adopting this reasoning in the late 1990s was largely attributable to the desire of these states to maintain some control over events in the region at a lower human and financial cost, and to avoid the public relations disasters that had attended the US intervention in Somalia and the French Turquoise operation in Rwanda.

The emergence of new state actors

Multilateral operations such as ACRI and RECAMP have proved difficult to get off the ground, partly because they have a relatively low priority for the Western powers, particularly since the events of 9/11. Their African partners have been relatively passive participants, willing to receive resources and assistance, but much less inclined to devote time and political capital to the multilateral objectives of the programmes. The scope of action for such multilateral forces is in any event circumscribed. Bilateral relations of power are likely to prove more important than multilateral ones as the nature of the interaction between African countries changes.

Nature abhors a vacuum, and the partial withdrawal of external actors in the 1990s from Africa resulted in the emergence of new political dynamics and different state actors. Both the decay of government structures in the region and the growing unwillingness of the West to use troops to protect regimes have combined to produce a number of new episodes of state collapse and civil war. In an earlier era, the Western powers might have intervened to avert the complete breakdown of law and order in Liberia, Sierra Leone, the Great Lakes region or Zaïre but, in the 1990s, these countries were allowed to fail. Western intervention limited itself to the protection of expatriate residents and some emergency aid for displaced civilians.

In each of these conflicts, new actors moved in to fill the void, claiming various objectives. The most obvious of these role players might have been expected to be leaders of the more powerful states within the region. To a certain extent, this has been true. Nigeria, for example, has sought to assert itself in the west African conflicts, notably through the West African Economic Monitoring Group (ECOMOG). Nigerian intervention has sometimes been justified within the context of an ambition to act as a 'regional policemen', the result of the traditional foreign policy objective of attempting to maintain peace in neighbouring countries. But the country's involvement in the affairs of other African states does not appear important to domestic peace in Nigeria itself, and seems neither to have been affected by, nor to have affected, the fall of the Abacha regime in 1999. Such intervention however brings some prestige to the otherwise discredited Nigerian military, in addition to substantial resources. These take the form both of support from the UN peacekeeping operation's Western backers, and of the important rent seeking opportunities afforded soldiers and their officers in Sierra Leone and Liberia. On the other hand, Nigeria's own internal weakness and the operational limits of its military have largely prevented it from taking up a more assertive regional posture.

In southern Africa, South Africa has flexed its muscles in several instances, most notably in restoring order in Lesotho in 1998. But both the Mandela and the Mbeki regimes have demonstrated considerable reluctance to project power in the region, being apparently unwilling to accept the mantle of regional *hegemon*. As a result, South Africa's initiatives have been limited to the diplomatic and peace making realm, most notably in the failed attempts to broker peace deals in Burundi.

More striking, however, have been the diplomatic initiatives undertaken by smaller states. In west Africa, President Campaore of Burkina Faso has adopted an aggressive regional policy, meddling in the affairs of a number of countries. Campaore seemed only slightly intimidated by Nigeria's opposition when he openly supported the Taylor regime in Liberia in the late 1980s. Throughout the 1990s, there were persistent and credible rumours of Burkinabe support for anti government forces in the Sierra Leone conflict. Most recently, Burkina Faso has discreetly provided backing for the military rebellion in northern Côte d'Ivoire, a geo strategic initiative which would have been virtually unimaginable in the heyday of *la France Afrique.*

Even more striking has been the activism of small states in East Africa. The Kagame regime in Rwanda and that of Museveni in Uganda have emerged as key players in the conflicts in central Africa, particularly in the DRC's civil war. These interventions represent a novelty in African international relations. In virtually unprecedented fashion, Uganda and Rwanda have seen their foreign policies as instruments of national state formation and consolidation. These cases remind one of Clausewitz's dictum that war is the continuation of politics by other means, in that governments project power abroad in order to promote security and political stability at home. Similarly, the Kagame regime has deployed its troops to the DRC as a way to destroy the remnants of the Hutu *Interhamwe* militias, which it believes are the most serious threat to the continuation of minority Tutsi rule in Rwanda. President Museveni has adopted an even more ambitious set of policy initiatives, not only with regard to the DRC, but also vis à vis Sudan, to shore up domestic stability.

Neither Uganda, Burkina Faso nor Rwanda can claim to have the economic might to play the role of regional *hegemon* credibly. On the other hand, during the 1990s Angola emerged as a more credible candidate, willing to fill the regional diplomatic vacuum by acting out an aggressive foreign policy. Because of its considerable oil revenues, Angola could afford its ambitions, and a long civil war had transformed its army into what is by regional standards an effective force. Even more than Uganda or Rwanda, Angola emerged as the kingmaker during the civil war in the DRC. In Congo Brazzaville, Angola helped Sassou Nguesso take back the presidency in 1997 by sending several battalions of experienced troops. However, the country's increasingly militant foreign policy was largely part of its main objective, that of defeating UNITA at home. Interference in the two Congos was seen as necessary in order to root out support for UNITA bases.

Thus, the most important consequence of the withdrawal of the superpowers from Africa since the 1990s has been the emergence of regional 'power politics', even though its most assertive practitioners are not, with the exception of Angola, the more important powers one might have expected to do so. The countries in the region that are able and willing to project power across their borders are finding fewer constraints in their way. The post colonial norms set by the OAU have not entirely disappeared, however. The old taboos forbidding secession and border changes remain, judging by regional public discourse regarding the collapsed state of the DRC. On the other hand, the norm of non interference has clearly been seriously eroded and can no longer prevent a number of countries from pursuing a variety of objectives in adjacent territories.

To return to a point previously made, it is striking that countries with the most assertive foreign policies are not the biggest powers in the continent. Rwanda in particular is a surprising case. It is only the 29th biggest economy in the region, according to the World Bank Development Indicators for 1998, and hardly a country one would expect to have a proactive foreign policy. Similarly, Angola is only the 17th biggest economic power in the region. To be sure, Nigeria, the region's second biggest economy after the RSA, has pursued a relatively dominant regional policy agenda. But some of the region's bigger economies, such as Kenya (the third biggest) or Côte d'Ivoire (the fourth) have continued to play by the old rules and have rarely sought to exert power abroad.

In this context, the role of the RSA, the economic giant of the region, is of interest. Everyone has assumed that the RSA will play an increasingly dominant role in the region's international relations. But while its economic power is increasingly felt throughout the continent, its diplomatic and defence posture has been relatively understated so far, particularly outside the countries that comprise southern Africa. With the exception of a brief foray into Lesotho in 1999, the South African armed forces have not intervened in the region. The RSA's diplomacy has been active in several African conflicts, but to no great effect. This is in part because its efforts have not been backed up by the threat of force. Instead, South African diplomacy has focused on initiatives such as the current Nepad[30] (which clearly harks back to the old post colonial regime in its focus on Western support for local regimes based on an official agenda for development). Whatever its merits, Nepad does not appear particularly relevant to the region's civil wars and is unlikely to affect the behaviour of 'revisionist' regimes such as Angola or Rwanda.

These patterns may change. In a normal system of interstate relations, one would expect regional powers to wield their strength more aggressively than smaller ones. The withdrawal of the West provides an opportunity for the bigger players to assert themselves. Perhaps Nigeria and RSA will progressively emerge as less inhibited regional powers, willing to flex their muscles on behalf of their regional interests.

Two factors, however, militate against such an evolution. First, both Nigeria and the RSA appear too focused on internal issues to take on such a leadership role at any time soon. Secondly, the region's outward oriented economic structures make this kind of development unlikely. Only the RSA has sufficient economic interests in the region to care about regional stability and peace. Nigeria, despite its relatively big domestic economy, exerts little sway over west Africa. Its manufacturing and agricultural bases are in tatters and little traded, while its oil, which constitutes by far the highest proportion of its traded sector, is sold outside the region. This is also true of Angola. In sum, the region's economic extraversion means that cases of state collapse in the region do not have a directly negative impact on neighbouring economies. To be sure, these 'neighbourhood' issues do give Africa a bad reputation which probably deters productive investment in the region by Western private interests, even in countries that have made great strides towards good governance and stability. But the lack of a more integrated regional economy does reduce the costs of state breakdown to other countries in the region. To give just one example, before its own collapse in 2002, Côte d'Ivoire's economy was little affected by the continuing problems experienced by Guinea and Liberia, largely because the mainstays of the Ivoirian economy were cocoa, coffee and cotton, with prices set by the world markets. The relatively low levels of trade within the region and the absence of a regional communications and infrastructure grid actually serves to protect individual states against economic collapse in others.

Conclusion

In this chapter, I have sketched the impact of African external relations on state formation over the course of the last half century, arguing that the system of international relations fashioned in the period after independence has helped to provide political stability to the region without creating strong and viable national states. The end of the Cold War and changing attitudes in the West about its relationship with Africa have conspired to alter this post colonial mindset. International relations in Africa are moving towards dynamics which are likely to be more open to change. In the absence of Western intervention, a handful of states have emerged that are willing to project power beyond their borders to promote their own domestic state formation projects. The two biggest powers in the region, Nigeria and the RSA, have yet to play a substantial regional role, but are likely to attempt to fill the void caused by the declining interest in the region shown by the West.

Table 1: The relationship of the 'big dysfunctional states' to the world economy (1990–1998)

	1990	1992	1994	1996	1998
Total external debt to GDP ratio (%)					
Angola	84	174	278	138	164
DRC	110	134	172	219	–
Ethiopia	126	168	206	168	150
Nigeria	117	89	140	89	70
Sudan	112	241	207	235	–
Net ODA from all donors, OECD source ($)					
Angola	269,430	350,530	451,010	544,150	–
DRC	897,710	269,150	245,450	167,410	–
Ethiopia	1,019,650	1,182,120	1,074,470	849,430	–
Nigeria	250,430	258,670	190,260	191,780	–
Sudan	826,570	549,550	413,040	230,250	–
Total merchant exports. (fob(($)					
Angola	3,884,000	3,833,000	3,017,000	5,087,000	3,509,000
DRC	–	1,245,700	1,255,400	1,727,000	–
Ethiopia	365,600	154,100	279,600	410,200	602,100
Nigeria	13,914,000	11,886,000	9,415,000	16,117,000	9,727,000
Sudan	442,800	–	–	620,300	595,700
Foreign direct invest (net) ($)					
Angola	-335,700	288,000	327,000	588,000	898,000
DRC	13,300	0		0	–
Ethiopia	–	–	–	–	–
Nigeria	602,000	714,000	588,000	759,700	1,351,300
Sudan	–	–	–	70,000	670,000

Endnotes

1   Jackson RH & CG Rosberg. 'Why Africa's Weak States Persist.' *World Politics*, 35 (1) October 1982, pp. 1-24.

2   Bayart J F. *L'Etat en Afrique: La Politique du Ventre*. Paris: Fayard, 1989.

3   Herbst J. 'War and the State in Africa',. *International Security*, 14 (4). Spring 1990, pp. 117-39.

4   Jackson RH & CG Rosberg. *op. cit.*, 1982; Clapham C, *Africa and the International System*. New York: Cambridge University Press, 1996.

5   Jackson RH & CG Rosberg. *ibid.*

6   Van de Walle N. *African Economies and the Politics of Permanent Crisis*. New York: Cambridge University Press, 2001, Ch 5.

7   Van de Walle N. *ibid*, 2001.

8   Stremlau JJ. *The International Politics of the Nigerian Civil War, 1967-1970*. Princeton, NJ: Princeton University Press, 1977.

9   Clapham C. *op. cit.*

10 Deng F, Kimaro S, Lyons T, Rothchild D & IW Zartman (eds.). *Sovereignty as Responsibility: Conflict Management in Africa*. Washington DC: The Brookings Institution, 1996, p. 160.

11 Clapham C. *op. cit.*, pp. 80-83.

12 Lemarchand R. 'Lybian Adventurism', In: Harbeson JW & D Rothchild (eds), *Africa in World Politics*. Boulder: Westview Press, 1991.

13 Callaghy T. 'Networks and Governance in Africa; Innovation in the Debt Regime', In: Callaghy T, Kassimir R & R Latham (eds). *Intervention and Transnationalism in Africa: Global-Local Networks of Power*. New York: Cambridge University Press, 2002, pp. 115-148.

14 Herbst J. *op. cit.*, p. 136.

15 Schatzberg M. *Mobutu or Chaos? The United States and Zaire, 1960 1990*. Lanham: University Press of America, 1991.

16 Clough M. *Free At Last? U.S. Policy toward Africa and the End of the Cold War*. New York: Council on Foreign Relations, 1992, p. 78.

17 Callaghy RK & R Latham (eds). *Intervention and Transnationalism in Africa: Global Local Networks of Power*. New York: Cambridge University Press, 2002, pp. 115-148.

18 De Waal A, 'What's New in the 'New Partnership for Africa's Development'?' *International Affairs*, 78 (3), 2002.

19 Reno W. *Warlord Politics and African States.* Boulder: Lynne Rienner Press, 1998.

20 Bayart JF, Ellis S & B Hibou., *La Criminilisation de l'Etat en Afrique.* Paris: Editions Complexe, 1997; Reno W. *ibid.*

21 Lake D & D Rothchild. *The International Spread of Ethnic Conflict: Fear, Diffusion, and Escalation.* Princeton: Princeton University Press, 1998, p. 124

22 Laidi Z. *The Superpowers and Africa.* Chicago: University of Chicago Press, 1988.

23 Chipman J. *French Power in Africa.* Oxford: Basil Blackwell, 1989.

24 Chafer T. 'Franco African Relations: No Longer so Exceptional?' *African Affairs* 101, 2002, pp.343-363; Utley R, 'Not to Do Less but to Do Better ... French Military Policy in Africa'. *International Affairs* 78, January 2002, pp. 129-46.

25 Adda J & MC Smouts, *La France Face au Sud: Le Miroir Brise.* Paris: Karthala, 1989.

26 Van de Walle N. *African Economies and the Politics of Permanent Crisis.* New York: Cambridge University Press, 2001.

27 Bennell P, 'Privatization in sub Saharan Africa: Progress and Prospects during the 1990s'. *World Development,* 25 (11), 1997, pp. 1785-1803.

28 Crook R & J Manor. *Democracy and Decentralisation in South Asia and West Africa.* Cambridge: Cambridge University Press, 1998.

29 Van de Walle N, *op. cit.*

30 De Waal A, *op. cit.*, pp. 463-75.

9

Conflict in Africa:

armies, rebels and geography

Jeffrey Herbst

Conflict occurs across Africa, but big states appear to be especially prone to war. All of the large states considered in this project – Angola, the Democratic Republic of the Congo, Ethiopia, Nigeria, South Africa and Sudan – have experienced conflicts or civil wars. Most of these have lasted for many years: indeed, only Nigeria's ended in less than a decade. Many of the conflicts have continued until this day. Only in the case of South Africa may it be possible to say that the conflict has definitely ended.

After developing a perspective on the dynamics of rebellion in Africa, this paper explores why the relatively large territories of some African states may make them especially prone to violent conflict. I depart from much of the recent literature on rebellion by arguing that it is the dynamics within African militaries, rather than the motivations of rebels, that actually drive these conflicts. Especially in mature insurgencies, rebels structure their forces according to the amount of military power that states can project. I go on to argue that the space available in large countries makes it especially unlikely that well developed insurgencies will be defeated. In addition, it may be particularly hard for large countries facing rebellion to win, because it is difficult to recruit soldiers for internal battles, and because foreign aid – a critical variable that determines the ability of many African governments to fight – is usually less available to large countries.

Early stages of rebellion

Rebel movements are important because they are armed threats to the state, a point surprisingly ignored in the increasingly complex attempts by analysts to parse the motivation, as opposed to the actions, of fighters. To understand rebels therefore it is important to understand their ability to undertake their fundamental task: combat. As such, most African rebellions begin life as extremely small and vulnerable operations. The eleven men who started the fighting in Eritrea,[1] the famous twenty seven fighters who began the National Resistance Movement (NRM) campaign in Uganda,[2] the approximately one hundred soldiers of the National Patriotic Front of Liberia (NPFL) who crossed into Liberia with Charles Taylor,[3] the thirty five trained soldiers who started the Revolutionary United Front (RUF) in Sierra Leone,[4] the 250 that founded the *Frente de Libertação de Moçambique* (Frelimo)[5] are representative of the low numbers and consequent weakness of rebel movements at the beginning. Of course, many of these insurgencies are defeated early, or simply collapse owing to internal divisions, never to be heard of again.

As a result, rebel leaders, literally from the start, are acutely conscious of the coercive power of the state and seek opportunities to take refuge from it. An unfortunate example of how divorced some aspects of social science have become from the real world of war is that the most commonly enunciated lesson of rebellion (that the terrain of struggle must be understood) is today largely ignored. For instance, Frelimo noted early on that 'our forces are far inferior to the enemy's'. Therefore, it designed a strategy to take its weakness into account by conducting a war of attrition.[6] Museveni's primary concern from the beginning was that his nascent movement should not be destroyed. All tactical concerns were made subordinate to that overriding goal: 'Loss of territory is, at this stage, of no consequence. In our case, the more important considerations are the preservation and expansion of our forces by avoiding unnecessary casualties, and destroying the enemy's means of making war'.[7]

African militaries and early insurgencies

It is when insurgencies are small that they are most likely to be defeated. Brockett concludes from central America: 'during "normal conditions"[...] that is, prior to the onset of a protest cycle, escalating repression will deter popular mobilisation against the regime. In contrast, in the ascendant phase of the protest cycle, the same repression is likely to provoke increased mass oppositional activities'.[8] It is not surprising that when the cost of repression falls heavily on members of a small rebel movement that are individually deterred (if not killed outright) the movement may be stopped at an early stage; but when governments find it impossible to keep the cost of repression for each individual from falling, the size of the insurgent group grows rapidly.

However, for African militaries, rebellions even in the relatively vulnerable early stages are difficult to defeat. Most governments in Africa lack systems to collect intelligence about what is actually happening on the ground, especially in rural areas distant from the capital. For instance, the presence of cells of the terrorist Osama bin Laden network in Kenya, revealed after the US Embassy in Nairobi was blown up in 1998, appears to have come as a surprise to the authorities. It is even harder for larger states to collect intelligence on the myriad groups who may be operating somewhere in their vast territories. Of course, militaries with intelligence services far more capable than those of African states routinely mistake insurgents for criminals in the early days of a rebellion, causing delay in the implementation of a counter insurgency campaign.[9]

Also, given that the basic local political structures of most African countries are so underdeveloped and that the leaders often tend to be authoritarian, African governments usually cannot confront a small insurgency by quickly addressing local grievances and so averting an armed conflict. Indeed, many leaders/regimes find any kind of local vision that might emerge from even a proto insurgency movement extremely threatening.[10] There are few governments in Africa that could duplicate the feat of Nelson Mandela in neutralising the military threat posed by the Zulu based Inkatha party after the non racial elections in South Africa in 1994. He managed to reduce deaths related to political violence from roughly 3,000 a year to below 100 by a complex political strategy. This involved making numerous concessions to Inkatha regarding the boundaries of KwaZulu Natal; overlooking the gross electoral fraud that allowed Inkatha to gain control of the province's government in 1994; giving the leader of Inkatha, Mangosuthu Buthelezi, the critical Home Affairs portfolio; and agreeing to pay subventions to a large number of Zulu chiefs, as well as other traditional leaders in Africa. The danger of a Zulu led insurgency was therefore avoided, but at a cost that few, if any, other African governments would have been able or willing to bear. Most African countries on the continent have no carrots, only sticks.

As a result, African militaries rely on relatively blunt strikes in the hope of defeating even small groups of rebels. Most governments in Africa feel that it is necessary to mobilise a significant amount of firepower in a short period to fight rebels when they are most vulnerable. The following description by Watts of Nigeria's reaction to the Prophet Maitatsine and his followers in Kano in 1980 is typical of what African states would at least *like* to do to small groups of insurgents:

> Federal Nigerian armed forces began a massive military assault on the sleepy residential and commercial quarter of 'Yan Awaki' in the walled city of Kano, in

northern Nigeria. Under ferocious aerial and ground bombardment, somewhere between five and ten thousand people were slaughtered, and another fifteen thousand injured. The body of the self proclaimed leader, *Maitatsine*, who was killed in the conflagration, was exhumed by the military authorities from a shallow grave outside the city walls where he had been laid to rest by his followers, and placed on display at the local police. Those federal authorities who engaged in the bloodletting and who self consciously sought to quite literally obliterate a leader and a community which saw itself as incontrovertibly Muslim in character and constitution, were acting on the instructions of a civilian administration presided [over] by an aristocratic northern Muslim [President Shagari] and a government that was widely held to be dominated by northern Muslim elites [the so called 'Kaduna Mafia'] [11].

Not many African armies would have been able to duplicate the firepower utilised by the Nigerians against this minor religious group, although few would hesitate if they could. More often, they attempt to use overwhelming force but fail, often with disastrous consequences. For instance, the following is an account of the reaction to the incursion of Charles Taylor's one hundred guerrillas of the NPFL in Nimba County in 1989:

Government forces in the area had responded to the first NPFL attack by detaining suspects, which in practice meant singling out young Gio men for arrest or murder while committing other brutalities in a region which the Krahn dominated military regarded as enemy territory. When the government imposed a curfew throughout Nimba Country, thousands of local people fled into Guinea and Côte d'Ivoire, leaving Armed Forces of Liberia (AFL) troops to loot the empty towns they found. AFL counter measures were ineffective since the army was receiving no support from any part of the population in Nimba County other than its Mandingo residents, many of them traders and shopkeepers. Substantial numbers of government soldiers were deserting.[12]

Although these blunt strikes usually do not work, they should not be seen as irrational, given the circumstances that African leaders face. Many of them may feel that they have no alternative other than lashing out blindly to stop insurgencies that they often cannot pinpoint and usually do not understand.

It might be reasonable to believe that rebellions are especially likely in large countries, given that they will, almost inevitably, have larger areas of under policed territory than small countries. However, intelligence and police services appear to be so inadequate in Africa that rebellions can occur even in fairly small countries. As Museveni noted, holding territory in the early phases of rebellion is not that much of an advantage. The fact that war is so prevalent in small west African states suggests that rebels can coalesce anywhere, and that every state is at risk.

Mature insurgencies

If a rebellion survives its infancy, its leaders then face fundamental questions as to how they should structure themselves. A critical dynamic, of course, is how much armed opposition the state itself presents. The strength of the force they are likely to meet has a profound effect on the dynamics of rebel movements, determining their need both to prepare for, and engage in, combat and to create an ideology. Leaders of rebellions, who face the constant risk of extermination from a relatively strong state, must build a cohesive fighting force in which the motivations of soldiers have been internalised through political and ethnic indoctrination, leavened by the usual amount of military coercion. Even the relatively low tech wars of Africa require a certain organisational coherence – to supply fuel and material and provide logistics. This means that rebellions whose main source of support comes from looting are usually not sufficiently disciplined or reliably supplied to face actual combat.

In contrast, other armed movements face states that are exceptionally weak. They may be in a process of advanced disintegration, only partially because of the insurgency itself. The declining economic fortunes of many African countries, combined with a reduction in external assistance for poorly performing states (as donors seek to reward 'winners') has caused atrophy in the security forces of some. States approaching collapse do not maintain their police and military services and may not even be paying their soldiers. As a result, their ability to project force is extremely limited. Rebels have been notably successful in overthrowing precisely those regimes that have been weakened because they have been cut loose by their superpower patrons after the Cold War. Examples are Barre's in Somalia, Doe's in Liberia, Mengistu's in Ethiopia and Mobutu's in Zaïre. Accordingly, the rebels who confront some African regimes may not have combat as their primary objective, because the state does not threaten their survival. Such opposition movements may use other means – including looting and coercion – to motivate their followers. That stealing and abduction will not yield effective combat forces with well honed fighting skills is not particularly important, because these organisations will rarely be called on to fight. They can often survive simply by terrorising the civilian population. These insurgencies can afford to be softer, more amorphous entities because they face softer, more amorphous states. Time consuming political and ethnic mobilisation may not be worth the investment required.

At one extreme on the continuum of the might that states can mobilise is the firepower and military competence associated with entrenched white settler regimes. Portugal, for instance, managed to field a credible force across three fronts (Angola, Guinea Bissau and Mozambique) for close to a decade. The Portuguese counter insurgency effort was notable for 'understanding of the struggle and adaptation to it at the theatre level and in successfully converting national strategy to battlefield tactics'. Among other things, Lisbon managed '[t]he complete reorientation of the entire Portuguese armed forces from a conventional force to one for counter insurgency'.[13] However, eventually distance, the terrain, and domestic weakness caused the government in Lisbon to collapse. Other formidable forces that fought against rebels included the British in Kenya during the Mau Mau uprising, the French against the National Liberation Front/*Frente de Liberation National* (FLN) in Algeria, the Rhodesians against the Zimbabwe African National Union (ZANU) and the Zimbabwe African People's Union (ZAPU), and South Africa against the South West African People's Organisation (SWAPO) in Namibia and the African National Congress (ANC) and the Pan African Congress (PAC) within its domestic boundaries.

White regimes were not the only ones able to mount large and relatively effective military campaigns against rebels. The Ethiopians fought a full scale conventional war against the Eritrean and Tigray liberation forces, while the Nigerians confronted the Biafrans with a relatively formidable military organisation. As a result, the Eritreans, Tigrayans, and Biafrans, like the national liberation forces that had fought against minority regimes, had to form themselves into conventional armies or be destroyed. For instance, the Eritrean People's Liberation Front (EPLF) in Eritrea had 20,000 fighters under arms, including brigade level heavy weapons, artillery, and engineering units. It also had 200 tanks and a 'navy' made up of fast attack speedboats.[14]

The rebels who confronted these competent armies recognised that they were not going to win by means of a quick, decisive battle. They understood that they had to mobilise relatively large groups of men to conduct combat operations over long periods. They also had to develop large cadres of supporters who would provide them with critical material support and sanctuary. Not surprisingly, this also required them to develop holistic ideologies to explain why their men were fighting, and to motivate them on political and ethnic grounds, since the fruits of victory would not be tasted for some considerable time. These movements also used ideology to try to weaken the other side. Perhaps the classic instance is the *Movemento Popular de Libertaçao de Angola* (MPLA) in Angola, which was not a particularly effective fighting force when measured against the strong Portuguese army. Rather, its 'major successes instead came in converting Portuguese military officers to its cause, thus mobilising political support in Lisbon for turning power exclusively over to the MPLA'.[15] This is not to say that profiteering or coercion were absent from these revolts, or that the leaders would not have preferred such means (especially if it meant enriching themselves) to developing a political ideology. Rather, all that it is necessary to assume is that leaders will do what is required to survive and to achieve eventual victory. That is why, after the rebellions were over, the leaders could treat their followers so badly (a question which still exercises the mind of some authors).

At the other extreme are rebel movements that do not, effectively, face a state or confront security forces, because the regime and its army are so weak that combat is hardly central to the mission of the rebel movement. Under such circumstances the insurgents can afford to operate as rather unimpressive military organisations and instead devote significant attention to other tasks, including enriching themselves. Kabila's Alliance of Democratic Forces for the Liberation of Congo Zaïre (ADFL) is perhaps the paradigmatic example of such a movement, as it did not really fight Mobutu's forces while it marched across what was then Zaïre. The state had delayed paying its military so often that most of its soldiers simply ran away when finally confronted by an armed enemy.[16] The logistics for Kabila's crossing of Zaïre - normally a difficult task which would require some organisational cohesion to fulfil - were handled by the Angolan military. The only fighting that Kabila's army did was when it briefly encountered the *União Naçional para a Independêncja Total d'Angola* (UNITA) forces near Kinshasa. Similarly, the *Resistência Nacional Moçambicana* (RENAMO) in Mozambique could operate a rough and ready organisation (a high percentage of its soldiers were abductees) only because the Frelimo government was so inept.[17] For instance, RENAMO obtained most of its weapons from fleeing Frelimo troops. Similarly, the Somali clans and the Congo (Brazzaville) militias can operate as looting agencies because they do not face a state that they have to fight. As was understood by the ancients, one should choose one's enemies carefully because one will become more like them.

One of the central reasons behind the more frequent occurrence of 'looting rebellions' in recent years is not, as Keen suggests[18], that rebel movements have become weaker. Rather, resistance movements operating through coercion and plunder are on the rise because *states* have become weaker. While insurrection in Africa was previously against strong settler states, it is now directed against weak and disintegrating independent governments. Rebel leaders who, like water, choose the path of least resistance, therefore can rely increasingly on intimidation and pillage. Accordingly, the child soldier problem is largely a post colonial phenomenon. Settler states could not have been defeated by children. The leaders of national liberation struggles were no more noble than many of the leaders of later rebellions, but they did need to organise on a fundamentally different basis to succeed.

African armies and mature insurgencies

A critical question, therefore, is whether African armies can mobilise and fight effectively once an insurgency begins. Hard as it is for the military forces of the states in Africa to fight small gangs of insurgents, more widespread warfare involving larger numbers of troops is even more difficult. As Thom notes:

> Counter insurgency is a most difficult job for any military to perform, and it requires African armies to perform in areas where they are the weakest; i.e., aggressive, multiple field operations with little short term payoff that must be sustained over long periods to achieve the ultimate goal. This requires good logistic support, mobility, maintenance, training in small unit tactics, good leadership, especially at the junior officer and NCO levels, and an ability to integrate military intelligence with field operations.[19]

In addition, counter insurgency places significant demands on a government, which has to co ordinate the various (very difficult) military tasks with a comprehensive political strategy. America's own doctrinal statement on low intensity conflict suggests just how difficult developing a comprehensive political/ military counter insurgency campaign can be:

> [Internal defense and development] focuses on building viable political, economic, military, and social institutions that respond to the needs of society. Its fundamental goal is to prevent insurgency by forestalling and defeating the threat insurgent organisations pose and by working to correct conditions

that prompt violence. The government often must overcome the inertia and incompetence of its own political system before it can cope with the insurgency against this system. This may involve the adoption of reforms during times of crisis, when pressures limit flexibility and make implementation difficult.[20]

After the first flurry of combat that reflects the government's initial attempt to obliterate the rebels and the insurgents' desire to inflict a psychological wound on the national army, rebels often establish a base in the countryside so as to organise a mobile force and recruit new soldiers. This was the pattern of insurgencies in Rwanda, Uganda and the Popular Movement for Salvation in Chad. After logistical lines have been consolidated, the rebels make a push for the capital. Some governments are so weak that they cannot defeat even this lightning strike, and the capital is overrun. Small countries are particularly vulnerable to this type of two phase campaign.[21]

Other insurgents are not able to adopt a quick capital first strategy, and become mired in the countryside. This may occur because the government is able to provide point defence of the capital (almost invariably the major city), or because the country is so big that the rebels' base is too far from the capital for their limited logistical ability to triumph over unyielding geography (as occurred in Angola and Sudan). At this point, it is possible for a stalemate to begin that may continue for many years. On the one hand, the rebels cannot defeat the government because defeat is defined by the international community as the military occupation of the capital.[22] On the other hand, the military prerequisites for fighting a protracted counter insurgency campaign are simply beyond the capabilities of most African armies.

As a result, states based in capitals and guerrillas anchored in relatively large country areas often reach a kind of equilibrium. The government knows that it is too costly to attack the guerrillas on the scale required to defeat them, and therefore attempts to define a territory that it can defend. It also realises that the regime will be politically viable as long as it controls the capital and some other towns. For instance, the Rhodesian notion of 'vital asset ground' – territory whose capture or control would result in, or significantly contribute to, the government's defeat – was developed in the terminal stages of the national liberation struggle in what is now Zimbabwe. The identification of what territory Salisbury had to control allowed a significant portion of the countryside to be ceded to the guerrillas. However, the Rhodesian strategy, while preventing outright military defeat, did not allow for government victory. Small groups of guerrillas could easily operate in territory that was not considered vital, and thereby gain popular support.[23] Similarly, President Mobutu of Zaïre was really little more than the mayor of Kinshasa in his declining years, while the governments of Sudan, Angola, and Mozambique, among others, lost control over significant parts of their territory during their civil wars although they did not suffer military defeat. Indeed, Collier and Hoeffler[24] have found some evidence that as the population becomes more dispersed, it becomes more difficult for the state's military to defend the entire landmass.

The ability to mobilise

The ability of an African army to defeat rebels therefore depends heavily on its ability to mobilise forces relatively quickly in the face of a growing enemy threat. Table 1 presents some examples of unsuccessful national defence in the face of an enemy, while Table 2 provides instances where African countries were able to raise sufficient military force to confront a growing enemy threat. I have used soldiers per thousand citizens as my major indicator of mobilisation, because budgetary data on African militaries are completely unreliable. It is, however, possible to present a reasonable account of the number of soldiers in an army. However, even this indicator has limited utility, as it cannot capture the use of informal militias, a favoured tactic of beleaguered governments as military institutions break down. However, it is probably as good an indicator of military prowess as per capita income, the statistic used by other studies as proxy for military capability.[25]

As far as possible, I have tried to show in the fifth column the year in which the enemy threat became most obvious, although some of the conflicts do not lend themselves to such neat chronologies. For instance, 1990 is the year that Doe was overthrown in Liberia; 1986 is the date that Museveni toppled the government in Kampala; 1997 is when Angola invaded Congo Brazzaville; while 1990 marks the year that the RPF initially invaded Rwanda. In other conflicts, it is more difficult to cite a precise time, as the conflicts emerged slowly and only gradually built to a crescendo. For instance, the threat to both Sierra Leone and Guinea grew progressively during the 1990s, as instability from Liberia spread westward. Frelimo's war with RENAMO in Mozambique and UNITA's battle with the MPLA government in Angola also escalated by degrees throughout the 1980s.

Table 9.1 Unsuccessful mobilisations during conflict

Country	Mobilisation during crisis (soldiers per thousand citizens)					
Congo-Brazzaville	1993	1994	1995	1996	**1997**	
	4.2	**4.1**	4	3.9	**3.8**	
Guinea	1987	1989	1991	1993	**1995**	1997
	4.5	**2.7**	2.4	2.2	**1.7**	1.6
Liberia	1986	1987	1988	1989	**1990**	1991
	2.6	**2.5**	2.8	2.7	**3.5**	2.9
Sierra Leone	1987	1989	1991	1993	**1995**	1997
	1.5	**1**	1.1	1.2	**1.1**	1
Somalia	1982	1984	1986	1988	**1990**	
	9.2	**6.9**	7.4	6.7	**5.6**	
Sudan	1980	1981	1982	1983	**1984**	1985
	3.4	**4.5**	4.3	4	**2.9**	2.8
Uganda	1982	1983	1984	1985	**1986**	1987
	0.7	**0.9**	1	1	**1**	0.9
Zaïre	1973	**1975**	1977	1979	**1981**	1983
	2.8	**2.2**	2	0.8	**1.5**	1.3

Bold type indicates year when threat has become obvious or most severe.
Source: Calculated from US Arms Control and Disarmament Agency, various years.

Table 9.2 Successful mobilisations during times of conflict

Country	Mobilisation during crisis (soldiers per thousand citizens)					
Angola	1979	1981	1983	1985	**1987**	1989
	7.2	7.6	7.4	8.7	**9.4**	12.9
Ethiopia	1974	1976	1978	1980	**1982**	1984
	1.3	1.8	6.1	6.5	**6**	4.5
Mozambique	1979	1981	1983	1985	**1987**	1989
	2.5	2.4	2.4	2.8	**4.6**	4.6
Rwanda	1990	1991	1992	1993	**1994**	1995
	0.8	4.1	4	3.9	**6**	5.5
Somalia	1973	1974	1975	1976	**1977**	1978
	8.3	9.7	9.4	9.7	**16.1**	15.9

Bold type indicates year when threat has become obvious or most severe.
Source: Calculated from US Arms Control and Disarmament Agency, various years.

It is notable, looking at the cases of failed mobilisation, that most of the wars had a distinctly civil nature although, as in almost any civil war, there was a significant international element. Thus, while Congo Brazzaville was invaded by Angola, Luanda was working in support of the former president, Denis Sassou Nguesso, who had striven for years to destabilise his successor. Similarly, the wars in Liberia and Sierra Leone are domestic conflicts, albeit fed by outsiders. Somalia in the 1990s, Sudan and Uganda are all civil wars, classically understood. Their failure to rise to the military challenge is quite remarkable. For instance, Siad Barre's army in Somalia actually shrank significantly as his country slid into civil war, while the authorities in Kampala were unable to augment their army during the endgame before Museveni took over.

The cases of successful action by national armies are more clearly linked to external invasion, although some of these cases cannot be easily categorised. Somalia went to war to reclaim what it viewed as the Somali portion of Ethiopia in 1977-78, while Ethiopia took to arms slightly later to defend itself. Similarly, the Hutu authorities in Rwanda readied the national army in anticipation of the attack by the RPF in 1994. Angola's and Mozambique's were clearly mainly civil wars, but both Maputo and Luanda had enemies (RENAMO and UNITA) that were directly tied to South Africa. Both governments could thus legitimately claim that they were under threat from a foreign power.

Why would governments find it easier to mobilise national forces in the face of foreign threats than to do the same for internal conflicts? Why do some armies seem to operate well across borders and yet to be unable to defeat rebels at home? At least part of the answer is that purely domestic conflicts within African countries are a reflection of basic failures in institutions and policies. Indeed, many failing African states cannot make any kind of military response to insurgency, because they do not have the resources or the capabilities to maintain even the agents of force in their country. (This is the more telling in that having a monopoly on legitimate violence is the defining characteristic of a state.) However, when one state is attacked by another, it may be for reasons originating with the invader, and not because the target is necessarily dysfunctional. Thus Somalia attacked Ethiopia because it wanted to be reunited with Somalis in neighbouring countries; not because of some fundamental institutional breakdown in Ethiopia. Therefore the latter was able to go to war in response to Somalia's attack, and to defeat the enemy. Similarly, Ethiopia attacked Eritrea.

Those states that are able to respond to armed threat are also often the recipients of foreign aid precisely because they are not dysfunctional, while states involved in civil wars do not receive much outside assistance because of the incorrigibility of their problems. For instance, foreign assistance (as measured by net overseas development assistance per capita from all donors) received by Somalia increased from $13 per capita in 1973 to $38 by the time of its invasion of Ethiopia in 1977.[26] Nor was the invasion punished by the foreign donors, who continued to give more money to Mogadishu. By 1980, foreign assistance had increased to $67 per capita. In contrast, starting in the late 1990s, foreign assistance to Somalia plummeted (in 1996, it was down to $12 per capita), with the result that when the Siad Barre government was under threat, there were few resources that could be devoted to the military.

Similarly, one of the reasons that the Hutu government in Rwanda was able to raise such a large number of soldiers after the initial RPF invasion in 1990 was that foreign assistance went from $37 per capita in 1988 to $51 in 1991. Nor was the ability of Mozambique to fund military operations during the war against RENAMO a surprise, given the vast amount of foreign assistance it received ($14 per capita in 1980, rising to $58 per capita in 1988). Angola did not require increases in foreign aid during the period of its civil war, because it could rely on its robust earnings from oil. Finally, the vast Ethiopian mobilisation during the 1998-2000 war with Eritrea was at least in part financed by foreign assistance. The willingness of the international community to provide food relief to Ethiopia meant that the government in Addis Ababa could devote a major proportion of its resources to the war, while the international community took on the responsibility of feeding the populous. The Ethiopian regime used this division of labour to gain maximum advantage.

In contrast, those countries that are declining receive less and less foreign assistance, especially now that donors believe that they must become more selective about funding African governments. States in trouble therefore find it much more difficult to raise military forces. For instance, President Doe of Liberia saw foreign assistance to his government decrease from $52 per capita in 1980 to $25 in 1989, leaving his regime vulnerable when Charles Taylor attacked it in 1989. Similarly Zaïre under Mobutu had its assistance cut from $24 per capita in 1990 to $4 per capita in 1996. That regime was therefore already tottering when Laurent Kabila began his march across the country.

238 / Chapter 9

Conclusion

Perhaps the only time when any African national armies – given their precarious state, and the difficulty they experience in mobilising to face domestic conflict – may have a good chance of defeating an insurgency is at the start of hostilities. Of course, that is precisely when African militaries are least prepared to fight. As an insurgency matures, a government may not be able to recruit sufficient forces for the army, especially if it is facing a domestic threat and if it does not receive foreign aid. It is not only scholars who may have been misled by the declining utility of force over time. African leaders may also systematically underestimate the threats that they face because they do not understand that they will quickly lose their advantage as an insurgency matures and their efforts to use the military to contain the rebellion fail.

Large states face particular problems fighting any insurgency. Originally, I thought the primary reason was that it might be particularly difficult for large states to detect insurgencies in their infancy. However, given the limited nature of most African countries' intelligence services, it seems that rebellions can begin in almost any size of state. Geography comes into play more centrally as insurgencies mature. It is more likely that an insurgency will end in a small country where victory is actually possible for either the rebels or the government, than it is in large countries, where the vast expanse of territory makes winning so difficult. The fact that it is hard to find soldiers to fight against internal threats only aggravates the problem for big countries. Large states are less likely (on a per capita basis) to receive foreign aid than small countries, with the result that it becomes even more difficult for them to commit their armies to military action.

The policy implication of these arguments is that big countries must invest more in 'first responders', especially police and intelligence services, so that they can detect and fight rebellions in their early stages. Once an insurgency matures, it is exceptionally difficult for a big state to fight, and it is therefore likely that a debilitating conflict will go on for many years. Indeed, civil conflicts that occur in an international environment where big states are not favoured by foreign donors are particularly difficult for the incumbent governments to resist. Prevention is therefore the best policy.

Endnotes

1   Pateman R. *Eritrea: Even the Stones are Burning.* Revised edition. Lawrenceville [NJ]: Red Sea Press 1998, p. 117.

2   Museveni Y. *Selected Articles on the Uganda Resistance War.* Kampala: NRM Publication, 1986, p. 7.

3   Ellis S. *The Mask of Anarchy: The Destruction of Liberia and the Religious Dimension of an African Civil War.* New York: New York University Press, 1999. p. 110.

4   Abdullah I & P Muana. 'The Revolutionary Front of Sierra Leone'. In: Clapham C (ed.). *African Guerillas.* London: James Currey, 1998, p. 177.

5   Frelimo. 'On the Necessity of Prolonged War'. In: de Bragança A & I Wallerstein (eds). *The Strategy of National Liberation.* London: Zed Press, 1982, p. 147.

6   *Ibid.* p. 147.

7   Museveni Y. *op. cit.,* p. 12.

8   Brockett CD. 'A Protest cycle Resolution of the Repression/Popular Protest Paradox'. In: Traugott M (ed.). *Repertoires and Cycles of Collective Action.* Durham: Duke University Press, 1995, p. 134.

9   Rich PB & R Stubbs. 'Introduction: The Counter insurgent State'. In: Rich PB & R Stubbs (eds). *The Counter Insurgent State: Guerrilla Warfare and State Building in the Twentieth Century.* London: Great Britain, 1997, p. 7.

10   Watts M. 'Black Gold, White Heat: State Violence, Local Resistance and the National Question in Nigeria, in Pile S & M Keith (eds). *Geographies of Resistance.* London: Routledge, 1997, p. 36.

11   *Ibid.* pp. 36-37.

12   Ellis S. *op. cit.,* pp. 77-78.

13   Cann JP. *Counter insurgency in Africa: The Portuguese Way of War,* 1961-1974. Westport CT: Greenwood Press, 1997, p. 11.

14   Pateman. *op. cit.,* p. 121.

15   Luke TW. 'Angola and Mozambique: Institutionalising Social Revolution in Africa.' *The Review of Politics,* 44, 1982, p. 421.

16   Thom WG. 'Congo-Zaïre's 1996-97 Civil War in the Context of Evolving Patterns of Military Conflict in Africa in the Era of Independence.' *The Journal of Conflict Studies* 19, Fall, 1999, p. 177.

17   Young T. 'A Victim of Modernity? Explaining the War in Mozambique.' In: Rich PB & S Stubbs (eds). *The Counter Insurgent State: Guerrilla Warfare and State Building in the Twentieth Century.* London: Macmillan, 1997, p. 145.

18   Keen D. *The Economic Functions of Violence in Civil Wars,* Adelphi Paper 320.

London: Oxford University Press on behalf of the International Institute for Strategic Studies, 1998.

19   Thom WG. *op. cit.*, p. 7.

20   Departments of the Army and Air Force. *FM100 20 and AFP 3 20: Military Operations in Low Intensity Conflicts.* Washington, DC: Department of Defence, 1990, pp. 9–10.

21   See generally, Young ET. 'The Victors and the Vanquished: The Role of Military Factors in the Outcome of Modern African Insurgencies.' *Small Wars and Insurgencies,* 7, Autumn, 1996, p. 185.

22   See, generally, Herbst J. *States and Power in Africa: Comparative Lessons in Authority and Control.* Princeton: Princeton University Press, 2000b.

23   Cilliers JK. *Counter Insurgency in Rhodesia.* London: Croom Helm, 1985, p. 249.

24   Collier P & A Hoeffler. 'On the Incidence of Civil War in Africa.' *Journal of Conflict Resolution,* 46, 2002, p. 18.

25   See, for instance, Fearon JD & DD Laitin. 'Ethnicity, Insurgency, and Civil War.' *American Political Science Review,* 97, 2003, p. 80.

26   All foreign assistance statistics in this and the next paragraph are from World Bank, *World Bank Africa Database,* CD Rom, 2003.

Africa's big states and organised crime

Gail Wannenburg

Introduction

Many African states suffer from endemic problems arising from organised crime and corruption. The World Bank has conservatively estimated that countries with widespread corruption have economic growth rates of 0.5-1 per cent less than would otherwise be the case, and that they are consequently more likely to experience civil conflict and instability.[1] In this book, it has been argued that big dysfunctional or failed states are even more prone to this malady. Problems of governance attributable to the sheer size of a country, its ethnic and religious diversity and the attempts within it to buy patronage (or conversely to emasculate opposition forces) can hasten political and economic decline. Nigeria and the Democratic Republic of Congo (DRC), frequently characterised as 'criminal states', would provide the best examples of this phenomenon. On the other hand, South Africa, which is also a big state, has been lauded for its transparency and accountability despite being home to several strong and competing racial and ethnic identities. Corruption is relatively low, but the country has experienced an exponential growth in organised crime in recent years, and a less than impressive growth rate.

In this chapter, the following questions will be considered:

· first, is there a link between dysfunctional or failed states and the proliferation of crime networks?
· second, do certain characteristics of dysfunctional states provide a more fertile environment for organised crime? Do the size, diversity and population distribution within the country, or the presence of abundant natural resources, affect levels of organised crime?
· third, does organised crime activity enhance state formation and free market reform? Or does it lead to disintegration of the state and the economy?

Dysfunctional states and organised crime: methodological questions

Failed and dysfunctional states are strongly associated with organised crime and terrorism in much of the literature on Africa and other continents. This is an intuitively compelling link, but is a difficult proposition to prove empirically, for several reasons. Firstly, organised crime is an interactive phenomenon. It may have its roots in specific historical conditions, but its trajectory is also shaped by the response of civil society, the state and the international community. It is therefore very difficult to isolate the most significant causal factors that may combine in different ways and in different circumstances.

The story of Pablo Escobar of the infamous Medellin cocaine cartel in Colombia perfectly illustrates this phenomenon. A notorious killer, he was regarded as a benefactor in the Medellin region, where the textile industry had been undercut by the dumping of synthetic fibres onto the world market. He ran a form of social welfare system for the poor, and was elected to Parliament. The American government, the main market for cocaine, lobbied the Colombian government to extradite Escobar and others to the US for trial. In a bid to avert this measure, the powerful Colombian drug cartels offered to pay the national debt and reinvest their profits in legitimate businesses. When the Colombian government refused, the Medellin cartel began a campaign of urban terror that continues in various guises today.

The Colombian government subsequently relented and repealed legislation allowing the extradition of drug traffickers to the US. There was no reduction in the flow of cocaine to America, as a myriad of small dealers took over the drug routes of the Medellin and other cartels.

Many commentators argue that the critical factor in the growth of organised crime and corruption of the Colombian state was its institutional weakness and perennial civil conflict, phenomena that predated the trade in cocaine. The roles of the different actors and their relative impact on organised crime goes relatively unexplored.

A second reason that a connection between non functioning states and organised crime is difficult to prove is that there is little consensus as to the boundaries between what constitutes illicit and licit activity in dysfunctional states. This creates problems of definition in analysing the phenomenon of organised crime. In the DRC, the extraction of minerals and other resources by the Kabila government was regarded as legitimate, whilst similar activity by the rebel movement, the

Rassemblement Congolaise Democratique (RCD Goma, in the territory they controlled, was considered illegal. Prior to the UN resolution on the exploitation of mineral resources and other commodities in the DRC, there was no provision for any sanction against other countries (such as Uganda and Rwanda) or private actors involved in exploitation of the extraction and sale of the country's assets by proxy or otherwise. However, this resolution and the expert panels appointed did not attempt to define what constituted illicit or licit extraction and their different permutations. Further, in the absence of UN resolutions on this subject in other dysfunctional or corrupt states, there are no limits set on the profiteering that may be taking place in other jurisdictions: even if it is morally repugnant, it is not necessarily illegal.

Thirdly, measuring the size and impact of organised crime networks is notoriously difficult even if sophisticated information collection systems exist. In South Africa in 1999, the police estimated that there were over 400 trans national crime groups operating in the country. In 2003, they claimed that they had disrupted the groups to such an extent that there are now only 238 such organisations in the Republic. This figure, whilst it might be helpful to the crime intelligence agencies, tells us very little about the extent of organised crime in South Africa. We would have to know, before making an assessment, whether these groups have merely consolidated their operations or whether the incidence of activities related to organised crime has diminished. This kind of information is not available in South Africa and in other African countries, where the infrastructure for information collection is weak and at times non existent.

Finally, there is little empirical information available as to the relative impact of market demand or market supply factors in the proliferation of crime networks. Most dysfunctional states are to be found in the developing world, where the consumption patterns of prohibited or illicit goods are low, even if the government and elite are corrupt and predatory. The market for such goods comes in the main from pockets of affluence in the region, and from the developed world. Many of these goods will therefore be sent to where the market is largest. This usually implies some complicity between individuals or groups in the source or recipient countries, which in turn raises further questions. At what point should the phenomenon be stopped, and what type of intervention is appropriate?

Organised crime networks in dysfunctional states

In the absence of empirical evidence, it is possible to argue that dysfunctional states are at least the weakest link in the international legal regime aimed at combating organised crime.

Crime networks and legitimate economic enterprises have much in common. They are risk averse and prefer a stable operating environment. This means that they generally require a relatively sophisticated infrastructure, modern economic systems, an environment that offers good cost/benefit ratios and a relatively low risk of prosecution. In failed states, the costs of doing business, illegitimate or legitimate, are generally prohibitive owing to the costs of transportation, general lawlessness and the possibility that numerous actors in any supply chain will demand bribes. The level of dysfunction of the state may be one of the key factors determining whether it is an attractive destination for trans national crime groups.

Doing business in dysfunctional or failed states may be prohibitive unless some of the following conditions exist:

- there is a logistical supply network that can circumvent degradation of infrastructure such as transportation systems;
- if there are no financial institutions, the commodity traded must be easy to exchange for cash, or there must be an enforceable system of promissory notes (such as the Hawala system);
- corruption must be centralised to a degree where costs are relatively predictable;
- the countries in which the transactions take place or through which they pass in transit must be accessible to target markets; and
- the risks of detection and apprehension must be relatively low in relation to the benefits anticipated from the illicit trade.

The weakness of a state may make it unattractive to organised crime, unless local warlords assume control over specific communities and geographic entities. This is exemplified in dysfunctional states such as Sierra Leone and the DRC. Both of these countries are rich in mineral resources that are attractive to organised crime networks. Many commentators have suggested that rebellions in these two countries have been motivated, or at least prolonged, by the extraction of mineral resources. In support of this view, rebel movements such as the Revolutionary United Front (RUF) in Sierra Leone and the RCD in the DRC have failed to articulate a coherent political ideology and objectives distinct from those of the regional sponsors of their groups. The UN reports on the illicit extraction of mineral and other resources in the DRC have suggested that these assets are being exploited by a range of private and state actors that have established organised crime networks and that these will persist despite the peace process in that country.

In Sierra Leone, the Truth and Reconciliation Commission (TRC) has been studying the war economy in relation to the diamond trade with the aid of statements from victims, perpetrators and witnesses. These investigations suggest that the RUF rebels acquired significant control over the diamond fields in Sierra Leone only between 1996-1997 - five years after the first RUF incursions into Sierra Leone. Prior to this RUF rebels plundered villages, and afterwards exchanged agricultural products (such as coffee and cocoa) and looted goods for weapons. Diamonds may have been among the items looted, but large scale diamond mining by the rebels was not the major focus of their activities. By 1992, according to the TRC, the rebels had acquired some control over areas like Kono, which was rich in diamonds, but this territorial advantage was insecure and the foothold gained often lasted only a couple of months before they were forced to retreat. Similarly in 1995, a private military company, Executive Outcomes, pushed the rebels out of many of the diamond rich areas.

The involvement of the rebels in large scale illicit trade in diamonds occurred in 1998 and 1999, when the RUF gained substantial access to, and control of, the diamond bearing parts of the country and began forcing civilians to work as miners under the supervision of rebel commanders. According to TRC investigators, some of these commanders sold diamonds for the RUF and diverted the profits to individuals.[2]

A similar pattern emerges in the DRC. The groups involved in the most systematic trade in natural resources not only had control over the territory in which they were found, but also had a logistical chain such as transportation networks and air companies to fly goods to various destinations. The smaller and less profitable criminal organisations are more likely to be involved in the so called 'triangle trade', which involves the exchange of diamonds (mainly alluvial) for guns and other goods. In areas controlled by the RCD, large amounts of income for their forces were raised by 'taxes' or the extortion of funds from businessmen rather than from direct trade in natural resources. Diamond industry insiders suggest that an estimated sixty per cent of diamonds in the DRC originate in Angola and exit through Congo Brazzaville, the only country that has the infrastructure to handle this trade.[3] Diamond *comptoirs* and bankers in the DRC have suggested that some of the trade relates to money laundering. At times, mysterious dealers undercut the trade by $50-100 per transaction, an unusual phenomenon in a trade that is highly monopolistic.[4]

Consequently, there is a degree of scepticism concerning some of the allegations made in the UN reports on the DRC, which are perceived to have focused on well known companies that appear to have very little to do with war financing. Some commentators in the DRC have suggested that there is little evidence of a national crime network, but rather of local groupings that are more or less organised. The more structured of these generally have better contacts within the transitional government, and are believed to be actively seeking out opportunities in the transportation sector, perhaps to facilitate illicit trade in the future. The less well run groups are generally more reliant on small scale extraction of resources and, increasingly, on banditry.

Organised crime activity (such as car theft and hijacking) which is prevalent in many other African countries, is still relatively unknown in the DRC. According to the police, bandits sometimes steal cars at night for transport, and abandon them the next day, because the roads out of Kinshasa are impassable.[5] In contrast, South Africa, which is a much more functional state, is the main source of sought after stolen consumer goods, such as cell phones and motor vehicles. In bilateral and multilateral police operations, under the aegis of the Southern African Police Chiefs Co operation Organisation (SARPCCO), the vast majority of the goods seized from criminals (between 96 and 99 per cent) originated in South Africa, and then found their way into countries throughout the continent, including the DRC and islands such as Mauritius.[6]

Due to their location at a midpoint between Asia and Europe, east African countries (Ethiopia, Kenya, Malawi and Tanzania) are the busiest transit routes for drug trafficking in Africa, far outstripping the southern African region. Sea and airport infrastructure in this region and its historical commercial and family ties with the East make it a significant hub for heroin and cocaine trafficking that originates in south east and south west Asia.

Big states and organised crime

There are certain attributes of failed or dysfunctional states that are valuable to organised crime syndicates. Phil Williams, Doug Brookes and Mark Shaw have argued that states attract transnational crime networks because they have the following characteristics:

- rudimentary legal systems;
- weak state capacity, including porous borders, poor customs control and ineffective and flawed criminal justice systems;
- weak civil societies; and
- corrupt governments that are characterised by clientelism and patronage.[7]

These attributes are particularly acute in countries that are experiencing civil war, public unrest or transitions to democracy. In these circumstances state resources are diverted from crime control, creating opportunities for crime networks to establish their operations.

Big states with highly diverse populations are frequently unable to create consensual legal frameworks that can mediate diverse political, social and economic conflicts. If, as occurs in many cases, the military and criminal justice officials are perceived as serving an elite, and lack legitimacy amongst large sectors of society, few citizens will respect the rule of law. Alternative political and governance systems may arise in those sectors of society and geographical areas that are on the margins of the centres of power and influence. In these circumstances it becomes difficult for governments to exert authority over the entire territory. In addition, alternative centres of power may be contiguous with, and enjoy the support of, neighbouring states, thus spreading instability across borders and into the region. The poor, the disaffected, the rebels or the militias, along with professional organised crime middlemen, may become involved in the extraction of and trade in natural resources and other commodities in exchange for food, armaments or profit. Many of the networks created during periods of civil war or instability may evolve and diversify in the post conflict era depending on the opportunities available.

Rudimentary legal systems and alternative systems of governance

In many big states, no regime for regulating trade (licit or illicit) has been established. There is no unified system of business law or, where it does exist, it is generally not enforced. This is frequently attributable to contestation over the division of state revenue between different regions of the country.

In the DRC, there is very little legislation governing the distribution of the state revenue of central government to the regions. Alternatively, where it exists, such law is not enforced. For example, local authorities in Bukava requested companies operating in their jurisdiction to pay taxes to them directly, so as to avoid revenue being sent to the Central Bank in Goma. In 2003, the DRC government received less than one sixth of the revenue anticipated from its provinces.[8]

This also means that the distinction between licit and illicit trade is practically non existent in practical terms. There is no way of knowing which goods are being traded legally, especially in a context where most goods are imported. Because business people cannot rely on the legal system, most transactions are conducted on the basis of personal relationships. Due to the risks involved, banks do not provide business loans. This makes the country more vulnerable to unscrupulous business people and criminal networks.

Many big states, including functional ones such as South Africa, have seen the formation of alternative (competing) forms of governance. They may be based on traditional leadership, religion or political identity.

To create a consensus on an appropriate legal system to control trade of all kinds is a complex endeavour. This is apparent in Nigeria, where twelve states have imposed a form of Islamic *shari'ah* law, which extends to criminal sanctions. In the DRC and in some parts of South Africa, traditional authorities still play a role in mediating conflicts over economic grievances and those with a criminal dimension. In South Africa, criminal groups (street gangs, the better organised family mafias and drug syndicates) ruled supreme in many communities on the Cape Flats and elsewhere in the country. As a result, in both Nigeria and South Africa, disillusionment with the legal system led to community vigilantism.[9] In contrast, in smaller states such as Mozambique and Sierra Leone, there is less evidence of this phenomenon. In the latter, the 'secret societies' reportedly induct young adults into community life by passing on norms and values, but there is little evidence that these societies play any role in organised crime networks.

Weak state capacity

Security officials in many big states in Africa do not have authority over the country. Not only do such states contain vast geographic areas, but there are long borders and coastlines to control. The security agencies generally have limited resources and insufficient technical capacity to fulfil this task. For example, in the DRC, which has a frontier of about 8,000 km, there are 60,000 uniformed police members and only 500 judicial police, who are responsible for the investigation of organised crime.[10] These police officers are paid less than $20 per month. Donors have not committed much funding to the police services in the DRC to date, in contrast to their more generous grants to the police in Sierra Leone, which is a smaller state. In addition, the DRC government is under some pressure to reduce its armed forces by at least fifty per cent, at a time when rebels and militia forces are being integrated into the new national army. While this is necessary to free up funds for poverty alleviation and economic development, military downsizing will reduce the capacity of the security agencies to exert control over the territory, and may result in a resurgence of conflict in some areas.

Generally, the growing sophistication of organised crime on the continent has not been matched by an increase in the sophistication, skill and resources of the police.

The task of rebuilding areas in which rebels and militias have held sway, bringing them back under central government control and establishing civilian structures such as local administrations, policing and the criminal justice system, is enormous. This is the case in big states such as Angola and the DRC, although there are many hindrances to such efforts. For example much of the countryside is rendered inaccessible by either the presence of landmines or by damaged infrastructure.

The fragile peace processes in some countries such as Sierra Leone and the DRC are under threat from former rebels or militia, who are prepared to work as mercenaries in the neighbouring countries that funded these opposition movements in the past. The presence of large numbers of firearms on the continent will continue to create opportunities for lawlessness in Liberia, Sierra Leone, the DRC and their neighbours. It will also increase the violence associated with criminal activities in regions such as southern Africa. Many civilian populations were militarised and armed in the conflicts Africa has experienced in recent years. The cessation of hostilities has, paradoxically, reawakened ancient disputes over land and resources at the local levels. This is evident in areas such as Ituri in the DRC, where Hema and Lendu militias have continued to fight after the signing of the peace accord.

Corrupt governments and weak civil societies

Many of the economies in big states in Africa, such as Nigeria, Angola and the DRC, are largely dependent on natural resources such as oil, diamonds and other commodities for revenue. State corruption in these sectors is rife.

In Angola it is estimated that $1 billion in oil revenue remained unaccounted for in 2000, whilst the population lives in dire poverty.[11] From 1985, illegal activities became a major contributor to Nigeria's shadow economy, with an estimated 1,000 million dollars annually (about fifteen per cent of government revenues) flowing through the criminal networks, often with the connivance of the country's elite.[12] While much has been staked on the civilian government of President Obasanjo, who took power in 1999, the country is still said to have the largest shadow economy in the world.[13]

The link between state corruption and the growth in organised crime activity is most clearly apparent in Nigeria. The oil sector produces about forty per cent of the country's GDP, and accounts for ninety six per cent of recorded exports.[14] The dramatic increases in the country's oil revenues after 1973 had important consequences for the development of criminal enterprises in the 1980s.

The country has been ruled by a succession of military governments from the north of Nigeria, while much of the oil is to be found along the coast in the south. This has led to dispute over the distribution of oil revenues to the regions.[15] The presence of oil has also created multiple opportunities for corruption, and has ensured that control of the state is the key to the accumulation of wealth. Economic decline accelerated during the Second Republic (1977-1983), the period immediately before the first increases in Nigerian involvement in illicit activities were noted by law enforcement agencies around the world.[16]

The weakening and criminalisation of the state in particular west African countries, notably Nigeria, Liberia and Ghana, has resulted in the heavy involvement of state actors themselves in criminal activities.[17] Paradoxically, this process of state capture and collapse has been central, as we have seen, in forcing some people to leave in search of new (and often criminal) opportunities because of the limited and declining economic scope at home, while ensuring that the instruments of the state – such as the police, the diplomatic service and various agencies responsible for the issuing of identity and travel documents – become heavily involved in illicit activity. The net result was often that the activities of the state and those of criminal groups became indistinguishable.[18]

The result by the early 1990s was a highly unstable and corrupt state with significant disaffected minorities. Nigeria and west Africa more generally developed into the hub of a world wide drug trafficking wheel that extended into almost every part of the globe.[19]

Civil society in these big corrupt states is not unaffected by the general malaise in government. Many civil society organisations (CSOs) are viewed as catalysts by those with political ambitions because they frequently mirror ethnic and other divisions within the state and society in general. However, there is no doubt that CSOs can play a vital role in exposing corruption linked to organised crime.

Other factors that contribute to organised crime

There are several other global factors, not unique to big dysfunctional states, which may contribute to the growth of crime networks. These would include factors such as:

- increased demand for illicit commodities (such as drugs) in developed and increasingly in developing countries, which creates opportunities for criminal groups;
- the privatisation of state assets, especially of transportation and border control entities, in Africa and elsewhere, which has sparked the interest of criminal groupings from around the world; and
- the explosion in information technology and increased ease of travel in the globalising economy.

Organised crime and the state

The distribution of the benefits and harm arising from organised crime activity needs to be interrogated if solutions to the problem are to be found. Trade, whether it is illicit or licit at source, may directly or indirectly benefit rather than harm nation building in dysfunctional states or in weak states at different stages of their development, although at the expense of other nations. Conversely, the relative benefits of organised crime may be much greater to the developed world if goods or services bought from developing countries are sold with greater profit margins than at source, or if the profits of these criminal activities are invested in the developed world.

There are three broad schools of thought on how transnational organised crime should be understood as having a bearing on the creation and maintenance of the integrity of the state. The first approach focuses on organised crime largely as an external threat to sovereign states, and is preoccupied with the structure and identity of these networks and their corrupting influence on governance. The second approach suggests that organised crime has been complementary to the development of new states, even if the after effects of this phenomenon may pose challenges to state makers later. The third approach views organised crime as symbiotic with the creation of the free market economy, and as taking the form of the development of an alternative (shadow) government.

Proponents of the first approach attribute to refugee, immigrant or other marginalised groups the creation of increasingly sophisticated crime syndicates that exchange goods or services with the connivance of largely low level government officials in stronger states, and with the elite or rebels in weaker or failed states. Much of the early literature about the Italian and Russian Mafias and West African crime networks encapsulates this approach, which throws the myth of the 'gangster or con artist as hero' into the mix. It follows that the solution to this problem would be to strengthen the dysfunctional state so that it is less likely to export crime to other countries, there to undermine their systems of governance.

The second and third approaches attempt to place organised crime in its broader historical, socio economic and political context. A proponent of the second approach is Charles Tilley, who argues that the history of state making in Europe illustrates that banditry and gangland rivalry belong on the same continuum as war for the purpose of capital accumulation and protection. The formation of the European state and its peculiar nature was a by product of the interplay between the cost/resource ratios of these processes, and was tempered only by the capacity of civil society actors to wring concessions from the ruling elite. In turn, the successful control of perimeters sharpened the distinction between internal and external relations.[20] Other authors have also argued that organised crime has been complementary to the evolution of the free market system, the mediation of conflicting social forces and the development of the state in the US, the Balkans and Russia. Crime may therefore enjoy some functional legitimacy amongst certain sectors of society.[21]

Proponents of the third approach, who include economists and criminologists, have suggested that free market forces have had the unintended consequence of facilitating both legal and illegal economic activity. For example, in a US hearing before the Sub Committee on Crime, Peter Andreas noted:

> Part of the problem is that legal and illegal markets are increasingly intertwined. The logic of liberal economic theory, after all, is for the state to conform to the dictates of the market... Neoclassical economics suggests that countries should specialise in exports in which they enjoy a comparative advantage. For some countries this has meant their market niche in exporting illegal drugs.[22]

Other economists have discussed the concept of an 'underworld government' or even a 'primitive state', supervising the illicit trade in prohibited commodities (mainly those related to personal vice), that runs parallel to the legal economy. Most commentators belonging to this school of thought have confined their study to the domestic arena. In the American context, researchers have diverged with regard to the implications of this phenomenon, possibly because different forms of criminal organisation are to be found in particular contexts. Those studies that concluded that the crime syndicate was hierarchical or monopolistic stressed that it gave illegal markets the same protection afforded to legal markets by tariff protection and control of access to markets. However, such enterprises may not be directly involved in the illicit trade; they may merely provide the infrastructure and protection for its operation.[23] Other researchers have found that the 'normal' crime organisation comprises small competitive networks in mutually beneficial relationships with other actors in the trade. They conclude that such arrangements are largely confined to local markets because they are unable to advertise their services except in a restricted environment, or to access legal capital to expand their businesses.

Both the second and third approach implicitly acknowledge that organised crime exists because states (or the international community) consciously or inadvertently place restrictions that are in conflict with market demands on products or the provision of goods and services. This type of crime is therefore not only the preserve of socially marginal actors in the domestic or international arena. This would suggest that criminal syndicates are a function of market demand and is primarily a domestic threat, even if our notion of 'domestic' hazards has to expand owing to increased economic integration and globalisation.

Endnotes

1   Harsch E. *Africa Recovery.* 13 (4), December 1999.

2   Interview with TRC Investigator, Sierra Leone, Freetown, December 2003.

3   Interview with staff of foreign embassies, Kinshasa, DRC, February 2004.

4   Interview with banker and diamond dealer, Kinshasa, DRC, February 2004.

5   Interview with judicial police, Kinshasa, DRC, February 2004.

6   Msuthu F. 'Responses to Organised Crime in SADC, Interpol and SARPCCO'. In: Goredema C (ed.). *Organised Crime in Southern Africa: Assessing Legislation,* Chapter 2, Monograph No. 56, Institute for Security Studies, June 2002, *www.iss.co.za,* p. 4.

7   Williams P & D Brooks. 'Captured States, Criminal States and Contested States: Organised Crime and Africa in the 21st Century'. *South African Journal of International Affairs,* 6 (2), Winter 1999, p. 86; Shaw M, 'The Development of Organised Crime in South Africa'. In *Policing The Transformation,* Monograph No. 3, Institute of Security Studies, April 1996.

254 / **Chapter 10**

7 Interview with IMF official, Kinshasa, DRC, February 2004.

9 In Nigeria, attempts were made to stop the operation of groups such as the Bakassi Boys but rising crime levels have led to a resurgence in their popularity.

10 Interview with judicial police, Kinshasa, DRC, February 2004.

11 Van Niekerk P & L Peterson. *Greasing the Skids of Corruption,* International Consortium of Investigative Journalists, p. 1, *www.icij.org.*

12 Lewis P. 'From Prebendalism to Predation: The Political Economy of Decline in Nigeria'. *Journal of Modern African Studies,* 34 (1), 1996, p. 97.

13 Schneider F & D Enste. *Shadow Economies around the World: Size, Cause and Consequences,* International Monetary Fund Working Paper, WP/00/26, p. 6.

14 Background information: Nigeria, Foreign and Commonwealth Office, *http://www. fco.gov.uk.*

15 Given that oil is produced in twelve of the 36 states, the country's constitution sets out a formula for how the wealth should be divided. Such intra state divisions point to the fragility of the federation itself. For an overview of recent tensions see *Africa Confidential,* 42, 15-27 July 2001.

16 See for example 'Combating International Crime in Africa: Hearing before the Subcommittee on Africa of the Committee on International Relations, House of Representatives', One Hundred Fifth Congress, Second Session, 15 July 1998.

17 The involvement of the Liberian government, for example, in drug trafficking is explored by Ellis S, *The Mask of Anarchy: The Destruction of Liberia and the Religious Dimensions of an African Civil War,* New York: New York University Press, 2001, pp. 169-172.

18 Williams P & D Brooks. 'Captured, Criminal and Contested States: Organised Crime in Africa'. *South African Journal of International Affairs,* 6 (2), Winter 1999.

19 The map is drawn from the US government's *International Crime Threat Assessment* completed for President Clinton in 2000, p. 102. Available from *http://www. terrorism.com/documents/pub45270/736502.gif.*

20 Tilly C, 'War Making and State Making as Organised Crime'. In: Evans P, Ruescemeyer D & T Skocpol (eds). *Bringing the State Back In.* Cambridge: Cambridge University Press, 1985.

21 See for example, Woodiwiss M. *Organised Crime and American Power.* Toronto: University of Toronto Press, 2001; Xenakis S. *The Challenge of Organised Crime to State Sovereignty in the Balkans: A Historical Approach,* Kokkalis Programme Conference Paper, 2001; Volkov V. *Violent Enterpreneurs: The Use of Force in the Making of Russian Capitalism.* Ithaca: Cornell University Press, 2002.

22   US Committee on Banking and Financial Service, Organised Crime and Banking: Hearing 28 February, Serial number 104 47, House of Representatives. 1996, US Government Printing Office.

23   Schelling T. *Choice and Consequence,* Cambridge, Massachusetts: Harvard University Press, 1984.

11

Leading large states

Joseph Ayee

Introduction

The need to study leadership in general and political authority in particular, and to derive useful insights into the conduct of leadership has never been so acute as in the case of Africa. To quote *Politics and Society in Contemporary Africa,* 'leadership is ... one of the many guides to the intricacies of political processes on the continent'.[1] In addition, the topic is important in defining the success (or otherwise) of good governance, a rare commodity in Africa. The richness of the continent's ancient heritage, the wealth of its abundant natural resources, and the vibrancy of its 700 million people conjure up the vision of a secure and prosperous future. But Africa has been reduced to a perilous and parlous state, lagging behind other regions in human development. Much of this is explained by the exploitation of the land and its peoples by a century or more of colonialism, whose dark legacy still lingers in the form of arbitrary cross ethnic national boundaries and the clandestine pursuit of post colonial foreign interests represented by multinational corporations. But equally, much is explained through the failures of Africa's leaders to promote long term policies and programmes that transcend not only national boundaries but regional ones. Mired in socio economic deprivation, and vulnerable to the vagaries of global epidemics and the predations of globalisation, Africa's peoples are crying out for transformational leadership which can bring about their common redemption.

In Africa, the persistent development crisis and the recent phenomenon of failing states are due in part to poor leadership, that is, leaders who are not committed to the development of their societies and who lack honesty and a commitment to democracy. Students of politics in Africa have pointed out that poor leadership has been a major factor in the development crisis across the continent since independence.[2] Indeed, it has been asserted that the problems experienced in Africa today are simply the result of a failure of leadership.

For instance, the World Bank study of sub Saharan Africa stated that: 'Underlying the litany of Africa's development problems is a crisis of governance'.[3] This has led to persistent instability, violence, ethnic conflict, hunger, disease, poverty and a lack of both transparency and accountability.

Against this background this chapter offers a comparative assessment of the leadership styles in Angola, the Democratic Republic of the Congo (DRC), Ethiopia, Nigeria, Sudan and South Africa, with emphasis on the particular challenges posed to leaders by the demands of governing large states. Specifically, the chapter addresses the following questions:

· what leadership styles have emerged in these six countries in the post colonial and post Cold War periods?
· do large size and internal diversity impose a need for a transactional leadership style? and,
· under what circumstances is it possible for leaders to transform the political systems within which they operate?

The chapter is divided into five sections. First, it offers a definition of leadership. Secondly, it analyses the contextual variables that have impacted on governance in Africa. Thirdly, it discusses the kinds of political regime which have emerged in varying degrees in the six countries, and argues that, irrespective of their different forms, they all exhibit, to a large extent, features of transactional leadership. Fourthly, it explores the relevance of size, diversity and other challenges in the six countries to the difficulties of political leadership. Fifthly, the chapter highlights the circumstances under which leaders can transform the political systems within which they operate.

The concept of leadership

Despite countless books and studies on the subject, no one has developed a widely accepted definition of what leadership is, nor of what makes some leaders effective and others ineffectual. In the absence of any consensual view on the meaning of the term, leadership in this chapter may be understood as a pattern of behaviour, a personal quality and a political value and process. As a pattern of behaviour, it is a social process in which influence is exerted by an individual or group over a larger body, to organise or direct its efforts towards the achievement of desired goals without the use or threat of violence. We expect leaders to influence non coercively, and to generate co operative effort toward goals that transcend the leader's narrow self interest. Leadership in terms of this definition is a property of the relationship between leader and follower.[4] People whom we call leaders are different from other people in at least two respects. First, they have more influence than those around them. Secondly, they try to persuade others to behave in ways that are beyond mere compliance with the rules and routines of the organisation or country.[5]

As a personal attribute, leadership refers to character traits which enable the leader to exert influence over others without coercion. This capacity is thus accurately equated with charisma, that is, qualities that provoke a certain kind of emotional commitment – a sense of mission, vision, excitement and pride. This feeling is typically associated with respect for, and trust in, the leader.[6]

As a political value and process, leadership refers to the ability in certain persons to offer guidance and inspiration, to mobilise others through moral authority or ideological insight, and to do so through a democratic system.

'Good' leadership, as defined by donors, is ethical leadership that supports the following values: democracy, justice, respect for human rights, accountability, responsibility, duty, freedom of speech, development, personal altruism and integrity.[7]

There are three main virtues of leadership. They are its ability to mobilise and inspire people who would otherwise be inert and directionless; to promote unity and encourage members of a group to pull in the same direction; and to strengthen organisations by establishing a hierarchy of responsibilities and roles. However, notwithstanding these virtues, leadership has its vices.[8] Some of its inherent risks are that it may concentrate power and thus lead to corruption and tyranny (hence the democratic demand that leadership should be checked by accountability); engender subservience and deference, thereby discouraging people from taking responsibility for their own lives; and stifle debate and argument because of its emphasis upon ideas flowing down from the top of the hierarchy, rather than up from the bottom.[9]

The context of political leadership in Africa

In order to understand the leadership styles that have emerged in the six countries under discussion in this volume and the particular challenges posed to the heads of state by the demands of governing large countries, a critical analysis of the key relationship between 'structure' and 'agency' is necessary. This makes it possible to distinguish between those constraints that must be taken as 'given', in determining the environment within which leaders have to operate and the scope that is available to individual rulers to help them effect change through their own vision, sense of direction and political and managerial competence. On one hand, African leaders have generally inherited from colonialism, incorporation into the global economy, and internal social fragmentation – a peculiarly difficult set of constraints. On the other hand the political systems in which they operate are characteristically highly personalised and leadership dependent. The tension between these is central to the understanding of the use of authority in Africa.

The African state has exhibited certain contextual variables that have in one way or another impacted on political leadership. They include:

- post colonial status, with all the implications that it has for the evolution of civil society;
- *a priori* problems regarding its territorial jurisdiction;
- heavy involvement in a restricted resource base (usually agriculture);
- relatively undifferentiated yet ethnically heterogeneous social infrastructure;
- salient processes of centralisation and consolidation of power by new ruling classes; and
- a pervasive dependency on external support.[10]

One of the more recent variables perceived as affecting political leadership is that the risks of office holding are very high. In other words, as Goldsmith demonstrates, African heads of state govern in a very perilous political environment.[11] In consequence, they tend to pursue short term, economically destructive policies. Of 180 leadership changes which took place between 1960–1999, by far the most common means for African rulers to lose power is through a *coup d'etat* or similar extra constitutional event (see Table 11.1). Therefore, to Goldsmith, the large proportion of '*coups*' can be construed as a sign that leaders in Africa typically employ high political discount rates'.[12]

Table 11.1 How leaders leave office in Africa, 1960–1999

Number of incidents						
Mode	1960–69	1970–79	1980–89	1990–99	Total	Mean time in office (years)
Overthrown in coup, war or invasion	27	30	22	22	101	5.7
Dead from natural or accidental causes	2	3	4	3	12	11.7
Assassination (not coup plot)	1	0	1	3	5	7.8
Retired	1	2	5	9	17	11.7
Lost election	0	0	1	12	13	14.8
Other (interim or caretaker regime, impeachment)	6	8	4	14	32	1.2
Regime transitions	37	43	37	63	180	7.2

Source: Goldsmith, op. cit., p. 80.

Styles of leadership that have emerged in the six countries

'Style of leadership' refers to the strategies and behavioural patterns through which a leader seeks to achieve his or her goals. Those who rule countries are not all alike, and their authority can be exercised in a number of different ways. The factors that shape the adoption of a particular leadership strategy or style are, of course, numerous. Among the most obvious are the personality and goals of the incumbent, the institutional framework within which he or she operates, the political mechanisms by which power is won and retained, the means of mass communication available, and the nature of the broader political culture.

Even though three distinctive styles of leadership, namely, *laissez faire, transactional* and *transformational,* have been identified in the general literature,[13] none of these seems to have been practised by any of the leaders of the six countries under discussion. In summary, *laissez faire* leadership, as its name suggests, refers to a decentralised, non participatory approach; transactional leadership is involved in exchange of goods and benefits between ruler and followers within a framework of self interest; whereas transformational leadership is ideological and visionary and concerned with altering the status quo. Leaders have, however, exhibited a mixture of nine different leadership styles,[14] which seem to be peculiar to African and other developing countries (see Table 11.2). These nine modes of governance are:

- *charismatic leadership*, based on popular appeal and personal loyalty;
- *patriarchal leadership*, centred on age, wisdom and the incumbent's standing as an elder statesman;
- *technocratic leadership*, grounded on administrative competence and professionalism;
- *popular prophetic leadership*, reliant on personality, ideological purity (especially religious) and demand for total loyalty;
- *tyrannical leadership*, based on personal coercive regimes;
- *mobilisation leadership*, dependent on the ability of an individual to rally the masses to a specific cause;
- *disciplinarian leadership*, focus on discipline and insistence that citizens comply with certain codes of behaviour;
- *reconciliatory leadership*, centred on the negotiation of compromise and consensus between different factions; and
- *monarchical leadership*, based on personal power elevated to regal and dynastic status.

These different methods of rule have not only been adopted because of a range of different factors as identified above. In addition, the large size and internal diversity of the states they governed has been an important determinant. For instance, General Murtala Mohammed adopted a disciplinarian style of leadership because of the general decadence that plagued Nigerian society after the end of civil war. In contrast, General Yakubu Gowon (who led the federal government during the civil war from May 1967–January 1970) and General Abdulsalami Abubakar (who provided a transition between tyranny and re democratisation) can be characterised as having adopted reconciliation as a style of leadership, because they attempted to find areas of compromise between widely divergent Nigerian viewpoints. On the other hand, Nelson Mandela, who took over as president of South Africa in 1994 after the transition from minority white rule to black majority rule, exhibited reconciliatory, patriarchal and charismatic leadership styles which (it can be seen with hindsight) were exactly what South Africa needed at that time.

Table 11.2 Styles of leadership in Angola, the DRC, Ethiopia, Nigeria, Sudan
and South Africa

Leaders	Date of leadership	Leadership styles
Angola (Date of independence: 11 November 1975)		
Augustino Neto	1975–1979	Mobilisation/technocratic
Jose dos Santos	September 1979–date	Mobilisation/technocratic
DRC (Date of independence: 30 June 1960)		
Patrice Lumumba	June–September 1960	Mobilisation/charismatic
Joseph Kasavubu	September 1960–1961	Tyrannical
Joseph Ileo	February–August 1961	Tyrannical
Cyrille Adoula	August 1961–July 1964	Technocratic
Moise Tsombe	July 1964–October 1965	Mobilisation/technocratic
Evariste Kimba	October–November 1965	Reconciliation
Mobutu Sese Seko	1965–May 1997	Tyrannical
Laurent D. Kabila	May 1997–January 2001	Mobilisation/tyrannical
Joseph Kabila	January 2001–date	Reconciliation
Ethiopia		
Haile Selassie	1930–September 1974	Patriarchal/tyrannical
Aman Andom	September–November 1974	Technocratic/reconciliation
Brig. Teferi Banti	November 1974–February 1977	Technocratic/tyrannical
Mengistu Haile Mariam	1977–May 1991	Tyrannical
Meles Zenawi	May 1991–1995 to date	Technocratic
Nigeria (Date of independence: 1 October 1960)		
Tafawa Balewa	1960–1966	Patriarchal
General Johnson Aguiyi-Ironsi	January 1966–July 1966	Technocratic
General Yakubu Gowon	July 1966–July 1975	Technocratic/reconciliation
Brigadier Murtala Mohammed	July 1975–February 1976	Disciplinarian
General Olusegun Obasanjo	February 1976–October 1979	Technocratic/tyrannical
Alhaji Shehu Shagari	October 1979–December 1983	Patriarchal
General M. Buhari	December 1983–August 1985	Disciplinarian/tyrannical
General Ibrahim Babaginda	August 1985–1993	Reconciliatory/tyrannical
Chief Ernest Shonekan	January 1993–November 1993	Reconciliatory
General Sani Abacha	Nov. 1993–June 1998	Tyrannical
General A. Abubaker	June 1998–May 1999	Reconciliatory
General Olusegun Obasanjo	May 1999- date	Mobilisation/reconciliatory

Leaders	Date of leadership	Leadership styles
Sudan (Date of independence: 1 January 1956)		
Ismail al-Azhari	1956	Mobilisation/technocratic
Abdulla Khalil	1956–1958	Mobilisation/technocratic
General Ibrahim Abboud	1958–1964	Technocratic/tyrannical
Sir El-Khatim Khalifah	1964–1965	Technocratic
MA Mahgoub	1965–1966	Technocratic
SS el-Madhi	1966–1967	Mobilisation/technocratic
MA Mahgoub	1967–February 1969	Technocratic
A. Awadallah	February 1969–May 1969	Reconciliatory
Gaafar Nimeiri	May 1969–April 1985	Reconciliatory up to 1983 and tyrannical 1983–1985
General Abdel al Dahab	April 1985–1986	Technocratic
Ahmed el-Mirghani	1986–May 1987	Reconciliation
SS el-Madhi	May 1987–June 1989	Reconciliation/tyrannical
General Omar al-Bashir	June 1989; President October 1993 to date	Reconciliatory/tyrannical
South Africa (31 May 1961 – Apartheid ended in April 1994)		
Dr Hendrik Verwoerd	1958–1966	Technocratic/Tyrannical
B.J. Vorster	1966–1978	Technocratic/Tyrannical
Pieter B Botha	1978–1989	Technocratic/Tyrannical
Chris Heunis	Jan–Sept. 1989	Technocratic/Tyrannical
Frederik de Klerk	Sept. 1989–May 1994	Technocratic/Reconciliatory
Nelson R. Mandela	May 1994–June 1999	Charismatic/Reconciliatory/Patriarchal
Thabo M. Mbeki	June 1999 to date	Technocratic/Mobilisation

From Table 11.2, it is possible to see that even though different leadership styles have been used by various African rulers, most of them, with the exception of Nelson Mandela of South Africa, Patrice Lumumba of the DRC and possibly Murtala Mohammed of Nigeria, practised methods which are akin to transactional leadership. As a result of circumstances in the countries they governed, most of them took the pragmatic course of adopting some form of personal rule, which carries no legitimacy or value independent of its effective use. They did this instead of relying on formal institutions, which were largely ineffective. Some of the important characteristics or practices of personal rule, as identified by Jackson and Rosberg,[15] are conspiracy, factional politics, clientelism, corruption, purges and rehabilitations and succession manoeuvres. These characteristics can be observed in five of the six countries (the exception is South Africa, which stands out among the six countries because of the relatively effective leadership qualities exhibited during both the apartheid and post apartheid periods). Personal rule can be generally effective in reducing or abating ethnic tensions and inequalities through imposing a need for transactional leadership.

According to Ndulo,[16] at independence, African states inherited from colonial rule undemocratic governments and bureaucracies that emphasised hierarchy, compliance and discipline, without addressing other equally important concerns such as public accountability, responsiveness and participation. In the post colonial period, the governments that emerged in the six countries (again with the exception of South Africa during the post apartheid period) became undemocratic, over centralised and authoritarian. Predictably, political monopolies, which emerged as a result of transactional leadership, led to corruption, nepotism and abuse of power. Most if not all of the political leaders simply replaced their colonial governors in fact and deed. Like them, they became the sole embodiment of the social will and purposes of the countries they ruled. Repressive single or no party systems of government emerged, in which power came to be concentrated in one man. Dissent, for which there had always been a secure and honoured place in traditional African society, came to be viewed with ill concealed hostility, almost as if it were treason. Multiple parties, even if originally formed as part of national agendas, generally tended to lead to ethnically based factions whose opposition to the regime made the five states ungovernable. Single party or military rule was often regarded as a viable and sometimes desirable way of controlling the ethnically based rival groups in the five states. Ultimately, the ruling party supplanted the machinery of the state, and the differences between the two became blurred.[17] To maintain themselves in power, most of the leaders in the six countries under discussion (and to a lesser degree in South Africa) had to construct stronger bases of social support through discretionary distribution of patronage and the development of clientelistic ties to key individuals and groups. This became the main form of political exchange.[18]

In the post Cold War era the transactional leadership style, characterised by extensive and destructive political corruption, continued. This is mainly because of what Olsen[19] refers to as an insecure grip on power by leaders who have to take steps to patronise favoured ethnic groups, often at the expense of the national economy. The reason for the insecurity of these heads of government was largely the proliferation of associational groups under structural adjustment programmes, which formed a rallying point for popular dissent in corrupt and unpopular regimes. The DRC's Mobutu Sese Seko is the archetypal example: he was a dictator who clung to power for thirty two years before being driven into exile in 1997. During his tenure he erased the line between public and private property, accumulating a vast personal fortune and bankrupting his country. His is an extreme case, yet every national leader has opportunities to profit individually from office. According to the premises of political economy, it is the head of government with the least certainty about his retention of power who has the strongest incentive to take his rewards while he can – and to take as much as possible. A more confident leader may calculate that it is safe to defer most personal financial gain until after he has left office.[20]

Once more with the exception of South Africa, where the presidency has grown in power *vis à vis* the other two organs of government, the transactional style of leadership exhibited in the post colonial and post Cold War periods has left the other five states in crisis, and, in some cases, collapse.

The characteristics of states which can be said to have failed include the following:

· highly centralised systems of governance;
· excessive state control, coupled with limited capacity to govern;
· arbitrary policy making and abuse of executive power;
· erosion of the boundaries between the state and civil society;
· weak institutions in both state and civil society;
· few countervailing forces to the executive branch of authority;
· bureaucracies that are not accountable to the citizenry;
· widespread corruption;
· unenforced or flawed legal systems;
· limited participation in governance by the general citizenry; and
· preferential access to power and resources often determined by religious, ethnic or geographical considerations.[21]

A comparative assessment of leadership styles in the six states under consideration, both in the post colonial and post Cold War periods, shows the number of transitions that have occurred in them relative to those of other African states (see Table 11.3). While Angola and South Africa (the latter mainly through elections in the apartheid and post apartheid periods) have had one and six transition(s) respectively, and are countries that show some stability, there is relative political insecurity in Ethiopia, the DRC, Nigeria and the Sudan, which have had five, eight and eleven transitions respectively (see Table 11.3).[22] (A transition is defined as a shift from an existing national leader to a new one, whether by legal or extra legal means.)

Table 11.3 Turnover of heads of government in Africa, 1960–2003

Number of transitions	Country
0	Eritrea, Namibia, Zimbabwe
1	Angola, Cameroon, Cape Verde, Djibouti, Equatorial Guinea, Malawi, Mozambique, Seychelles
2	Botswana, Gambia, Mauritius
3	Gabon, Mali, Sao Tome & Principe, Swaziland, Togo, Zambia, Guinea, Guinea Bissau, Mauritius, Tanzania, Senegal, Congo Republic, Kenya, Congo Republic
4	Cote d'Ivoire, Rwanda, Mauritania
5	Central African Republic, Burkina Faso, Ethiopia, Somalia
6	Chad, Lesotho, Niger, South Africa, Uganda
7	Madagascar
8	Liberia, Democratic Republic of Congo
9	Ghana, Burundi, Comoros, Sierra Leone
10	–
11	Nigeria, Sudan
12	Benin

Note: Leaders serving non-consecutive terms are counted twice. Adapted from Goldsmith (2001) whose analysis ended in 1999. The update of turnover from 1999–2003 was supplied by the author.

Large size, internal diversity and leadership

The six countries discussed in this study are 'sprawling giants' with substantial internal diversity in their populations. As a result of these and other circumstances, there are huge disparities between these and other African countries in their potential for nation building, economic development and stability. The large size and internal diversity of these states has resulted in the following endemic problems that need to be addressed. These are:

· a crisis of identity, which must be resolved so that the people learn to identify themselves as citizens of the nation state rather than as members of a particular ethnic sub group;

· a crisis of legitimacy, which must be met by governments to ensure the development of the sense, on the part of the governed, that the government in power has the right to rule;

· a crisis of penetration, which must be addressed to build the state's capacity to enforce all decisions in every province within its territorial jurisdiction;

· a crisis of participation, which requires of government the provision of means and opportunities for the citizens to influence state decisions;

· a crisis of distribution, which entails the evolution by the ruling authority of the will and the means to solve at least the most glaring aspects of social, political and, especially, economic inequalities; and

· a crisis of factionalism, which must be avoided to prevent ethnicity, clientelism and the exclusion of groups from the decision making process.[23]

These liabilities (large size, ethnic, religious and linguistic diversity) have contributed in no small way to political disaster in the countries concerned.

The argument is often made that it is more difficult, for obvious reasons, to govern large states with diverse ethnic populations than small ones. This argument has also been commonly dismissed because countries of small size that have relatively homogeneous ethnic compositions (like Somalia, Sierra Leone and Rwanda) have suffered worse political, social, economic and human disasters than the six large states discussed here. Consequently, certain analysts argue that there is no necessary correlation between size, internal diversity and political governance. Even though this is a valid point, size and diversity in a country pose problems for leaders that cannot be easily glossed over. The frequency of civil wars and the contagious nature of ethnic and religious violence, coupled with the perennial risk that a resurgence of crisis may occur at any time, are far more marked in large states than in small ones. Nigeria, where ethnic and religious violence are rife, is a case in point. Furthermore, the costs of such uprisings, both in terms of material and human resources, are far greater in large states than small ones.

With the exception of Angola, which has had relative political stability (having had only two leaders since independence in 1975) and South Africa, which had a smooth transition from white minority rule to black majority rule, the other four countries under analysis in this volume have witnessed a succession of leaders. Changes of regime have been brought about mostly through *coups d'état,* with Nigeria and Sudan the worst sufferers. In a nutshell, leaders in the six countries are faced with particular challenges related to the contradictory and enormous demands of governing large states. The popular saying that 'small is beautiful while big is ugly' is equally applicable to the problems posed by large states.

Conclusion: Conditions that would make it possible for leaders to transform their political systems

There is no doubt that the enterprise of socio economic development and the reduction of poverty cannot be carried out in Africa without good political leadership. Indeed, governance of the right kind is so important that the World Bank asserts that 'Africa can claim the 21st century with determined leadership'.[24] How much has Africa's governance been shaped by the quality of its rulers? And might good leadership, where it exists, shape the political institutions of the 21st century?

Research in sub Saharan Africa indicates that political and administrative leaders in government are conservative, 'preferring an unacceptable present to an unpredictable future'.[25] These characteristics have resulted in a neglect of policy issues, development goals, and public welfare. In Africa, leaders do not display the acumen necessary to undertake management or institutional reforms because of the high risks involved when authoritarian management systems and hierarchical controls are replaced. A willingness to take risks and to challenge the system is closely bound up with the notion of transformational leadership.

The only incontrovertible point that one can make about the quality of leadership needed in sub Saharan Africa is that it should be development oriented. Leaders should be committed to the development of the entire society over which they rule. They can do this by ensuring that the formulation and implementation of public policies and programmes are aimed at enhancing the quality of life of all their citizens. This is essentially a transformational task, that is, the moving of a country from a lower level of development to a higher level. Development should be manifested in reduced poverty and improvements in basic education, health, food and housing as well as in the promotion of good governance (which includes democracy, justice, respect for human rights, accountability, responsibility, duty, freedom of speech, personal altruism and integrity).

There is evidence that the effectiveness of political leadership in Africa can be measured by examining the extent to which the central authority is effectively exercised throughout the territorial area of the state, and assessing the progress made in the field of socio economic development. The state in five of the countries discussed in this book remains dysfunctional because the central authority has had to cope with civil wars, revolts, other forms of conflict, corruption and patronage. The fragility of these states has also been evident in the number of *coups d'état* most of them have experienced. Furthermore, probably with the exception of South

Africa, these countries have not been able to promote policies and programmes that will improve the standard of living of their people.

There are certain circumstances under which it may be possible for leaders to transform the political systems within which they operate. In other words, we must recognise that the socio cultural environment in which leaders function in Africa is not particularly conducive to, or receptive of, ethical leadership. Consequently, this aspect of the social environment should be altered to strengthen Africa's good cultural values and norms. This entails a good governance approach to leadership. The following actions could enable states to transform the political systems:

- cultivate transformational leaders whose experiences can be shared with potential successors who can use them to serve as their role models;
- nurture inventive political practitioners, because statesmen are to political development what entrepreneurs are to economic development;
- regard leadership as an institution and not as vested in individuals;
- see leadership as entailing teamwork rather than the glorification of one person;
- pursue an electoral policy that favours inclusive government, which will allow vulnerable and minority groups to participate in the decision making process;
- cultivate and nurture a leadership mentoring system to develop leaders who are ethical and morally upright;
- develop, strengthen and enforce leadership codes, which will prevent abuse of leadership positions;
- reform and strengthen institutions such as local government units, so that they can provide a training ground for future leaders;
- build and strengthen credible institutions such as political parties, and give them the task of selecting and recruiting leaders at all levels to remove partisan or sectional interests;
- emphasise character formation in educational institutions from primary to tertiary levels;[26]
- strengthen civil society organisations by encouraging them to develop the culture of internal democracy, provide them with resources and allow them to act as a counterweight to state power; and
- encourage leaders to appreciate the importance of preferring the general good to their personal interests.

Leaders whose lives have had a profound, beneficial influence on their followers in their own day, and who continue to be models for others to emulate thereafter, are those who have been true to the noble ideal expressed by John Ruskin: 'That man is richest who, having perfected the functions of his own life to the utmost, has also the widest helpful influence, both personal, and by means of his possessions, over the lives of others'.[27]

Endnotes

1   Chazan N, R Mortimer, J Ravenhill & D. Rothchild. *Politics and Society in Contemporary Africa.* Boulder: Lynne Rienner, 1992, p. 168.

2   See, for example, Mazrui A. 'Leadership in Africa', *New Guinea,* 5 (1), 1970, pp. 33-50; Mazrui A, 'The Monarchical Tendency in African Political Culture'. In: Doro M & NE Stultz (eds). *Governing in Black Africa.* Englewood Cliffs, NJ.: Prentice Hall, 1971, pp. 18-38; Mazrui A. *Pan Africanism, Democracy and Leadership in Africa: The Continuing Legacy for the New Millennium.* Inaugural Abdulsalami Abubakar Lecture, Chicago, 23 February 2001 (unpublished).

3   See *Sub Saharan Africa: from Crisis to Sustainable Growth,* Washington: World Bank, 1989, pp. 6-7.

4   Cohen M & JG March. *Leadership and Ambiguity.* New York: McGraw Hill, 1974; Burns JM. *Leadership.* New York: Harper, 1978; Grint K. *The Arts of Leadership.* Oxford: Oxford University Press, 2000.

5   Paige GD. *The Scientific Study of Political Leadership.* New York: Free Press, 1977; Hollander EP. *Leadership Dynamics.* New York: The Free Press, 1978; Macoby M. *The Leader.* New York: Ballantine, 1981; Kuhnert KW. 'Leadership Theory in Postmodernist Organisations'. In: Golembiewski RT (ed.). *Handbook of Organisational Behaviour.* New York: Marcel Dekker, 1993, pp. 189-202.

6   Bass BM. *Bass and Stogdill's Handbook of Leadership: Theory, Research and Managerial Applications,* 3rd edition. New York/London: New York Press, 1990; Bass BM. 'Leadership and Performance beyond Authority'. In: Pennock JR & JW Chapman (eds). *Authority Revisited: Norms, XXIX.* New York: New York Press, 1985; Rosenbach WE & RL Taylor (eds). *Contemporary Issues in Leadership,* 3rd edition. Boulder, CO.: Westview Press.

7   See Ayee JRA. *Leadership in Contemporary Africa: An Exploratory Study.* United Nations University Leadership Academy Occasional Papers Academic Series No. 3, December 2001, pp. 7-12; UNDP. *Public Sector Management, Governance,*

and Sustainable Development. New York: UNDP, 1995; UNDP. *Reconceptualising Governance.* Discussion Paper 2. New York: UNDP, 1997.

8   Bass BM. *op. cit.*; Burns JM. op. cit.; Grint K. *Leadership: Classical, Contemporary and Critical Approaches.* Oxford: Oxford University Press, 1997.

9   Bass BM. *ibid.*; Bass BM. 'Leadership: Good, Better, Best'. *Organisation Dynamics,* 13, pp. 26-40; Heywood A. *Key Concepts in Politics.* Hampshire/New York: Palgrave, 2000.

10   Doornbos M. 'The African State in Academic Debate: Retrospect and Prospect', *Journal of Modern African Studies,* 28 (2), 1990, p. 180.

11   Goldsmith AA. *op. cit.*

12   *Ibid.,* p. 80.

13   For example, the three leadership styles have been identified in the studies of such scholars as Grint K. *op. cit.*; Hollander EO. *op. cit.*; Hollander EP & LR Offerman. 'Power and Leadership in Organisations', and in Rosenbach WE & RL Taylor (eds). *op. cit.,* pp. 62-68.

14   Nine related leadership styles (which seem to vary from period to period) have been identified in the literature. See, for example, Mazrui A. 'Leadership in Africa', *New Guinea,* 5 (1), 1970, pp. 33-50; Mazrui A. 'The Monarchical Tendency in African Political Culture'. In: Doro M & NE Stultz (eds). *Governing in Black Africa.* Englewood Cliffs, NJ.: Prentice Hall, 1971, pp. 18-38; Mazrui A. *op. cit.*

15   See Jackson RH & CG Rosberg. 'Personal Rule: Theory and Practice in Africa'. In: Lewis P (ed.). *Africa: Dilemmas of Development and Change.* Boulder, CO.: Westview, 1998, Chapter 1.

16   Ndulu M. 'Constitution making in Africa: Assessing Both the Process and the Content'. *Public Administration and Development* 21, 2001, pp. 101-117.

17   *Ibid.*

18   Gordon DL. 'African Politics'. In: Gordon AA & DL Gordon (eds). *Understanding Contemporary Africa,* 3rd edition. Boulder/London: Lynne Rienner, 2001, pp. 55-99.

19   Olsen M. 'Dictatorship, Democracy and Development'. *American Political Science Review,* 83 (3), 1993, pp. 567-576.

20   See Goldsmith AA. *op. cit.*

21   Ndulu M. *op. cit.,* p. 104.

22   See Hughes A & R May. 'The Politics of Succession in Black Africa', *Third World Quarterly,* 10 (1), 1988, pp. 1-22; Lodregan J, Bienen J & N van de Walle. 'Ethnicity and Leadership Succession in Africa', *International Studies Quarterly,* 39 (1), 1995, pp. 1-25; Breytenbach W. *Democratisation in Sub Saharan Africa: Transitions,*

Elections and Prospects for Consolidation, 2nd edition. Pretoria: Africa Institute of South Africa, 1997.

23 See Hyden G. *op. cit.*; Doornbos M. *op. cit.*; Chabal P. *Political Domination in Africa.* New York: Cambridge University Press, 1986; Jackson & Rosberg. *Personal Rule in Black Africa, op. cit.*

24 World Bank, *Can Africa Claim the 21st Century?* Washington, DC: World Bank, 2000, p. 11.

25 Montgomery JD. 'Probing Managerial Behaviour: Image and Reality in Southern Africa'. *World Development,* 15 (7), 1987, pp. 911-929.

26 The idea of 'if you trample on another's right to seek your own, you will be disappointed in the end' must be inculcated in students. See Gyekye K. *African Cultural Values: An Introduction.* Philadephia, PA/Accra: Sankofa Publishing, 1996, pp. 7-8.

27 John Ruskin, quoted in Barlett J, *Familiar Quotations: A Collection of Passages, Phrases, and Proverbs Traced to Sources in Ancient and Modern Literature.* Boston: Little, Brown, 1968, p. 8.

Africa and its boundaries, a legal overview:

from colonialism to the African Union

Garth Abraham

In contemplating the cause and implications of the Rwandan genocide, Nigeria's prize winning writer and political satirist, Wole Soyinka, has commented: 'We should sit down with square rule and compass and redesign the boundaries of African nations.'[1]

Not surprisingly, the 80,000 km of boundaries bequeathed to the continent by its sometime colonial masters have contributed significantly to Africa's many problems. They unite those who should be divided, and divide those who should be united. They limit access to resources that were once part of a shared heritage and they exacerbate economic and bureaucratic inefficiencies. The borders of African states, it might be argued, have served to hinder continental development.

Disputes over boundaries lie at the heart of many of the manifestations of continental malaise. At best, this type of problem is addressed through international adjudication. At worst, the 103 disputed borders[2] may be linked, directly or indirectly, to incidences of internal and external strife that have claimed the lives of millions[3] - whether because of ethnic violence (which is associated with refugee catastrophes and genocide) or because of political ineptitude (reflected in endless coups and state failures).[4]

That Africa's borders should be the cause of much dispute is not surprising. A 'tea and macaroons' approach to boundary delimitation during the process of colonisation - culminating in the Berlin Conference of 1884-1885 - rendered this inevitable. Lord Salisbury, commenting on the demarcation of territory in 1890, held:

> We have been engaged ... in drawing lines upon maps where no white man's feet have ever trod; we have been giving away mountains and rivers and lakes to each other, but we have only been hindered by the small impediment that we never

knew exactly where those mountains and rivers and lakes were.[5]

Astronomical lines determine forty four per cent of African borders, mathematical lines determine thirty per cent, while geographical features make up a mere twenty six per cent.[6]

The arbitrariness of many of Africa's boundaries has made instability inevitable in a world order still characterised by a nineteenth century understanding of international law which links sovereignty to the notion of territorial integrity.[7] States are territorially defined – 'they are created and function and draw their sustenance within a specific spatial setting. States have no meaning outside this context.'[8] In the *Island of Palmas* case, Judge Huber held:

> Territorial sovereignty is, in general, a situation recognised and delimited in space, either by so called natural frontiers as recognised by international law or by outward signs of delimitation that are undisputed, or else by legal engagements entered into between interested neighbours, such as frontier conventions, or by acts of recognition of states within fixed boundaries.[9]

Borders serve both to demarcate the extent of state sovereignty and the reach of the domestic legal order. It is within its boundaries that a state establishes and exercises its jurisdiction. Acts of state sovereignty are thus linked directly to, and restricted by, defined territory. Territorial sovereignty and boundaries configure the state. 'To "define" a territory is to define its frontiers'.[10]

The usefulness of boundaries as the foundation for territorial sovereignty, however, is premised on their stability, their finality and their permanence. The International Court of Justice (ICJ) in the *Temple of Preah Vihear* case declared that:

> when two countries establish a frontier between them, one of the primary objects is to achieve stability and finality. This is impossible if the line so established can, at any moment be called in question, and its rectification claimed ... Such a frontier, so far from being stable, would be completely precarious[11].

As has been emphasised by Sir Robert Jennings, 'in a properly ordered society ... territorial boundaries will be among the most stable of all institutions'.[12] Where the coherence of the society is fragile and where boundaries are arbitrary, stability is illusory.

However, despite the obvious imperfections of colonial boundaries, African states elected consciously in 1964 to continue to respect them. That decision has since been reaffirmed in the Constitutive Act of the African Union.[13] A radical revisitation of boundaries is not an option that African states have - thus far - been prepared to contemplate. However, if Africa's many disputes concerning borders are to be successfully resolved, a re examination might well be required.

Any such reconsideration must commence with an assessment aimed at understanding why Africa is configured as it has been. What was the legal justification used by the colonial powers for their acquisition of territory in Africa? Having considered their origin, one must then ask why it is that the states of Africa continue to accord binding legal status to these boundaries.

The acquisition of colonial territory by the European powers in Africa - reflective of what Georges Scelle has termed the *'obsession du territoire'*[14] - as in Asia and the Americas, was legally justified in one of three ways: occupation, consent or conquest.

By occupation was meant the Roman civil law concept of *occupatio* of movable property belonging to no one - the so called *res nullius*. In terms of the doctrine of *occupatio*, the first person to seize the *res nullius*, if accompanied by the requisite animus - intention - to become its owner, was possessor of the property for so long as he controlled it.[15] For the Roman jurists the concept of *occupatio* had no territorial dimension; nor did it have any association with the acquisition of sovereignty. However, during the formative period of public international law, the utility of the doctrine was soon appreciated. The transition from *occupatio* of *res nullius* to *occupatio* of *terra nullius* - territory belonging to no one - was relatively easily achieved. It was soon accepted that in international law *terra nullius* constituted territory over which there existed no legal sovereign or owner. This understanding posed no problem in circumstances where the territory was abandoned (*res derelicta*), uninhabited, or inhabited by relatively few persons who lacked any real social or political organisation.

Where the territory was in fact inhabited by recognisable entities, the appropriateness of the Roman legal analysis was more doubtful. In such circumstances various theses were advanced. While a number of the founding fathers of international law (for example Vitoria, Soto, Las Casas, Ayala, Gentili, Selden and Grotius) tended to treat indigenous peoples in colonial territory as though they did enjoy 'legal sovereignty', 'legal sovereignty' could alternatively be interpreted to mean exclusively a form of state or government that resembled those of the European countries. It was this approach that dominated throughout much of the nineteenth century, particularly in the treatment of Africa by European powers.[16]

Thus, if an indigenous population was in possession of territory but did not enjoy 'sovereignty' in respect of the territory, then it was not in legal occupation and the territory might be classed as *terra nullius*. It would thus be open to European occupation.

Over time what was meant by occupation was refined to mean 'effective occupation'. Mere discovery of *terra nullius* was insufficient for title by way of occupation. Grotius proclaimed in *Mare Liberum* (1609):

> No one is sovereign of a thing which he himself has never possessed and which no one else has ever held in his name ... To discover a thing is not only to capture it with the eyes but to take real possession thereof ... The act of discovery is sufficient to give clear title of sovereignty only when it is accompanied by actual possession.[17]

To this extent developing international law accorded with Roman civil law – detection does not accord the finder title: what is required is actual appropriation, the assumption of possession.

In the words of Judge Huber in the *Island of Palmas* case, evidence of 'continuous and peaceful display' of actual sovereign control within the boundaries of the territory was needed. What amounted to 'effective control', in his considered opinion, varied according to the circumstances of the case, for example the geographical nature of the region and the presence or absence of competing claims.

Despite the significant support given for the acquisition of territory by way of occupation during the process of colonisation, international law no longer gives legal currency to the treatment of African territory as *terra nullius*. In the *Western Sahara* case, the ICJ gave as its opinion:

> Whatever differences of opinion there have been among jurists, the State practice of the relevant period [1884] indicates that territories inhabited by tribes or peoples having a social and political organisation were not regarded as *terra nullius*. It shows that in the case of such territories the acquisition of sovereignty was not generally considered as effected unilaterally through 'occupation' of *terra nullius* by original title but through agreements concluded with local rulers. Such agreements with local rulers, whether or not considered as an actual 'cession' of the territory, were regarded as derivative roots of title, and not original titles obtained by occupation of *terra nullius*.[18]

If the territory could not be acquired by way of *occupatio* - because the community of the indigenous peoples reflected sufficient organisation to satisfy the requirement of 'legal sovereignty' - then that territory might be acquired by way of consent or conquest.

Consent ordinarily refers to the acquisition of territory by way of treaty. Indeed this was the most common method for the delimitation of African boundaries.[19] Clearly, by the time Africa was partitioned, international law - in its understanding of the legal personality of indigenous peoples - had made some progress since the settlement of the Americas. Castellino and Allen comment

> [t]hat the imperial powers agreed that treaties of cession had to be signed to legitimate transfer of territory in Africa suggests a greater respect for the existence of a people than was granted to Latin American indigenous peoples, even though in both cases the imperial powers ultimately achieved their end result - the acquisition of territory.[20]

However, the legal validity of the treaties negotiated with indigenes is dubious.[21] A treaty, negotiated either by an appointed representative of the imperial power or by a delegated agent, such as a chartered company, would ordinarily take the form of a cession agreement[22], but might also constitute recognition of a 'sphere of influence', or an instrument of jurisdictional capitulation - both alternatives being possible precursors to ultimate annexation. The cession of territory, however, raises questions of consideration, capacity and subject matter. These were not agreements between sovereign, equal and independent states, even though they were held to be necessary in order to justify the acquisition of territory. At best, such agreements constituted proof of the transfer of rights. The Berlin Conference of 1884, while not itself partitioning Africa, institutionalised the process by which territory was acquired on the continent. Alexandrowicz argues that this process 'was in the first instance not a race for occupation of land by original title, but a race for obtaining derivative title deeds which the European powers had to acquire according to the rule of international law relating to negotiation and conclusion of treaties'.[23] At their worst, these agreements, as Judge Huber said in the *Island of Palmas Case*:

> ... are not, in the international law sense, treaties or conventions capable of creating rights and obligations such as may, in international law, arise out of treaties. But, on the other hand, contracts of this nature are not wholly void of indirect effects on situations governed by international law; if they do not

constitute titles in international law, they are none the less facts of which that law must in certain circumstances take account.[24]

Conquest, as the word suggests, involved the taking possession of enemy territory through recourse to military force in an armed conflict.[25] While today outlawed as a means for the acquisition of title to territory,[26] it was certainly a valid though exceptional source of title during the nineteenth century,[27] because conquest, it has been suggested, involves 'an implicit recognition of the international legal personality of the opposing party'.[28]

What is reflected in this brief discussion on the modes by which territory was acquired in Africa is that the legal justification of rights to title had little to do with relations between the European powers and their new African dependants. The concern of the former was rather to 'legalise' the division of Africa - even *ex post facto* - and thereby limit potential conflict between the European powers *inter se*. Africa's boundaries were determined and agreed, not in the interests of the newly subjected peoples but so as to ensure peace and stability in the international relations of nineteenth century Europe. 'European colonisers typically agreed among themselves on arbitrary borders that simplified administration and enforcement.'[29]

Despite the dubious legality of these demarcations, during the process of decolonisation the colonial powers and the majority of the new indigenous political elites across Africa agreed to continue to respect colonial boundaries.[30] If not for reasons of 'cautious pragmatism',[31] the rationale was the achievement of territorial stability and consequently the maintenance of continental peace.[32] Furthermore, adoption of the principle ensured that no territory constituted *terra nullius* at the time of independence, thus pre empting any possible claims for occupation by alien powers. The message for internal consumption was also clear - secession or adjustment of borders in order to accommodate the aspirations of minorities was not to be contemplated.

This decision to continue to respect colonial boundaries is equated with the Roman civil law doctrine of *uti possidetis*; which doctrine, in turn, is rooted in the norm *uti possidetis ita possidetis* - 'as you possess, so you possess'. In terms of Roman law, *uti possidetis* was one of the possessory interdicts developed by the praetor (the administrator of justice) of republican Rome. The essence of the interdict was to the effect that when two parties claimed ownership of real property, the praetor would award temporary possession to the most recent possessor - the aim being to prevent the 'disturbance of the existing state of possession of immovables as between two individuals'.[33] The only qualification to the temporary award of possession, however, was that the property had to have been acquired from the other party *nec vi, nec clam, nec precario* - 'without force, secrecy or permission'.[34] During the litigation - ordinarily an action for ownership (*vindicatio*) - the temporary possessor would have defendant status, effectively placing the onus of proof on the party not in possession of the property. Thus, *uti possidetis* constituted an award of interim possession as a preliminary to the determination of real ownership.

Contrarily, when the concept was incorporated into international law, not only did it apply to public (as opposed to private) land, but, more radically, it transformed provisional possession (even if obtained by way of military conquest, and thus in a manner contrary to the Roman civil law qualifications) into permanent ownership, 'a complete reversal of the Roman law concept'.[35]

Recourse had been made to the concept of *uti possidetis* during the Spanish and Portuguese decolonisation of Latin America. With some exceptions, the frontiers of Latin America were determined on the basis of the administrative boundaries between the *capitanías* and *virreinatos* of the old Spanish and Portuguese empires as they existed in 1810 and 1821. For South America the relevant year is 1810, while for Central America it is 1821.[36] The exceptions were: the relation between the Spanish and Portuguese areas;[37] the colonial enclaves of other European Powers in Guyana;[38] and one single territory[39] on the Central American isthmus.[40]

The relative success of the concept in preventing violence during the withdrawal of the colonial powers from Latin America marked it for further reinterpretation in the decolonisations of the twentieth century. The horrors of the two world wars meant that, for the colonial powers, the paramount concern was that decolonisation should proceed as peacefully as possible. The self determination of colonial peoples was thus to be interpreted within the caveat of order.[41] *Uti possidetis* provided an ideal principle in terms of which the colonisers and the colonised might negotiate the configuration of post independence Africa.

Contrary to some pre independence discussion,[42] the Organisation of African Unity (OAU) in its Cairo Declaration of 1964 formally adopted the principle, though it was not referred to by name.[43] The date of departure of the colonial power was to be the 'critical date', after which the physical dimensions of the new state would be considered finalised.

In the *Frontier Dispute Case (Burkina Faso/Republic of Mali)*,[44] the court was able to declare that the principle of *uti possidetis* is now considered 'a firmly established principle of international law where decolonisation [is] concerned'.[45] The court defined *uti possidetis* in the following terms:

The essence of the principle lies in its primary aim of securing respect for the territorial boundaries at the moment when independence is achieved. Such territorial boundaries might be no more than delimitations between different administrative divisions or colonies all subject to the same sovereign. In that case, the application of the principle of *uti possidetis* resulted in administrative boundaries being transformed into international frontiers in the full sense of the term.[46]

The principle, however, is not necessarily limited exclusively to circumstances of decolonisation. The attempted application of the principle within the context of transforming internal administrative boundaries into international frontiers has been applied within a number of contexts in eastern Europe over the past decade.[47] Perhaps the most successful was its application in Czechoslovakia. The 'Velvet Divorce' of 1993, and the creation of the new states of Slovakia and the Czech Republic saw a return to the historical Moravian–Hungarian border. However, as Castellino and Allen observe, the principle of *uti possidetis* fails to take account of nomadic peoples. Thus, in the case of the Czech/Slovak divide, the position of the Roma peoples on both sides of the boundary was not addressed.[48]

The principle was also applied relatively successfully in the case of the dissolution of the former Soviet Union, although the internal boundary configurations were of more recent creation and were essentially the product of efforts on the part of Stalin to enhance his political strength and emasculate ethnic and nationalist aspirations.[49] Although it was rejected by the Baltic states of Estonia, Latvia and Lithuania – all of whom had lost considerable territory after their forcible incorporation following the Molotov Ribbentrop Pact – the remaining states of the Soviet Union agreed to the application of internal *uti possidetis:* existent administrative borders were to be respected. The Minsk Agreement of 8 December 1991 stated that 'the High Contracting Parties acknowledge and respect each other's territorial integrity and the inviolability of existing borders within the Commonwealth.'[50]

These sentiments were later confirmed in the 1993 Charter of the Commonwealth of Independent States, although of course the former republics continue to have claims against each other for territorial rearrangement.

More problematic was the case of Yugoslavia. The internal administrative boundary configuration created in terms of the treaty of Saint Germain en Laye was significantly overhauled by Tito after the World War II. The result was six republics that accorded closely with the pre 1918 political units of the territory. These units incorporated significant ethnic minorities. The commencement of the dissolution of Yugoslavia after 1991 prompted the international community quickly to declare that the internal frontiers of the constituent republics were not to be altered by recourse to force. The European Community (EC), the Conference on Security and Co operation in Europe, and the UN Security Council all issued statements to the effect that if Yugoslavia were to dissolve, 'the only predictable way would be along the lines of the republics'.[51] Indeed, the EC Arbitration Committee of 1991 stated that:

> ... it is well established that, whatever the circumstances, the right to self determination must not involve changes to existing frontiers at the time of independence *(uti possidetis juris)* except where the States concerned agree otherwise.[52]

But for the boundary between Slovenia and Croatia, however, the attempt to apply *uti possidetis* within a post Cold War context was rejected by the actions of the parties involved.

Thus, despite its contested application in Yugoslavia, there is recent precedent for the successful application of the principle to the internal administrative boundaries of states undergoing a process of dissolution. These internal demarcations, however, might well pose problems similar to those of international borders. As was the case in the former Soviet Union, these boundaries might well serve the interests of effective political control, but divide ethnic and cultural groupings and so violate a competing international legal claim to that of *uti possidetis* - that of the right to self determination.[53]

As early as 1960, in UN Resolution 1514 (XV) (*Declaration on the Granting of Independence to Colonial Countries and Peoples),* Paragraph 2 states that 'all peoples have the *right* to self determination'. The right was reinforced in the two International Covenants on Human Rights, adopted by resolution of the General Assembly on 16 December 1966. Article 1, Part I, of both the International Covenant on Civil and Political Rights and the International Covenant on Economic, Social and Cultural Rights proclaim that 'all peoples have the right to self determination', and that the signatories 'shall promote the realisation of that right, in conformity with the provisions of the Charter of the United Nations'. Further, in the 1970 *Declaration on Principles of International Law Concerning Friendly Relations and Cooperation Among States in Accordance with the Charter of the United Nations,*[54] it is declared that peoples have the right 'freely to determine, without external interference, their political status and to pursue their economic, social and cultural development'.

However, the manner in which the two concepts have been dealt with in international law is contradictory. Despite its lofty assertions, the 1970 *Declaration on Principles of International Law* is immediately qualified in the following respect: 'Nothing in the foregoing paragraphs shall be construed as authorising or encouraging any action which would dismember or impair, totally or in part, the territorial integrity or political unity of sovereign and independent states'.

Similarly, in the *Frontier Dispute Case (Burkina Faso/Mali)* the Court decided that:

> At first sight [*uti possidetis*] conflicts outright with ... the rights of peoples to self determination. In fact, however, the maintenance of the territorial status quo in Africa is often seen as the wisest course, to preserve what has been achieved by peoples who have struggled for their independence, and to avoid a disruption which would deprive the continent of gains achieved by much sacrifice. The essential requirement of stability in order to survive, to develop and gradually consolidate their independence in all fields, has induced African states judiciously to consent to the respecting of colonial frontiers, and to take account of it in the interpretation of the principle of self determination of peoples.[55]

Thus, for the international community, territorial stability (peace) trumps justice, equity and fairness (the right to self determination). Self determination is interpreted as a right limited only to the inhabitants of non independent territories. As a principle conferring the right to secede upon an identifiable group within an already independent state, self determination has been rejected. It is thus of no relevance once a colony or territory has attained sovereignty and independence. The failures to win international support for the attempted secession of the Katanga of Moïse Tshombé in 1960 and the Biafra[56] of Chukwuemeka Odumegwu Ojukwu between 1967-1970 both serve to illustrate this conclusion. (In both examples, it has been argued, the territory of the aspirant secessionists had itself been demarcated by the former colonial power, and was no less artificial than the territory of the larger state itself. The secessionist movements had more to do with gaining control of major revenue sources of the state than with self determination.)[57]

For similar reasons, the applications to secede of Southern Sudan[58] and Somaliland have also been rejected by the international community. In the case of Somaliland, the boundaries of the territory claimed are precisely those demarcated by the British following their victory over the Italians in the Second World War, the British and Italian territories having been united in 1960 to form the independent Republic of Somalia. The Somali problem, however, is compounded. Not only is there a secessionist movement within a portion of the territory, but significant

Somali minorities are to be found in Djibouti, Ethiopia, and Kenya. The artificiality of the borders with Ethiopia and Kenya, in particular, has led to constant conflict between these territories. In 1985, the Somali president, Abdirashiid Ali Shermaarke, complained,[59]

> Our misfortune is that our neighbouring countries … are not our neighbours. Our neighbours are our Somali kinsmen whose citizenship has been falsified by indiscriminate boundary arrangements. They have to move across artificial frontiers to their pasture lands. They occupy the same terrain and pursue the same pastoral economy as ourselves. We speak the same language. We share the same creed, the same culture and the same traditions. How can we regard our brothers as foreigners?

Somalia however has received very little support for its case.[60]

The ICJ has endorsed the concept of self determination as predominating on only one occasion - in the *Western Sahara* case, and this precisely because it did not conflict with the doctrine of *uti possidetis*. Morocco had made extensive claims to Mauritania, Western Sahara and parts of Algeria on the basis that these territories had historically belonged to the old Moroccan empire. This argument was initially viewed as an essentially political stance with little, if any, legal relevance. However, in 1975 the ICJ accepted that there did indeed exist historical ties between the tribes of Western Sahara and those of Morocco and Mauritania, concluding as follows:[61]

> The material and information presented to the Court show the existence at the time of Spanish colonisation, of legal ties of allegiance between the Sultan of Morocco and some of the tribes living in the territory of Western Sahara. They equally show the existence of rights, including some rights relating to land, which constituted legal ties between the Mauritanian entity, as understood by the Court, and the territory of Western Sahara. On the other hand, the Court's conclusion is that the materials and information presented to it do not establish any tie of territorial sovereignty between the territory of Western Sahara and the Kingdom of Morocco or the Mauritanian entity. Thus the Court has not found legal ties of such a nature as might affect the application of resolution 1514 (XV) in the decolonisation of Western Sahara and, in particular, of the principle of self determination through the free and genuine expression of the will of the peoples of the Territory.

It is precisely because the Polisario seeks self determination for the Sahrawi peoples within the context of boundaries determined by the Spanish colonial power that the territory has been accepted as a state by the OAU, and its successor the African Union (AU), since 1984.[62]

The only incidence of successful secession within Africa is that of Eritrea. Eritrea had, following a UN resolution, been federated with Ethiopia in 1952. Ten years later, in 1962, Eritrea became part of the Ethiopian Empire. Thereafter Eritrean secessionist groups, such as the Eritrean People's Liberation Front (EPLF), battled constantly against the troops of the Ethiopian government. In the years following the overthrow of Emperor Haile Selassie the fighting was particularly fierce. Eritrea claimed that because it had been federated without the express consent of its population, and because of the extent of its subjugation by the authorities in Addis Ababa, it had acquired a right to 'self determination'. This claim was finally acknowledged by the Ethiopian government following the military defeat of its forces. Eritrea gained independence from Ethiopia in 1993. This independence, again, conformed to the principle of *uti possidetis* in that the boundaries of the territory were those of 1952 - as determined by the colonial powers.

Despite the overriding endorsement of the principle of *uti possidetis* and its adoption by the new African elite, widespread armed conflicts over boundaries have continued to characterise post colonial Africa. Is it not ironic - or, in the phrase of Herbst, 'paradoxical'[63] - that the primacy accorded to *uti possidetis* over self determination lends legitimacy to the often unlawful manner in which Europe despoiled Africa? McCorquodale and Pangalangan comment:

> By ignoring natural boundaries and by ensuring that new states, and the boundaries of new states, are decided in the interests of the existing states, the international legal system recreates and affirms the dispositions by colonial powers. The sad irony is that, at their moment of triumph, the states that came into existence due to the process of decolonisation, turned away from the right of self determination and their own communal organisations towards an acceptance of both the very boundaries created artificially by past colonial powers and an international legal order based on precise territorial boundaries of states.[64]

Surely in a new world order premised on the idea of 'rights', the nineteenth century concept of the territorial state must be revisited? The 'impermeability of statehood' and 'territorial inviolability' - conceptual baggage that originated in the age of the princedom - serve to privilege certain voices at the expense of others.[65] 'It allows the elites in a territory to gain and exercise power, particularly political and economic power, at the expense of most of the people living in that territory.'[66] In his criticism of the OAU's adoption of the principle of *uti possidetis* in 1964, President Nyerere of Tanzania held that 'we [African leaders] must be more concerned about peace and justice ... than we are about the sanctity of the boundaries we inherit'.[67]

However, while recognising the injustice of many colonial boundaries, what are the alternatives to the European concept of sovereignty premised on defined territory? A revisitation of boundaries resulting in the redrawing of the map of Africa so as to create 2,000 new entities that are reflective of the continent's variety of tongues and tribes is not a feasible option. Quasi ethnic mini states based on pre colonial boundaries, apart from being of questionable economic sustainability, are not necessarily better alternatives. The boundaries of Rwanda and Burundi are those of kingdoms whose configuration was established long before the arrival of European administrators.

Must sovereignty inhere in a territorial state? Does the solution lie with the pre colonial African allegiance to the tribe or people rather than to territory?[68] Or do we need to develop a more porous concept of territory, such as characterised ancient Asian societies?[69] Such boundaries were 'living' in the sense that they were subject to the pressures of constant change.

Perhaps individual boundary problems will be overtaken by international changes. In an increasingly globalising world, boundaries are being 'de signified'. Regional entities need to be fostered and developed instead. Alternatively, it is globalisation itself that will necessitate a radical rethinking of traditional notions of state sovereignty. The World Bank, for example, has declared:

> The State defines the policies and rules for those within its jurisdiction, but global events and international agreements are increasingly affecting its choices. People are now more mobile, more educated, and better informed about conditions elsewhere. And involvement in the global economy tightens constraints on arbitrary State action, reduces the State's ability to tax capital, and brings much closer financial market scrutiny of monetary and fiscal policies.[70]

Increasingly the territorial state is having to accommodate trans national imperatives. International law, at some stage, will have to address the problem. A rigid adherence to the sanctity of territorial boundaries must not be allowed to become a barrier to successful development.

Or is it not about imposed colonial boundaries at all? Might one not argue that the causes of conflict between - and within - the territorial states of Africa have little, if anything, to do with their boundaries? After all, although the doctrine of *uti possidetis* - essentially a defence of the colonial status quo on African boundaries - has, on the one hand, been used by African states to deny statehood to aspirant secessionists, on the other, it has been used by the self same secessionists to justify their claims to statehood. The boundaries of Eritrea, a successful secession, conforms to the Italian colony prior to its federation with Ethiopia in 1952; the boundaries of Somaliland, a secession that has yet to receive international recognition, conforms to the British colony of Somaliland prior to the creation of the Republic of Somalia in 1960; the boundaries of the Southern Sudan, a potential secession, conforms to the three provinces of the southern Sudan during the period of British colonial administration.

Thus, the question as to whether a reworking of African boundaries will solve the shared problems of governance and statehood faced by many of the continent's big states is not only moot but wide of the political mark. Collectively, Africa has shown no interest in embarking on this road; individually, those entities that have shown a willingness to interrogate boundaries have also relied on colonial boundary delimitation - albeit internal administrative delimitation prior to the critical date of independence. A vast proportion of Africa's dominant elite, instead of interpreting imposed colonial boundaries as an obstacle, have embraced those boundaries. There is no reason to suspect that this strategy will be revisited.

Endnotes

1   *http://www.sas.upenn.edu/African_Studies/Articles_Gen/colon_bound.html.*
2   *http://news.bbc.co.uk/2/hi/africa/2316645.stm.*
3   One million persons were apparently killed in the suppression of the Ibos of Biafra between 1967-1970. What the cost in terms of lives is in the conflicts raging in the Sudan and in Central Africa can only be guessed at.
4   Griggs R. 'Boundaries for an African Renaissance: Reshaping the Continent's Political Geography', *http://ccrweb.ccr.uct.ac.za/two/3/p21.html.*
5   Lord Salisbury, speaking in 1890, as quoted in the 'Separate Opinion of Judge Ajibola', in *Territorial Dispute* (Libya v Chad). ICJ Reports, 6, 53, 1994; and as further cited in McCorquodale R & R Pangalangan, 'Pushing back the Limitations

of Territorial Boundaries'. *European Journal of International Law*, 12 (5) 2001, p. 867.

6   Engelbert P. *State Legitimacy and Development in Africa.* Boulder: Lynne Rienner, 2000, p. 88.

7   McCorquodale R & R Pangalangan. *op. cit.*, p. 868.

8   Shaw MN. 'The Heritage of States: The Principle of *Uti Possidetis Juris* Today', *British Yearbook of International Law,* 67, 1996, pp. 76-77.

9   *Reports of Arbitral Awards (RIAA),* 1928 (2), pp. 829-828; cited in Shaw MN. *ibid.*, p. 77.

10   *ICJ Reports 1994,* p. 26, cited in Shaw MN. *op. cit.,* p. 77.

11   *ICJ Reports 1962,* p. 34, cited in *ibid.*, p. 83.

12   Jennings R. 'The Acquisition of Territory in International Law', 1963, p. 70; cited in *ibid.*, p. 83.

13   Despite President Mbeki's comments to the contrary in the South African parliament on 29 May 2002.

14   Scelle G. *'Obsession du Territoire'.* In: *Symbolae Verzijl,* 347, 1958, cited in Ratner SR. 'Drawing a Better Line: *Uti Possidetis* and the Borders of New States', *American Journal of International Law,* 90, 4, 1996, p. 590.

15   Buckland WW. *A Textbook of Roman Law from Augustus to Justinian,* 3rd edition, 1963, pp. 204-208.

16   Shaw M. *Title to Territory in Africa: International Legal Issues,* 1986, p. 32.

17   Cited in Waldock CHG. 'Disputed Sovereignty in the Falkland Island Dependencies', *British Yearbook of International Law,* 25, 1948, p. 322.

18   'Western Sahara Case, Advisory Opinion', *ICJ Reports 1975,* para 80.

19   Jennings R & A Watts (eds). *Oppenheim's International Law,* I, 9th edition, 1992, cited in Harris DJ. *Cases and Materials on International Law,* 5th edition, 1998, p. 235.

20   Castellino J & S Allen. *Title to Territory in International Law: A Temporal Analysis,* Aldershot : Ashgate, 2003, p. 25.

21   See Touval S. 'Treaties, Borders, and the Partition of Africa'. *Journal of African History,* 7 (2), 1966, pp. 279-280.

22   Shaw M. *Title to Territory in Africa: International Legal Issues,* 1986, p. 38, holds that 'the prime method of acquiring territory in Africa in the period of colonisation was by way of cession'.

23   Alexandrowicz CH. *The European African Confrontation.* Leiden: Sijthoff, 1973, p. 7, cited in *ibid.*, p. 39.

24   'Island of Palmas Case'. *RIAA*, 1928 (2), p. 858.

25   See, for example, Porch D. Wars of Empire, London: Cassell, 2000; and Vandervort B. *Wars of Imperial Conquest in Africa, 1830-1914,* Bloomington: Indiana University Press, 1998.

26   War as an instrument of state policy was outlawed in the Peace of Paris in 1928; a position confirmed in the Charter of the United Nations.

27   Shaw M. *Title to Territory in Africa: International Legal Issues,* 1986, p. 46.

28   *Ibid.,* p. 46.

29   Engelbert P. *op. cit.,* p. 88.

30   Ratner SR. *op. cit.,* p. 595.

31   Okafor OC. 'After Martyrdom: International Law, Sub state Groups, and the Construction of Legitimate Statehood in Africa'. *Harvard International Law Journal,* 41 (2) 2000, p. 512.

32   Ratner SR. *op. cit.,* p. 591; McCorquodale R & R Pangalangan. *op. cit.,* p. 875.

33   See Shaw MN. 'The Heritage of States: The Principle of *Uti Possidetis Juris* Today', *op. cit.,* p. 98.

34   Jolowicz HF & B Nicholas. *Historical Introduction to the Study of Roman Law.* Cambridge: Cambridge University Press, 1972, p. 259.

35   Ratner SR. *op. cit.,* p. 593.

36   Verzijl JHW. *op. cit.* p. 517.

37   'After their original delimitation by Pope Alexander VI (1493) and the treaty of Tordesillas (1494) nothing much would seem to have occurred with regard to the boundaries between these areas for a considerable period. A more precise demarcation was, however, undertaken in the Spanish-Portuguese treaty of Madrid of 13 January 1750 ... and that of San Ildefonso of 1 October 1777 ... by which the borderline was in part fixed along rivers, such as the Río de la Plata and the River Uruguay. In a later period the frontiers of independent Brazil towards her independent Spanish speaking neighbours have also been fixed on the basis of *uti possidetis,* by separate treaties with Venezuela (5 May 1859, NRG, XVII, 161); Bolivia (27 March 1867, *ibid,* NRG, XX, 613); Paraguay (9 January 1872, *ibid,* NRG, IV, 573); Argentina (28 September 1885, *ibid,* NRG, XII, 584, and 6 October 1898, *ibid,* XXXII, 397); and Ecuador (6 May 1904, *ibid,* NRG, XXXIV, 519).' Verzijl JHW. *International Law in Historical Perspective: Part III, State Territory.* Leyden: AW Stijthoff. 1970, p. 548.

38   French, British and Dutch Guyana.

39   British Honduras or Belize.

40   Verzijl JHW. *op. cit.,* p. 548.

41 Castellino J & S Allen. *op. cit.*, p. 12.

42 In December 1958, at the Accra All African Peoples Conference, a resolution was adopted calling for the early abolition and adjustment of existing boundaries. 'This was seen as a desirable prelude to the formation of regional groupings, based on cultural, linguistic, and religious affinity, that would eventually become an African Commonwealth. The 1958 Accra resolution, however, was passed at a time when very few African countries had attained independence, and a modification of the former attitude was displayed at the inaugural summit conference of the Organization of African Unity, held in Addis Ababa in May 1963. The vast majority of delegates to this conference emphasised that whatever might be the moral and historical argument for a readjustment of national boundaries, practical attempts to reshape the map of Africa at the present day might well prove disastrous.' McEwen AC. *International Boundaries of East Africa*, Oxford: Oxford University Press, 1971, pp. 23-24.

43 At the first OAU Heads of State and Government meeting, held in Cairo in July 1964, Resolution 16(1) expressly affirmed that member states of the OAU 'pledge themselves to respect the borders existing on their achievement of national independence'. Cited in Castellino and Allen (see note 41 above). p. 114 n 71.

44 International Court of Justice Reports, 1986.

45 *Ibid.* p. 554.

46 *Ibid.* p. 566.

47 See Ratner SR. *op. cit.*, pp. 596-598; and Castellino J & S Allen. 'The Doctrine of *Uti Possidetis*: Crystallisation of Modern Post colonial Identity'. *German Yearbook of International Law,* 43, 2000, pp. 215-218.

48 Castellino J & S Allen. *Title to Territory in International Law: A Temporal Analysis, op. cit.*, p. 20.

49 Ratner SR. *op. cit.*, p. 597.

50 Cited in Castellino J & S Allen. *Title to Territory in International Law: A Temporal Analysis, op. cit.*, p. 19.

51 Ratner SR. *op. cit.*, p. 596.

52 Cited in Castellino J & S Allen. 'The Doctrine of *Uti Possidetis:* Crystallization of Modern Post Colonial Identity', *op. cit.*, p. 215.

53 Whether 'self determination' constituted a 'right' in international law in terms of the Charter of the United Nations is a matter of some debate. However, it is generally accepted that by the 1960s self determination had developed into an international right. See McEwen AC, *op. cit.* p. 32.

54 UN General Assembly Resolution 2625 (XXV), 24 October 1970.

55 'Frontier Dispute (Burkina Faso/Republic of Mali).' *ICJ Reports,* 1986, pp. 566–567.

56 Biafra's independence was recognised by Tanzania, Zambia, Gabon and the Ivory Coast. However, its position was compromised in the eyes of most African states by the approval given to it by South Africa, Southern Rhodesia and Portugal.

57 See Clapham C. 'Boundaries and States in the New African Order'. In: Bach DC (ed.). *Regionalisation in Africa: Integration and Disintegration,* Bloomington: Indiana University Press, 1999, p. 55.

58 See Lloyd AM. 'The Southern Sudan: A Compelling Case for Secession'. *Columbia Journal of Transnational Law,* 32 (1) 1994, p. 419.

59 Cited in Engelbert P. *op. cit.,* p. 85.

60 Shaw MN. International Law. 4th edition, 1997, p. 355.

61 'Western Sahara Case.' Advisory Opinion, *ICJ Reports* 1975, para 162.

62 See Zoubir YH. 'The Western Sahara Conflict: A Case Study in Failure of Prenegotiation and Prolongation of Conflict.' *California Western International Law Journal,* 26, 1996, p. 173.

63 Herbst J. 'The Creation and Maintenance of National Boundaries in Africa', *International Organisation,* 43, 1989, p. 673, cited in Okafor OC. 'After Martyrdom: International law, Sub state Groups, and the Construction of Legitimate Statehood in Africa', *Harvard International Law Journal,* 41 (2) 2000, p. 512.

64 McCorquodale R & R Pangalangan. 'Pushing back the Limitations of Territorial Boundaries'. *European Journal of International Law,* 12 (5) 2001, p. 877.

65 *Ibid.*

66 *Ibid.*

67 Radan P, 'Post secession International Borders: A Critical Analysis of the Opinions of the Badinter Arbitration Commission'. *Melbourne University Law Review,* 24, 2000 p. 70.

68 Ford AN. 'A Question of Boundaries.' *African Business, September 2001. http:// dspace.dial.pipex.com/icpubs/ab/sept01/cover2.htm* argues: 'In general, African pre colonial polities were far more fluid than European states. In order to cope with the harsh natural environment, flexibility proved to be a far more effective method of political organisation than fixed Western style states. Where drought or disease struck one ethnic group, a state of any size was able to contract or even move itself wholesale. Political authority tended to follow trade routes, as with the Swahili in East Africa, and sovereignty was invested in people rather than land.'

69 McCorquodale R & R Pangalangan. *op. cit.,* p. 878.

70 *World Development Report 1997,* Washington: World Bank, 1997, p. 12, cited in

13

Conclusion: policy options for the problems of Africa's big states

Christopher Clapham

Introduction

The theme of this book is that Africa's biggest states constitute a 'problem' - or rather, a complex of interconnected predicaments - that generates a significant challenge to the continent's prospects of political and economic transformation. To be sure, no one would claim that this is Africa's only challenge, still less that carving up its largest states into supposedly more 'manageable' pieces would provide any panacea for the difficulties that they face. But the fact is that on the three main indices of state functionality - peace and personal security, economic development and public welfare, and democracy and 'good governance' - the largest states lag significantly behind the continental norm, and still further behind the levels of measurable progress on all three fronts that Africa's best performing states have shown to be possible. The policy challenge is then to discern to what extent, and how, this extremely disappointing performance can be rectified.

Just as the problems of Africa's big states display their effects on three main levels, so also there are three corresponding points at which policy options can be considered. First, there is the level of the states themselves. Second is that of their neighbours and the continent as a whole, which are affected both by the immediate impact of state dysfunctionality beyond their borders, and also by the influence of the largest states on the wider project of African governance and recovery, to which these states are disproportionately critical. Third is the level of the global system, for which much of Africa figures as a stain on legitimate expectations that human well being will improve, as well as a significant and growing threat to their own security in its widest sense. This conclusion will examine policy options at each of these levels in turn.

The domestic arena

One key finding of this study is that the exceptional problems of Africa's largest states derive overwhelmingly from the domestic political constitution of these states themselves. Obviously no state in the world, least of all in Africa, can be treated as an island unto itself; and the peculiarly damaging way in which the continent was historically incorporated into the global system continues to exercise its baleful influence - not least, for our purposes, in the arbitrary way in which colonialism designated a few very large territories in addition to a large number of small ones. But this is not a distinctive challenge for large states: indeed, the smallest states may plausibly be regarded as most subject to the dangers of external dependence. Pan Africanists from Kwame Nkrumah onwards have characteristically identified a need for Africans to unite into larger political units (ideally a continental union), precisely in order to reverse the consequences of colonial 'balkanisation'. That such larger units might have their own problems did not figure in pan Africanist thinking.

Another key reason to give primacy to the domestic arena is that by far the most important sufferers from the dysfunctionality of many of Africa's largest states are the citizens of those states. However long and painful the learning process may be, these citizens are in the best position to work out how best to improve their own conditions in the light of both their own values and aspirations, and their diagnosis of where their problems lie. Outsiders certainly have legitimate concerns, and for all their well publicised failures, external attempts to improve the condition of Africa have not been entirely counter productive. Many Africans, for example, have reason to be grateful for the external support given to democracy in the continent since the end of the Cold War, though regrettably not beforehand. But the interests of outside parties, both in Africa and in the rest of the world, can be lastingly achieved only by working with the citizens of affected states to help them manage their own problems.

This is not always an easy task. One of the most worrying indicators of the difficulties of Africa's largest states is that these countries have generally proved far less able than most of their continental fellows to sustain democratic systems of government, which in turn provide the most effective mechanism through which people can constructively influence their own futures. In most of the countries with which we are concerned in this book, people have instead been forced into a situation where violence (ranging from outright civil war to the anti apartheid campaign in South Africa) has been the only available means through which to pursue their aspirations. Even now, of the six states under consideration, only in Nigeria and South Africa are opposition parties at least reasonably free to operate, while in none of them (with Nigeria as the only doubtfully possible exception) is there any plausible prospect that any opposition party might be able to assume power in the near future through a peacefully contested election.

One important finding of this study is nonetheless that several of Africa's largest states have themselves – of necessity in most cases – started to devise mechanisms to cope with the consequences of size, and have done so in significantly different ways. South Africa is in this respect in a category of its own. It is the one state in our sample for which size can generally be regarded as a strength rather than a drawback, due to its capacity to develop a single integrated economy linked by an effective communication structure, and – not least – a nation wide political community united especially by the African National Congress (ANC). Its problems lay in the peculiar structure of its pre 1994 domestic political order, and once this had been resolved, other problems were reduced to relative manageability. Nigeria, however, has also developed a thoroughly *political* approach to the problems of diversity, through its own distinctive form of federalism, and the highly complex processes of bargaining and coalition building through which politics at the federal level is conducted. This system is both violent (it would seem increasingly so) and corrupt. It is likewise deeply strained by the progressively greater mismatch between the fragmentation of its domestic political constituencies (most clearly indicated by the issue of *shari'ah* law in the Moslem part of the country, and the problems of the oil producing south east), and its dependence on the single and highly centralised funding structure created by oil revenues. The future of the Nigerian experiment is a matter for deep concern; but at least no one could accuse Nigeria's politicians of failing to recognise the 'federal character' of their country.

In two of our most troubled examples, Ethiopia and Sudan, the survival of the state in its current territorial form is under much greater challenge than in Nigeria. In each case, some kind of 'federalism' has been identified as appropriate, though in different ways from Nigeria, or indeed South Africa. In each case, too, the current leaders have parted company both with previous regimes in their own countries, and with continental norms that emphasise 'territorial integrity', by explicitly recognising circumstances under which the territory that they govern can be divided into separate sovereign states. In Ethiopia these take the form of constitutional provisions that acknowledge the rights of the country's constituent nationalities to self determination 'up to and including secession'. In Sudan the route is conceding to the Southern Sudanese the right to a referendum on their future status after a period of six years following the introduction of the proposed peace settlement to the country's long lasting civil war. In Ethiopia, indeed, the Ethiopian Peoples' Revolutionary Democratic Front (EPRDF) government acknowledged the separate independence of Eritrea as one of its first actions after gaining power in 1991. Even though, as the country chapters make clear, the formal concession of a right to secession is in practice often belied by the actual behaviour of the regimes concerned, the formalities are nonetheless vitally important, in that they open up policy options which have previously been denied, and impose a real incentive to ensure the success of the federalist alternatives that each government regards as vastly preferable to fragmentation. The Union of Soviet Socialist Republics (USSR) has in any event shown how provisions that were regarded at the time of their introduction as no more than the merest formalities may eventually come to have a life of their own.

Our last two cases present a much more mixed picture. In Angola, the *Movimento Popular de Libertaçoa de Angola* (MPLA)'s outright victory in the long civil war against *União Naçional para a Independêngia Total d'Angola* (UNITA) appears to have closed off, rather than opened up, the options for creating a more accountable political structure. In the Democratic Republic of Congo (DRC) on the other hand, the recent civil war has revealed a medieval mixture of local fiefdoms and contested territories, which endless negotiations are unlikely to convert into any approximation of an effectively decentralised modern state. Nonetheless, the basic proposition holds: local actors provide the point from which any attempt to manage the problems of big states must start, even if this means that external actors must engage with unwelcome options and unhelpful participants. At the same time, none of those states that have sought to address the problems of scale has as yet emerged with any remotely stable and effective way of doing so. The federal systems devised in both Nigeria and Ethiopia remain deeply problematic. In Nigeria the reason is essentially the clash between devolved politics and centralised finance; in Ethiopia it is attributable to the still unresolved tension between ethnic devolution and a deeply entrenched tradition of centralised statehood. This can be compared with the situation in Sudan, where the current peace settlement (even if it holds) has ensured an extremely fraught period of political contestation leading up to the projected referendum. The continued fragility of domestic solutions in turn argues the case for international involvement.

Regional and continental arenas

African leaders have characteristically sought to address the problems of the continent in terms of an ethic of 'African unity', and a belief in the desirability of 'African solutions to African problems'. Given the size of the continent, and the regional clusters within which states are deeply affected by developments among their neighbours, this approach has often in practice led to devolved processes of regional conflict management. These have taken place under the overall aegis of Africa wide structures such as those provided by the Organisation of African Unity (OAU), or more recently the African Union (AU) and the New Partnership for Africa's Development (Nepad). There seems to be every reason to follow this precedent in the cases with which we are concerned here, given the impact of the difficulties of large states on their neighbours, and the urgent need to devise solutions that can address the often closely interlinked problems of domestic and regional conflict. The war in DRC, with its internal and external elements, provides the classic example. The Nepad initiative appears to offer a particularly conducive framework for conflict management at a regional level, given its emphasis on 'good governance' as the key to African development, and the envisaged role of a supportive process of 'peer review' in helping to achieve it.

In practice, however, it is at best uncertain whether regional and continental networks are actually capable of playing the constructive role that this scenario envisages. All of the principles of regional stability start from the presumption that large states within each broad geographical area must act as the major stabilising influences for that part of Africa, and must form the core of regional organisations through which conflict is managed. Large but dysfunctional states are unable to create or manage effective regional organisations, not only because they are likely to be preoccupied with their own domestic problems, but because those problems may themselves serve as a source of instability. South Africa provides a classic example. During the apartheid years, when the regime destabilised neighbouring southern African states in a vain attempt to preserve its domestic power structure, there was little that these states could do to protect themselves. It was only after the transition to majority rule that South Africa could emerge as a force for stability. In west Africa, Nigeria has been an active regional hegemon, notably in contributing by far the largest element of the Economic Community of West African States (ECOWAS) peacekeeping forces in both Liberia and Sierra Leone. However, the intensely fractious structure of its domestic politics has increasingly undermined this role.

Another problem is ideological. African regional and continental organisations and their constituent states remain, in practice, deeply committed to the principles of territorial integrity and non intervention enshrined in the charter of the now superseded OAU. The commitment to territorial integrity has been carried over into the charter of its successor, the AU; and even though the commitment to non intervention in the internal affairs of other states has in principle been greatly diluted by the AU and especially by Nepad, much of the former attitude remains. Nowhere is this clearer than in the reluctance of the South African government to take Zimbabwe to task for blatant breaches of Nepad's ideals; and what goes in this respect for a large state dealing with a much smaller regional neighbour may be expected to apply *a fortiori* when the positions are reversed. Even so, it remains paradoxical that regional organisations should retain a commitment to 'territorial integrity' even when, as with Ethiopia and Sudan, the states most concerned have ceased to apply it to themselves.

Nor, conversely, can the smaller regional states, even acting together, be expected to exercise any very significant role in helping to stabilise the large ones. The southern African regional system played a negligible part in the momentous transformation within South Africa. Again, were Nigeria to succumb to the pressures that threaten to split it apart, to expect other west African states to make any significant contribution to its stabilisation would be futile. International relations theory makes no provision for circumstances in which a large and potentially hegemonic regional state is itself the major source of instability, and it remains extremely doubtful whether effective regional management structures can operate under these circumstances. There may well be specific instances in which some kind of tacit cross border regime can be developed, with international support, to help manage flashpoints such as the Rwanda-Burundi-DRC frontier region or the Bakassi peninsula. But on the whole, the most that one can plausibly ask of regional and continental actors is that they should do whatever they can to discourage neighbouring states from actively contributing to the process of destabilisation within states such as the DRC and Ethiopia.

This leaves open the major question of how leadership structures can be developed for African regional systems, or for the continent as a whole. It goes without saying that in a continent comprising over fifty states, with a strong sense of its own identity and an active set of regional and continental organisations, some states must in practice come to take a greater initiative than others. One effect of Africa's strong historic emphasis on the sovereign equality of states has been that this initiative has often in the past come from medium sized or even small states. What has mattered has been that these states - or often in practice their leaders

- have come to symbolise aspirations with a wider continental relevance. In the era of decolonisation, for example, Kwame Nkrumah exercised an influence out of proportion to the scale of the state that he ruled, partly because Ghana was the first sub Saharan state to become independent from colonial rule, but also because of his own capacity for leadership. One of Africa's tiniest states, The Gambia, played a pivotal role in the adoption of the African Charter of Human and Peoples' Rights, because (at that time at least) it exemplified qualities to which other African states aspired. More recently, the creation of the AU has owed much to Libyan initiative. The way is open for those states that best demonstrate the social and political values espoused by Nepad to come to the fore. Such leadership can however only operate at a very 'soft' level, through example and through aspiration. It is unable to develop the kind of hegemonic role for which the classic correlates of power are needed. The conclusion must be that action at the regional and continental level has only a limited and subordinate contribution to make towards managing the problems with which we are concerned.

The global arena

Major external actors - whether states or international organisations - inevitably pay most attention to the larger states in Africa, because these are the ones that matter most. Given the scale and complexity of the problems that these states face, they often have a prominent role on global agendas. Crafting a specific approach to these difficulties is, however, another matter. During the Cold War, there was in practice a distinctive policy regime for big African states, simply because these were regarded as especially significant allies in the global contest between the superpowers. They were therefore accorded critical support by superpower patrons, which - in collaboration with the norms of the international system as a whole - enabled them to manage (after a fashion) the dilemmas of governability arising from their large size. Ethiopia was a client first of the US, and then (after the 1974 revolution) of the Soviet Union. Angola remained throughout in the Soviet camp, while Congo (or Zaïre, as it was for much of the period) stayed with the West. Nigeria gained military aid from both sides in the Cold War during its civil conflict in the late 1960s, while Sudan shifted between them. This policy regime had mixed results, and helped to maintain undemocratic and often extremely brutal regimes, with lasting and damaging consequences. But in the short term, at least, it broadly promoted the objective of state survival.

With the end of the Cold War, the policy environment changed, and the incentive that had prompted international powers to maintain large African client states disappeared. In its place, a common external policy regime was erected which applied to all African states, regardless of their size. This assumed that the global norms of liberal multi party democracy and 'good governance', together with market oriented economic policies, would help to resolve the domestic political problems from which almost all African states suffered to some degree. It was expected that these reforms would in turn lay the foundations for managing the related problems of territorial integrity and regional security, which were (rightly, in most cases) ascribed to failures of internal governance.

Though this policy regime has helped to achieve significant results in much of Africa, it has proved to be peculiarly ill adapted to the distinctive challenges of large states. First of all, these states have complex and multipolar domestic political structures, which make the application of the liberal democracy formula much more problematic than in small and medium sized states. Where - as is commonly the case - these states encompass different large population groups with distinct territories of their own, which often have a very slight physical or emotional connection with a national centre, multi party politics is much more likely to lead to a challenge to the territoriality of the state itself than in small countries dominated by their national capitals. The failure of Africa's largest states to develop viable democracies reflects these difficulties. Secondly, such states often have special problems of administrative capability, especially in projecting power over large distances, which affect the application of the 'good governance' formula. Governing a huge territory such as Sudan or the DRC is always going to be problematic, and there is a limit to what can be achieved through the largely technical formulae of externally inspired capacity building programmes. Thirdly, the international community has much less leverage over very large states than over smaller ones. Military intervention and externally managed reconstruction on the scale seen in Sierra Leone, for example, is simply not an option in the DRC. To put it another way, these states are at least as difficult to 'manage' for the international community as they are for their own governments.

Furthermore, while distinct policy options need to be devised to cope with the problems of large states, equally these options need to be crafted to suit the specific circumstances of each of these states separately. One size fits all solutions have at least the merit of simplicity when dealing with smaller states; but the big ones are both varied and important enough to justify separate treatment. As the case study chapters show, each of them has a distinctive geography and historical trajectory, and although the difficulties that they face have significant elements in common, the potential solutions often vary. Not only the governments but the peoples of large states have developed different approaches to their problems, which external actors must take into account. However paradoxical it may be, for example, that the peoples of the Congo appear to share a commitment to its maintenance as a single territorial unit, this remains an important element in the search for a viable political outcome. Conversely, in Sudan it now seems unlikely that the peoples of the southern part of the country can ever be brought to acknowledge a commitment to a single Sudanese state governed from Khartoum, and this opens up very different avenues for conflict management.

Equally, any consideration of policy options must recognise that the international community has very limited resources and leverage with which to tackle the problems of large African states, and must adapt its approaches accordingly. Developments in Afghanistan and Iraq are testing the capacity of the US and the international system as a whole to carry through large scale projects of state reconstruction, and must necessarily limit both the resources and the political incentives to engage in such projects elsewhere. Military intervention and multinational peacekeeping on the scale achieved in a tiny country such as Sierra Leone are effectively ruled out in the case of large states, where direct military action is extremely improbable, and even peacekeeping operations are likely to be restricted to point defence of key towns or installations. Policy leverage is likewise much harder to apply in large states than small ones. Not only are the states considered here generally low level recipients of international aid (which itself provides a very uncertain source of leverage in key political issues), but these states are equally in a position to apply 'reverse leverage' over the international system. Most of them hold significant mineral resources, notably oil in Nigeria, Angola and Sudan, and a variety of other important minerals in the DRC and Angola. As previous chapters have shown, the effective management of these natural assets is both a key to stability and requires close collaboration between global and local actors. Similar considerations apply to the closely related issue of the control of international crime. Still more persuasively, the governments of large states can claim (with varying degrees of plausibility) to provide a bulwark against state collapse and the still greater dangers that this would entail for continental and global stability, and use this to secure support for their own approaches to state maintenance. Their leaders must of necessity develop sophisticated bargaining skills that apply as much to the external as to the domestic arena.

The central conclusion to this study is thus that expectations should be modest, and that the old formulae for coping with diversity – territorial integrity, non intervention in the internal affairs of other states, democracy, governance, federalism – however admirable in themselves, actually sound quite hollow. External actors should be flexible, and different approaches should be considered in response to different situations. Some basic precepts follow.

· Commitment to territorial integrity should be limited to repelling aggression from the outside. The international system needs to protect countries from being attacked, but it should not try to offer a guarantee of survival to countries threatened by internal factions. Rather than declaring commitment to the territorial integrity of a state, outsiders should put all the political forces in a country on notice that the survival of their state is in their hands. It is likewise crucial that the international community maintain a realistic view of what constitutes external aggression.

· Partition should not be advocated as the solution to the problems of big states. Even less should outside actors try to decide where the lines of partition should be, but they should accept partition if it happens. Africa does not need another Berlin conference and more lines drawn on maps. Nor does it need stubborn international determination to keep alive states that were dysfunctional when they became independent and are even more dysfunctional forty years later.

· Federalism should not be promoted as an all purpose solution. Although federalism may remove or reduce the demand for partition in some cases, this will only happen if the component units of the system reflect political reality. In the big, troubled African states, federalism will predominantly be based on ethnicity and/or religion. The role of the international community is not to dictate the boundaries of the component units, but to help the participants reach the necessary compromises.

· Where there is a reasonably effective government which itself has a strategy for coping with the problems of size and diversity, the 'default option' for the international community should be to give this regime critical support. Only in rare cases, where the internal strategy is clearly failing and does not take account of key political forces in the country, will it be feasible to attempt to develop an alternative.

· Democracy, while a good thing in itself, is not a solution to the problems of big, dysfunctional African states. A democratic process can take place only in a functioning state. Elections do not build states. They can succeed only where there is already a basis for national unity, reasonably effective governance and political compromise.

- The big African states, with the exception of South Africa, are too dysfunctional to be encouraged to deal with conflicts in the smaller countries of the region. Even South Africa cannot carry too large a burden. Big African states will become a force for stability and peace in their regions only if can they find ways to manage their own considerable political and economic problems. They should be encouraged to focus on their domestic challenges first.

- Rather than seeking to engage other regional actors in managing the problems of big states, a preferable approach would be to seek to *disengage* regional actors, by discouraging involvement by regional states in the affairs of their large neighbours. At the same time external powers should do whatever is possible to protect smaller states against the effects of the crises being experienced by their neighbours.

- The international community should seek to develop good relations with those African states that exemplify 'best practice' in the continent regardless of size. It should use these where appropriate as its interlocutors in guiding its own engagement with Africa, while recognising that they cannot be expected to exercise a hegemonic role, or to serve as surrogates for external influence.

- The West should accept that in twenty years the map of Africa is unlikely to look like that of today or of forty years ago. Africa needs to be given the space to adapt its states and institutions to its own needs, and these cannot always be expected to reflect the lines imposed by colonialism a century ago.

Index